X-DAY

ALSO AVAILABLE FROM TOKYOPOP®

MANGA

.HACK//LEGEND OF THE TWILIGHT
@LARGE (December 2003)
ANGELIC LAYER*
BABY BIRTH*
BATTLE ROYALE*
BRAIN POWERED*
BRIGADOON*
CARDCAPTOR SAKURA
CARDCAPTOR SAKURA: MASTER OF THE CLOW*
CHOBITS*
CHRONICLES OF THE CURSED SWORD
CLAMP SCHOOL DETECTIVES*
CLOVER
CONFIDENTIAL CONFESSIONS*
CORRECTOR YUI
COWBOY BEBOP*
COWBOY BEBOP: SHOOTING STAR*
CYBORG 009*
DEMON DIARY
DIGIMON*
DRAGON HUNTER
DRAGON KNIGHTS*
DUKLYON: CLAMP SCHOOL DEFENDERS*
ERICA SAKURAZAWA*
FAKE*
FLCL*
FORBIDDEN DANCE*
GATE KEEPERS*
G GUNDAM*
GRAVITATION*
GTO*
GUNDAM WING
GUNDAM WING: BATTLEFIELD OF PACIFISTS
GUNDAM WING: ENDLESS WALTZ*
GUNDAM WING: THE LAST OUTPOST*
HAPPY MANIA*
HARLEM BEAT
I.N.V.U.
INITIAL D*
ISLAND
JING: KING OF BANDITS*
JULINE
KARE KANO*
KINDAICHI CASE FILES, THE*
KING OF HELL
KODOCHA: SANA'S STAGE*
LOVE HINA*
LUPIN III*
MAGIC KNIGHT RAYEARTH*

MAGIC KNIGHT RAYEARTH II* (COMING SOON)
MAN OF MANY FACES*
MARMALADE BOY*
MARS*
MIRACLE GIRLS
MIYUKI-CHAN IN WONDERLAND*
MONSTERS, INC.
PARADISE KISS*
PARASYTE
PEACH GIRL
PEACH GIRL: CHANGE OF HEART*
PET SHOP OF HORRORS*
PLANET LADDER*
PLANETES*
PRIEST
RAGNAROK
RAVE MASTER*
REALITY CHECK
REBIRTH
REBOUND*
RISING STARS OF MANGA
SABER MARIONETTE J*
SAILOR MOON
SAINT TAIL
SAMURAI DEEPER KYO*
SAMURAI GIRL: REAL BOUT HIGH SCHOOL*
SCRYED*
SHAOLIN SISTERS*
SHIRAHIME-SYO: SNOW GODDESS TALES* (Dec. 2003)
SHUTTERBOX
SORCERER HUNTERS
THE SKULL MAN*
THE VISION OF ESCAFLOWNE
TOKYO MEW MEW*
UNDER THE GLASS MOON
VAMPIRE GAME*
WILD ACT*
WISH*
WORLD OF HARTZ (November 2003)
X-DAY*
ZODIAC P.I. *

For more information visit www.TOKYOPOP.com

*INDICATES 100% AUTHENTIC MANGA (RIGHT-TO-LEFT FORMAT)

CINE-MANGA™

CARDCAPTORS
JACKIE CHAN ADVENTURES (November 2003)
JIMMY NEUTRON
KIM POSSIBLE
LIZZIE MCGUIRE
POWER RANGERS: NINJA STORM
SPONGEBOB SQUAREPANTS
SPY KIDS 2

NOVELS

KARMA CLUB (April 2004)
SAILOR MOON

TOKYOPOP KIDS

STRAY SHEEP

ART BOOKS

CARDCAPTOR SAKURA*
MAGIC KNIGHT RAYEARTH*

ANIME GUIDES

COWBOY BEBOP ANIME GUIDES
GUNDAM TECHNICAL MANUALS
SAILOR MOON SCOUT GUIDES

080103

X-DAY

Volume Two

By Setona Mizushiro

Los Angeles • Tokyo • London

Translator - Shirley Kubo
English Adaptation - Lisa Blank
Editor - Elizabeth Nix
Retouch and Lettering - Brian Bossin
Cover Layout - Raymond Makowski
Graphic Designer - James Lee

Editor - Julie Taylor
Managing Editor - Jill Freshney
Production Coordinator - Antonio DePietro
Production Manager - Jennifer Miller
Art Director - Matt Alford
Editorial Director - Jeremy Ross
VP of Production - Ron Klamert
President & C.O.O. - John Parker
Publisher & C.E.O. - Stuart Levy

Email: editor@TOKYOPOP.com
Come visit us online at www.TOKYOPOP.com

A  Manga

TOKYOPOP Inc.
5900 Wilshire Blvd. Suite 2000
Los Angeles, CA 90036

KANOJO TACHI NO X-DAY VOL. 2
© 2003 SETONA MIZUSHIRO. ALL RIGHTS RESERVED.
FIRST PUBLISHED IN JAPAN IN 2003 BY AKITA PUBLISHING CO., LTD., TOKYO
ENGLISH TRANSLATION RIGHTS ARRANGED THROUGH AKITA PUBLISHING CO., LTD.

English text copyright ©2003 TOKYOPOP Inc.

ISBN: 1-59182-380-3

First TOKYOPOP printing: October 2003

10 9 8 7 6 5 4 3 2 1
Printed in the USA

＊*X*-DAY coming there＊

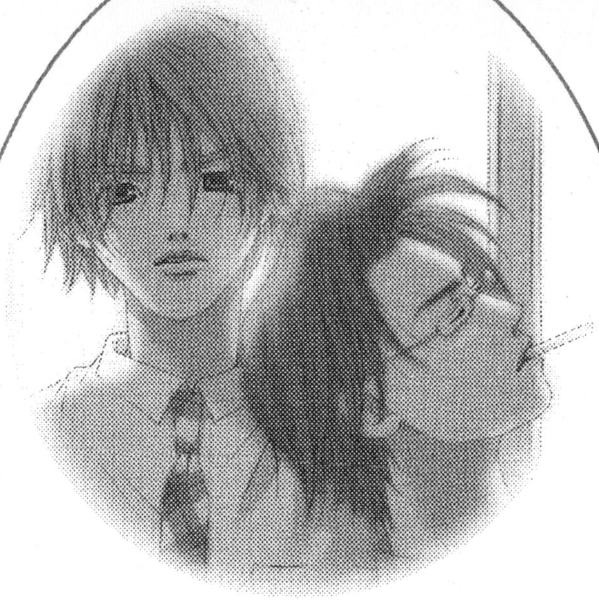

X-DAY coming there

2

CONTENTS

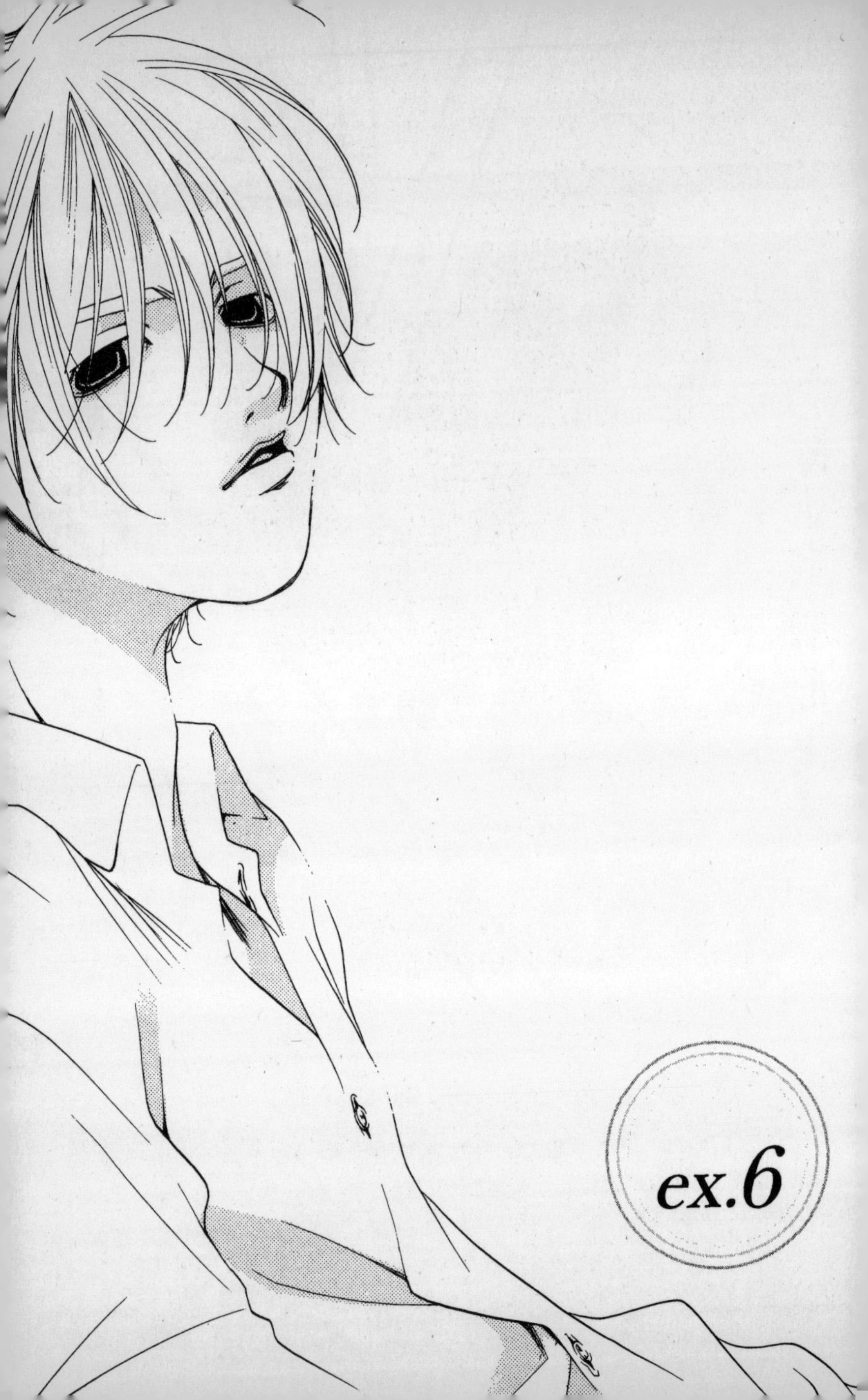
ex.6

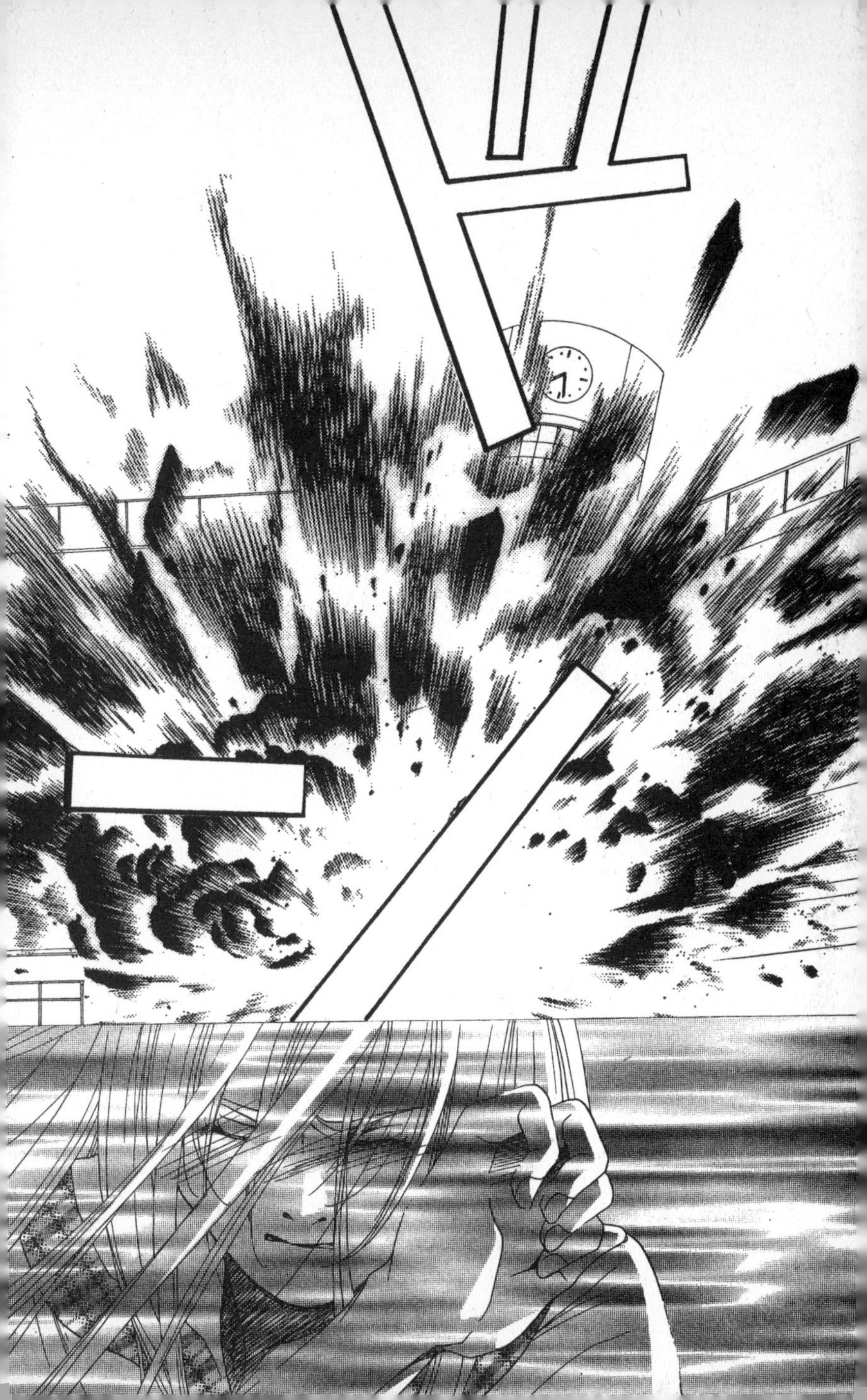
ドン

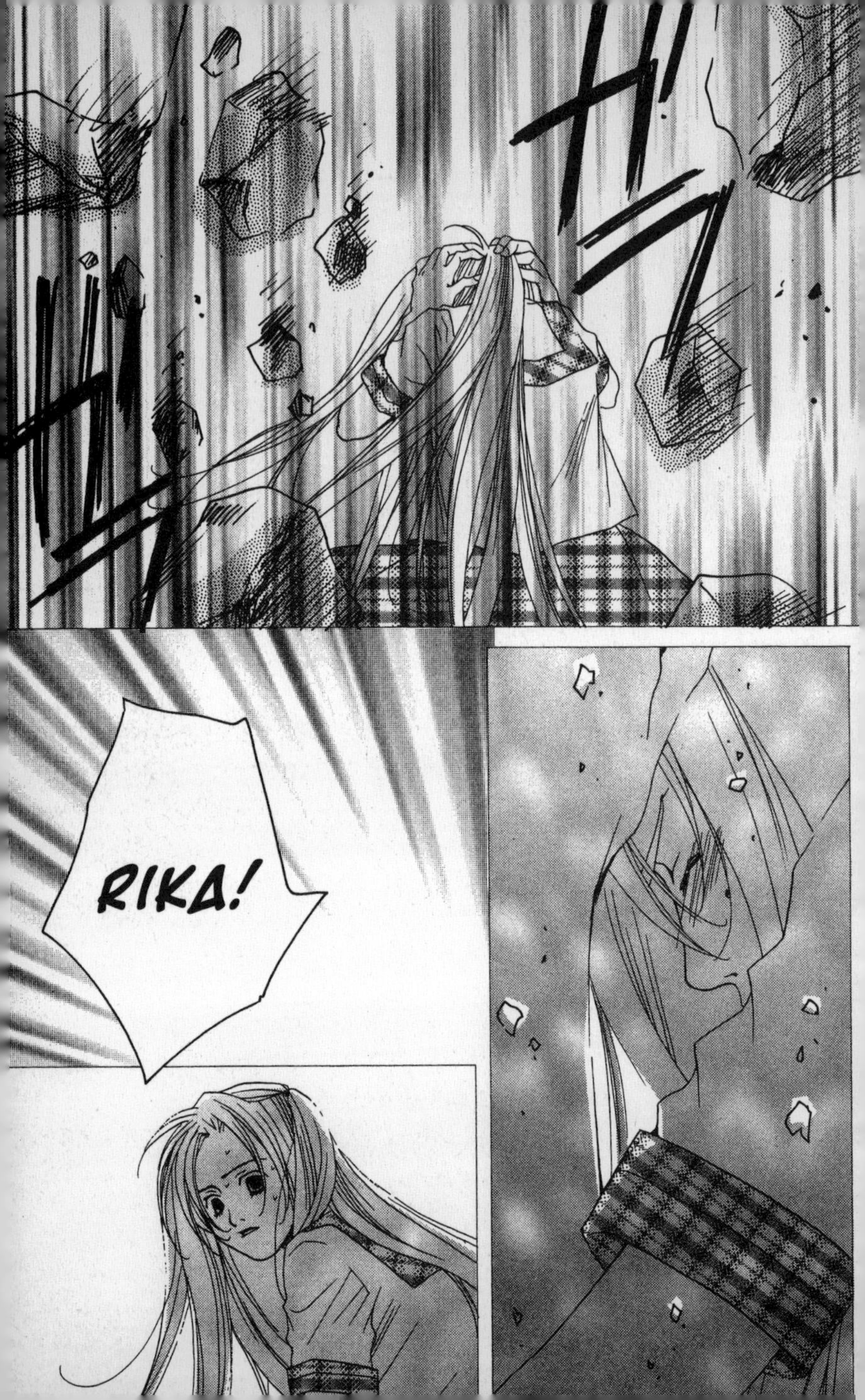
RIKA!

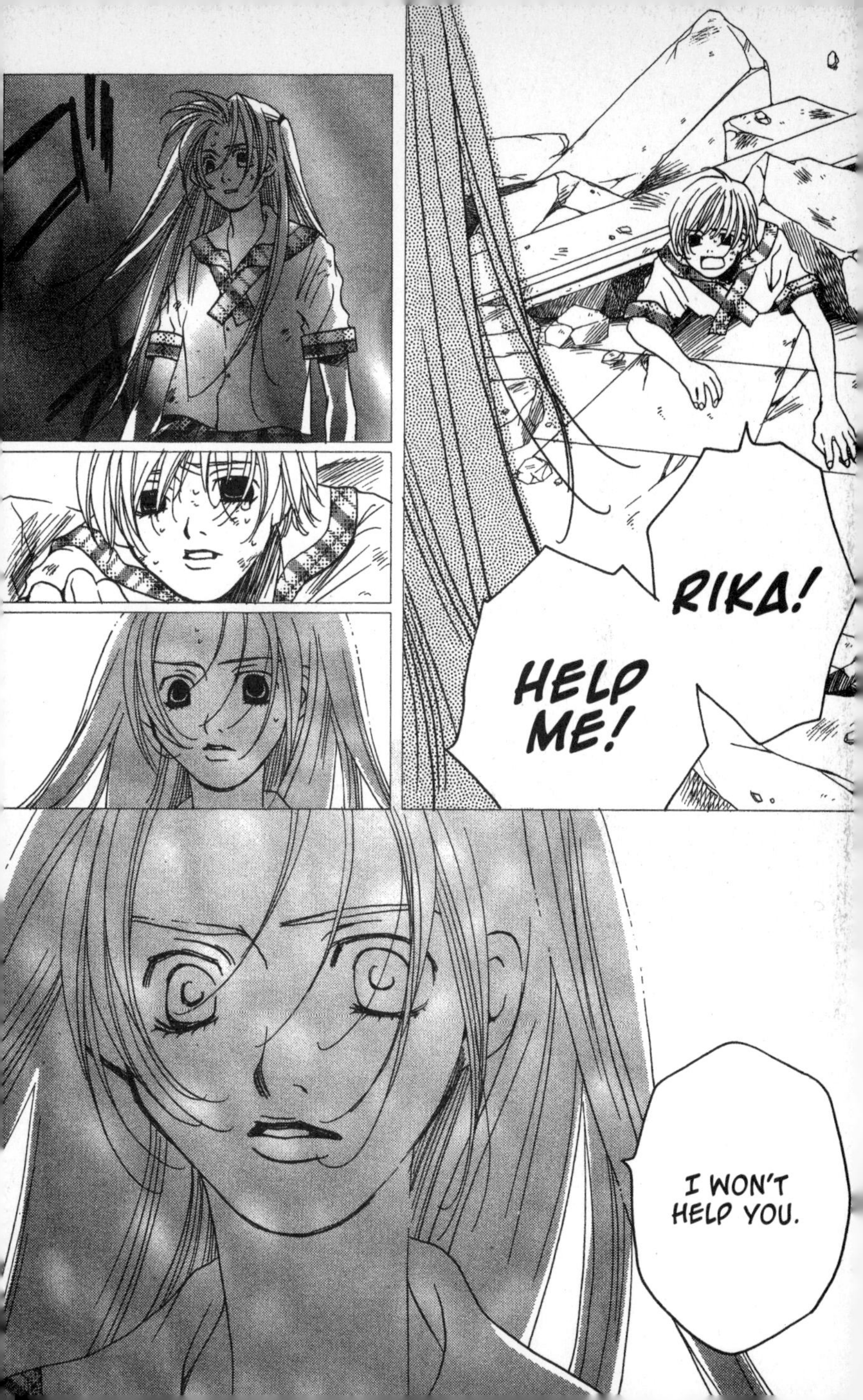
RIKA!
HELP ME!
I WON'T HELP YOU.

THERE'S
NO WAY...

...I'LL
HELP
YOU.

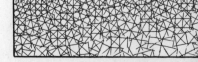

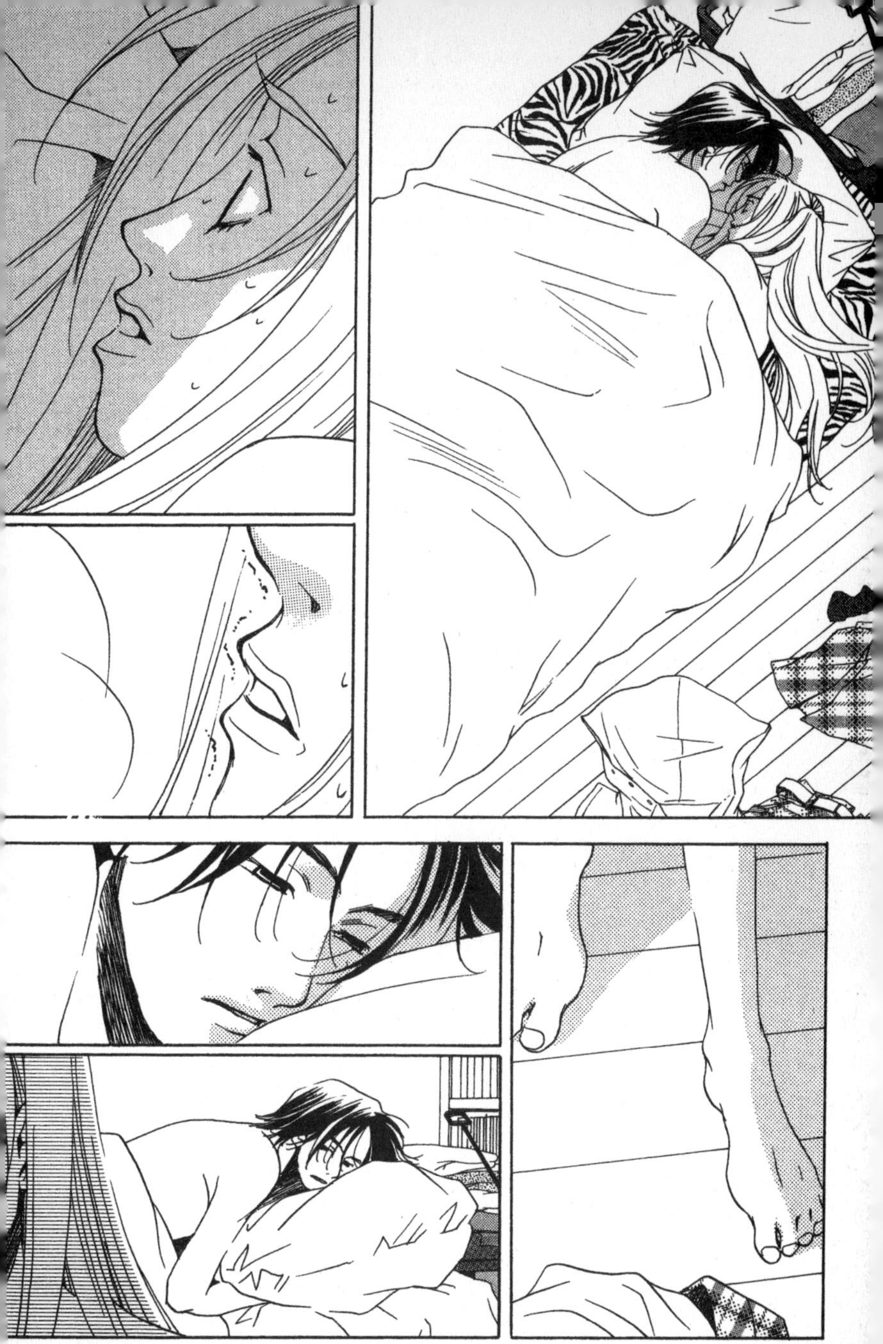

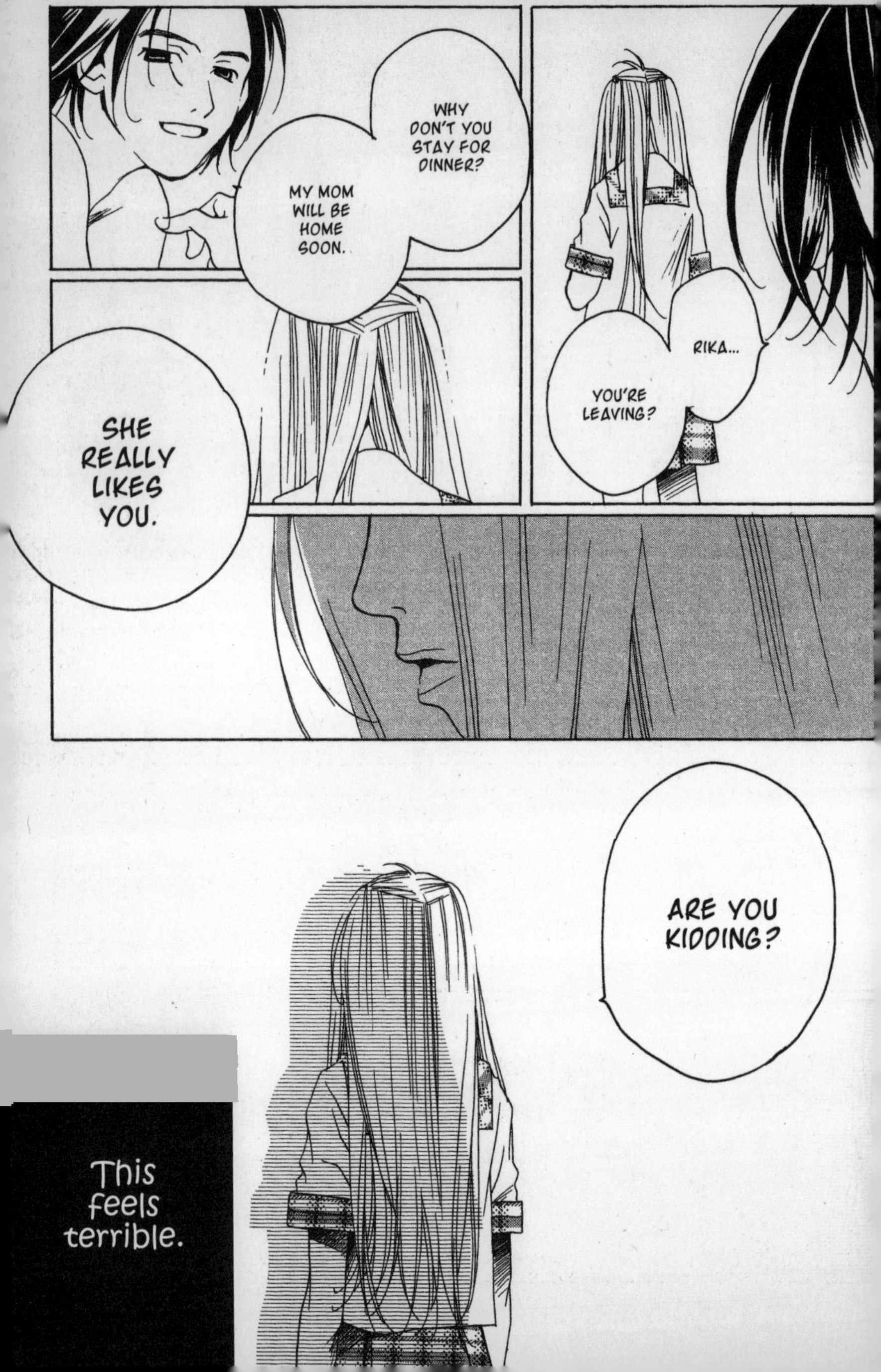
RIKA...
YOU'RE LEAVING?
WHY DON'T YOU STAY FOR DINNER?
MY MOM WILL BE HOME SOON.
SHE REALLY LIKES YOU.
ARE YOU KIDDING?
This feels terrible.

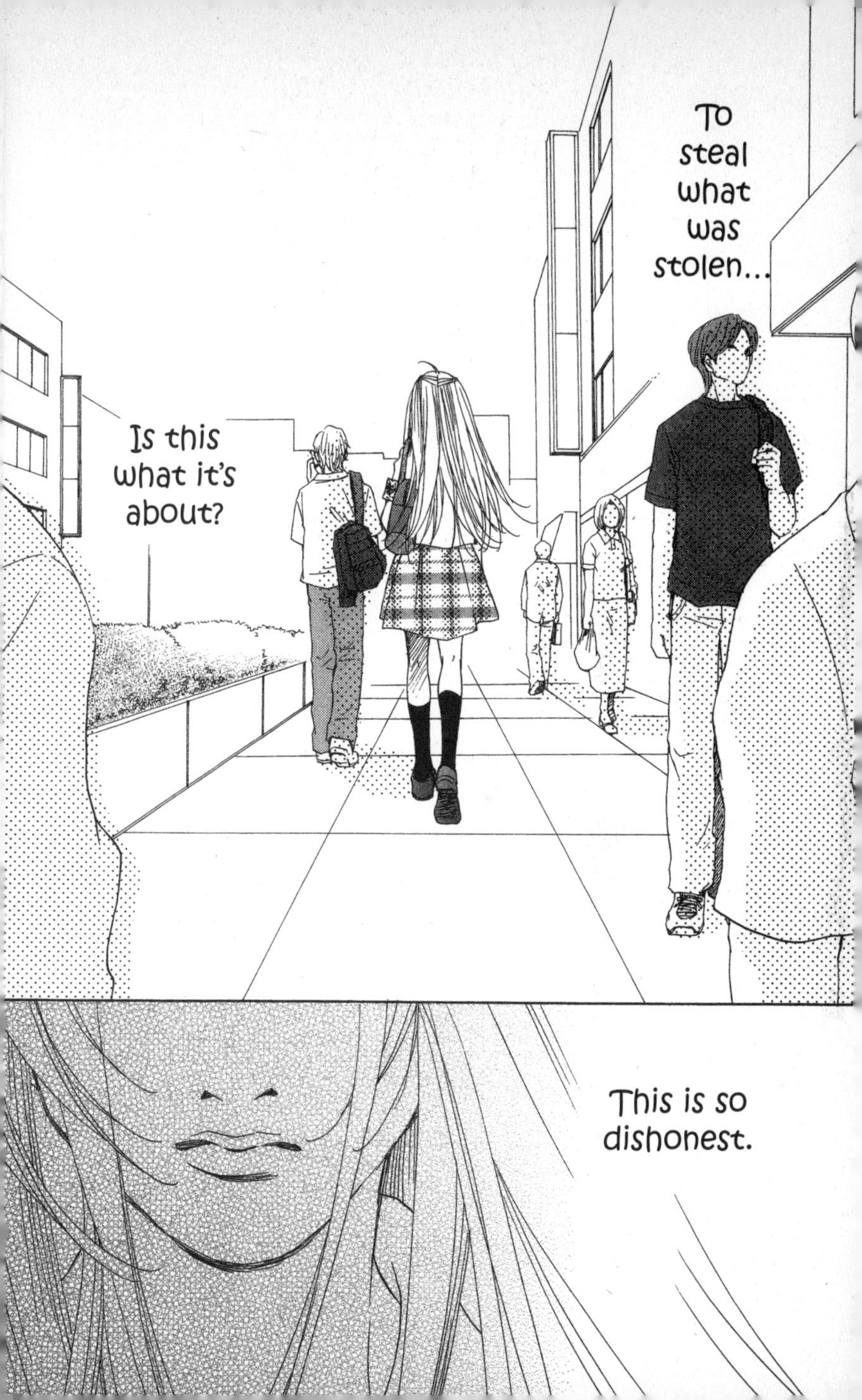
To steal what was stolen...
Is this what it's about?
This is so dishonest.

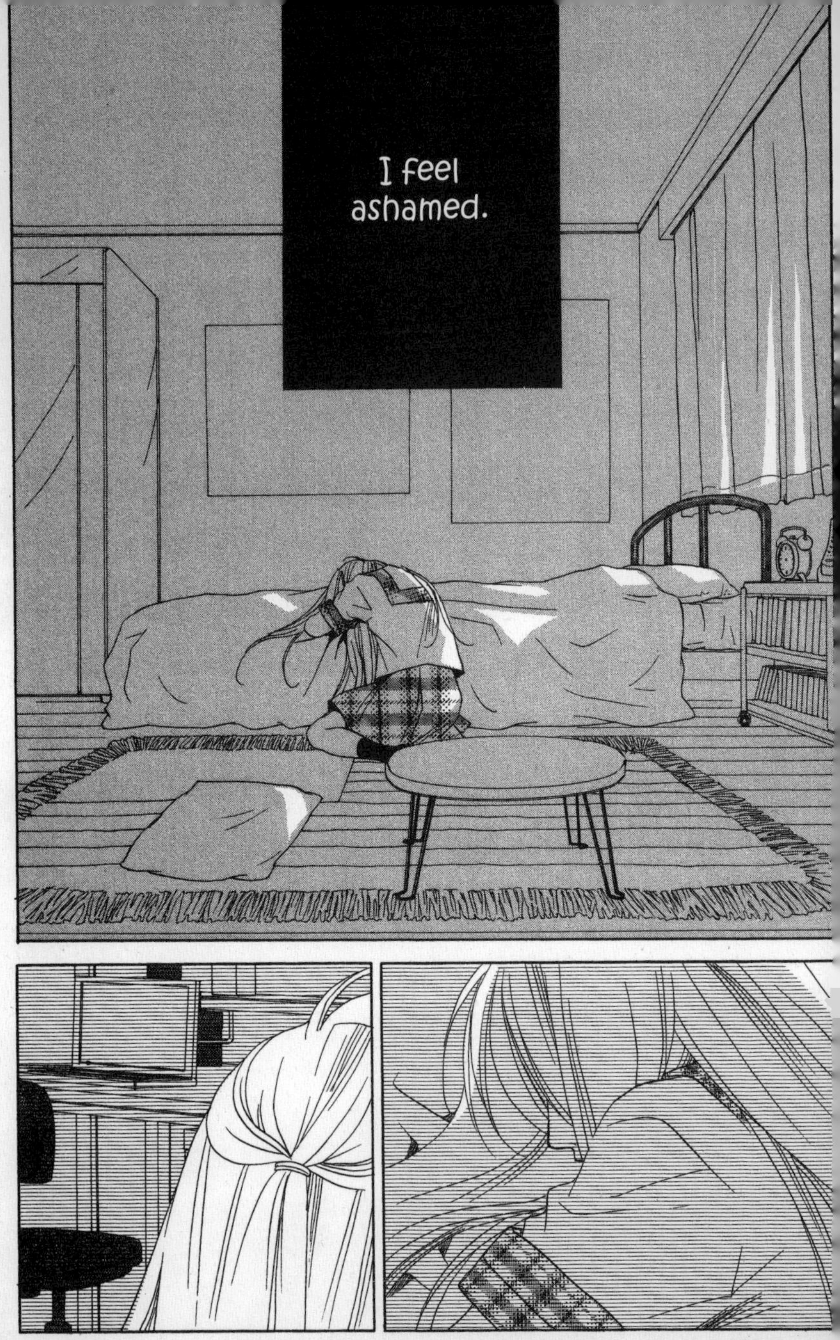
I feel
ashamed.

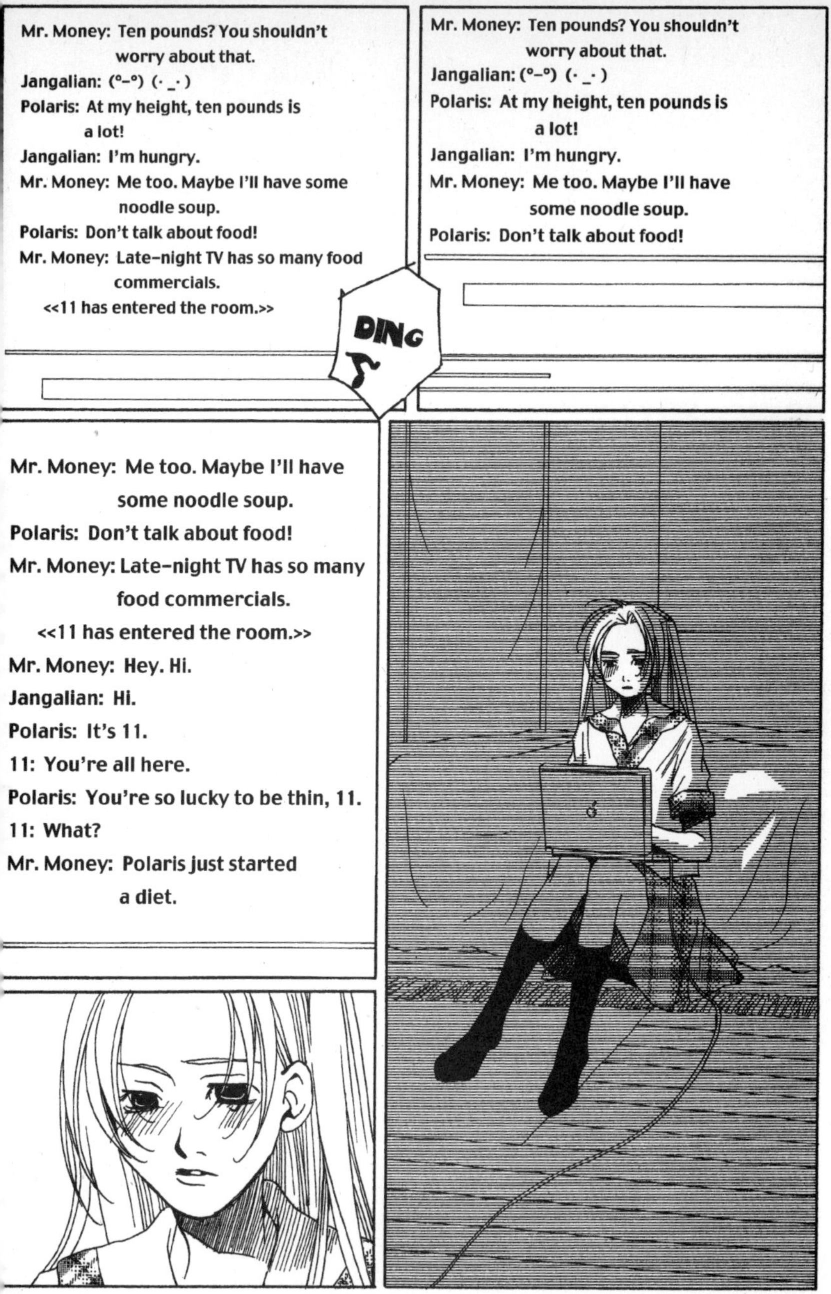
Mr. Money: Ten pounds? You shouldn't worry about that.
Jangalian: (°–°) (·_·)
Polaris: At my height, ten pounds is a lot!
Jangalian: I'm hungry.
Mr. Money: Me too. Maybe I'll have some noodle soup.
Polaris: Don't talk about food!
DING
Mr. Money: Ten pounds? You shouldn't worry about that.
Jangalian: (°–°) (·_·)
Polaris: At my height, ten pounds is a lot!
Jangalian: I'm hungry.
Mr. Money: Me too. Maybe I'll have some noodle soup.
Polaris: Don't talk about food!
Mr. Money: Late-night TV has so many food commercials.
<<11 has entered the room.>>
Mr. Money: Me too. Maybe I'll have some noodle soup.
Polaris: Don't talk about food!
Mr. Money: Late-night TV has so many food commercials.
<<11 has entered the room.>>
Mr. Money: Hey. Hi.
Jangalian: Hi.
Polaris: It's 11.
11: You're all here.
Polaris: You're so lucky to be thin, 11.
11: What?
Mr. Money: Polaris just started a diet.

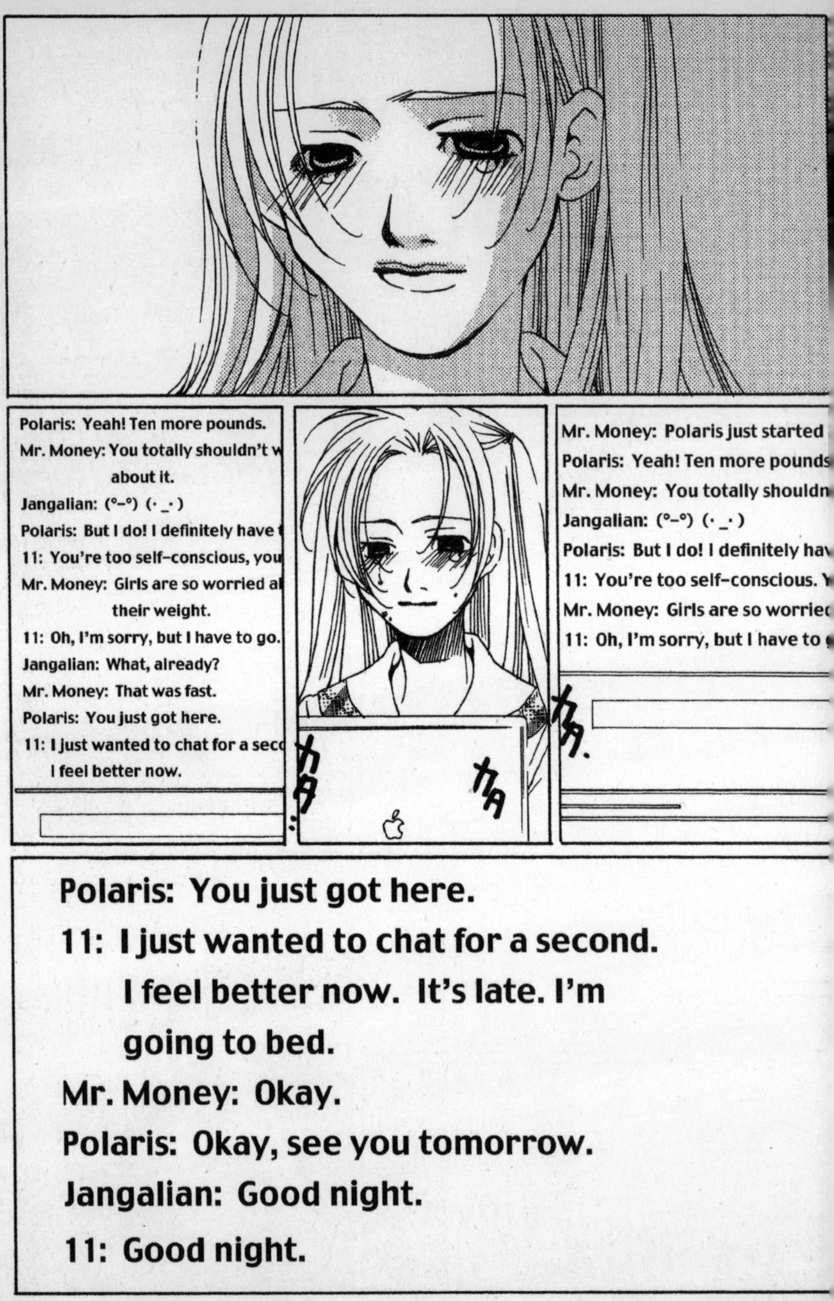
Mr. Money: Polaris just started
Polaris: Yeah! Ten more pounds
Mr. Money: You totally should
Jangalian: (°–°) (·_·)
Polaris: But I do! I definitely ha
11: You're too self-conscious.
Mr. Money: Girls are so worrie
11: Oh, I'm sorry, but I have to
カタ
カタ
カタ
Polaris: Yeah! Ten more pounds.
Mr. Money: You totally shouldn't
about it.
Jangalian: (°–°) (·_·)
Polaris: But I do! I definitely have
11: You're too self-conscious, you
Mr. Money: Girls are so worried a
their weight.
11: Oh, I'm sorry, but I have to go.
Jangalian: What, already?
Mr. Money: That was fast.
Polaris: You just got here.
11: I just wanted to chat for a sec
I feel better now.
Polaris: You just got here.
11: I just wanted to chat for a second.
I feel better now. It's late. I'm
going to bed.
Mr. Money: Okay.
Polaris: Okay, see you tomorrow.
Jangalian: Good night.
11: Good night.

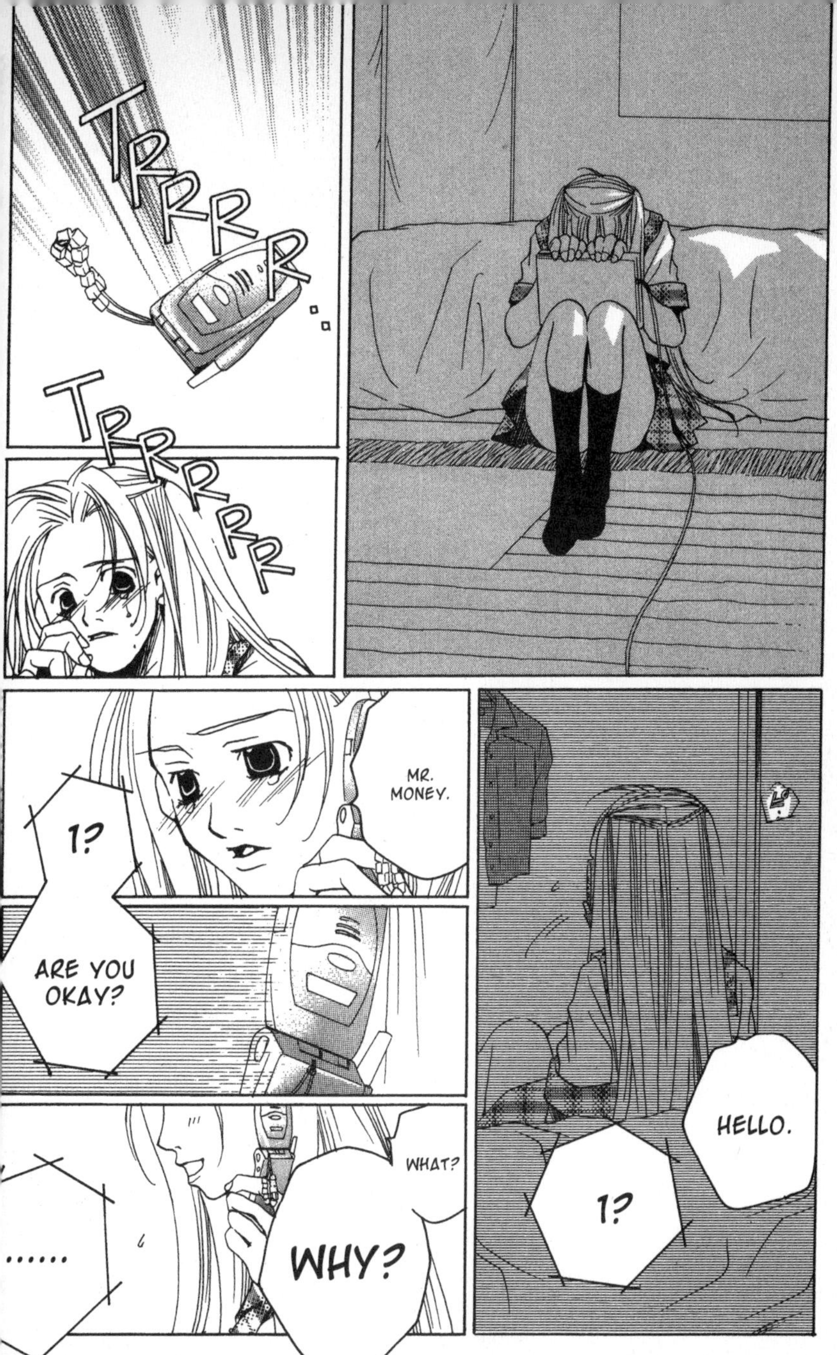
TRRRR
TRRRRR
HELLO.
!?
MR. MONEY.
!?
ARE YOU OKAY?
WHAT?
WHY?
......

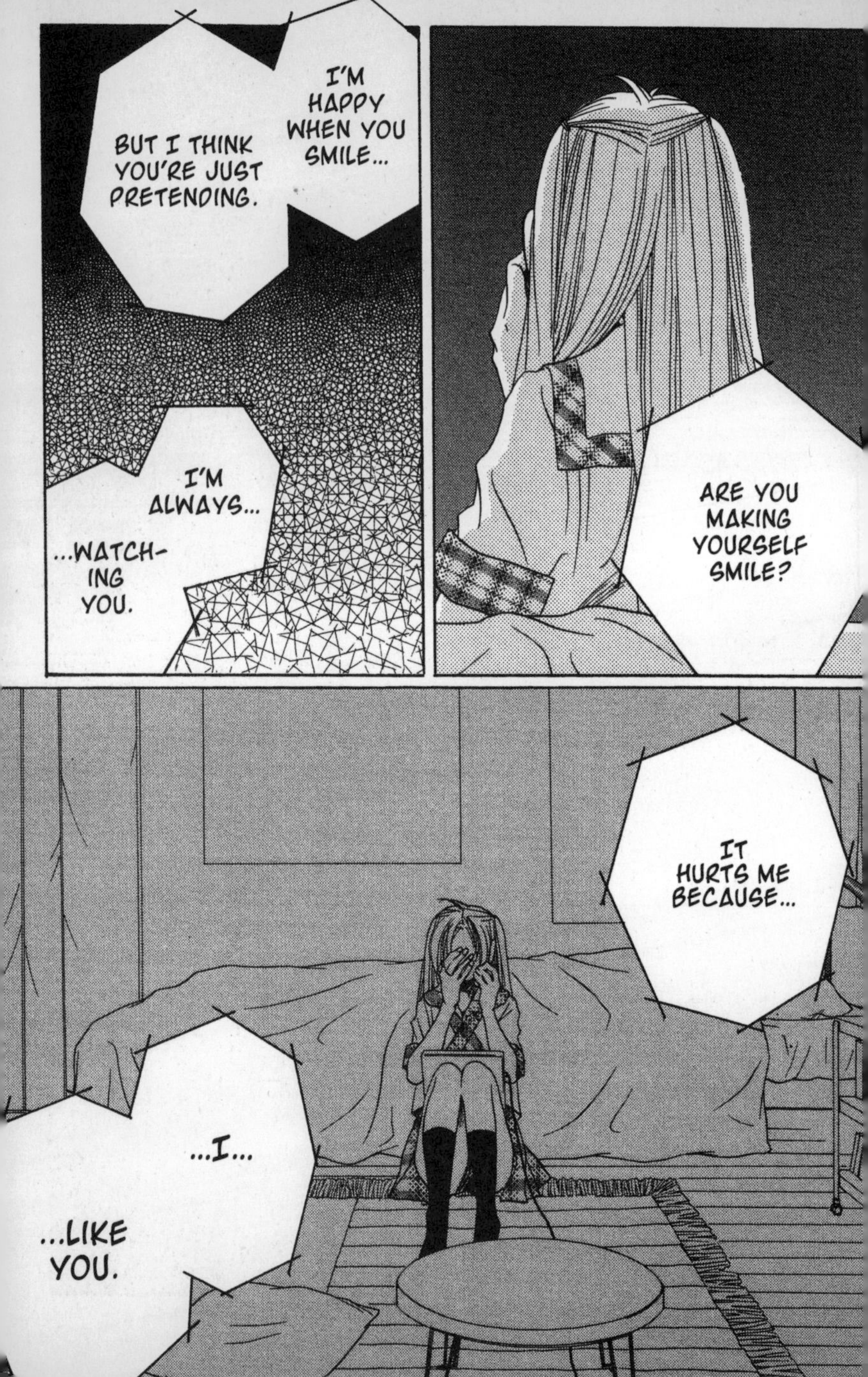
ARE YOU MAKING YOURSELF SMILE?
I'M HAPPY WHEN YOU SMILE...
BUT I THINK YOU'RE JUST PRETENDING.
I'M ALWAYS...
...WATCHING-ING YOU.
IT HURTS ME BECAUSE...
...I...
...LIKE YOU.

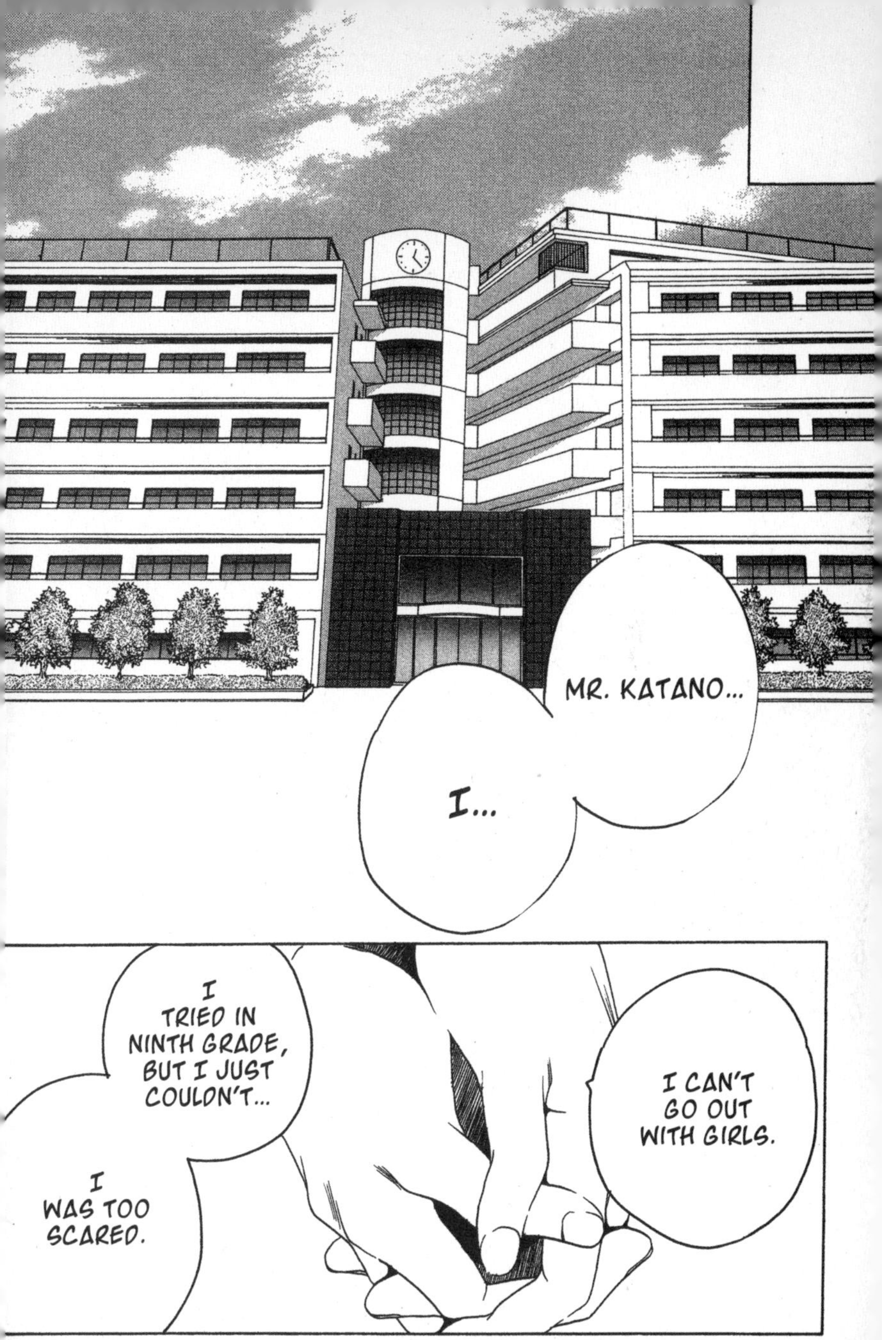
MR. KATANO...
I...
I CAN'T GO OUT WITH GIRLS.
I TRIED IN NINTH GRADE, BUT I JUST COULDN'T...
I WAS TOO SCARED.

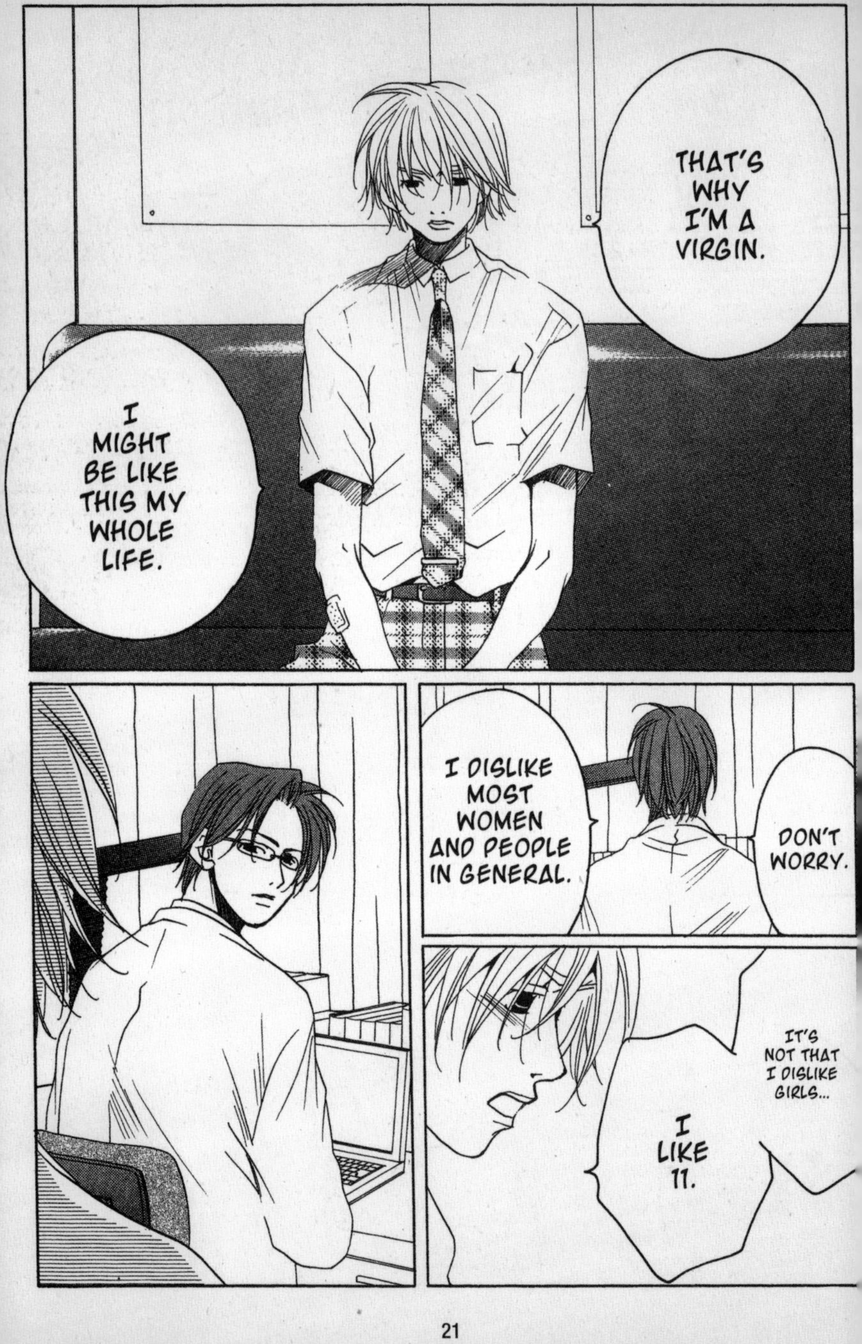
THAT'S WHY I'M A VIRGIN.
I MIGHT BE LIKE THIS MY WHOLE LIFE.
DON'T WORRY.
I DISLIKE MOST WOMEN AND PEOPLE IN GENERAL.
IT'S NOT THAT I DISLIKE GIRLS...
I LIKE IT.

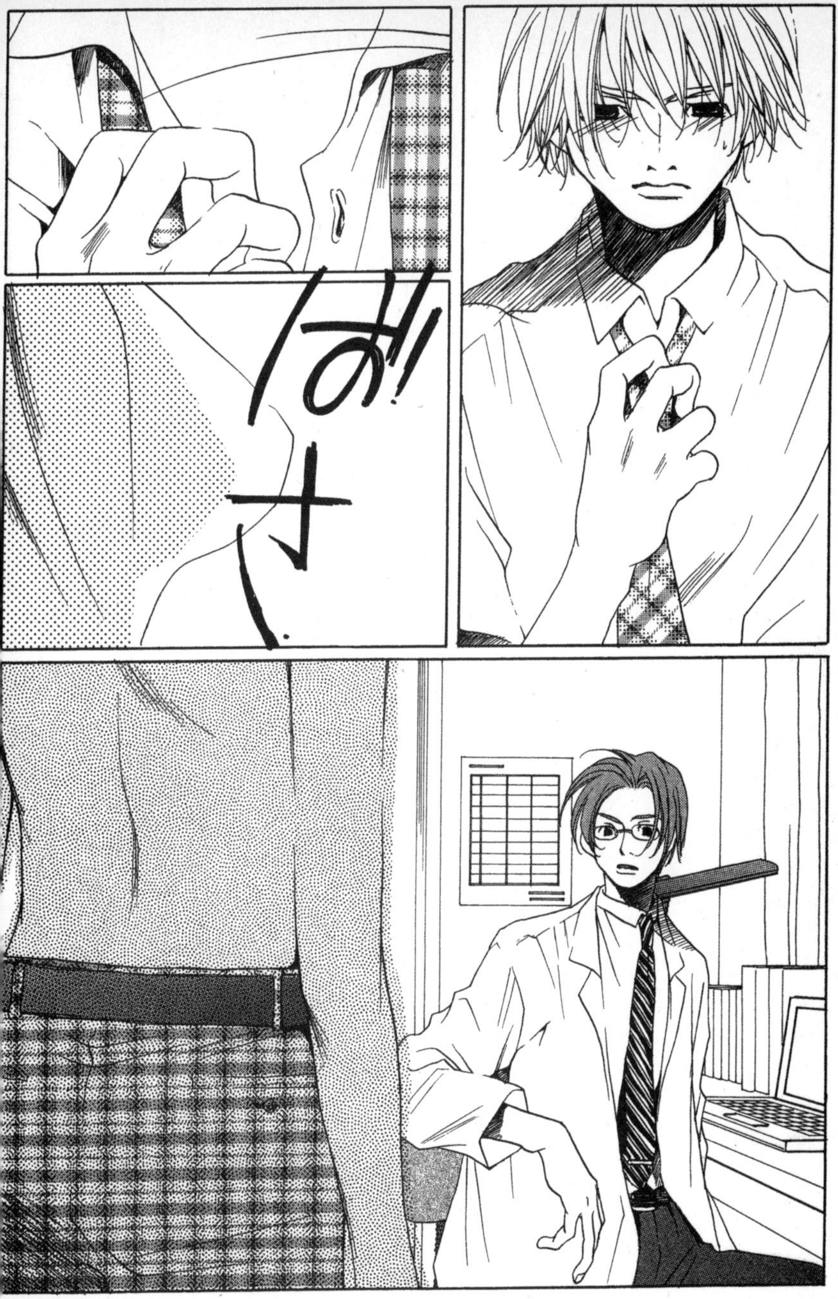
ばさ

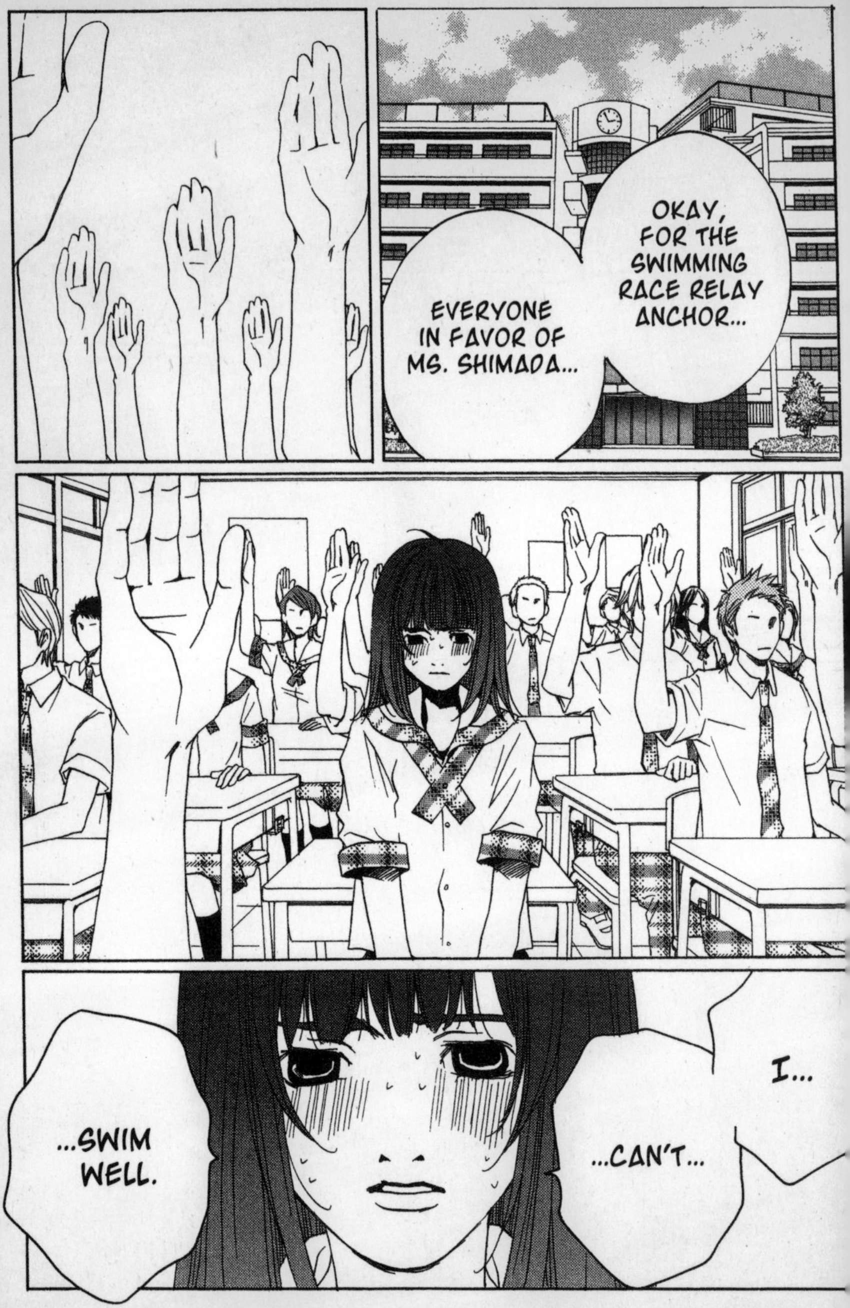
OKAY, FOR THE SWIMMING RACE RELAY ANCHOR...
EVERYONE IN FAVOR OF MS. SHIMADA...
I...
...CAN'T...
...SWIM WELL.

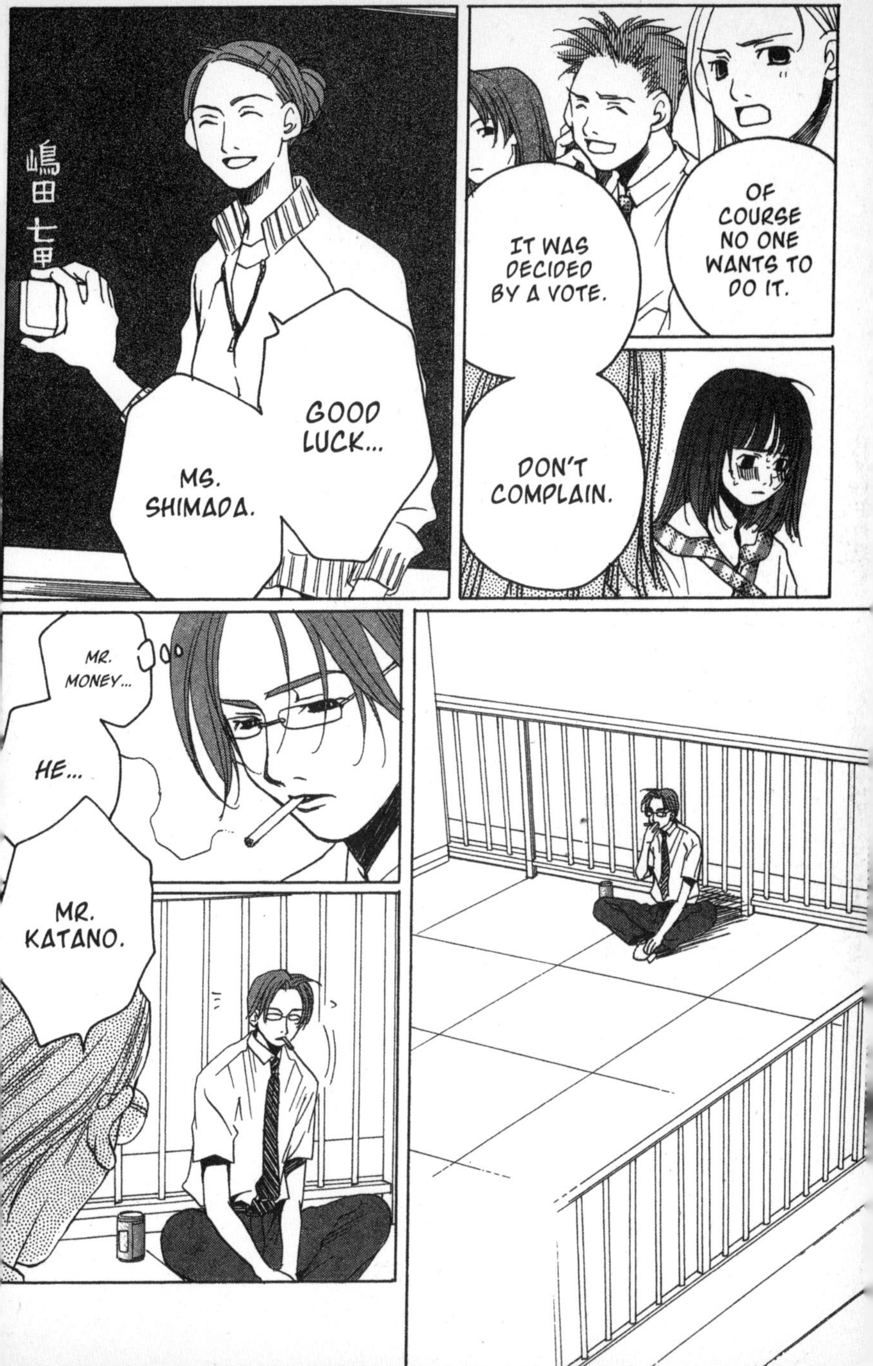

OF COURSE NO ONE WANTS TO DO IT.
IT WAS DECIDED BY A VOTE.
DON'T COMPLAIN.
嶋田七
GOOD LUCK...
MS. SHIMADA.
MR. MONEY...
HE...
MR. KATANO.

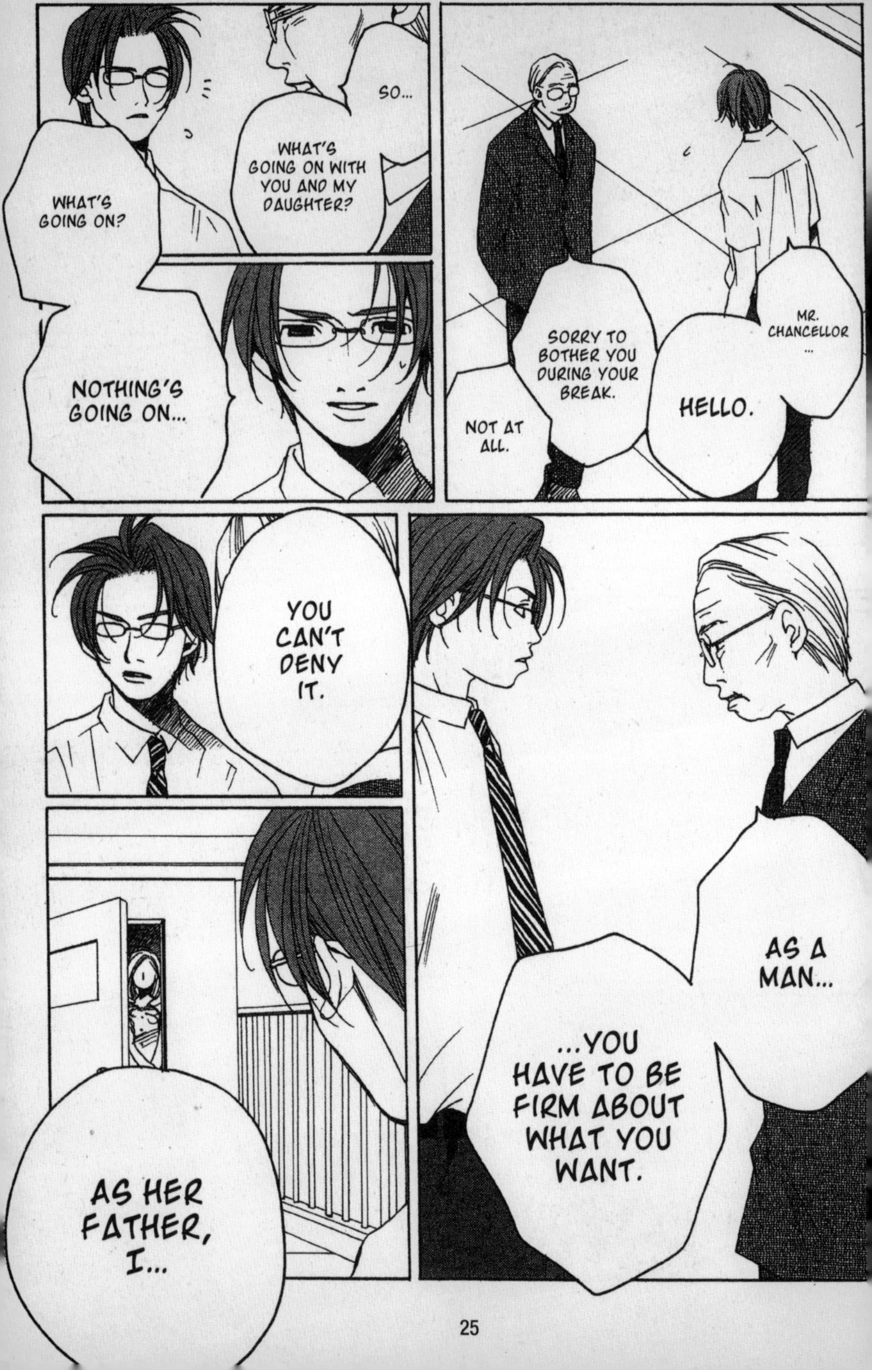
MR. CHANCELLOR ...
HELLO.
SORRY TO BOTHER YOU DURING YOUR BREAK.
NOT AT ALL.
SO...
WHAT'S GOING ON WITH YOU AND MY DAUGHTER?
WHAT'S GOING ON?
NOTHING'S GOING ON...
AS A MAN...
...YOU HAVE TO BE FIRM ABOUT WHAT YOU WANT.
YOU CAN'T DENY IT.
AS HER FATHER, I...

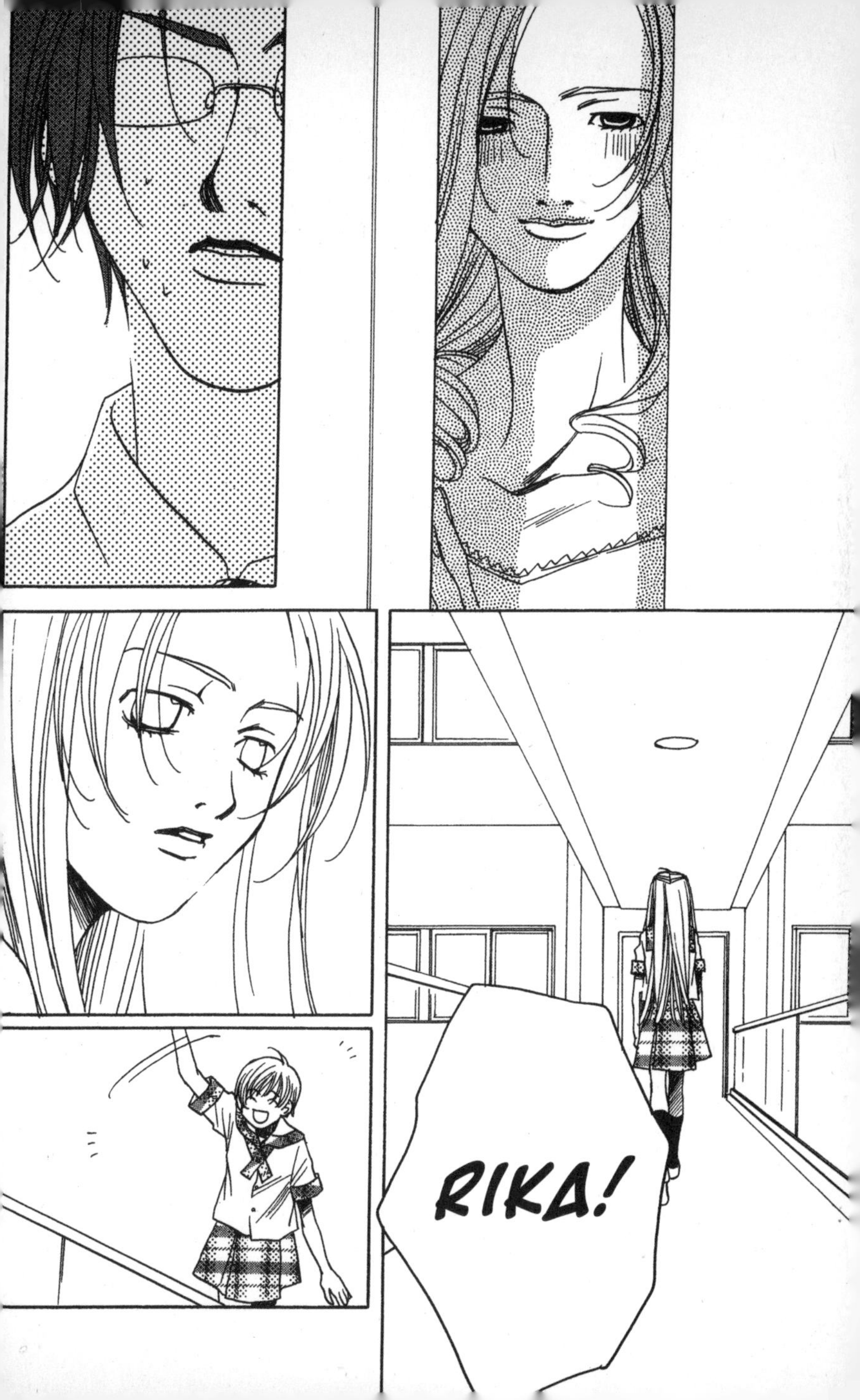
RIKA!

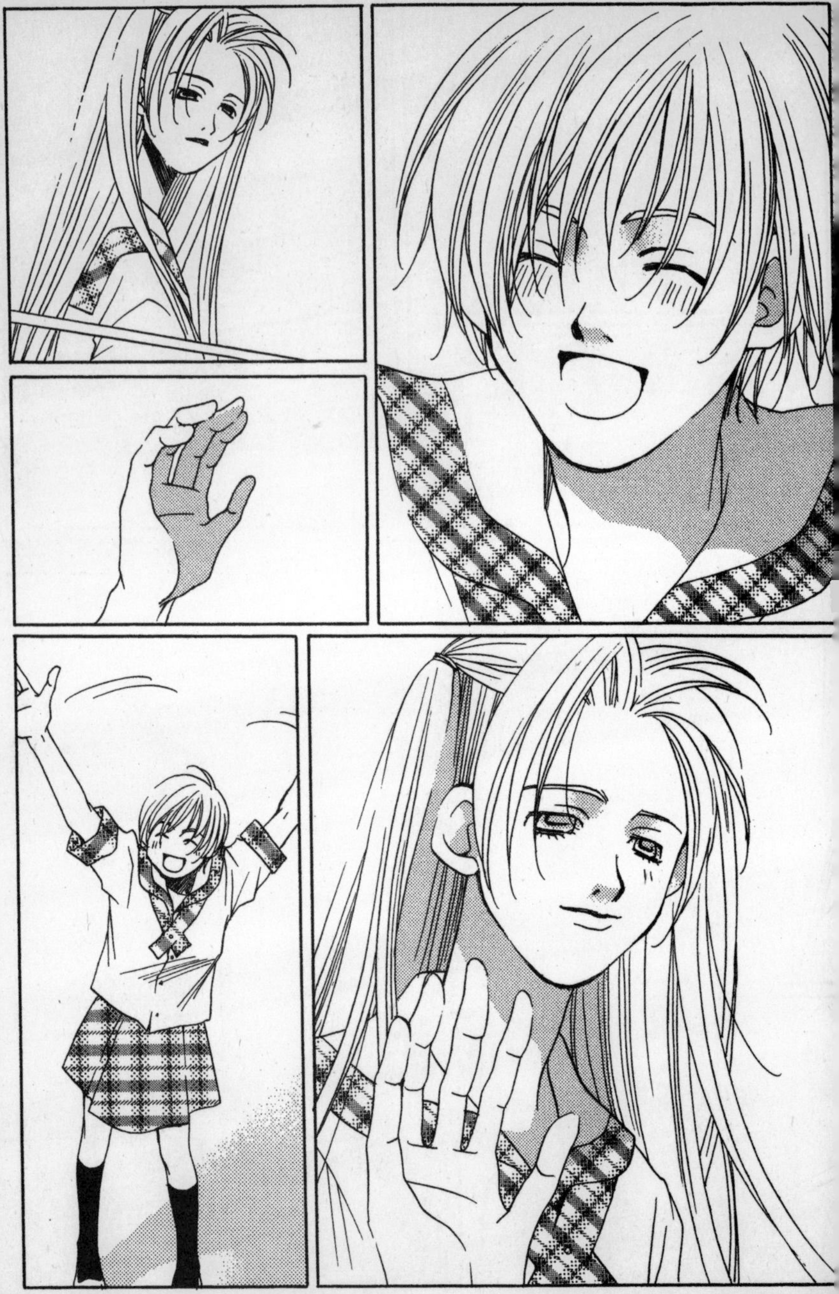

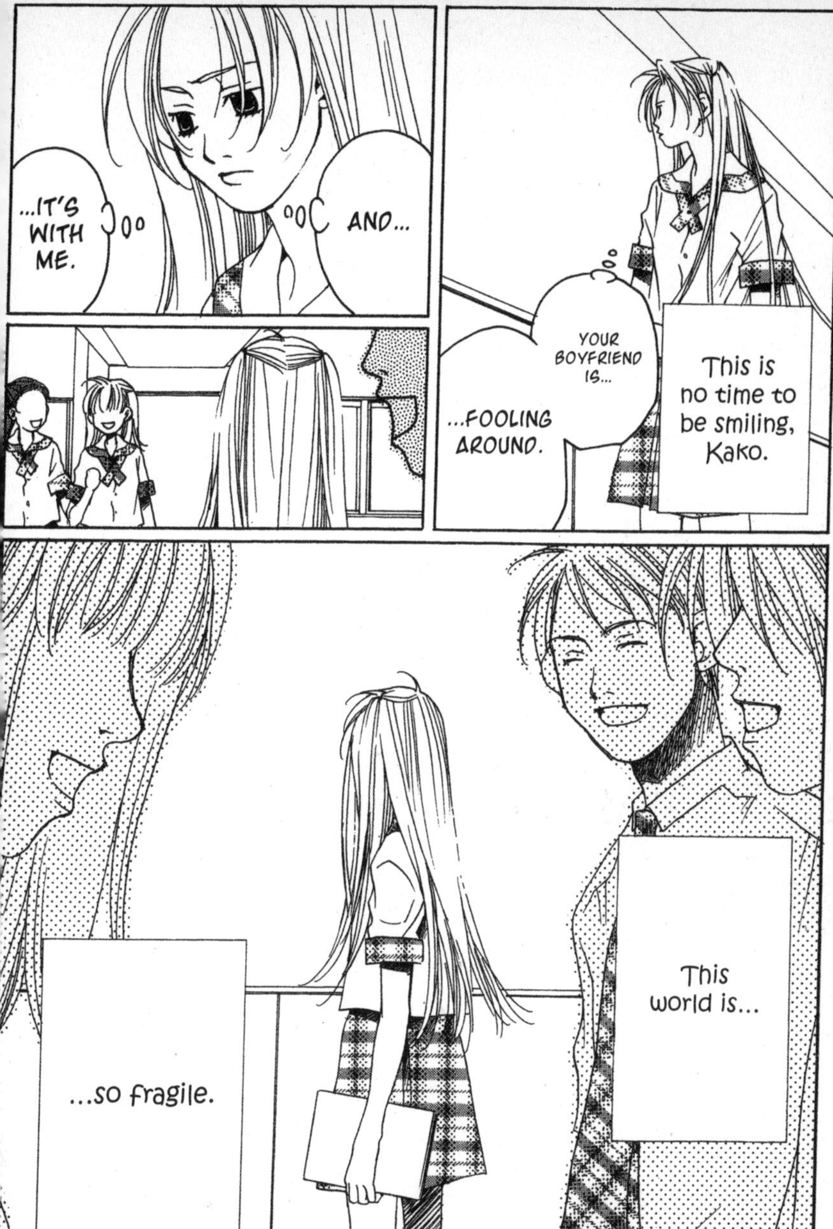
YOUR BOYFRIEND IS...
...FOOLING AROUND.
This is no time to be smiling, Kako.
AND...
...IT'S WITH ME.
This world is...
...so fragile.

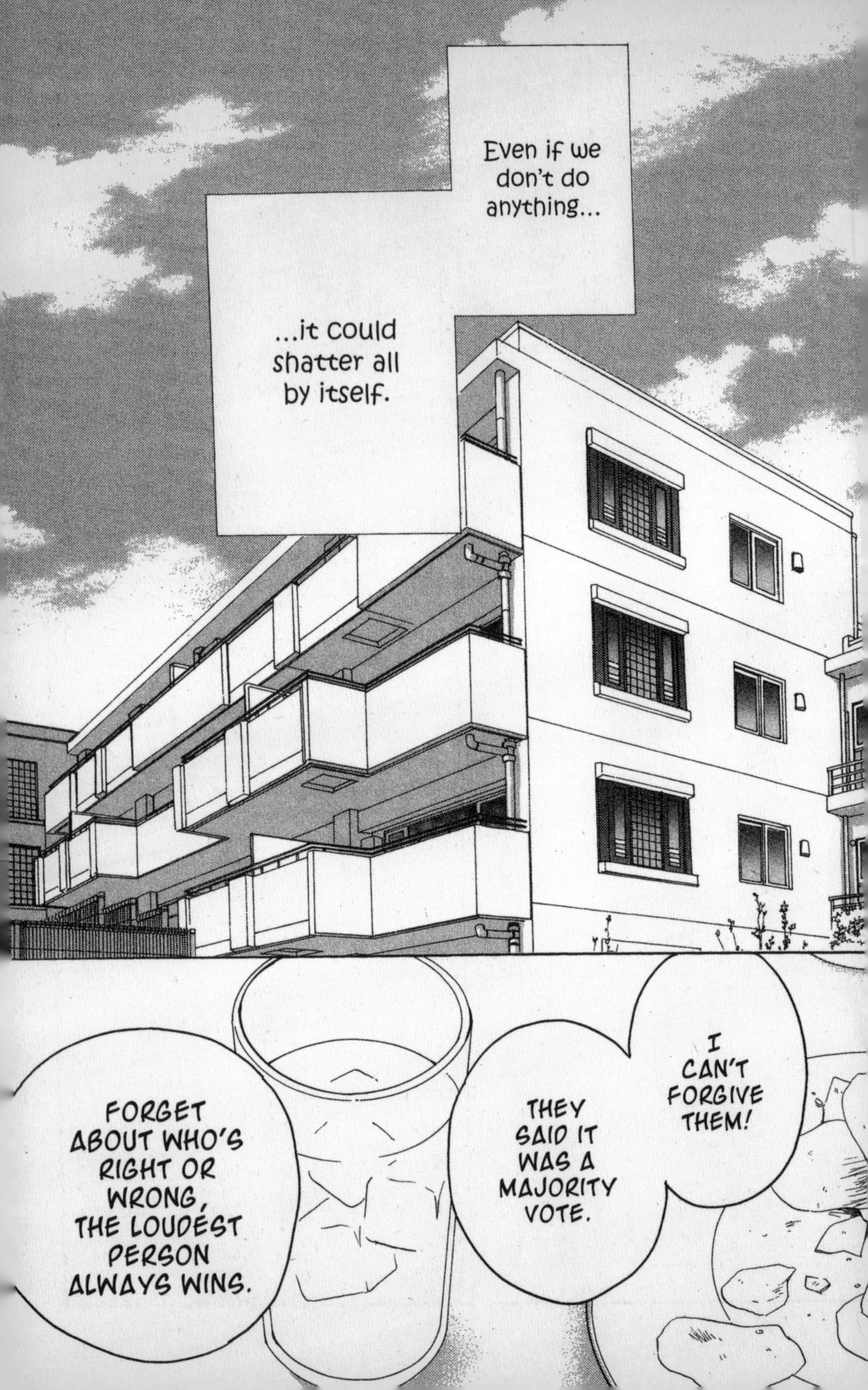
Even if we don't do anything...
...it could shatter all by itself.
I CAN'T FORGIVE THEM!
THEY SAID IT WAS A MAJORITY VOTE.
FORGET ABOUT WHO'S RIGHT OR WRONG, THE LOUDEST PERSON ALWAYS WINS.

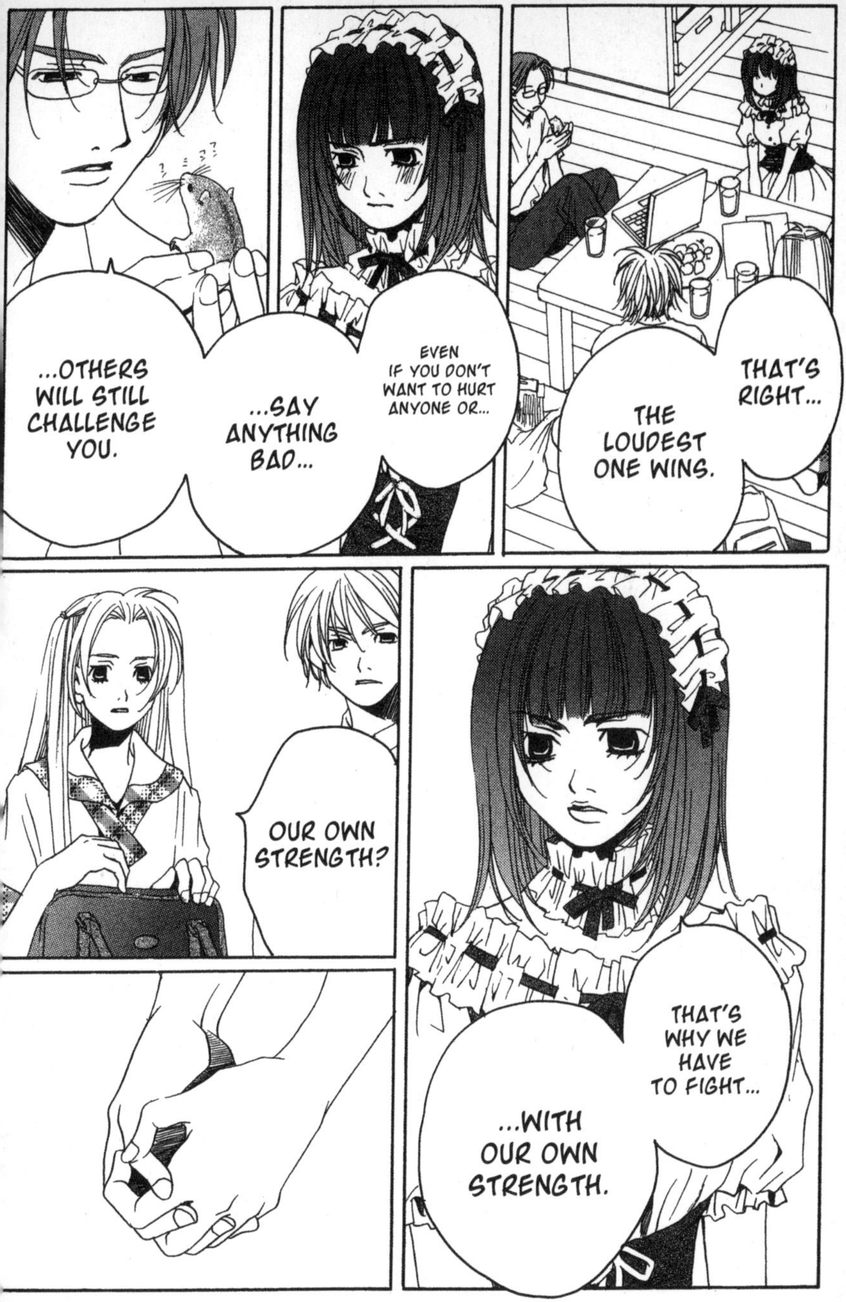
THAT'S RIGHT...
THE LOUDEST ONE WINS.
EVEN IF YOU DON'T WANT TO HURT ANYONE OR...
...SAY ANYTHING BAD...
...OTHERS WILL STILL CHALLENGE YOU.
THAT'S WHY WE HAVE TO FIGHT...
...WITH OUR OWN STRENGTH.
OUR OWN STRENGTH?

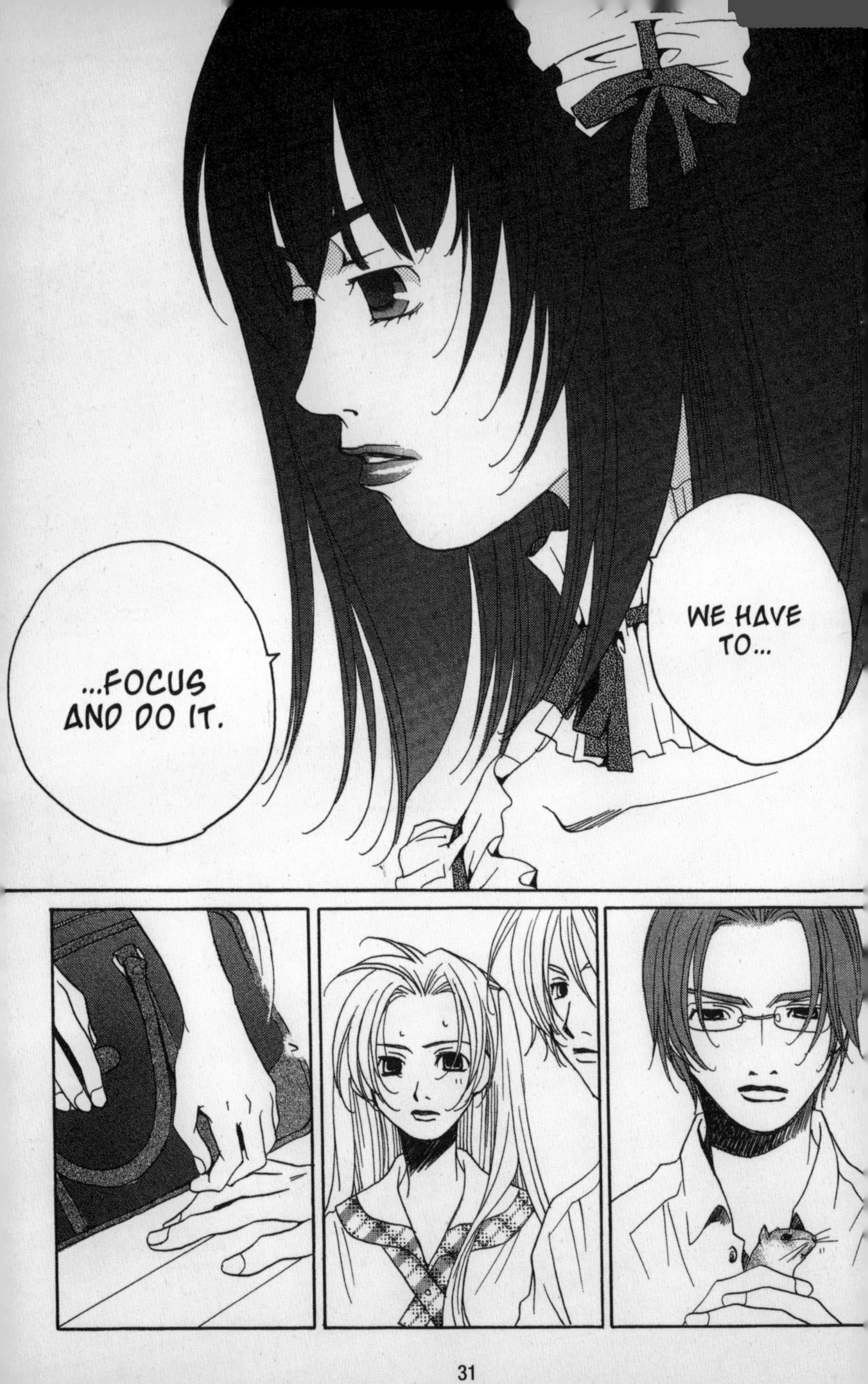
WE HAVE TO...
...FOCUS AND DO IT.

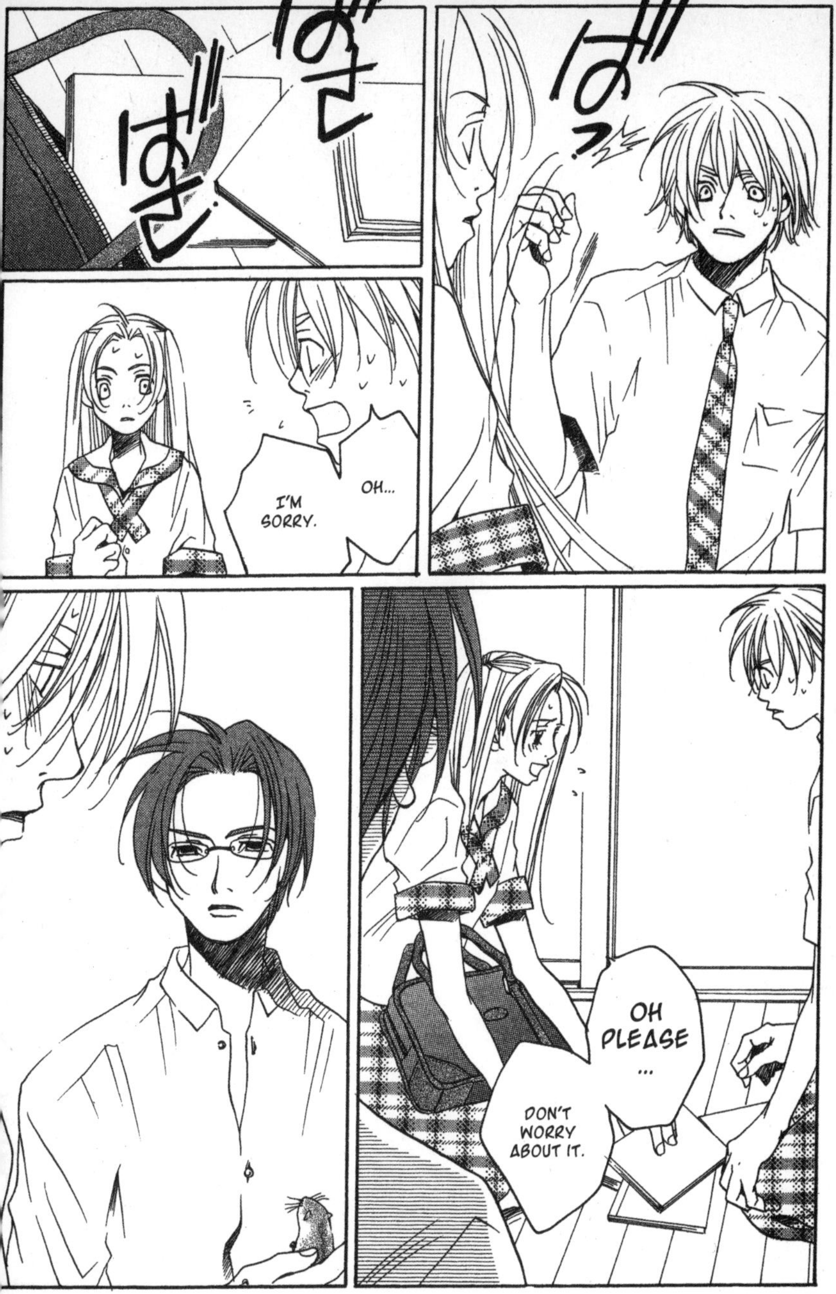
ばっ
ばさ ばさ
OH...
I'M SORRY.
OH PLEASE ...
DON'T WORRY ABOUT IT.

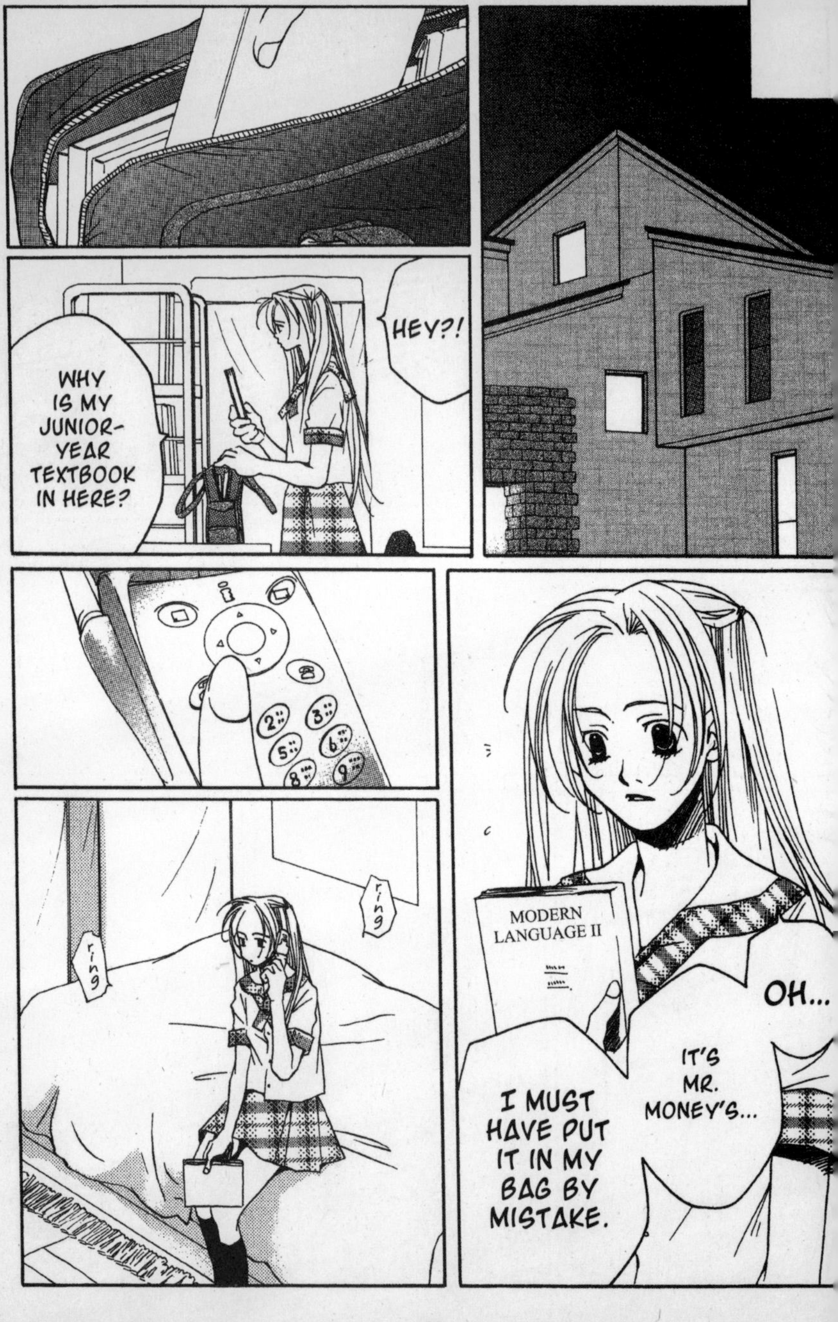
HEY?!
WHY IS MY JUNIOR-YEAR TEXTBOOK IN HERE?
MODERN LANGUAGE II
OH...
IT'S MR. MONEY'S...
I MUST HAVE PUT IT IN MY BAG BY MISTAKE.
ring
ring

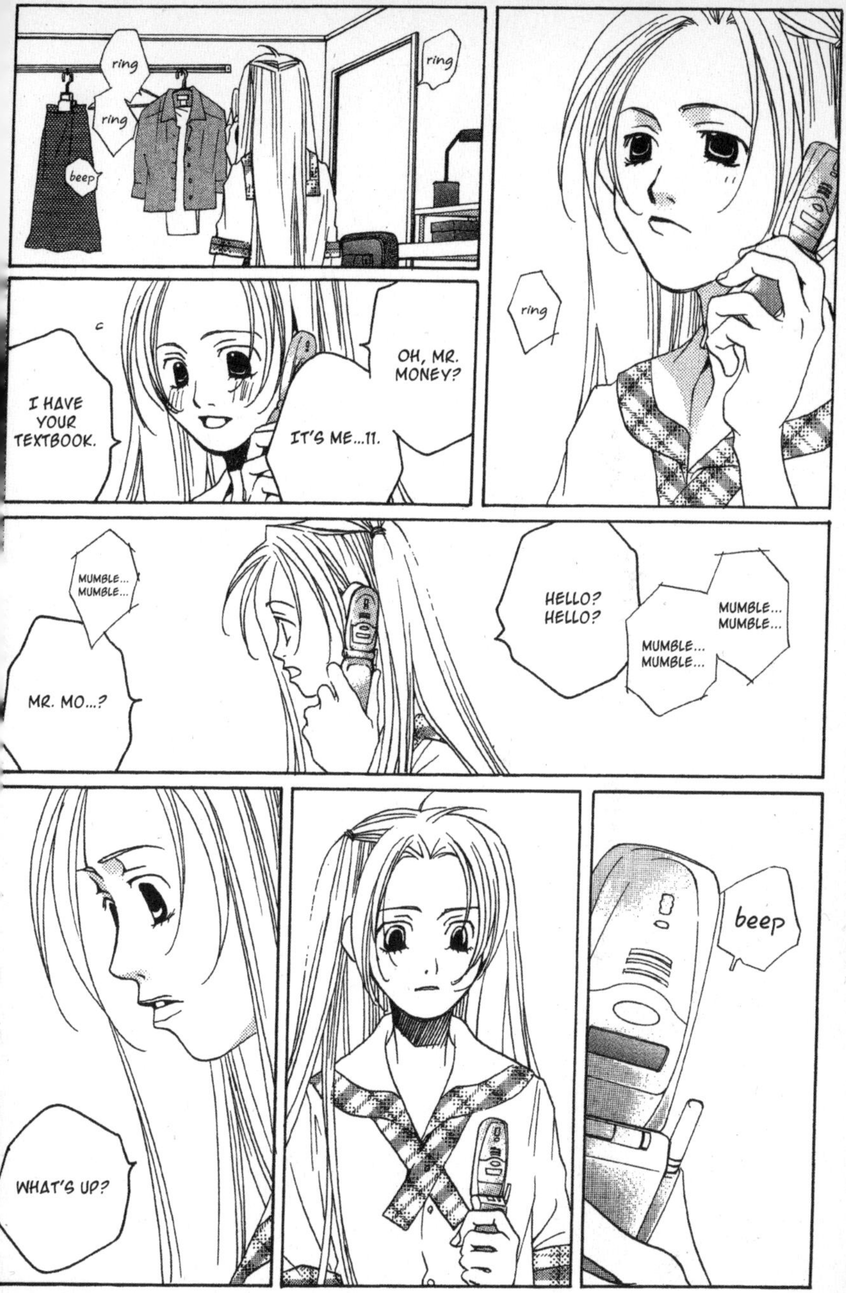

ring
ring
ring
ring
beep
OH, MR. MONEY?
IT'S ME...11.
I HAVE YOUR TEXTBOOK.
MUMBLE... MUMBLE...
HELLO? HELLO?
MUMBLE... MUMBLE...
MUMBLE... MUMBLE...
MR. MO...?
beep
WHAT'S UP?

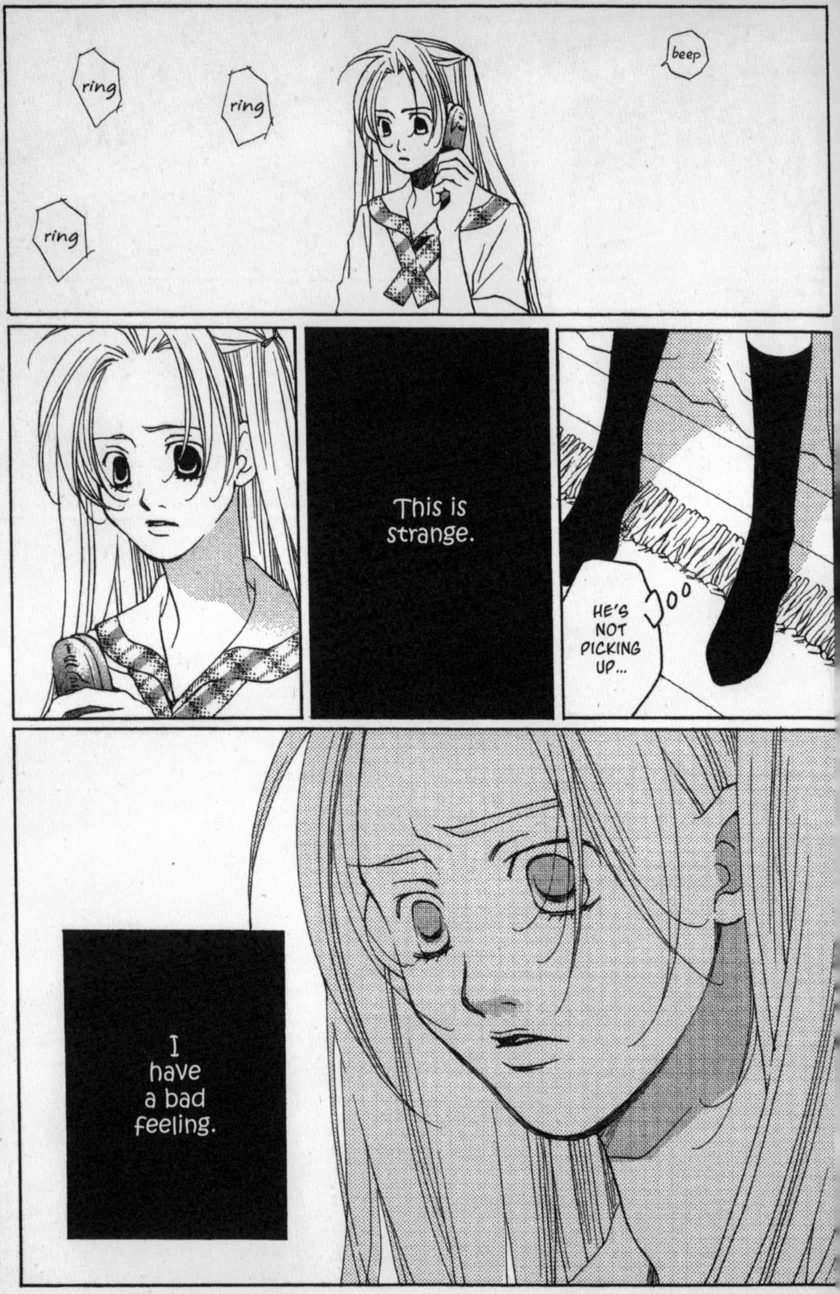
beep
ring
ring
ring
HE'S NOT PICKING UP...
This is strange.
I have a bad feeling.

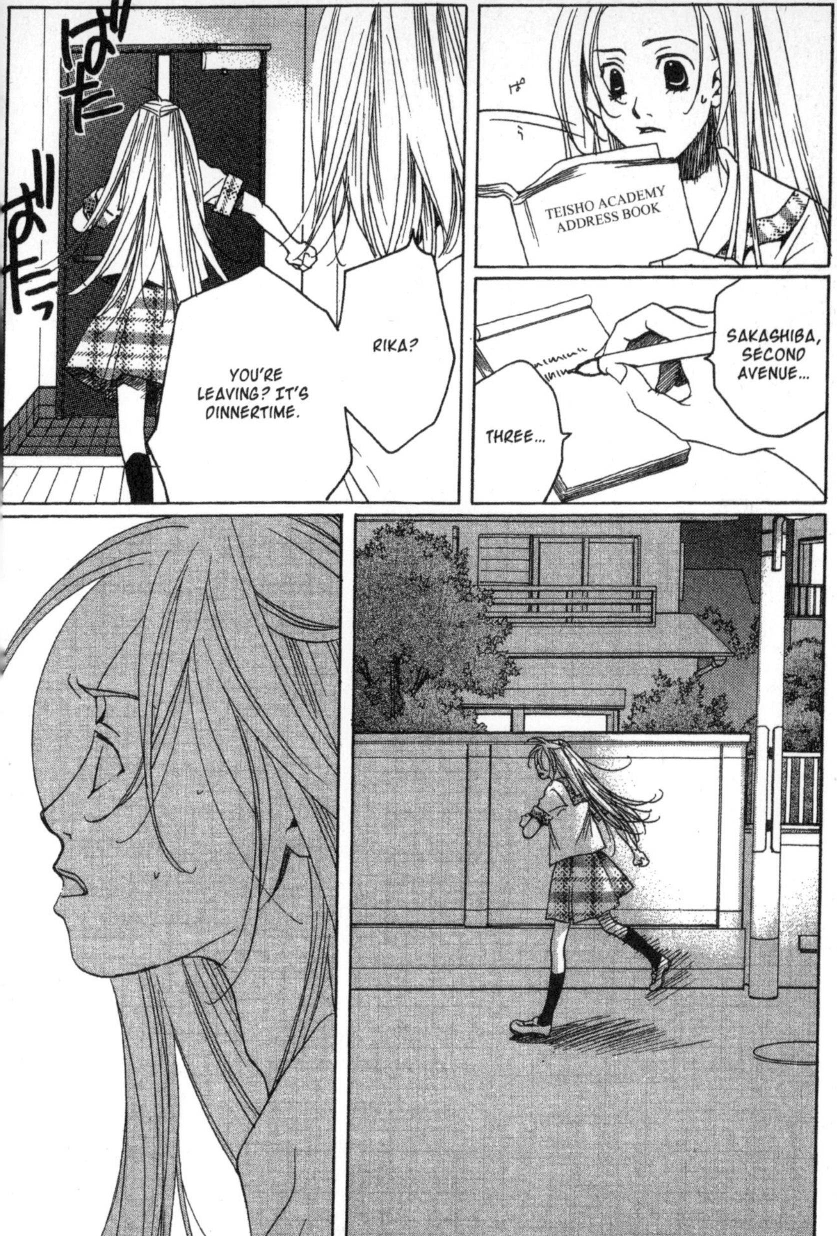
ぱら
TEISHO ACADEMY ADDRESS BOOK
SAKASHIBA, SECOND AVENUE...
THREE...
ばた
ばたっ
RIKA?
YOU'RE LEAVING? IT'S DINNERTIME.

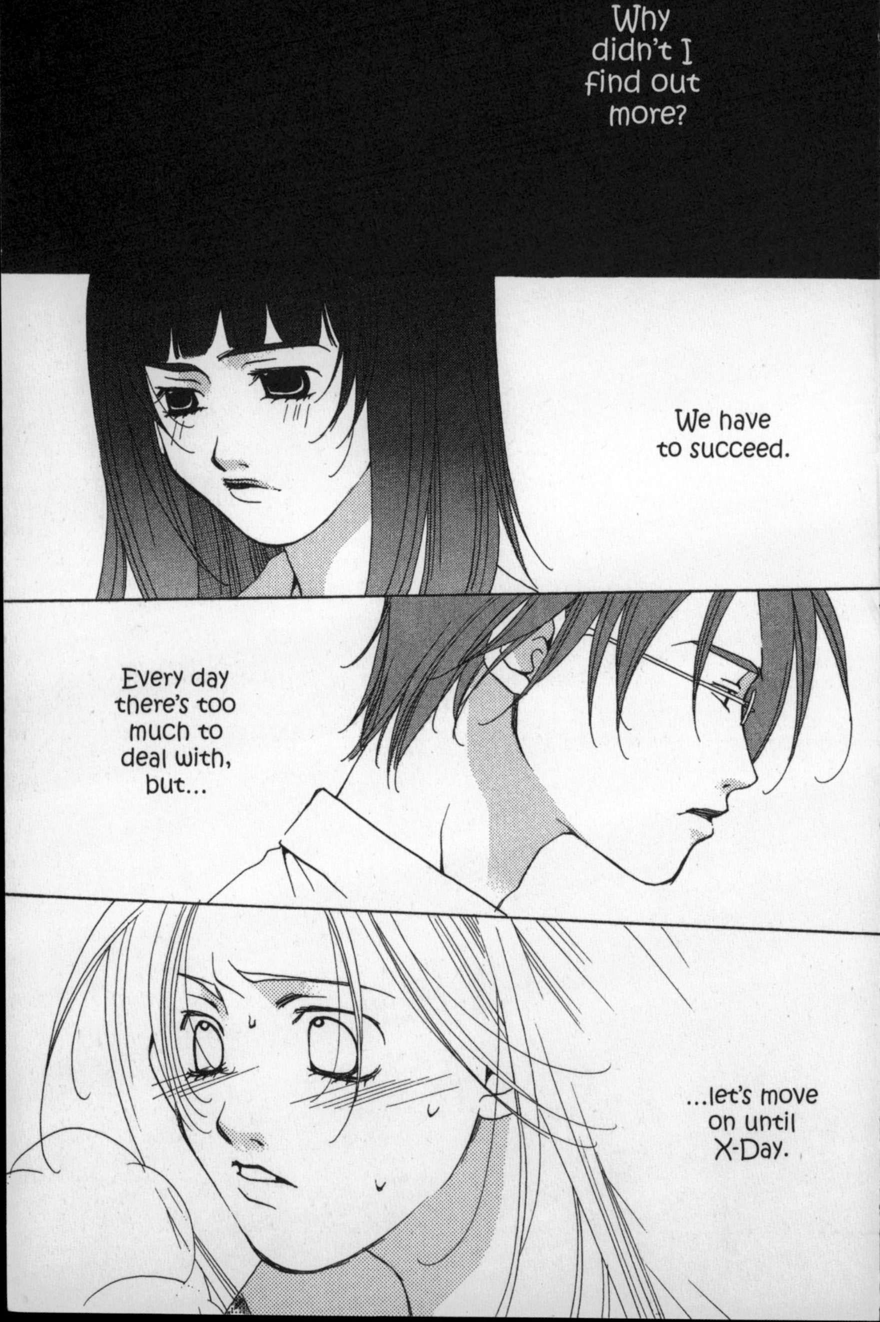
Why didn't I find out more?
We have to succeed.
Every day there's too much to deal with, but...
...let's move on until X-Day.

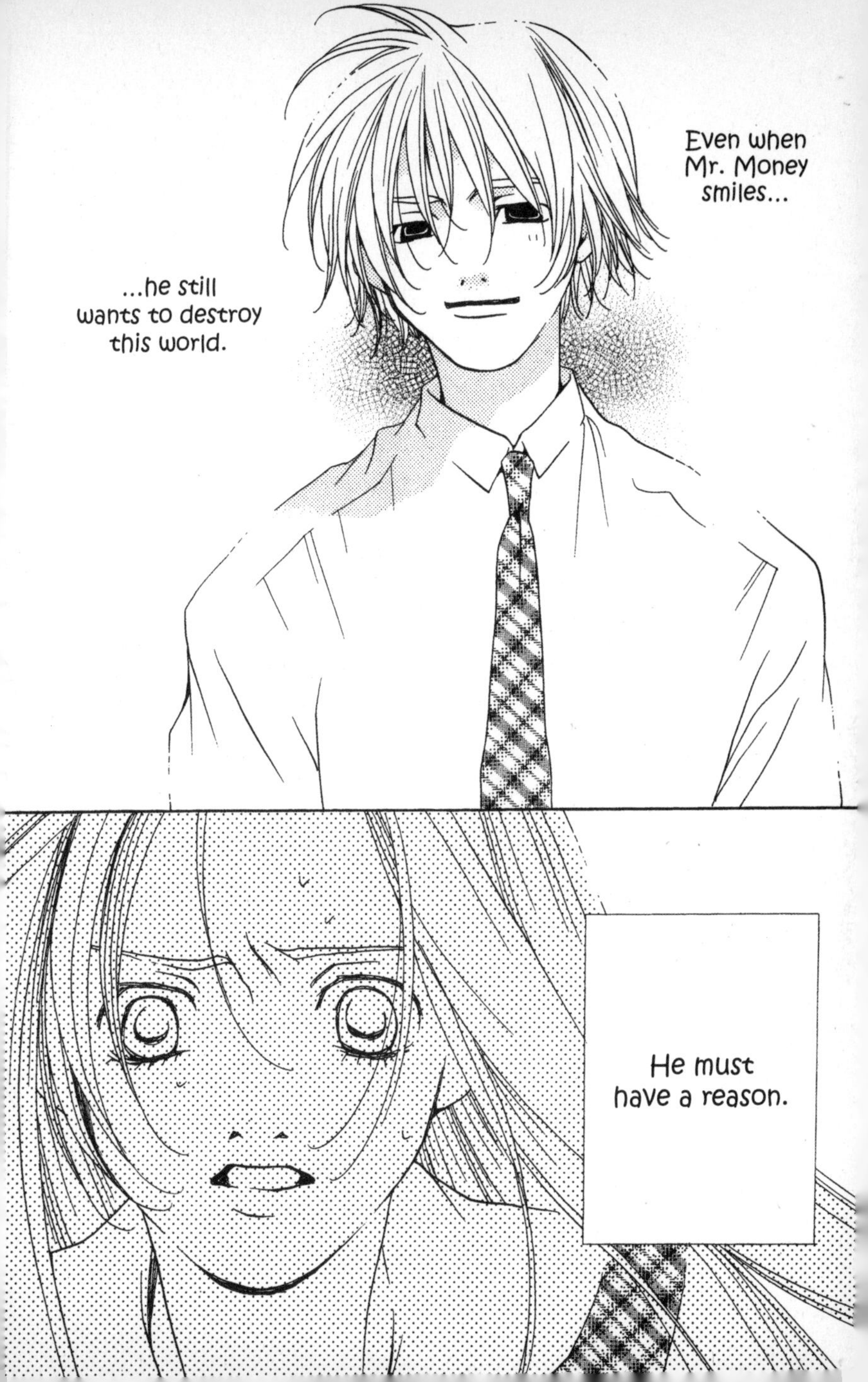
Even when Mr. Money smiles...
...he still wants to destroy this world.
He must have a reason.

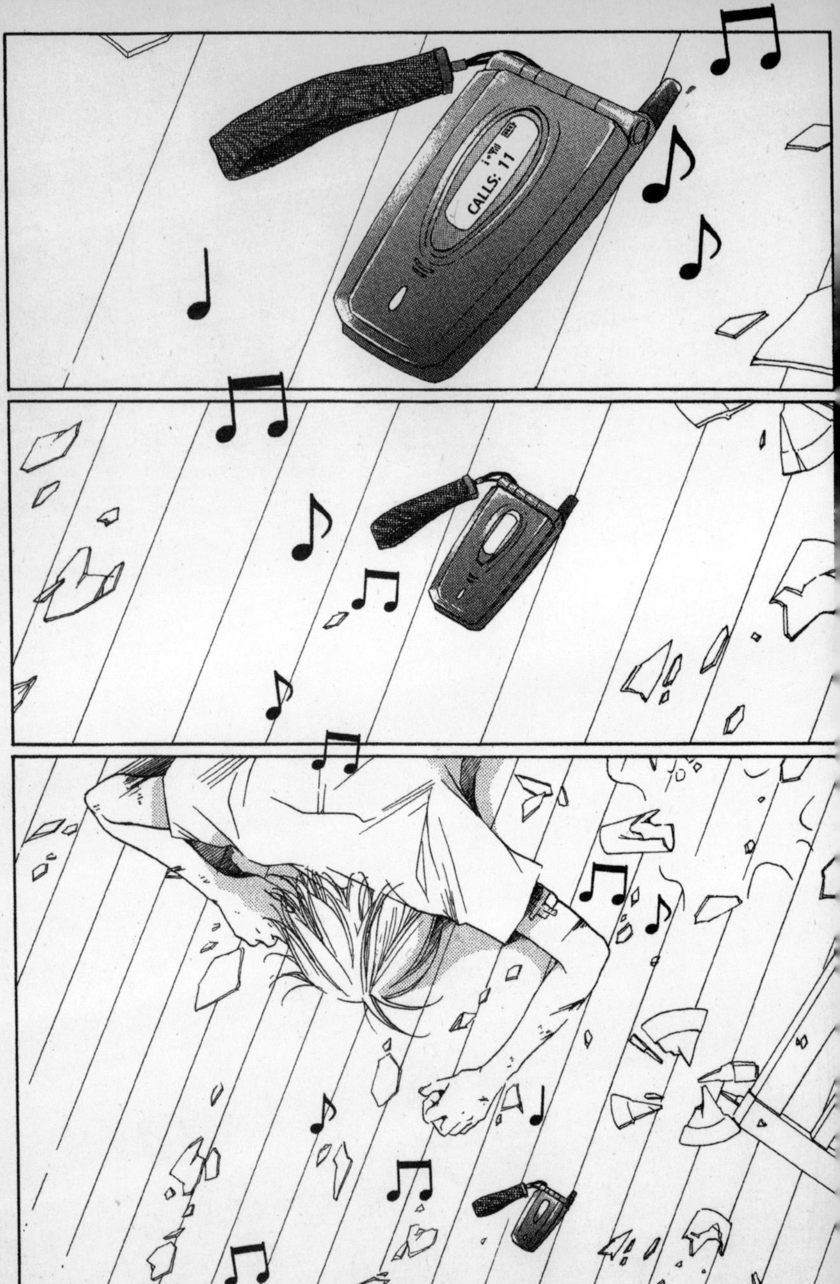
CALLS: 11

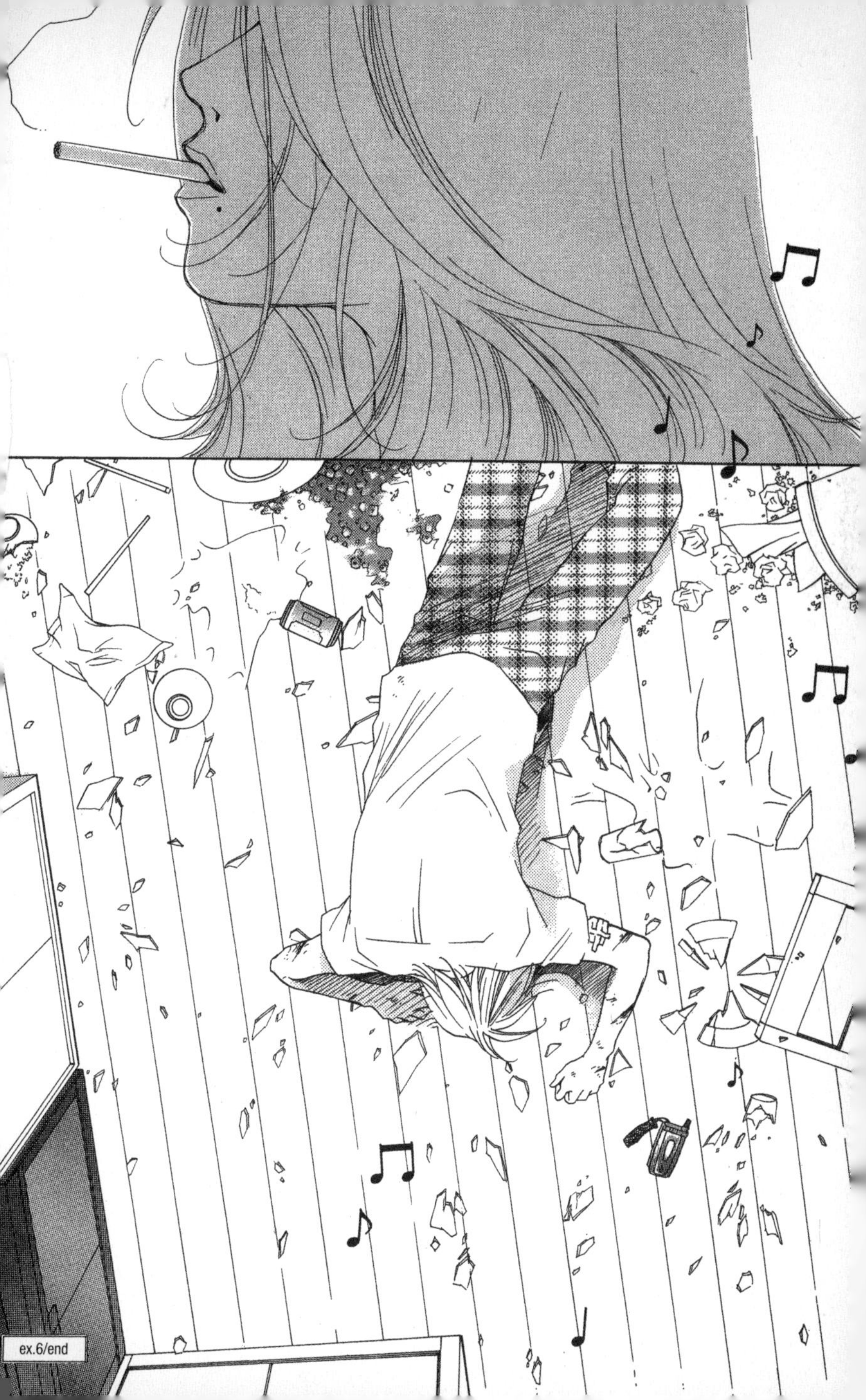
ex.6/end

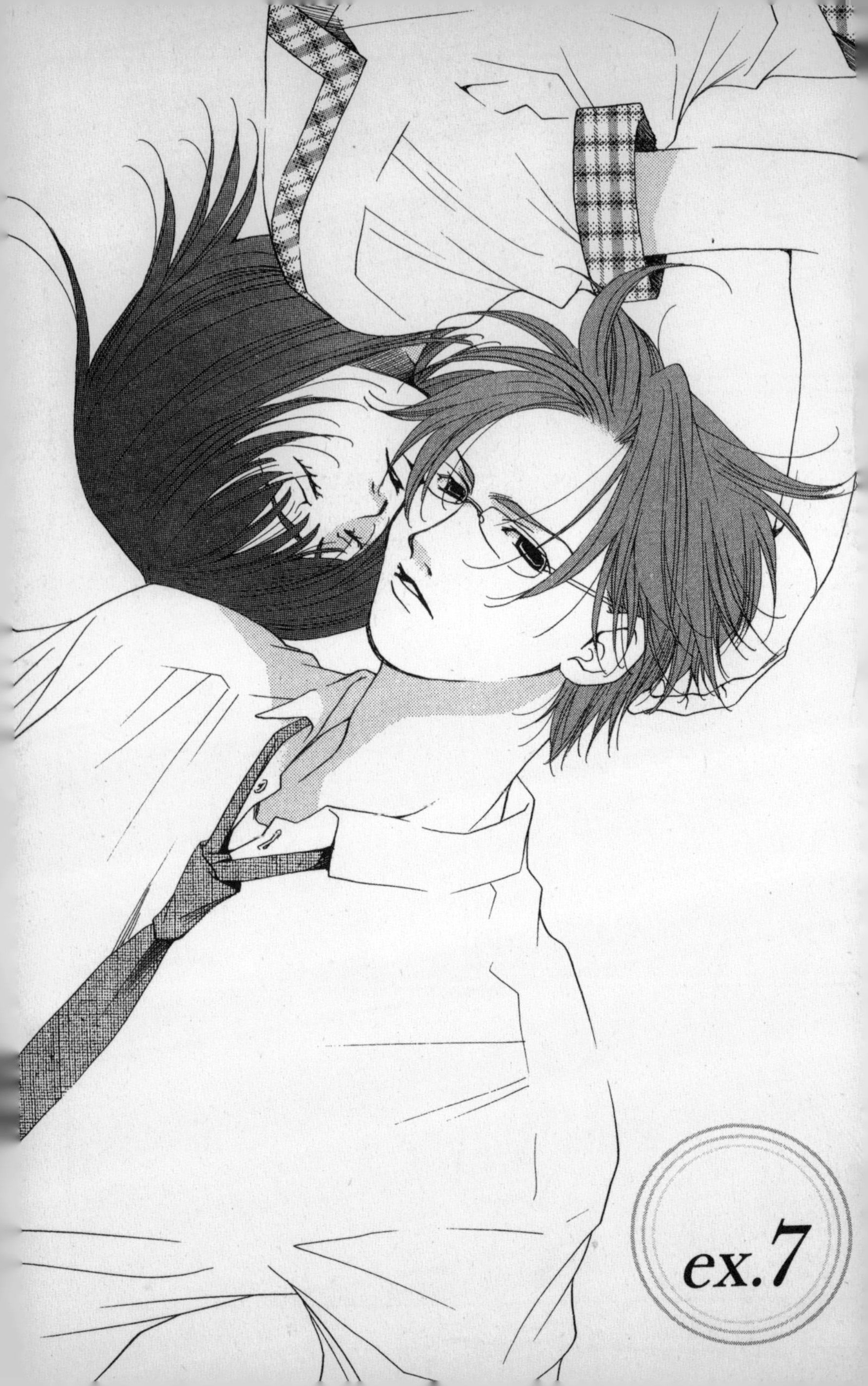
ex.7

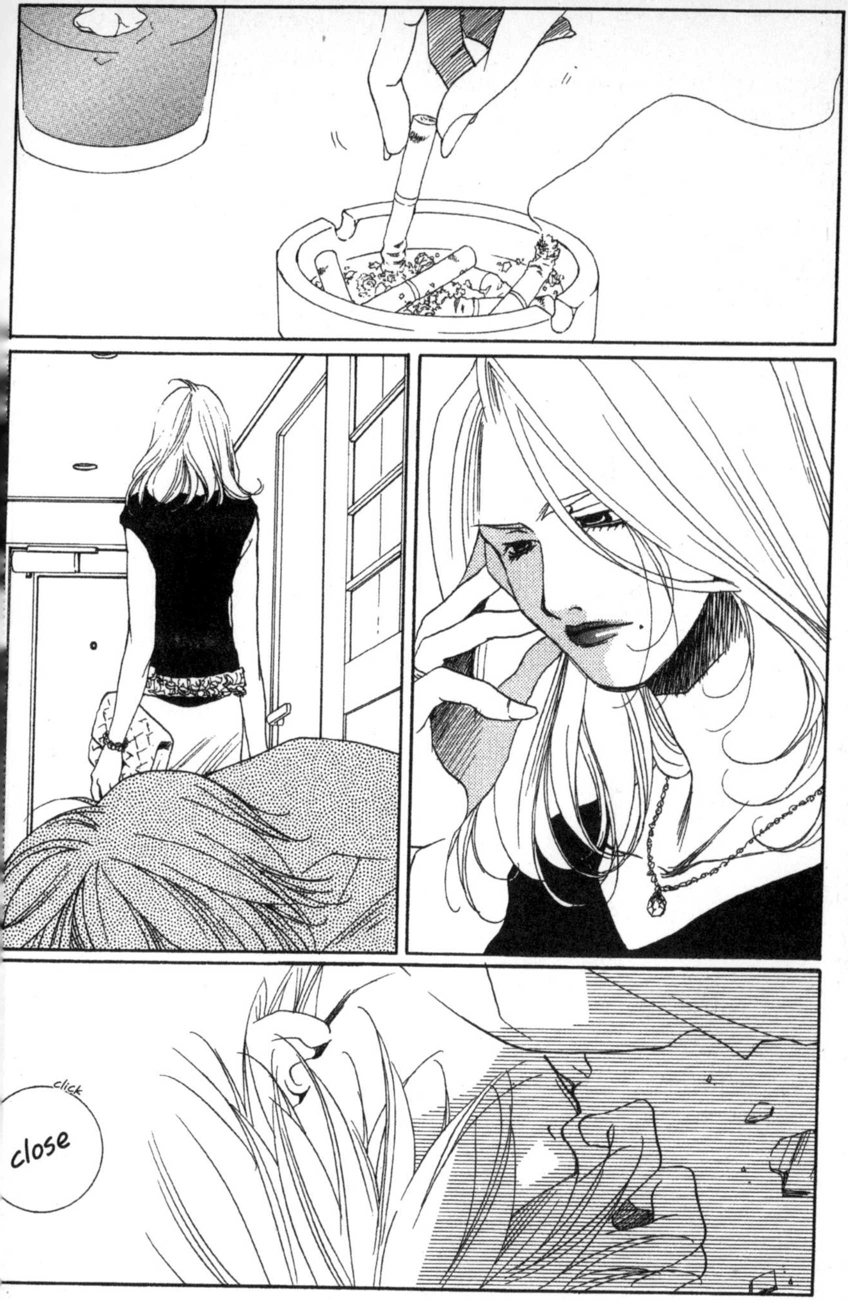
click
close

カン.
カン
カン.
カン..
カン
カッ

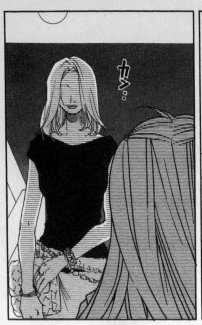

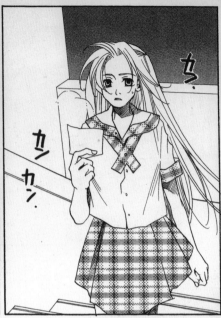

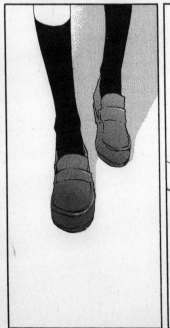

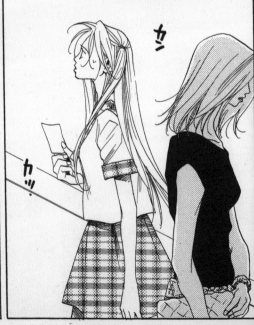

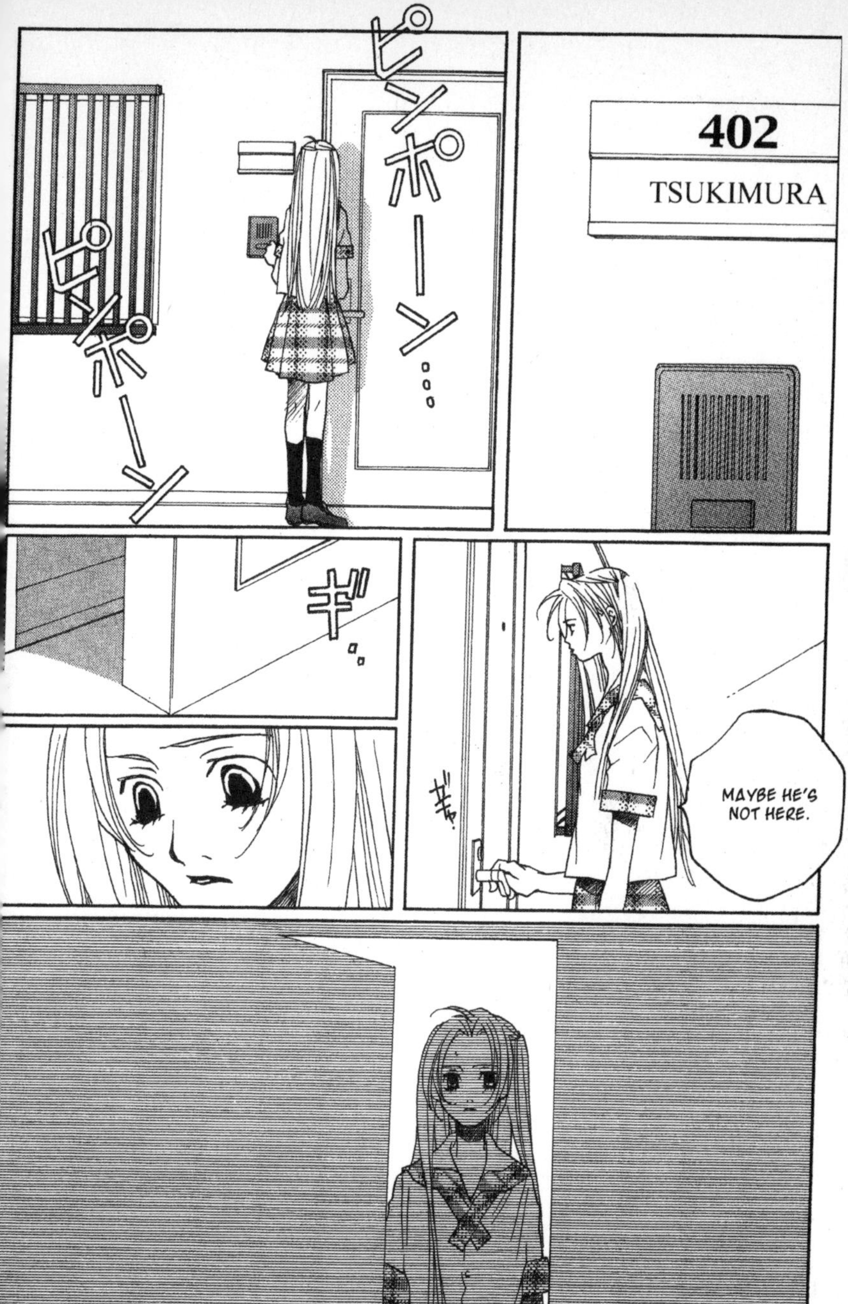

402
TSUKIMURA
ピンポーン。。。
ピンポーン
ギャ
MAYBE HE'S NOT HERE.
ギ。。

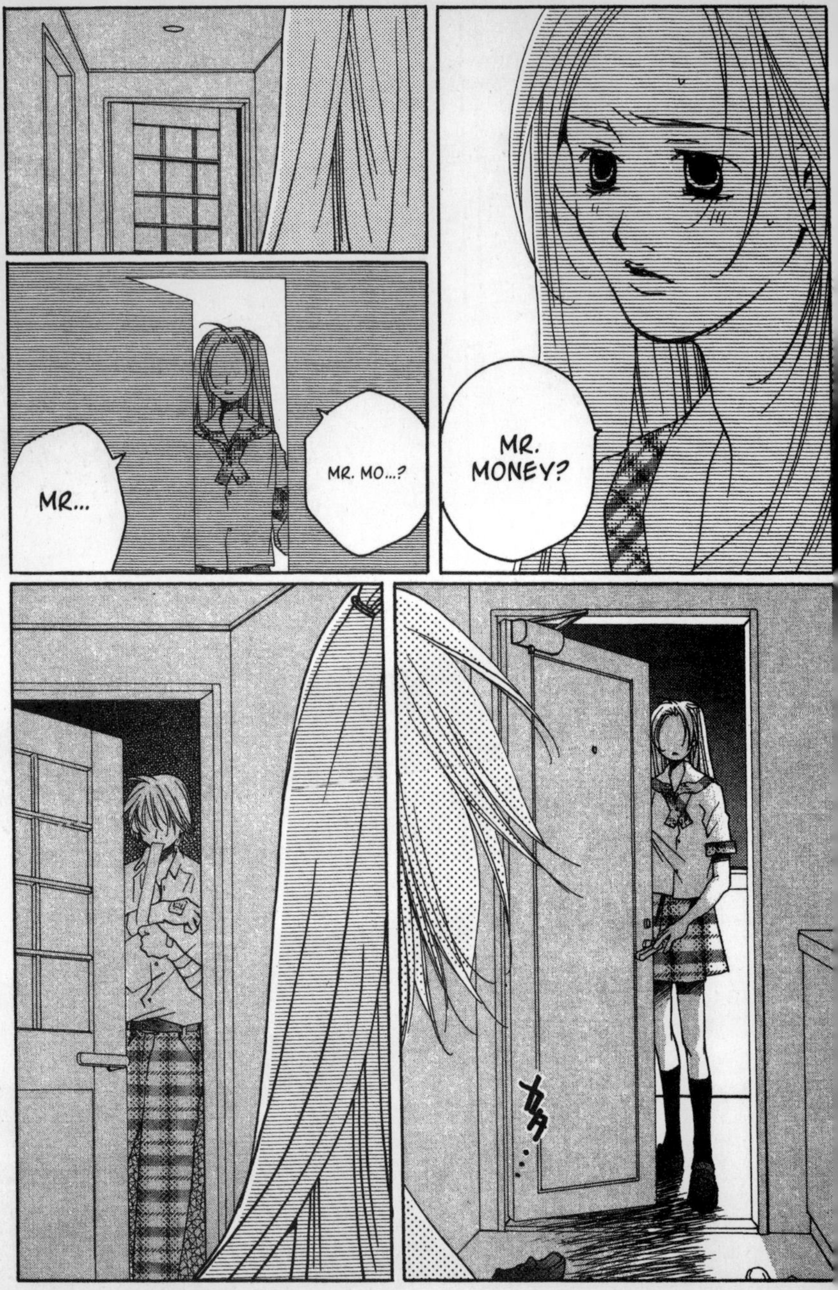
MR.
MONEY?
MR. MO...?
MR...
カタ...

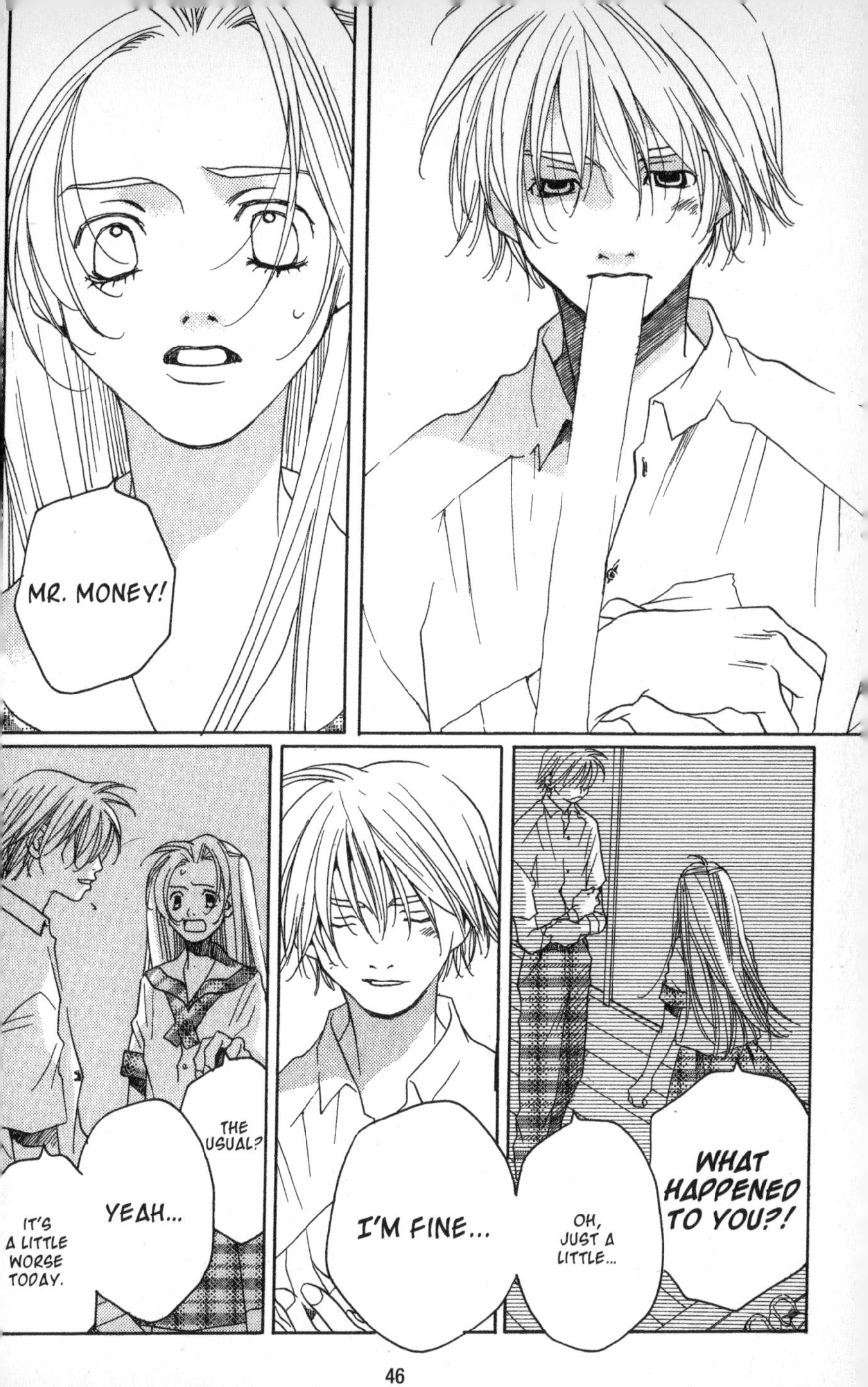
MR. MONEY!
WHAT HAPPENED TO YOU?!
OH, JUST A LITTLE...
I'M FINE...
THE USUAL?
YEAH...
IT'S A LITTLE WORSE TODAY.

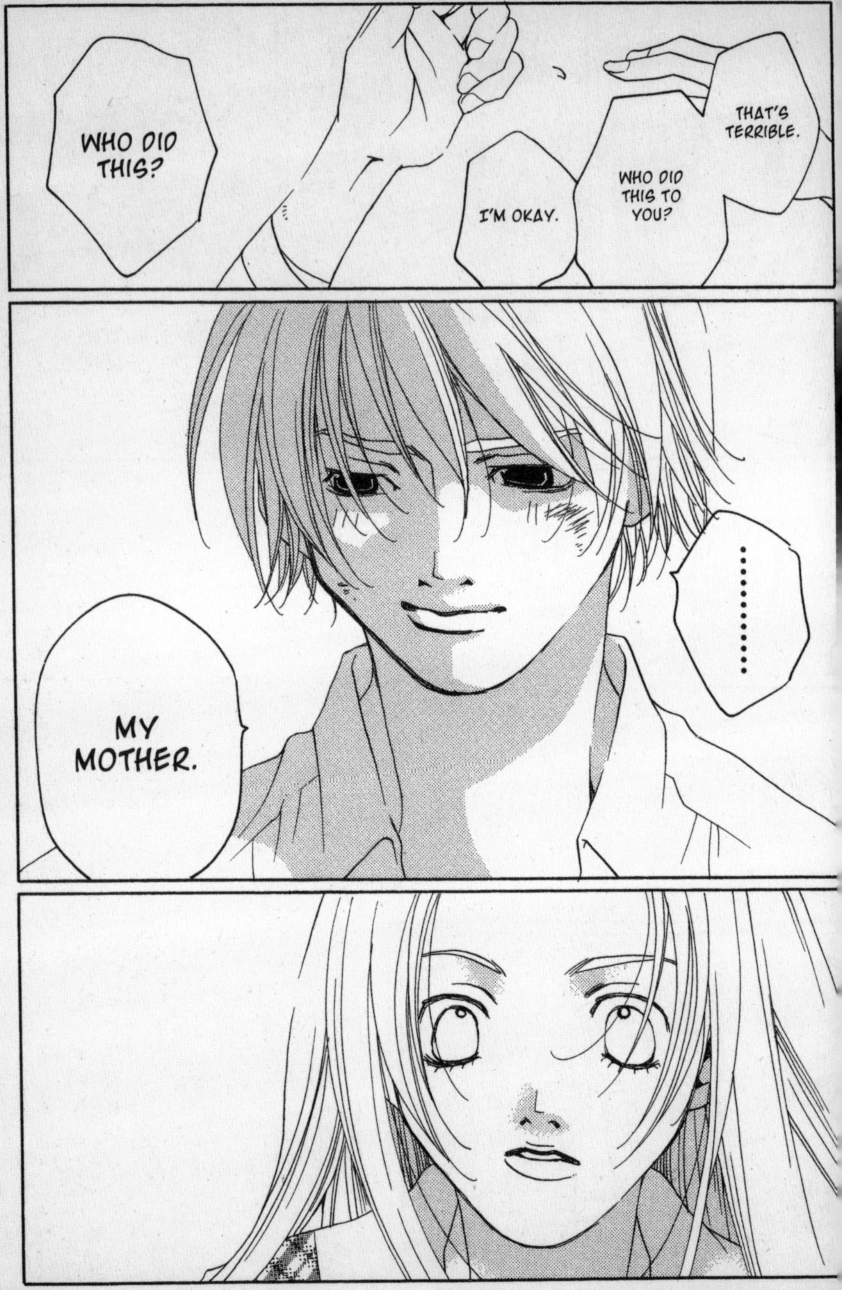
THAT'S TERRIBLE.
WHO DID THIS TO YOU?
I'M OKAY.
WHO DID THIS?
....
MY MOTHER.

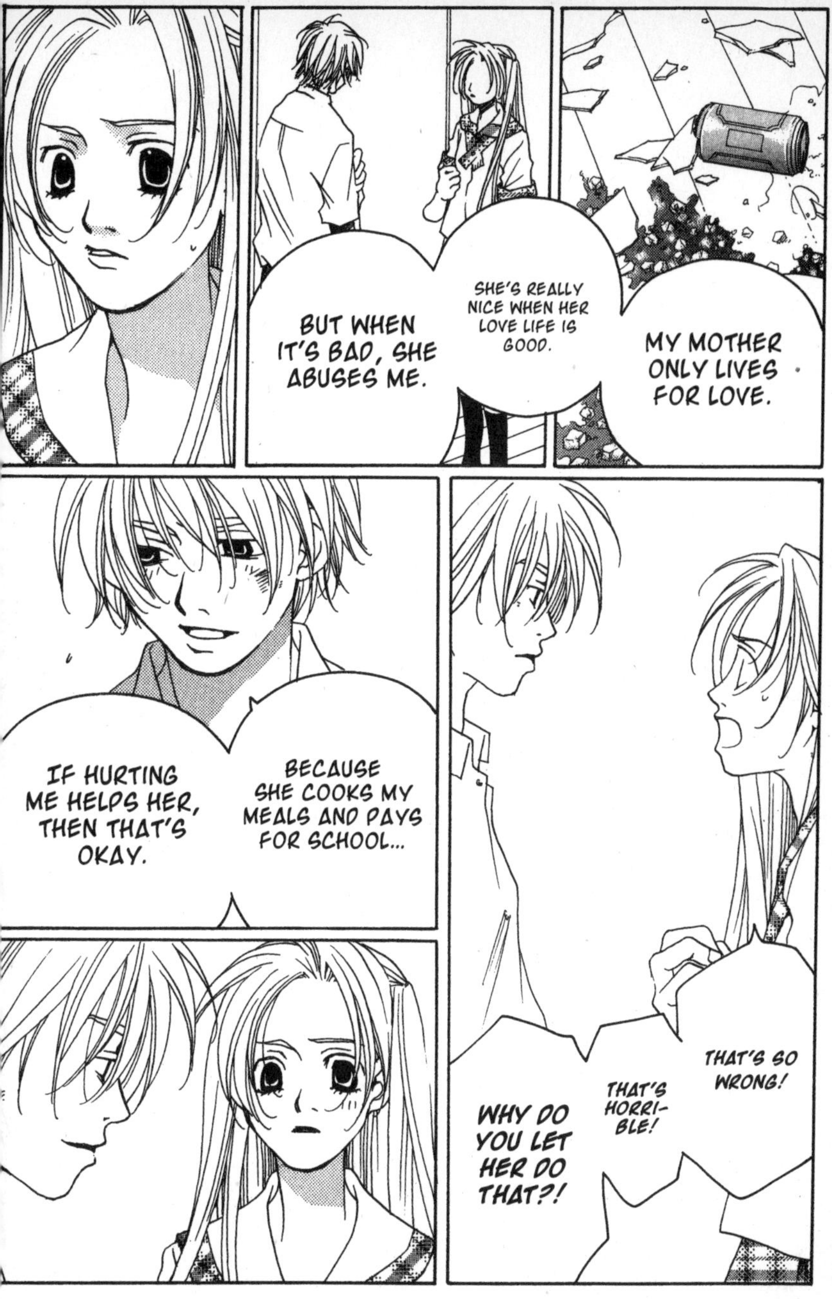
MY MOTHER ONLY LIVES FOR LOVE.
SHE'S REALLY NICE WHEN HER LOVE LIFE IS GOOD.
BUT WHEN IT'S BAD, SHE ABUSES ME.
THAT'S SO WRONG!
THAT'S HORRI-BLE!
WHY DO YOU LET HER DO THAT?!
BECAUSE SHE COOKS MY MEALS AND PAYS FOR SCHOOL...
IF HURTING ME HELPS HER, THEN THAT'S OKAY.

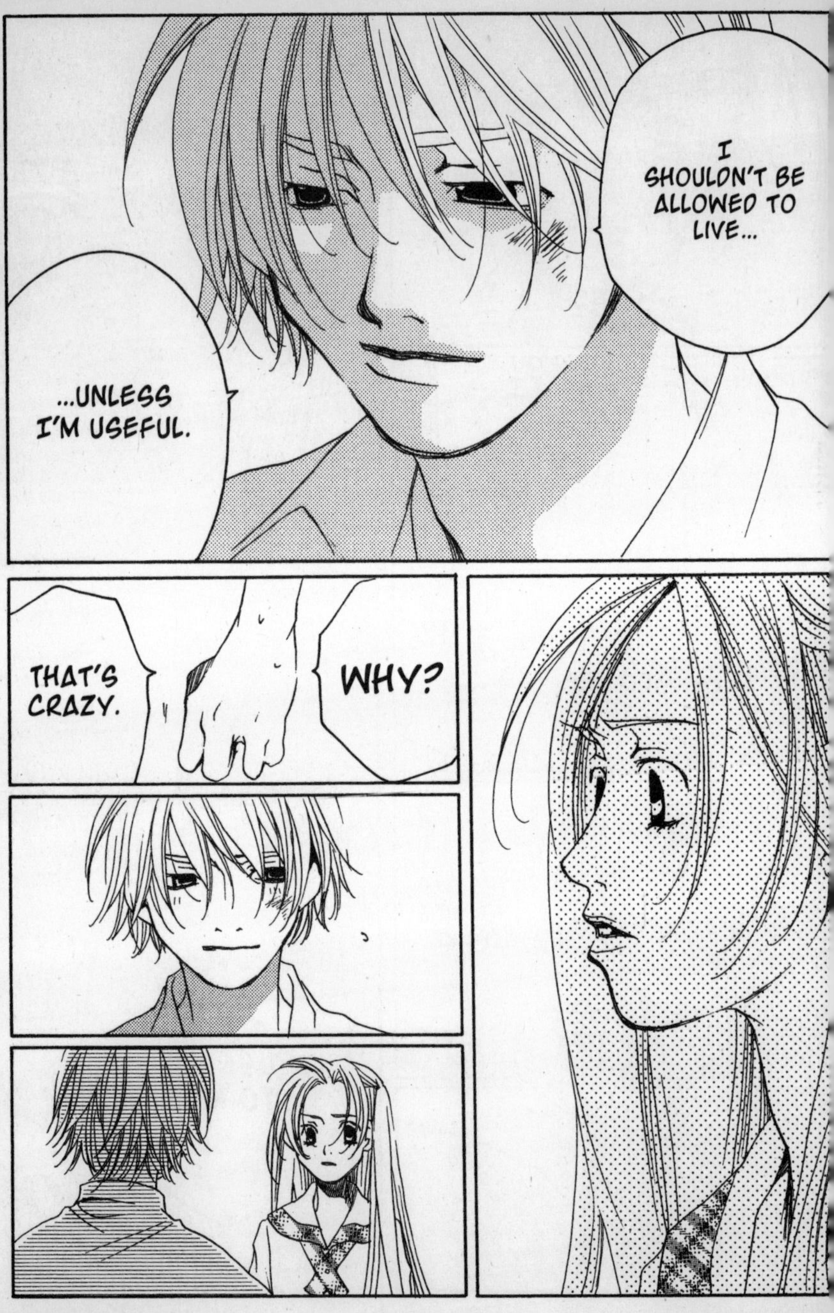
I SHOULDN'T BE ALLOWED TO LIVE...
...UNLESS I'M USEFUL.
WHY?
THAT'S CRAZY.

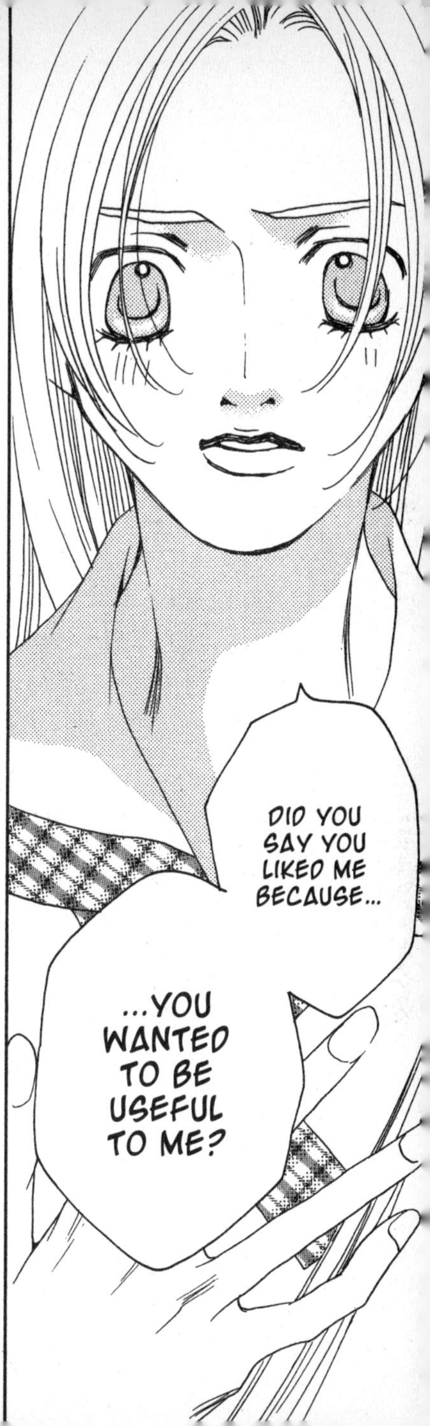
DID YOU SAY YOU LIKED ME BECAUSE...
...YOU WANTED TO BE USEFUL TO ME?

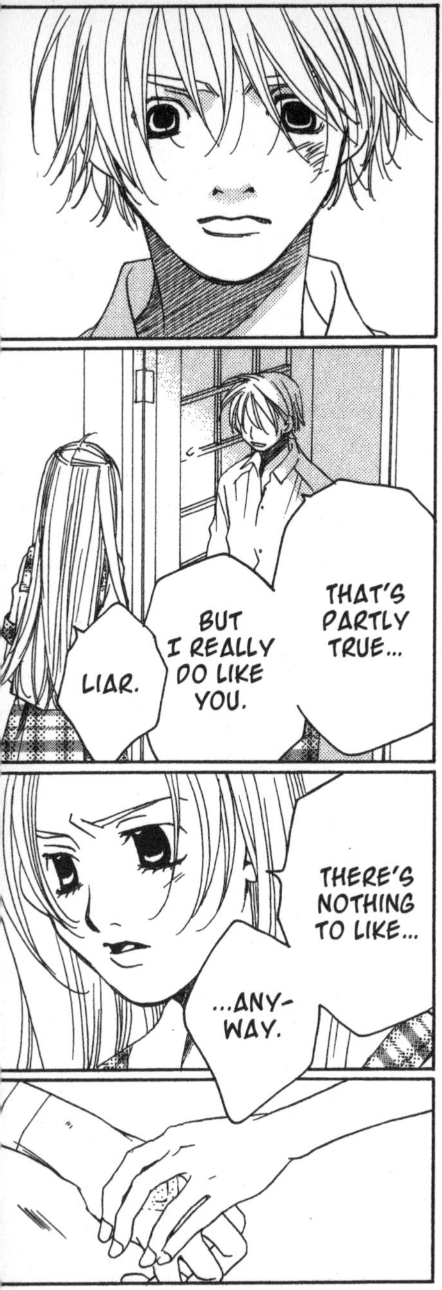
THAT'S PARTLY TRUE...
BUT I REALLY DO LIKE YOU.
LIAR.
THERE'S NOTHING TO LIKE...
...ANY-WAY.

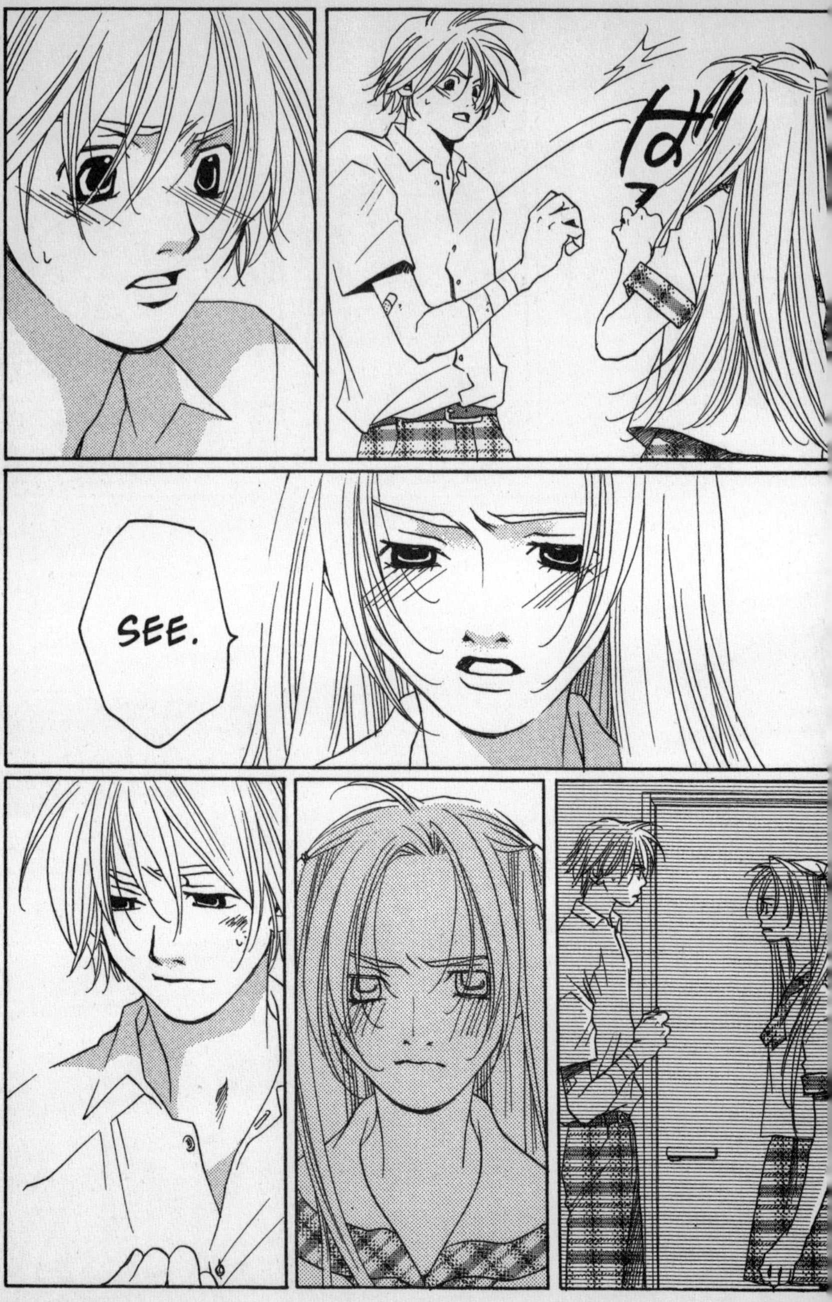
SEE.

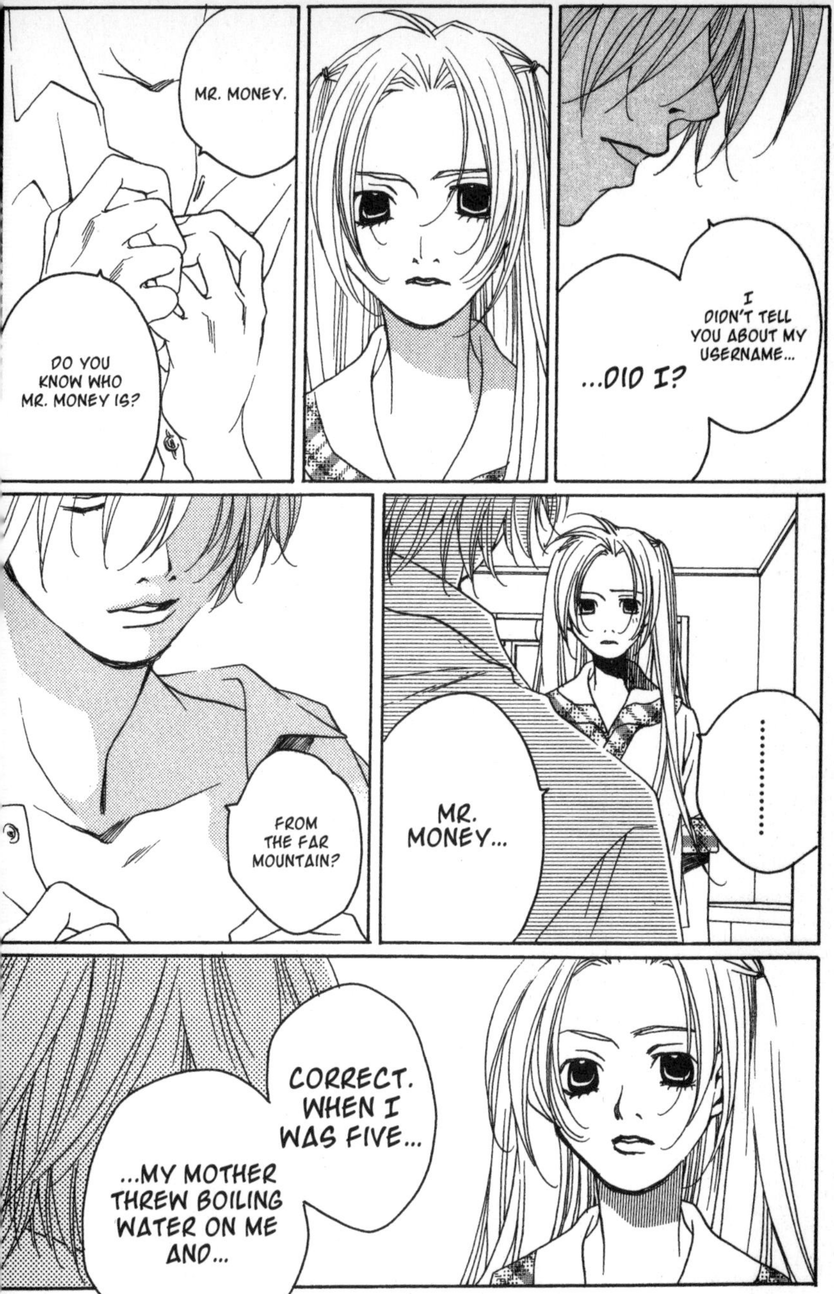
I DIDN'T TELL YOU ABOUT MY USERNAME...
...DID I?
MR. MONEY.
DO YOU KNOW WHO MR. MONEY IS?
....
MR. MONEY...
FROM THE FAR MOUNTAIN?
CORRECT. WHEN I WAS FIVE...
...MY MOTHER THREW BOILING WATER ON ME AND...

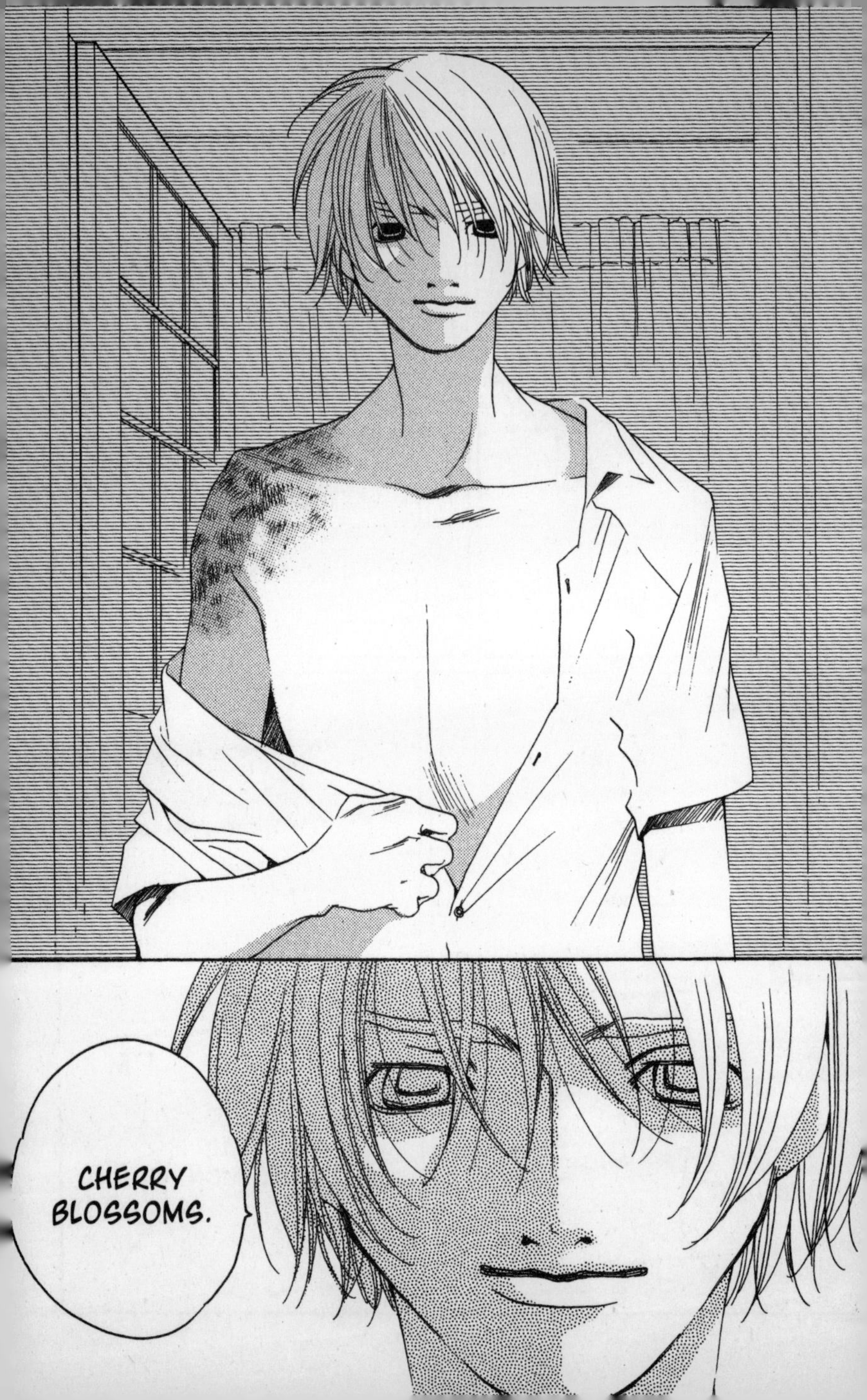
CHERRY BLOSSOMS.

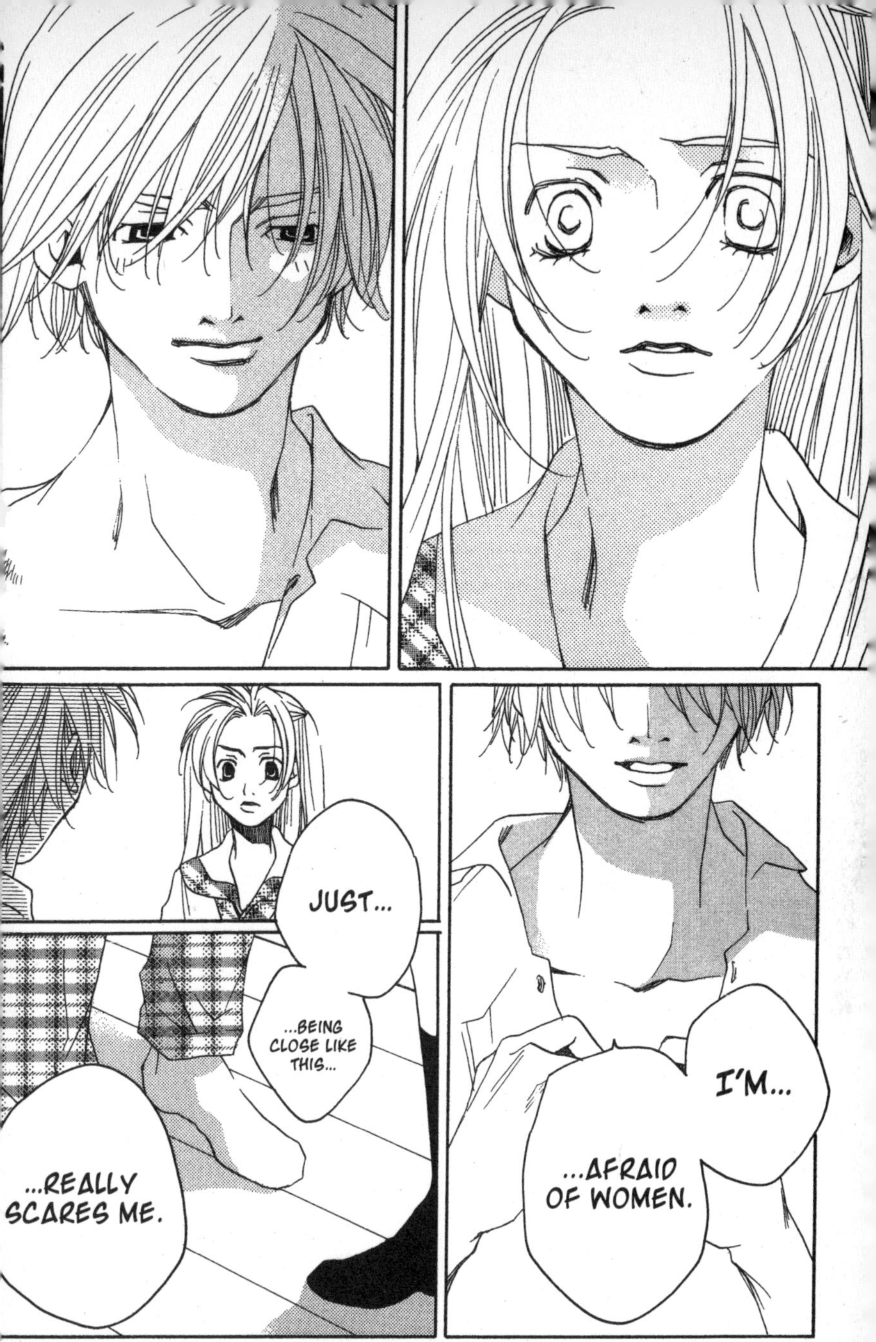
I'M...
...AFRAID OF WOMEN.
JUST...
...BEING CLOSE LIKE THIS...
...REALLY SCARES ME.

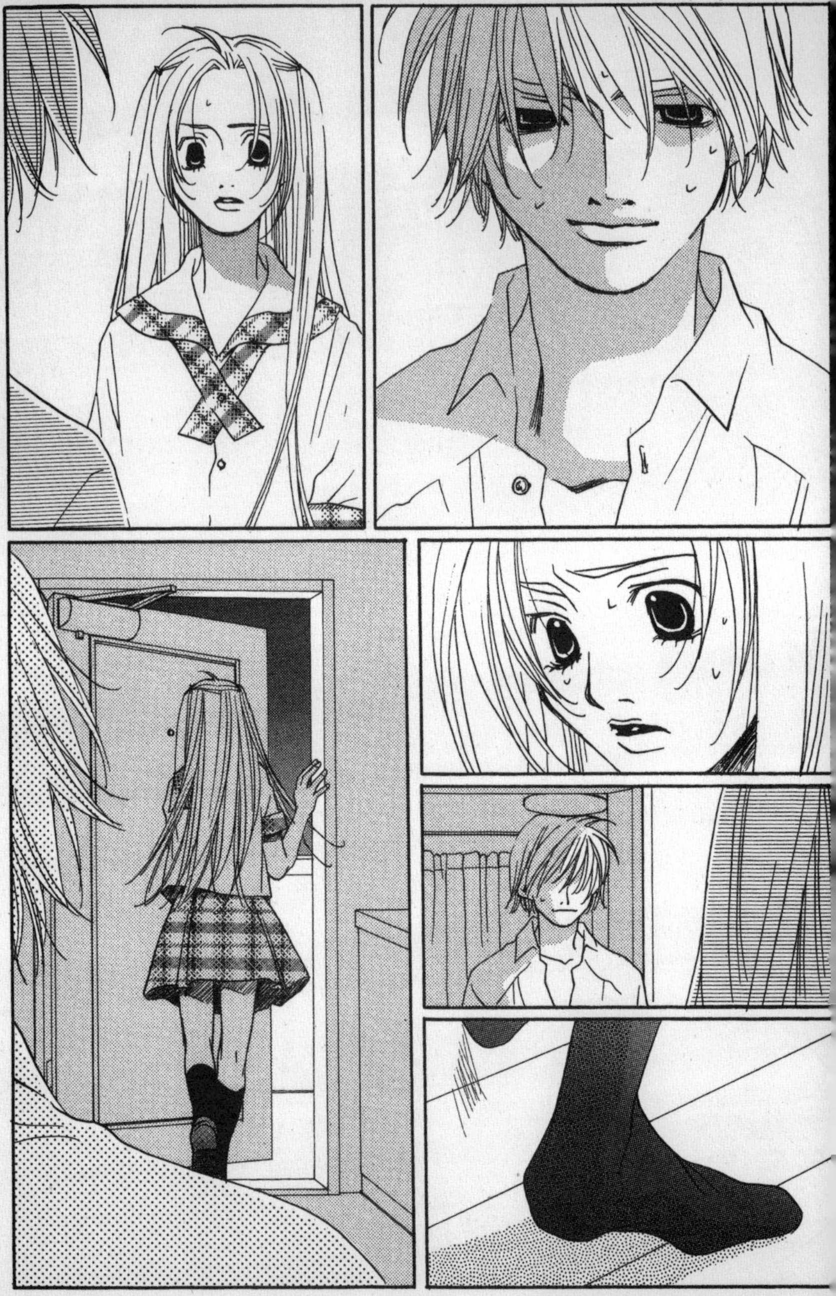

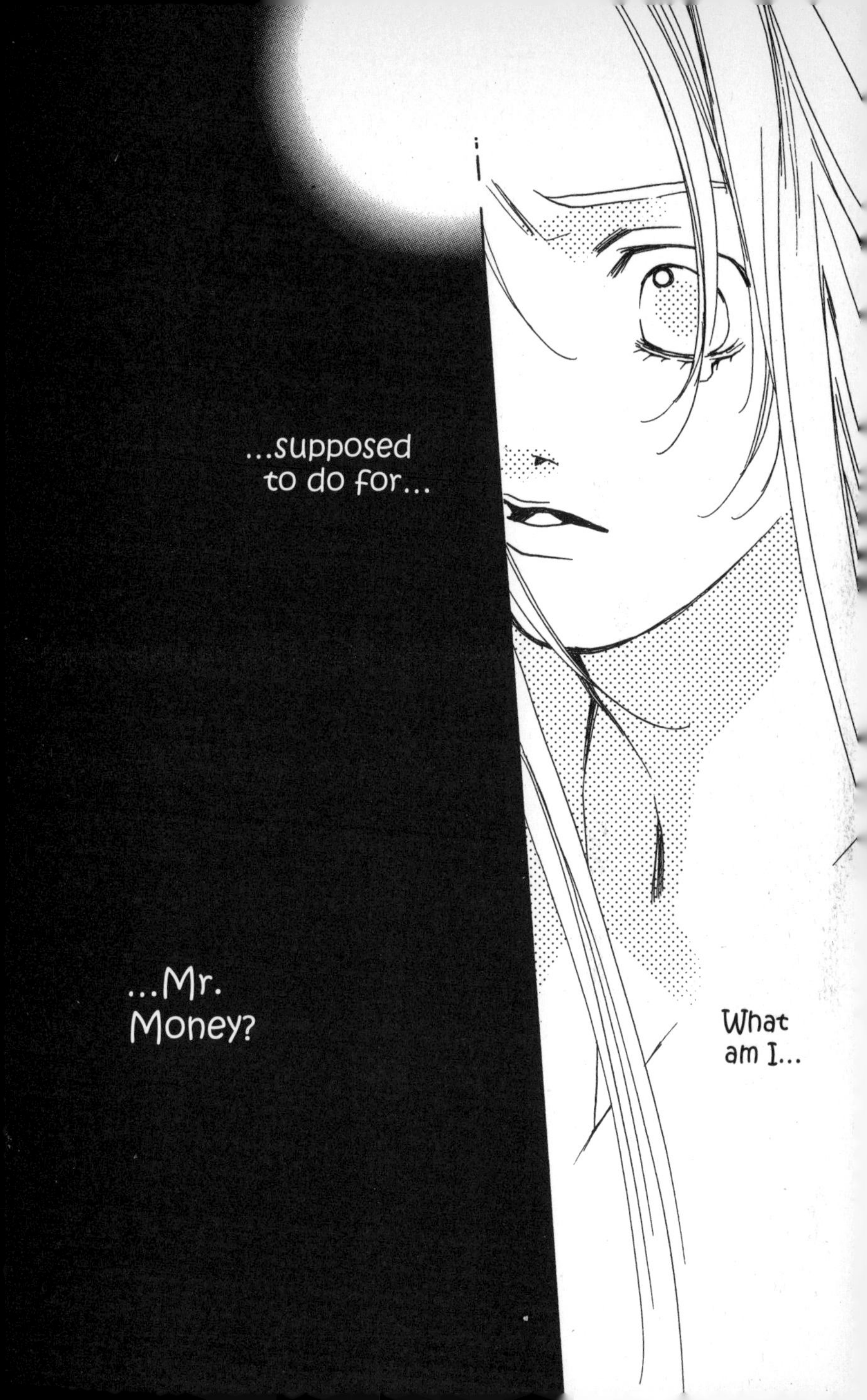
What am I...
...supposed to do for...
...Mr. Money?

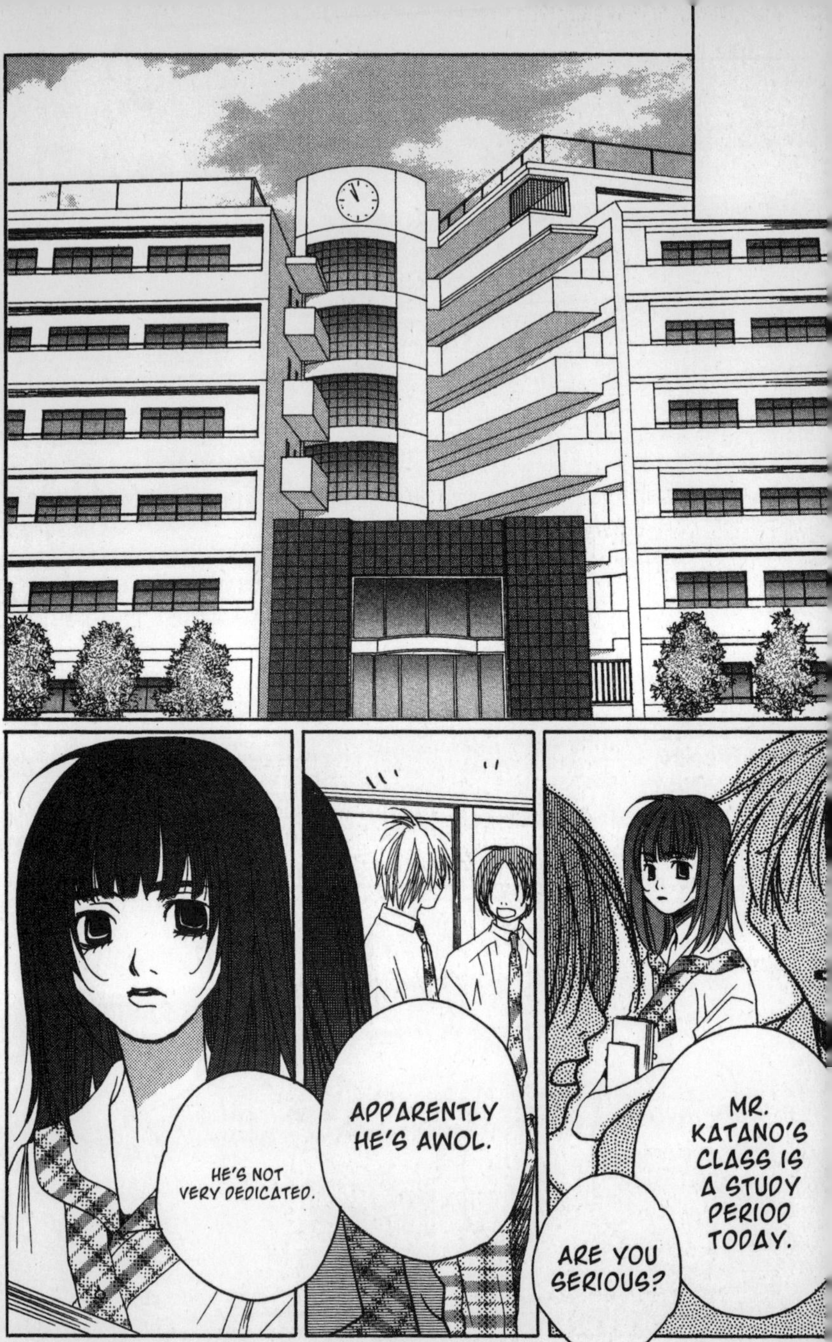
MR. KATANO'S CLASS IS A STUDY PERIOD TODAY.
ARE YOU SERIOUS?
APPARENTLY HE'S AWOL.
HE'S NOT VERY DEDICATED.

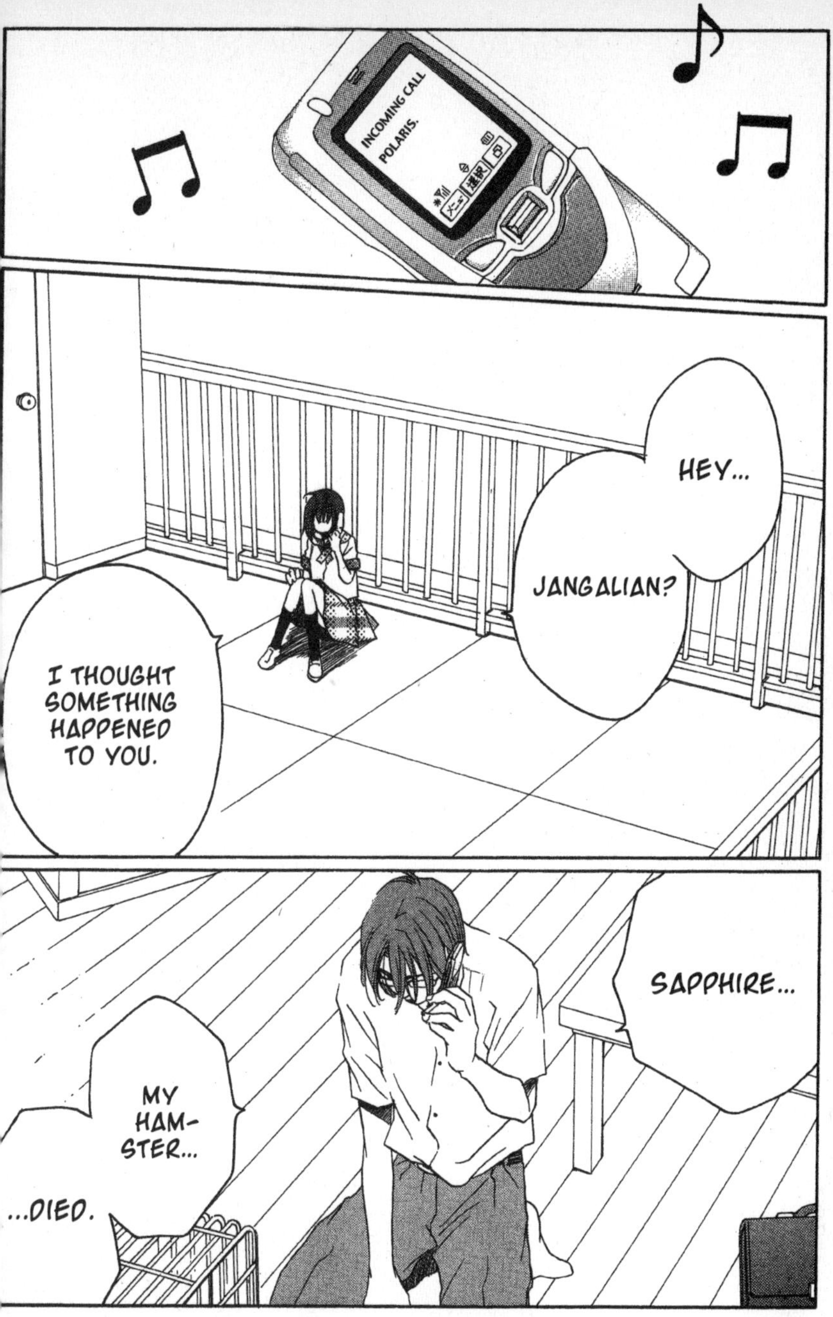
INCOMING CALL
POLARIS.
HEY...
JANGALIAN?
I THOUGHT SOMETHING HAPPENED TO YOU.
SAPPHIRE...
MY HAM-STER...
...DIED.

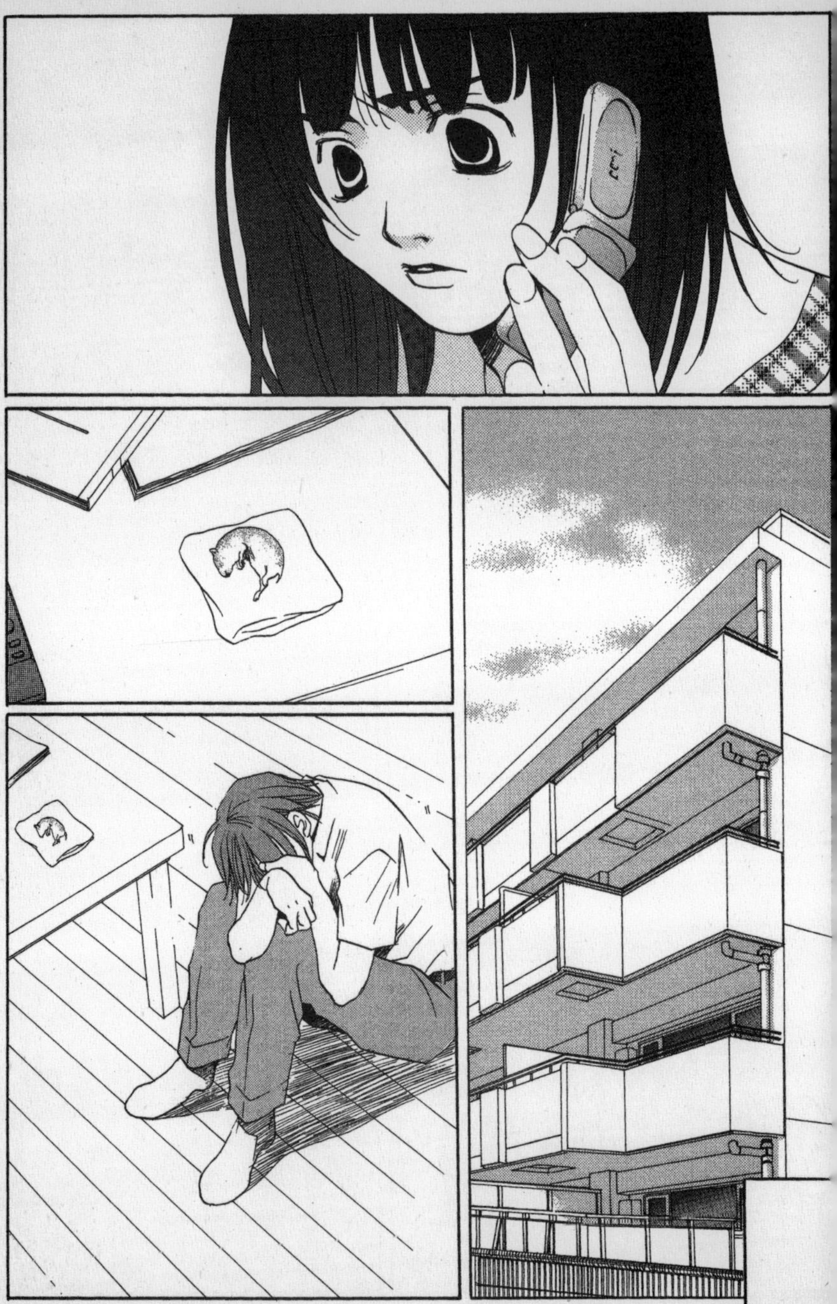

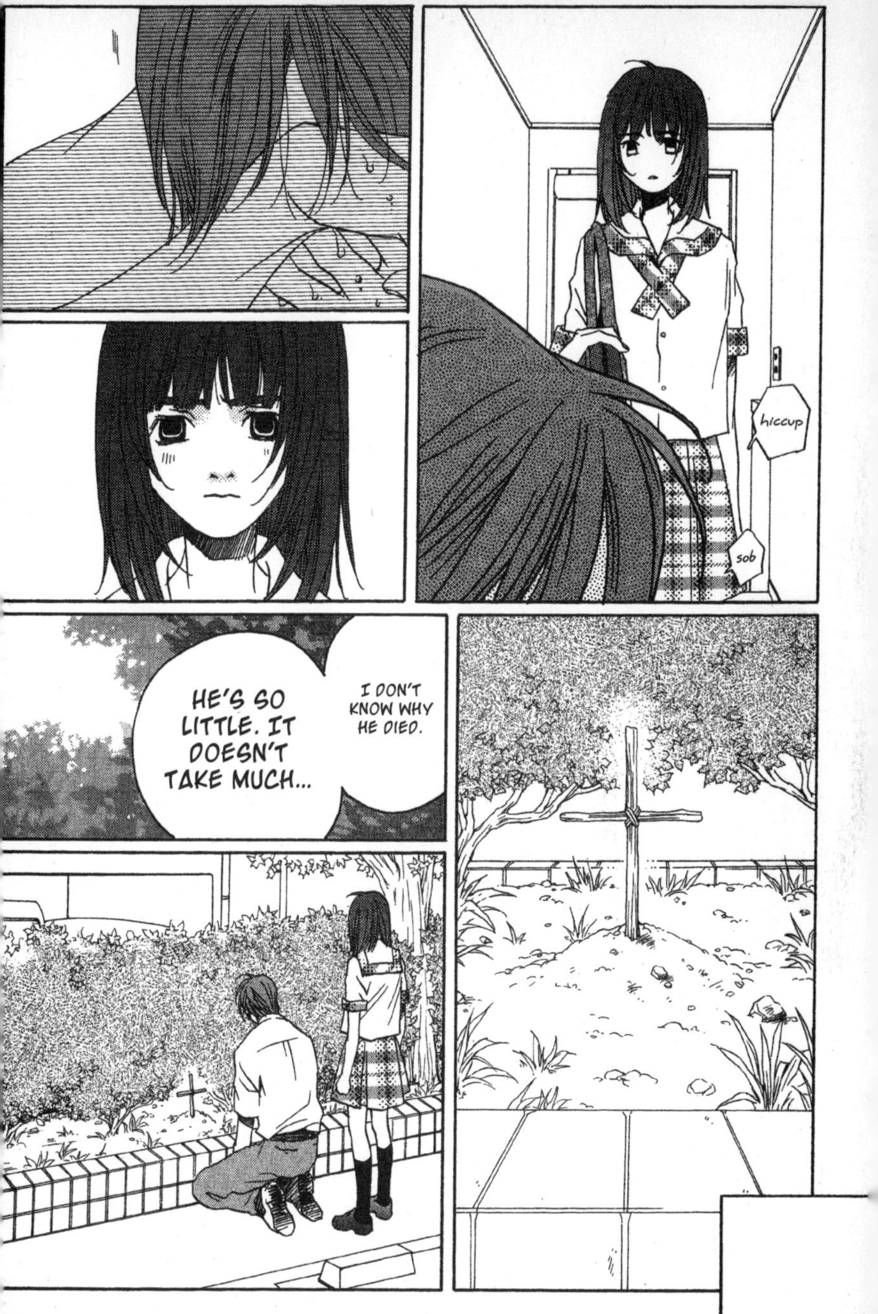
hiccup
sob
I DON'T KNOW WHY HE DIED.
HE'S SO LITTLE. IT DOESN'T TAKE MUCH...

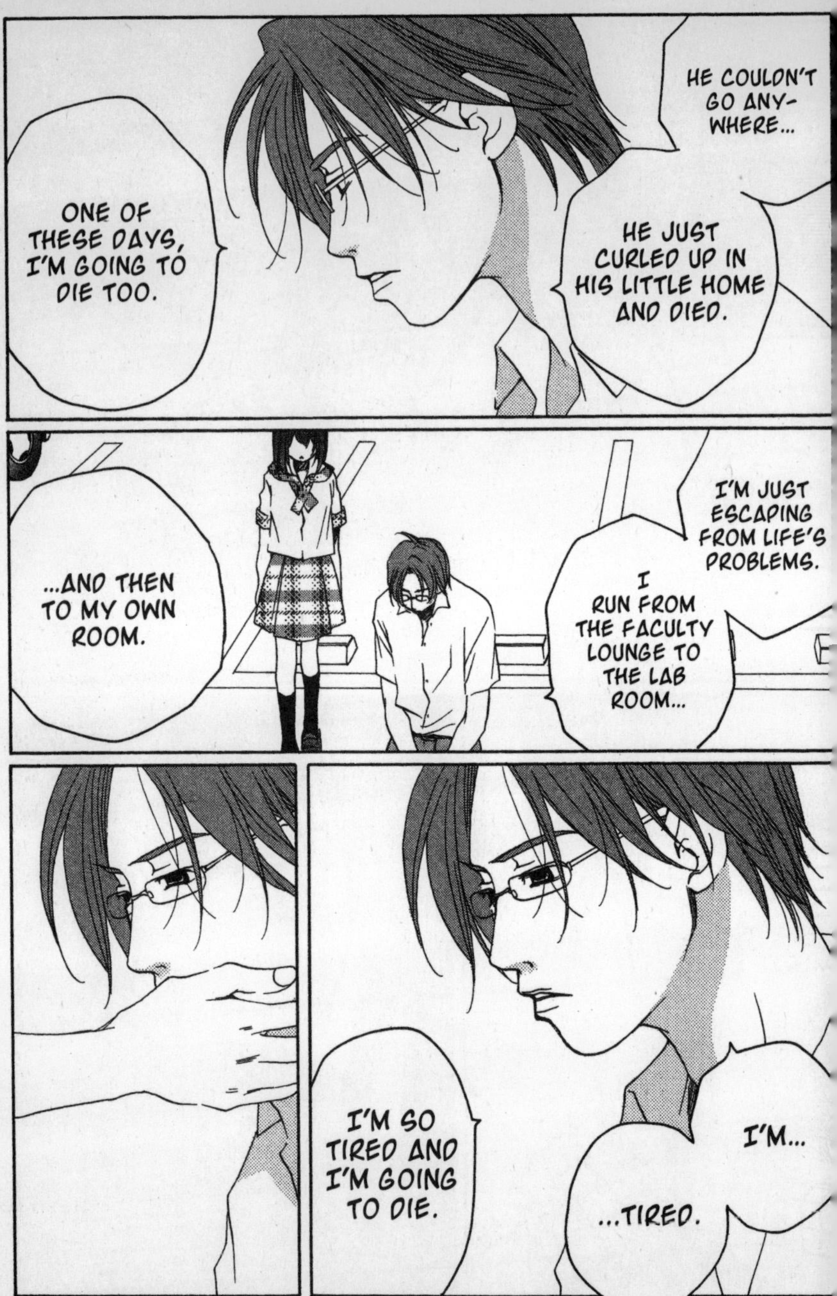
HE COULDN'T GO ANY-WHERE...
HE JUST CURLED UP IN HIS LITTLE HOME AND DIED.
ONE OF THESE DAYS, I'M GOING TO DIE TOO.
I'M JUST ESCAPING FROM LIFE'S PROBLEMS.
I RUN FROM THE FACULTY LOUNGE TO THE LAB ROOM...
...AND THEN TO MY OWN ROOM.
I'M...
...TIRED.
I'M SO TIRED AND I'M GOING TO DIE.

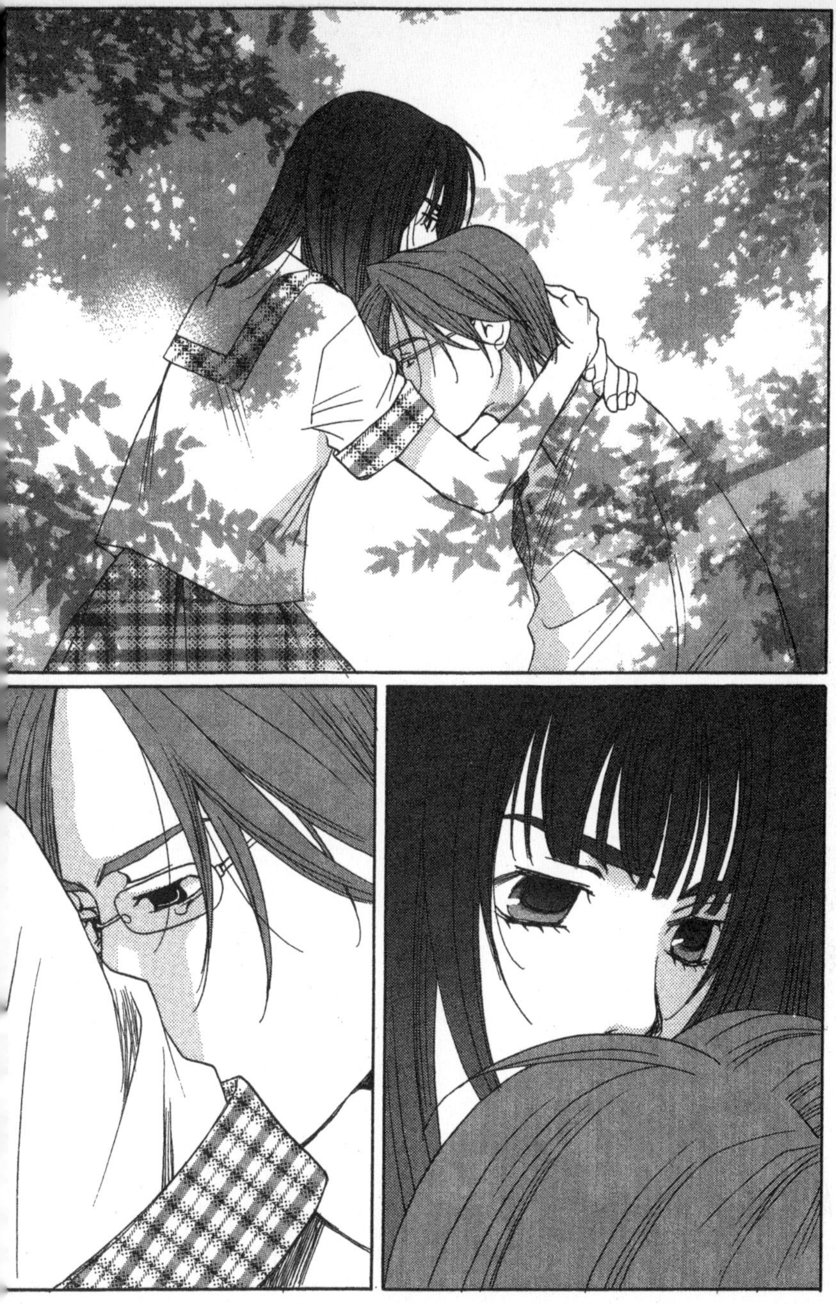

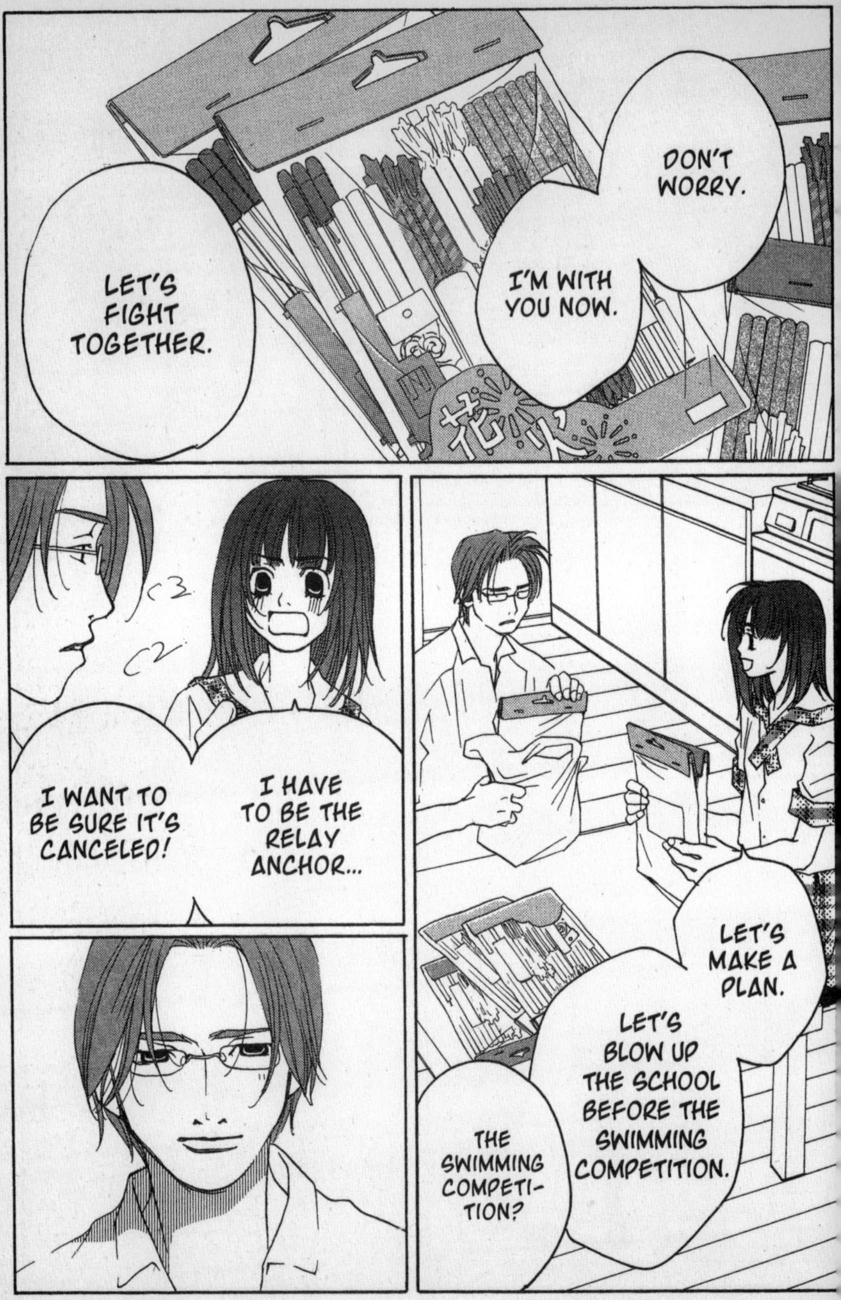
DON'T WORRY.
I'M WITH YOU NOW.
LET'S FIGHT TOGETHER.
花火
LET'S MAKE A PLAN.
LET'S BLOW UP THE SCHOOL BEFORE THE SWIMMING COMPETITION.
THE SWIMMING COMPETITION?
I HAVE TO BE THE RELAY ANCHOR...
I WANT TO BE SURE IT'S CANCELED!

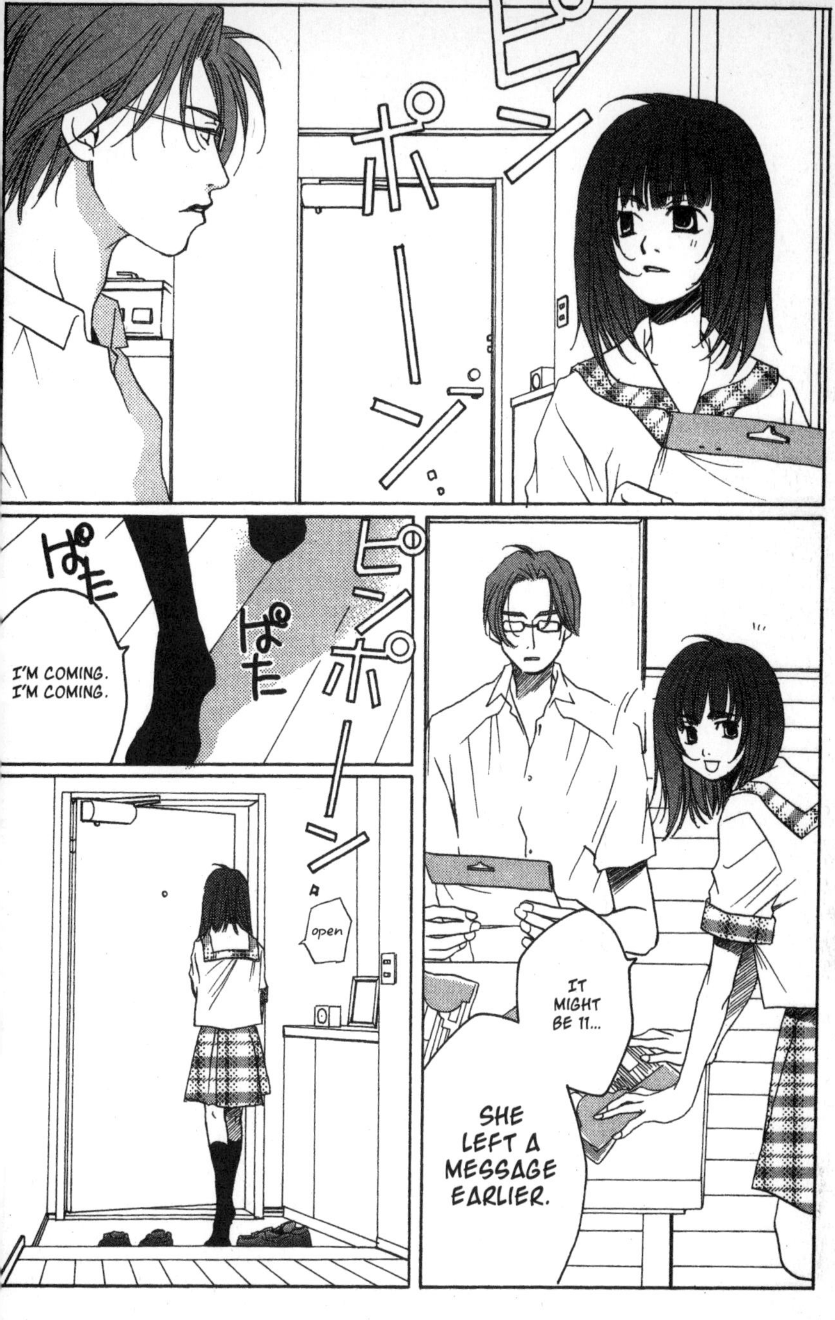
ピンポーン
ぱた
ぱた
ピンポーン
I'M COMING. I'M COMING.
open
IT MIGHT BE 11...
SHE LEFT A MESSAGE EARLIER.

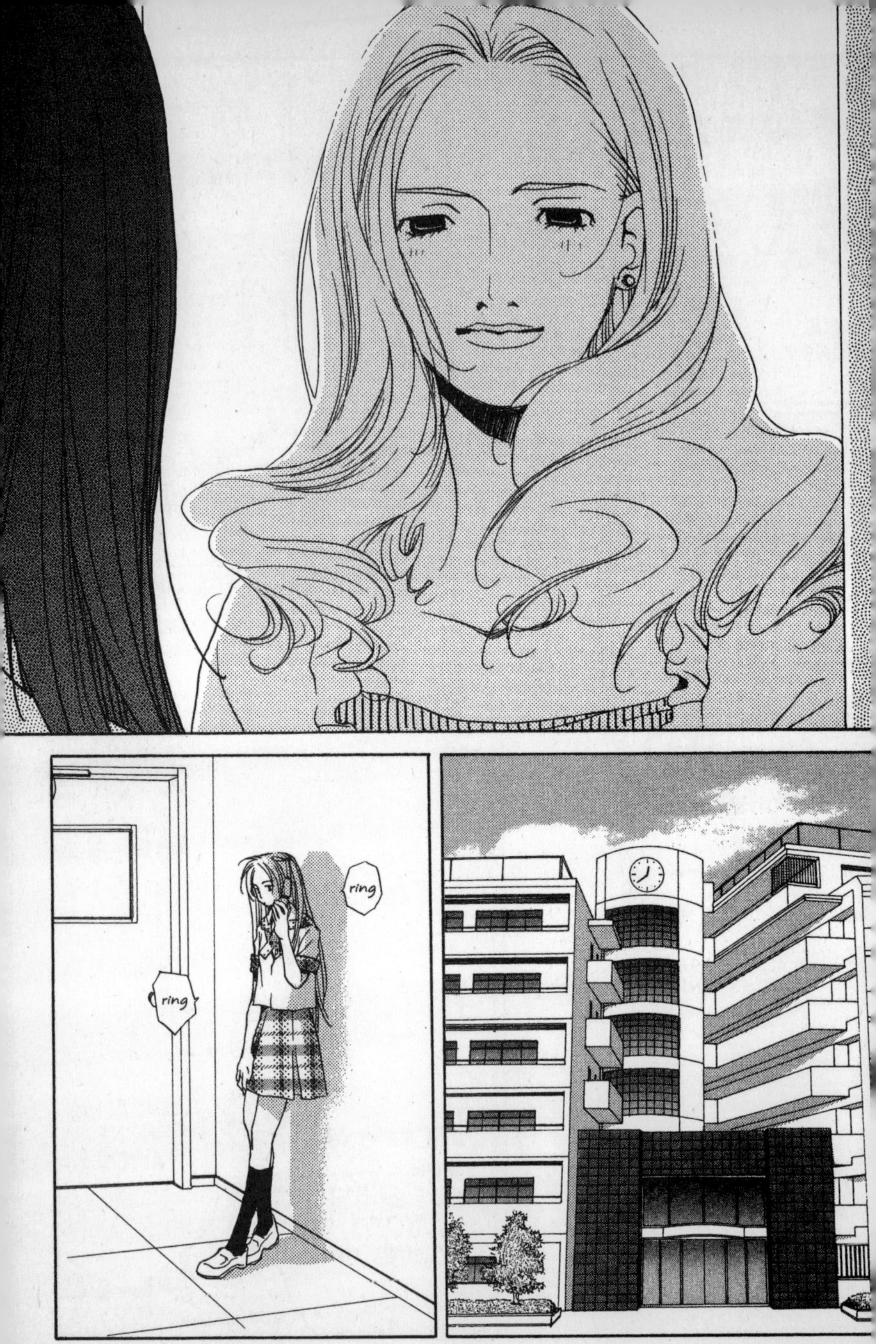
ring
ring

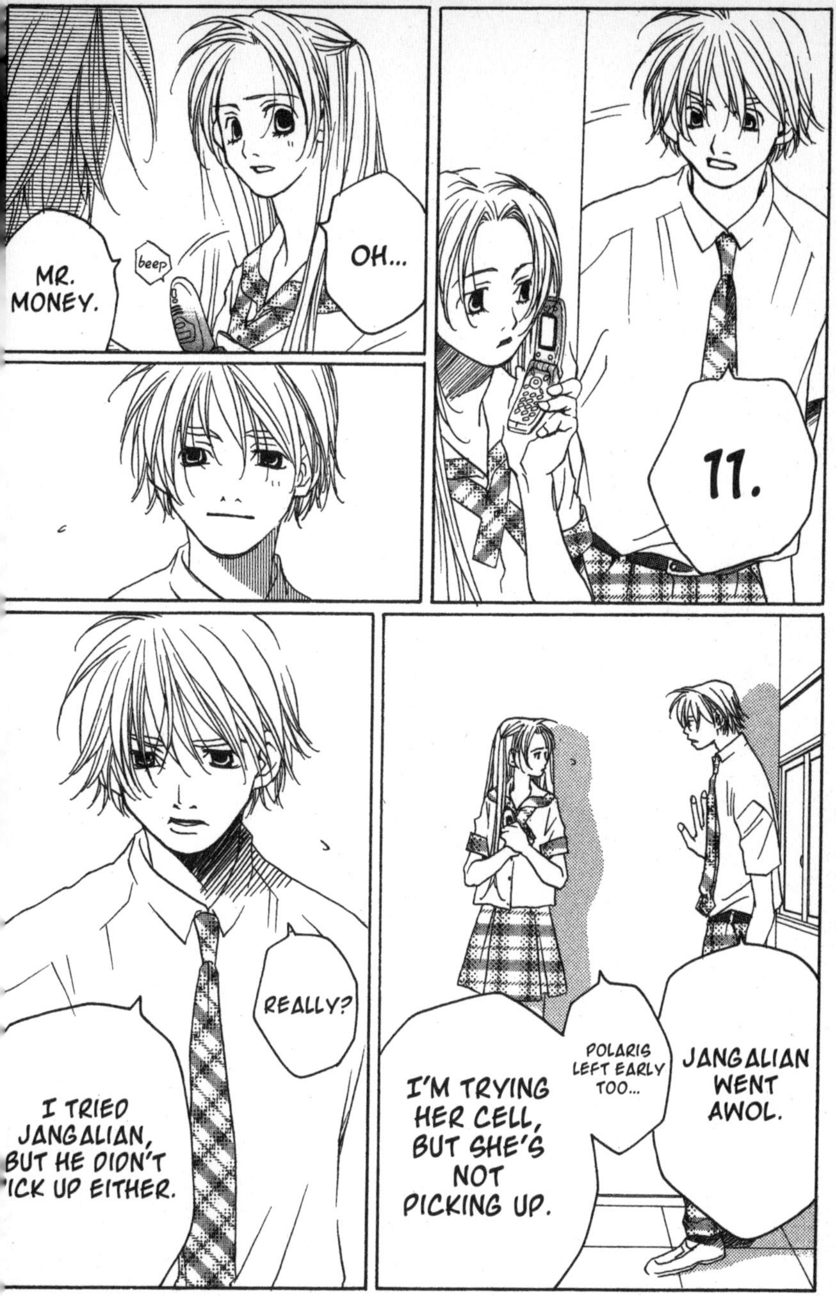
11.
OH...
beep
MR. MONEY.
JANGALIAN WENT AWOL.
POLARIS LEFT EARLY TOO...
I'M TRYING HER CELL, BUT SHE'S NOT PICKING UP.
REALLY?
I TRIED JANGALIAN, BUT HE DIDN'T
ICK UP EITHER.

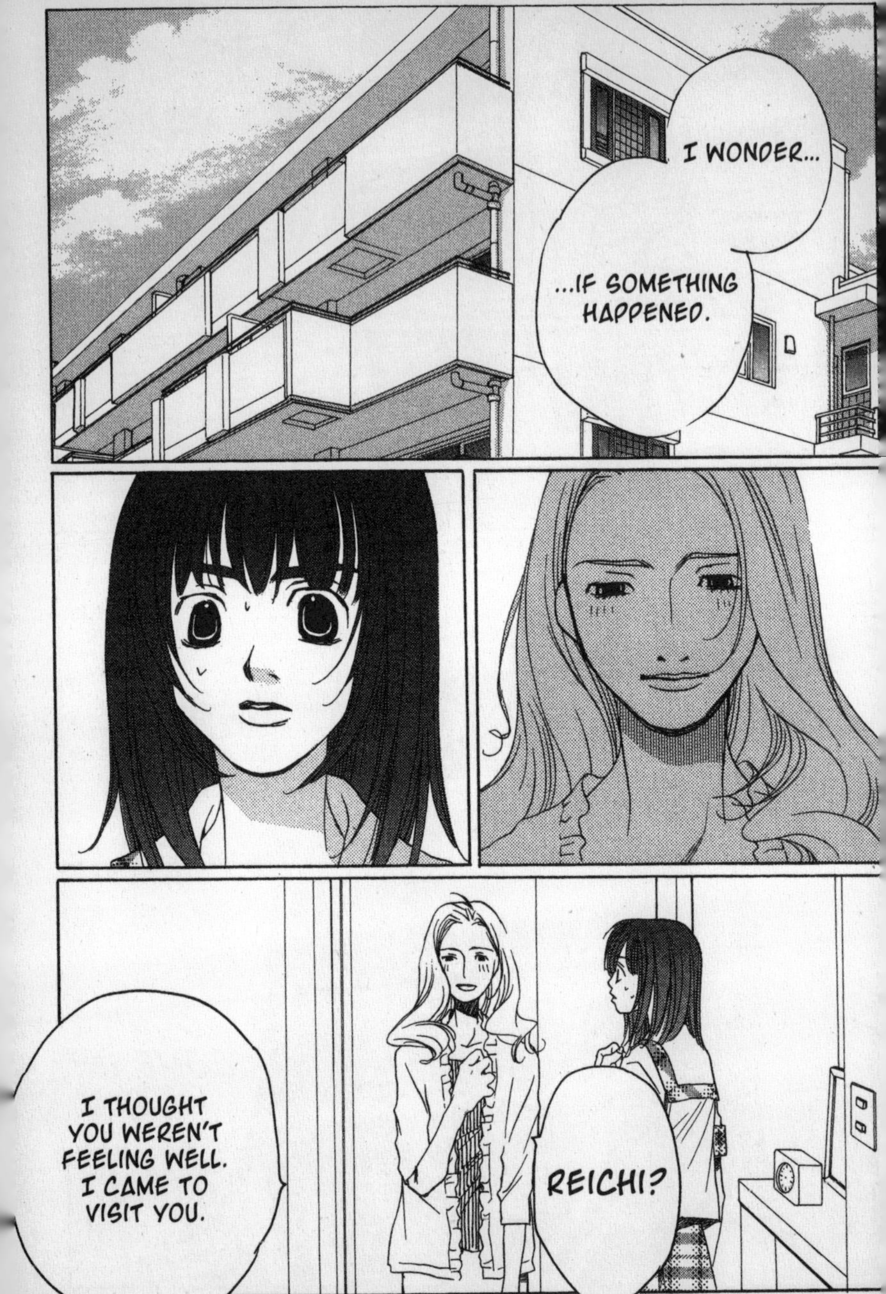
I WONDER...
...IF SOMETHING HAPPENED.
REICHI?
I THOUGHT YOU WEREN'T FEELING WELL. I CAME TO VISIT YOU.

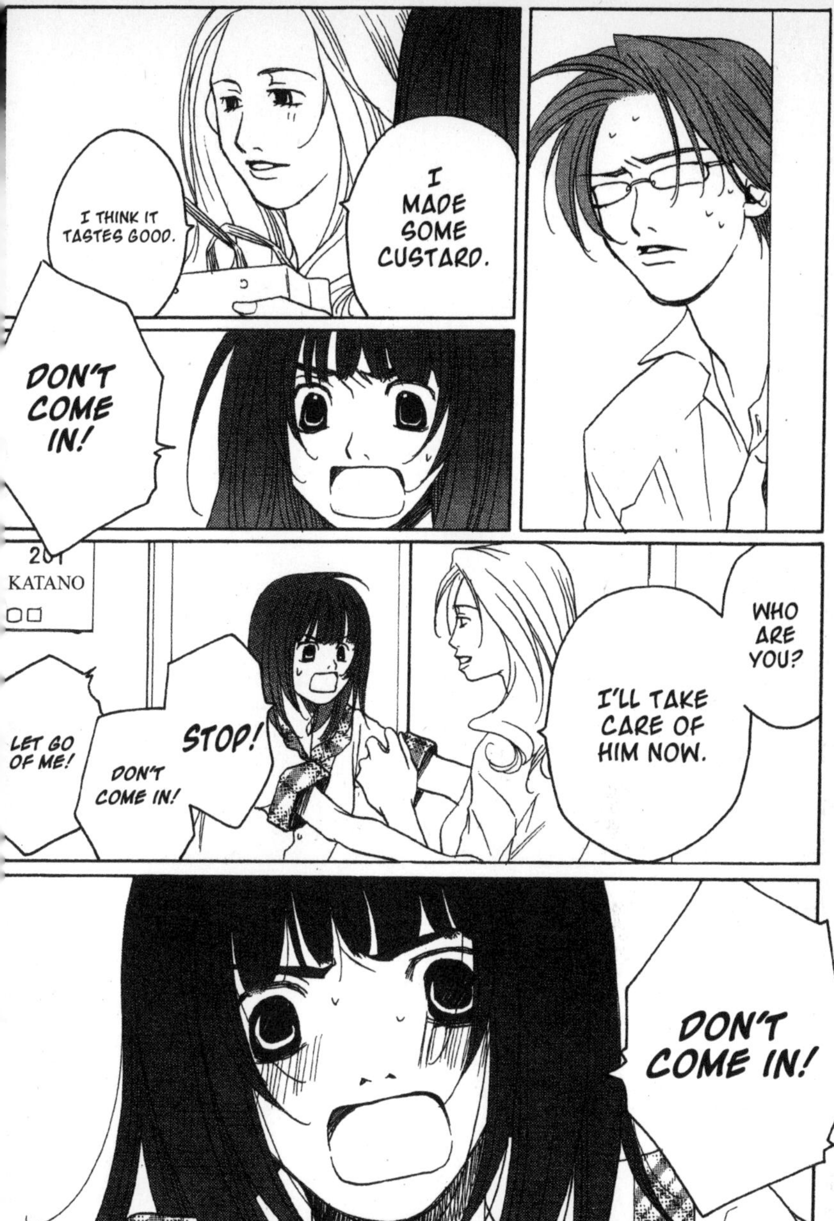
I MADE SOME CUSTARD.
I THINK IT TASTES GOOD.
DON'T COME IN!
WHO ARE YOU?
I'LL TAKE CARE OF HIM NOW.
201
KATANO
STOP!
DON'T COME IN!
LET GO OF ME!
DON'T COME IN!

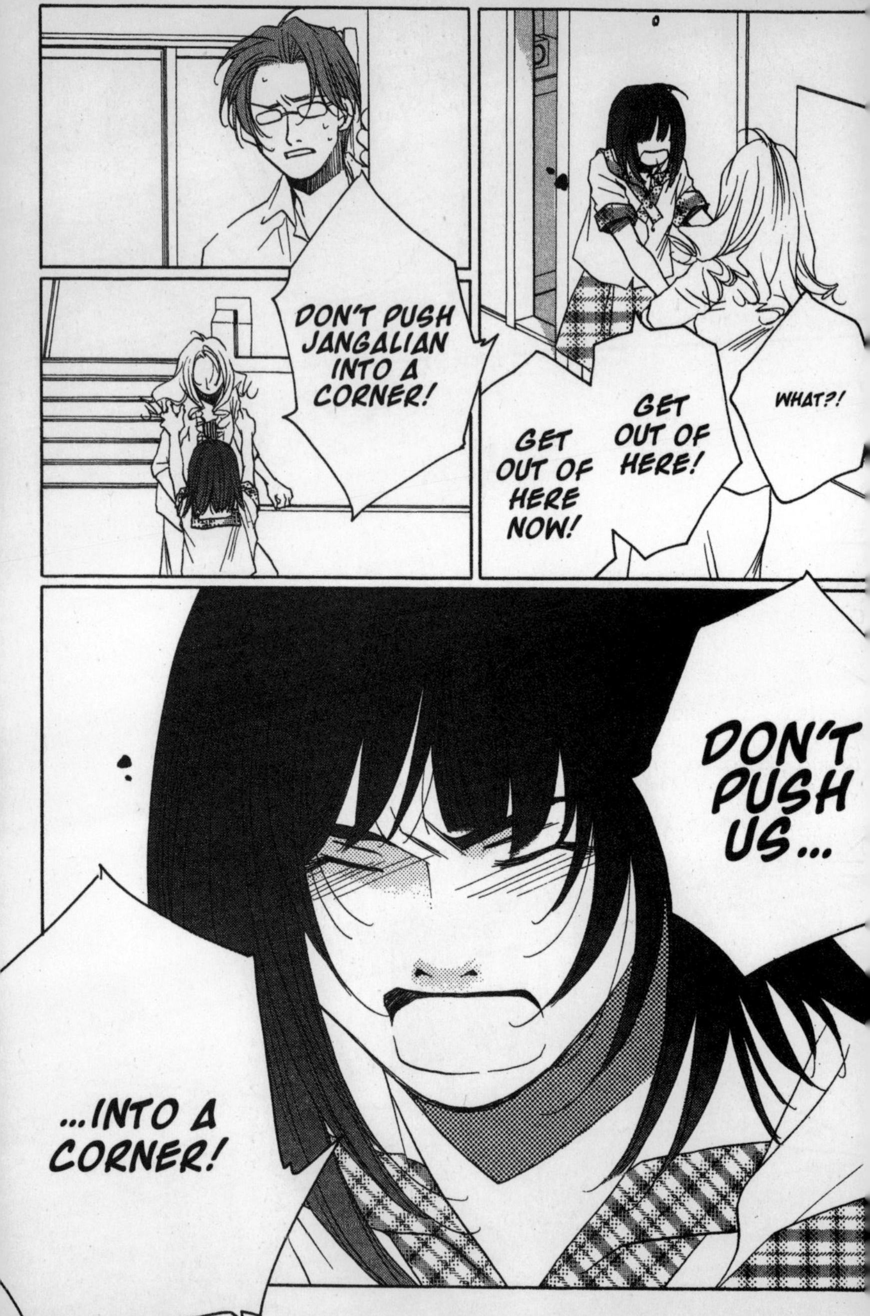
WHAT?!
GET OUT OF HERE!
GET OUT OF HERE NOW!
DON'T PUSH JANGALIAN INTO A CORNER!
DON'T PUSH US...
...INTO A CORNER!

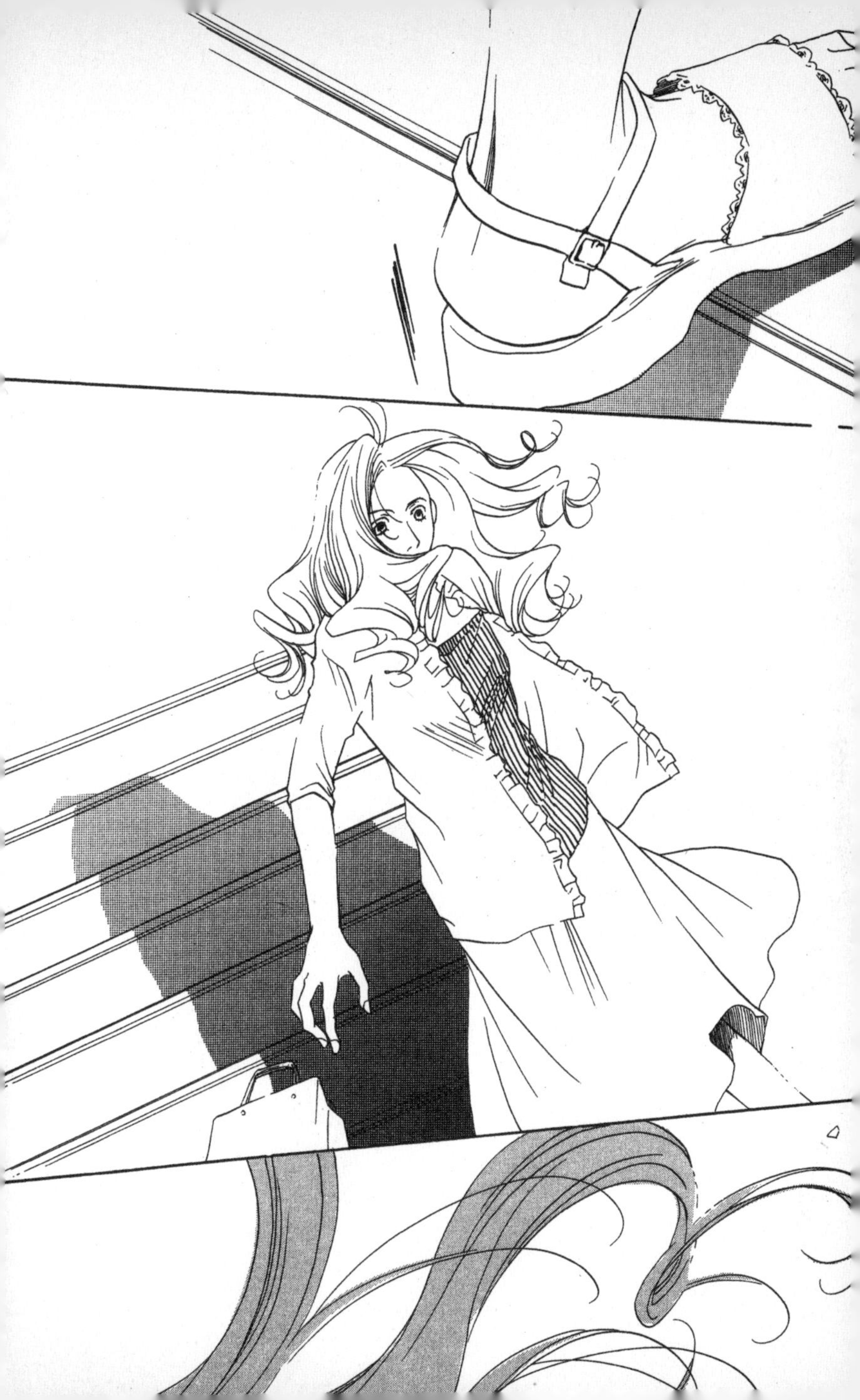

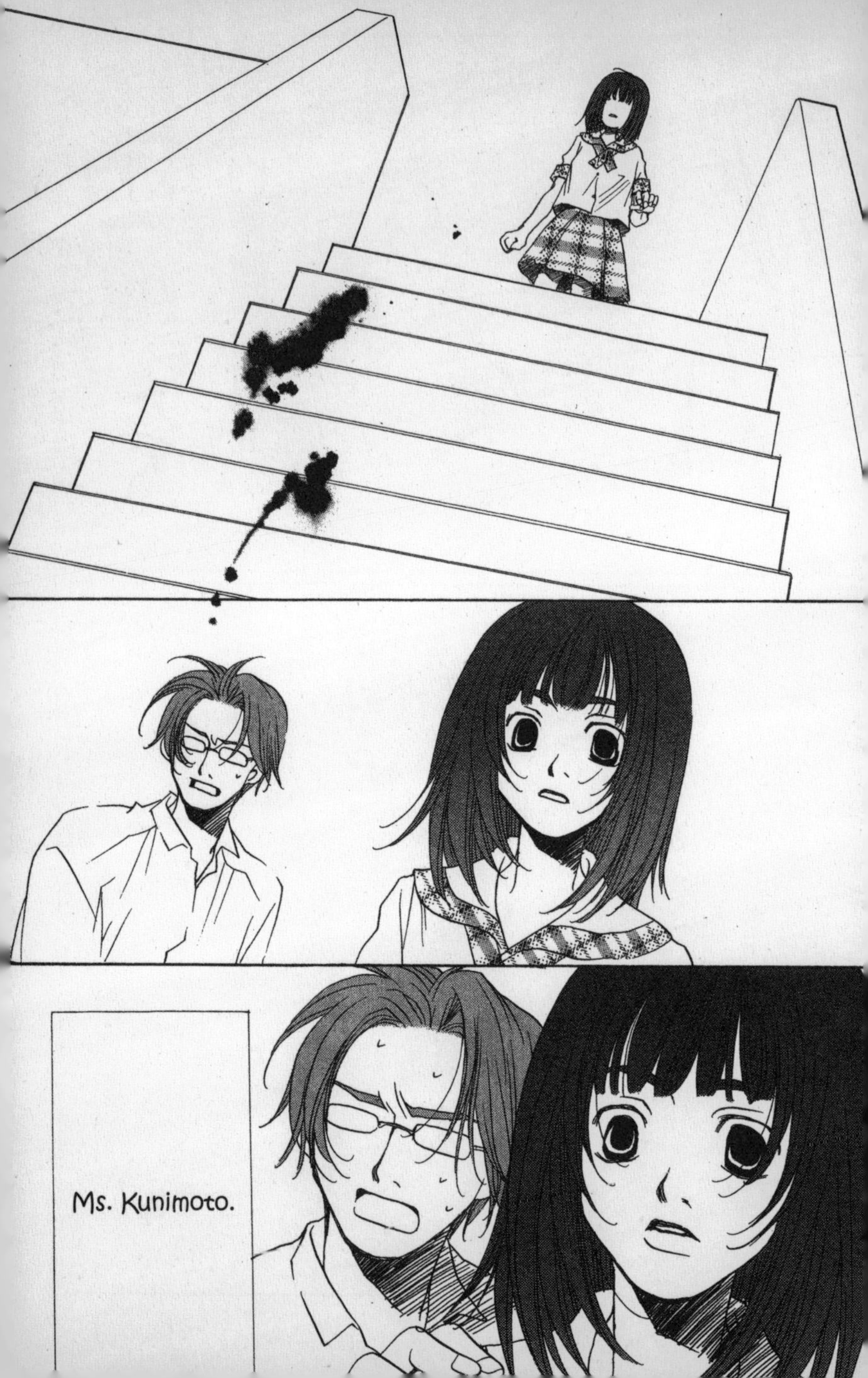
Ms. Kunimoto.

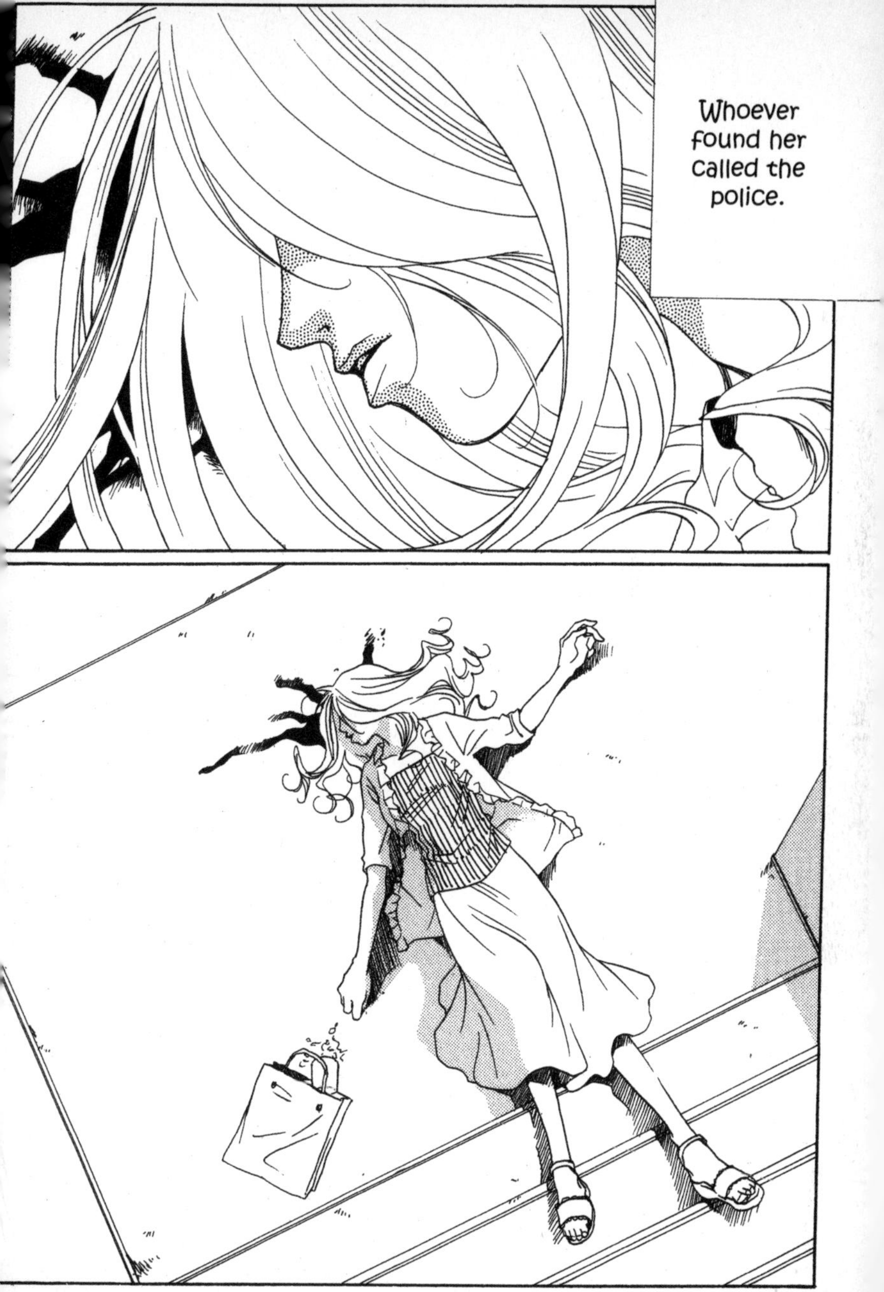
Whoever found her called the police.

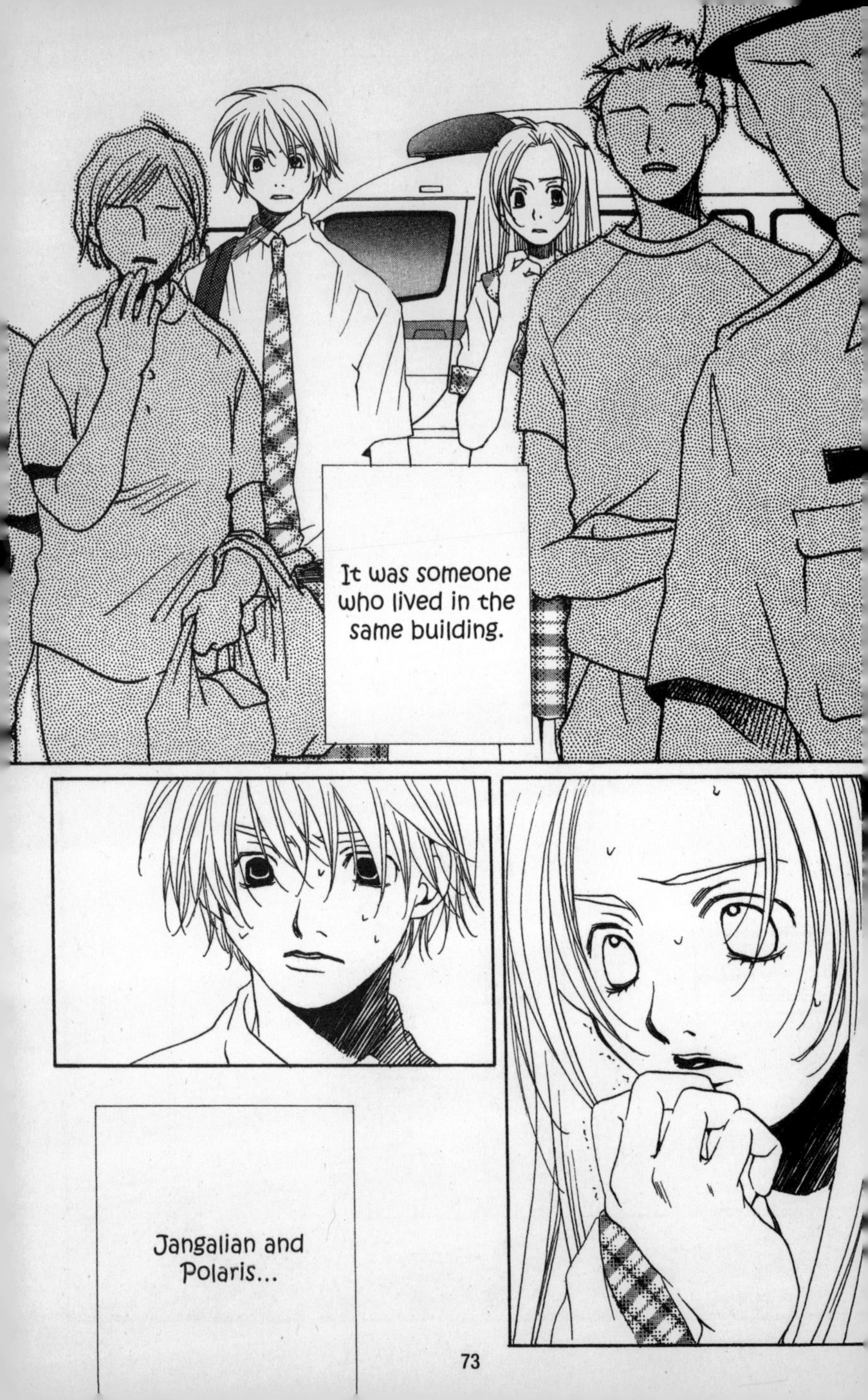
It was someone who lived in the same building.
Jangalian and Polaris...

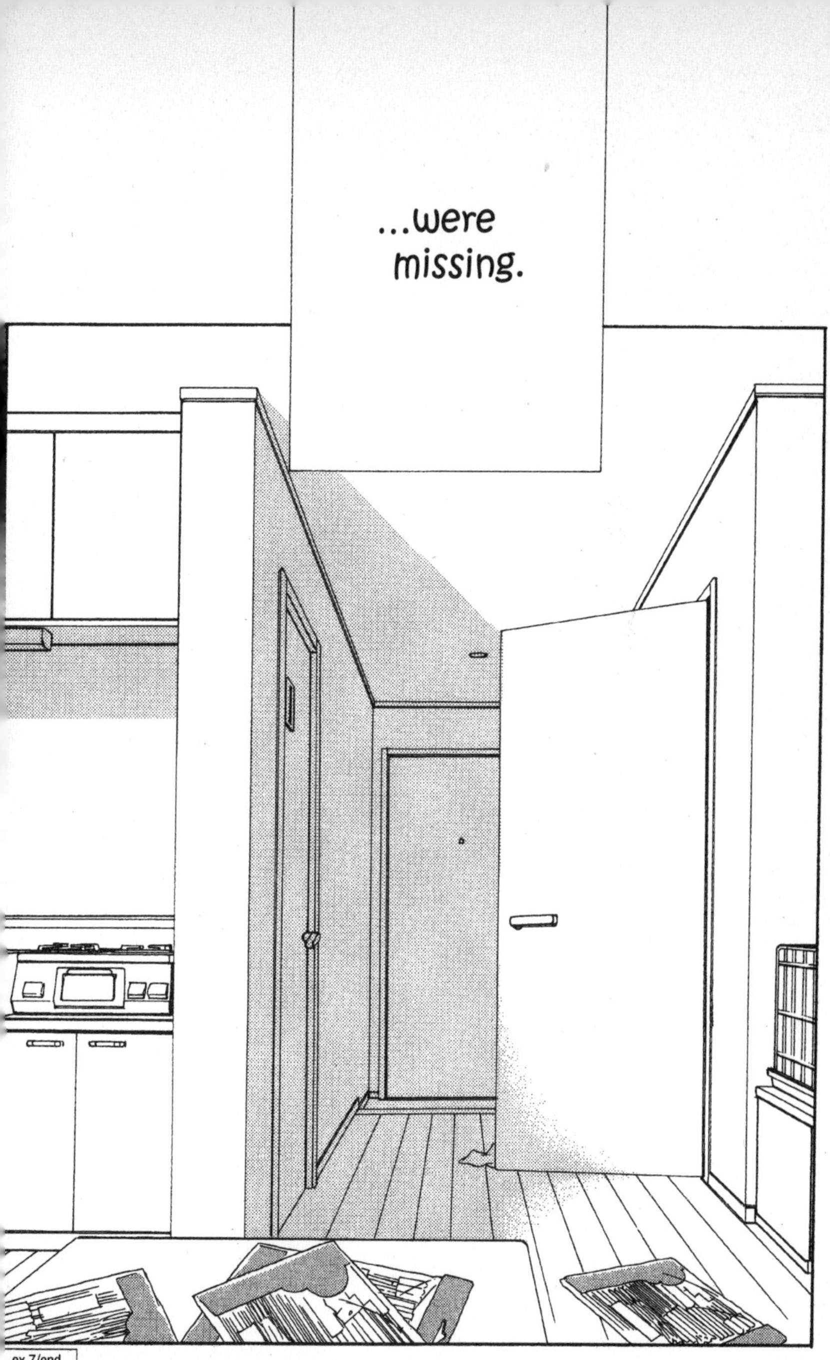
...were
missing.

ex.7/end

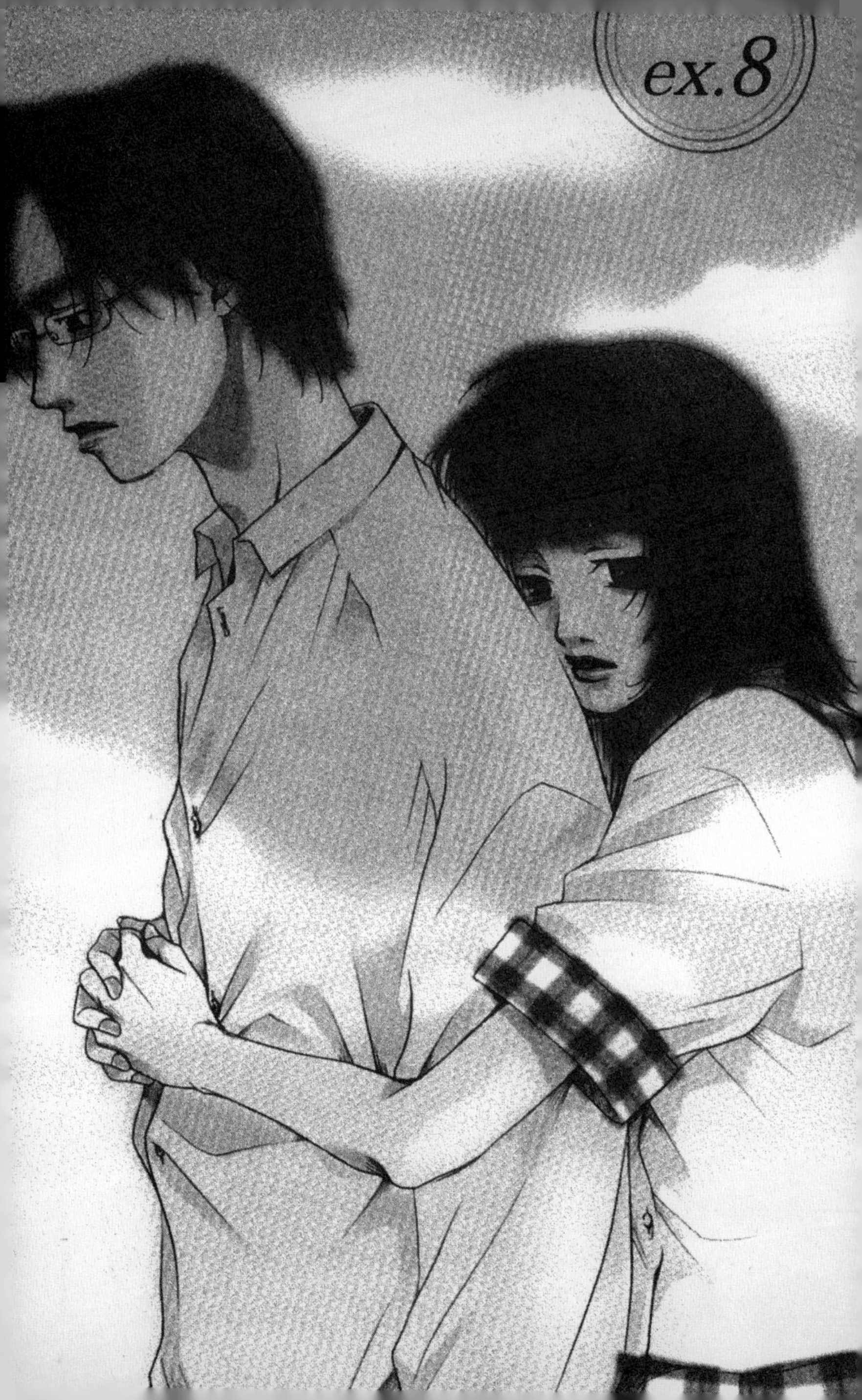
ex.8

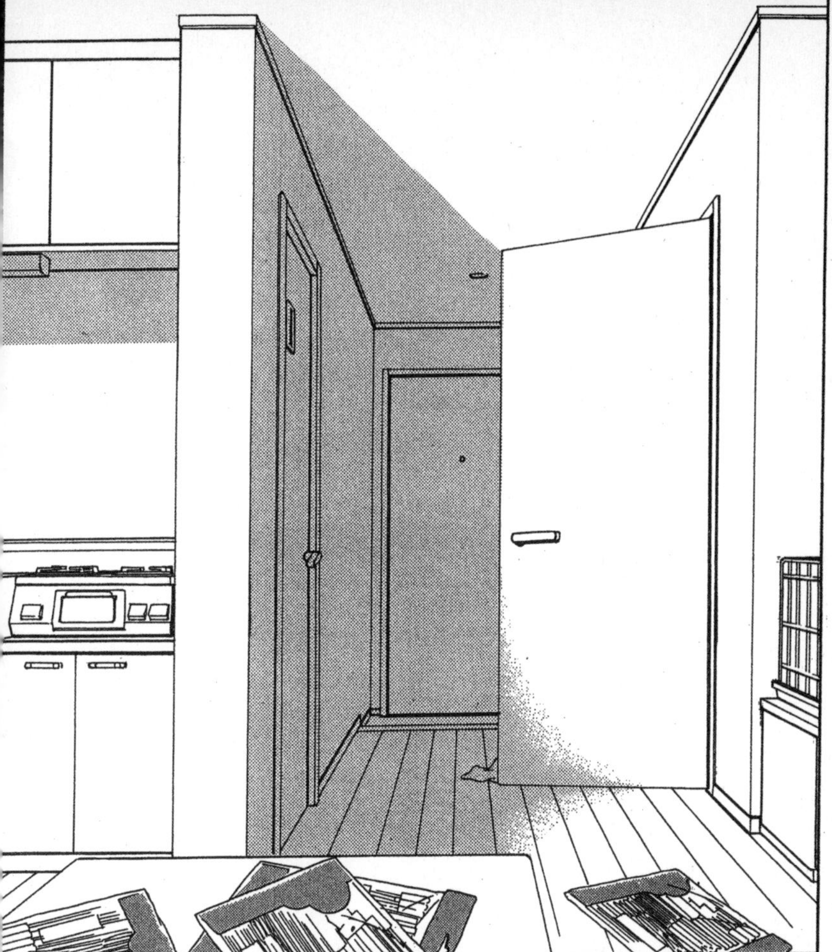
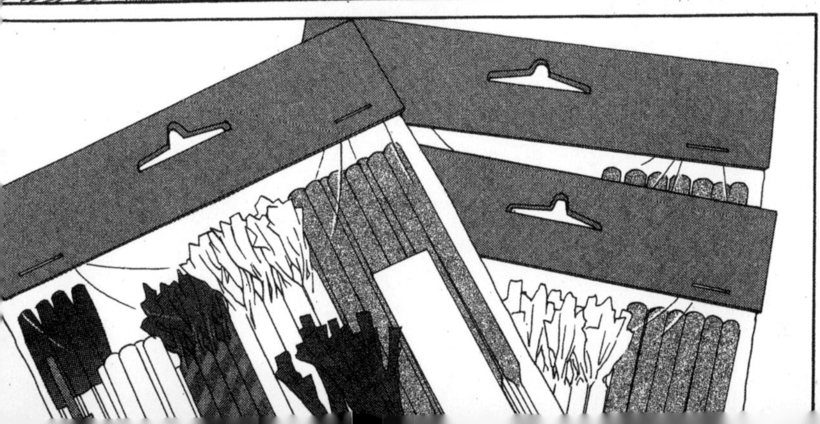

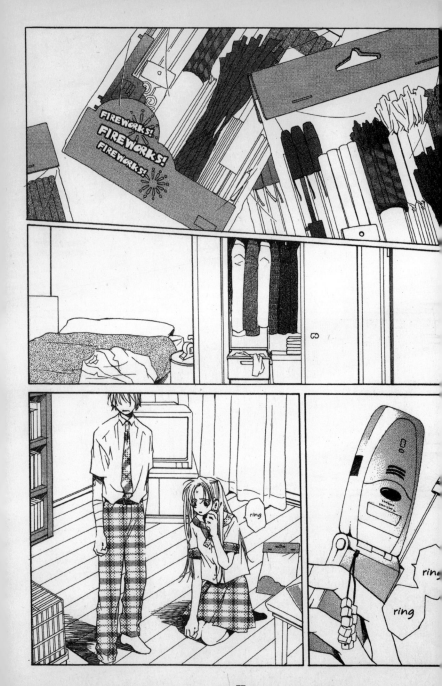

FIREWORKS!
FIREWORKS!
FIREWORKS!

ring

ring

ring

77

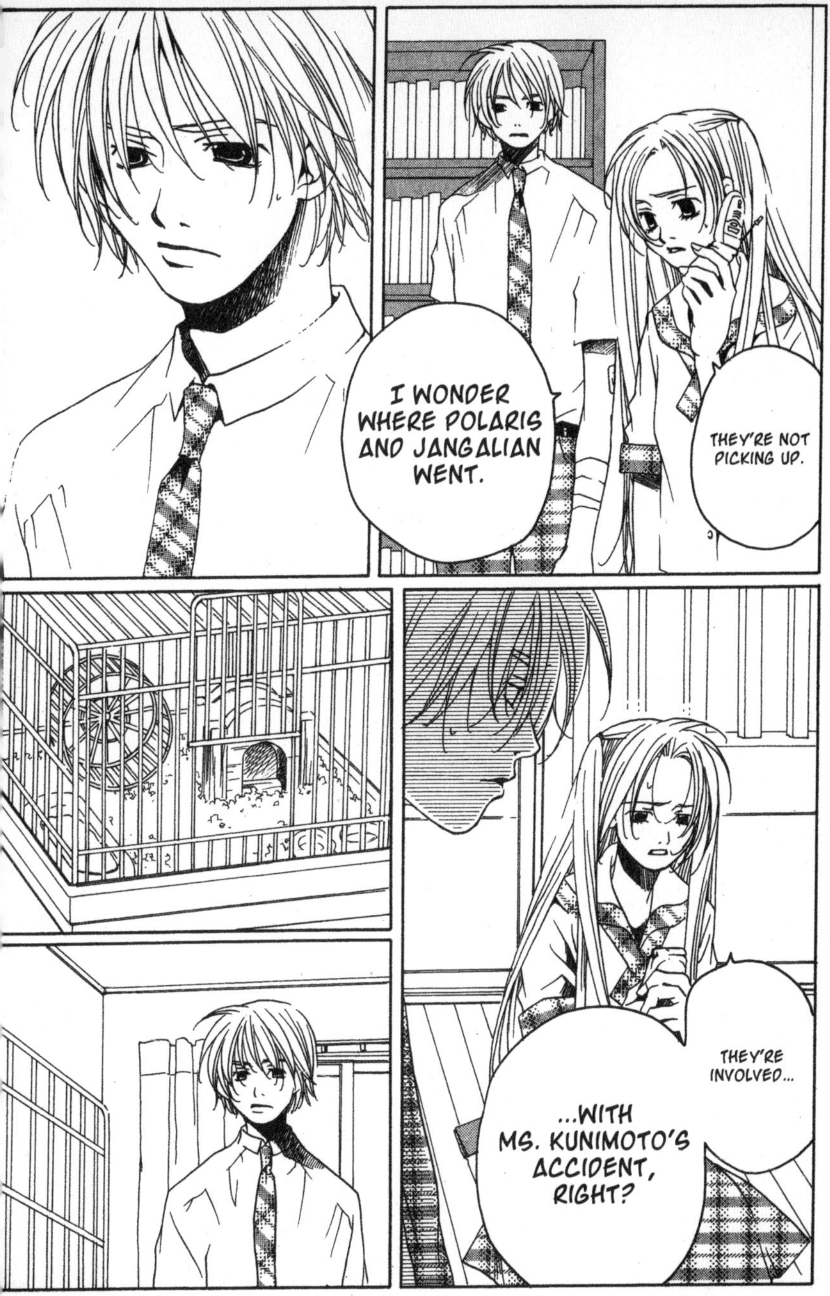
THEY'RE NOT PICKING UP.
I WONDER WHERE POLARIS AND JANGALIAN WENT.
THEY'RE INVOLVED...
...WITH MS. KUNIMOTO'S ACCIDENT, RIGHT?

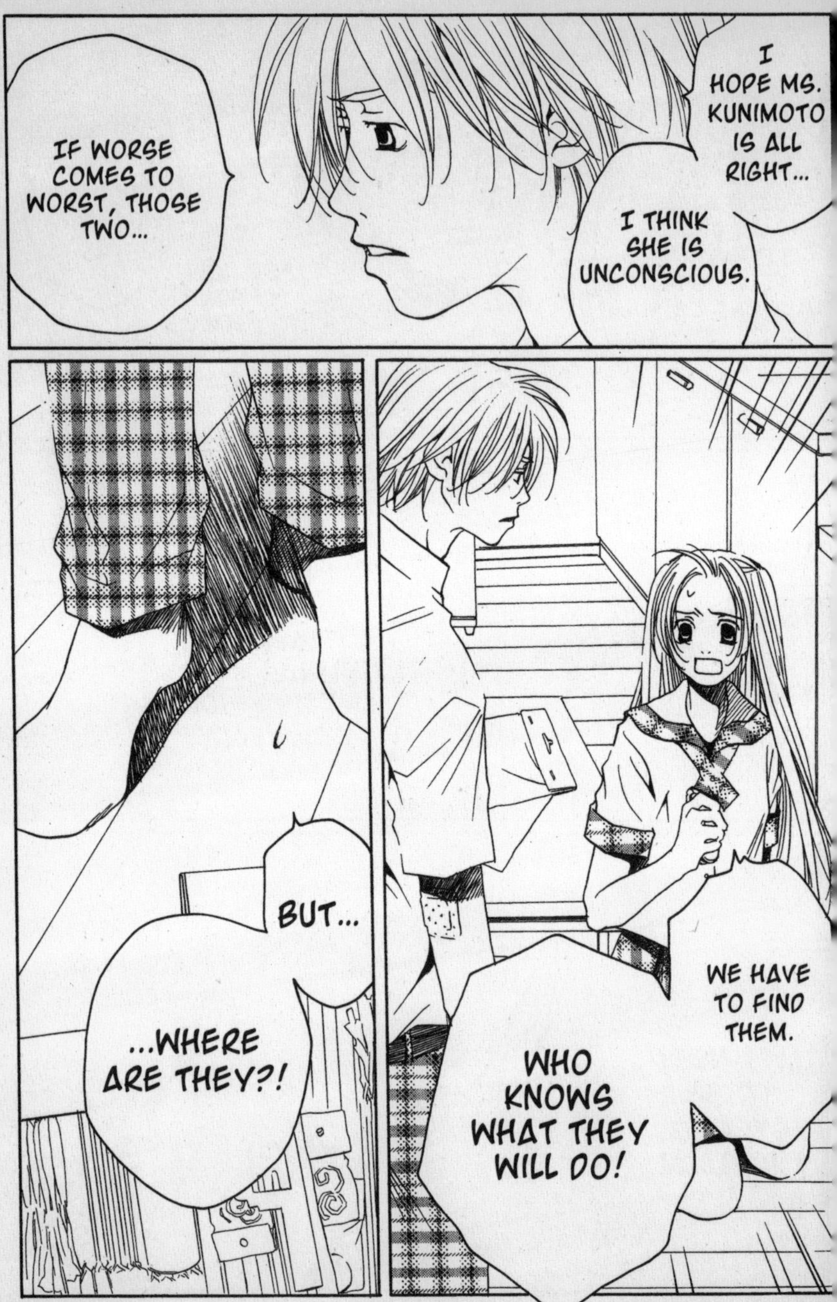
I HOPE MS. KUNIMOTO IS ALL RIGHT...
I THINK SHE IS UNCONSCIOUS.
IF WORSE COMES TO WORST, THOSE TWO...
WE HAVE TO FIND THEM.
WHO KNOWS WHAT THEY WILL DO!
BUT...
...WHERE ARE THEY?!

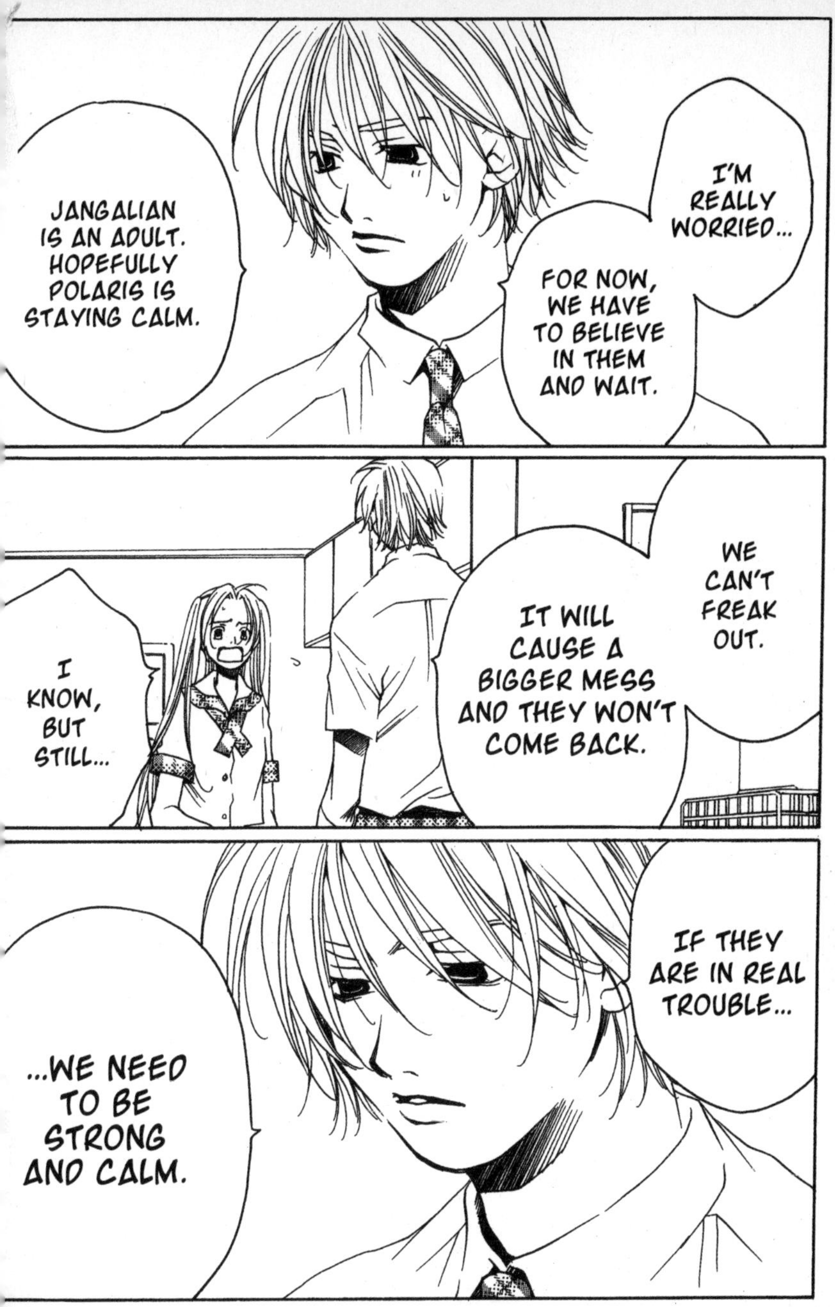
I'M REALLY WORRIED...
FOR NOW, WE HAVE TO BELIEVE IN THEM AND WAIT.
JANGALIAN IS AN ADULT. HOPEFULLY POLARIS IS STAYING CALM.
WE CAN'T FREAK OUT.
IT WILL CAUSE A BIGGER MESS AND THEY WON'T COME BACK.
I KNOW, BUT STILL...
IF THEY ARE IN REAL TROUBLE...
...WE NEED TO BE STRONG AND CALM.

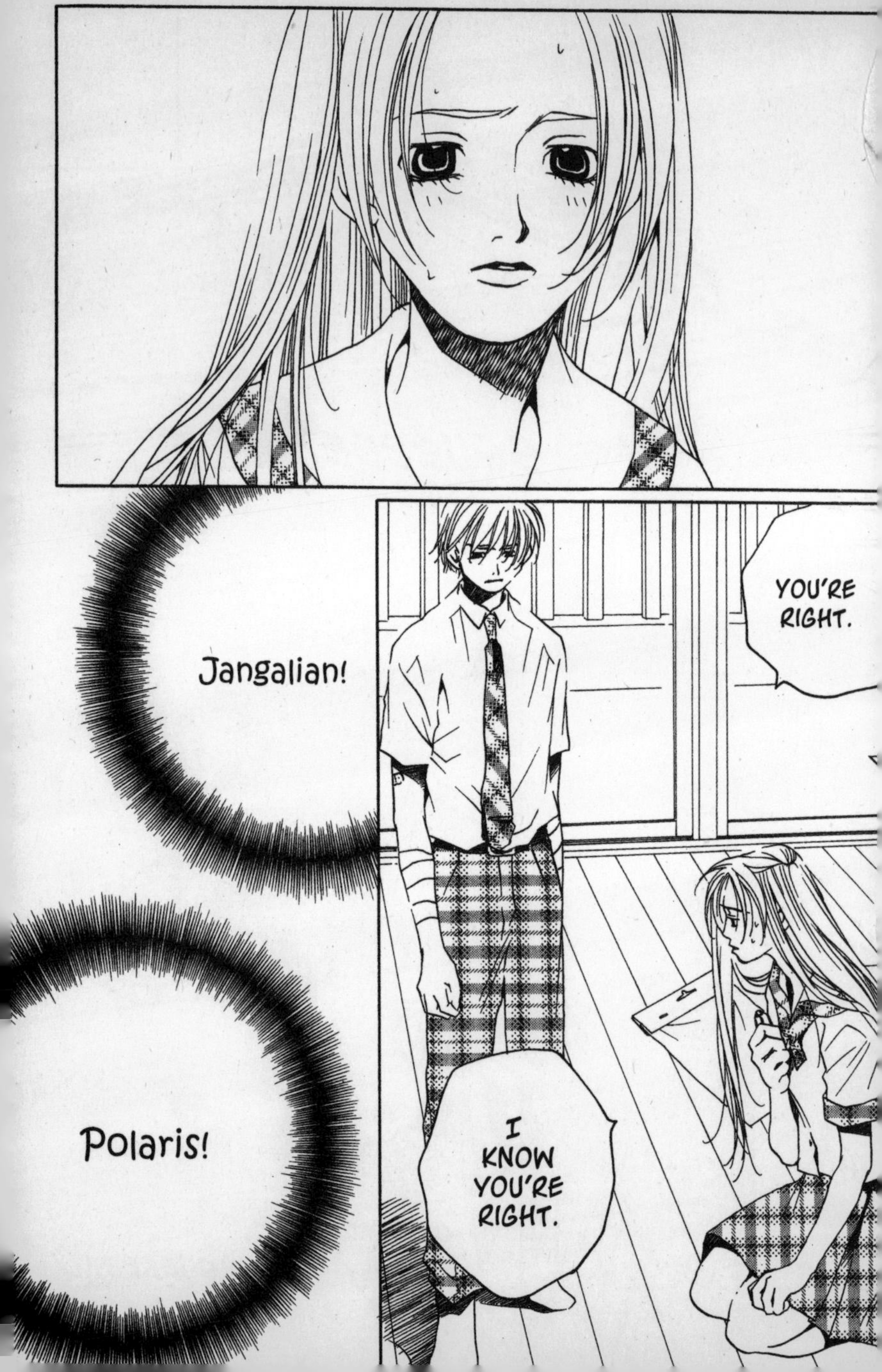
YOU'RE RIGHT.
I KNOW YOU'RE RIGHT.
Jangalian!
Polaris!

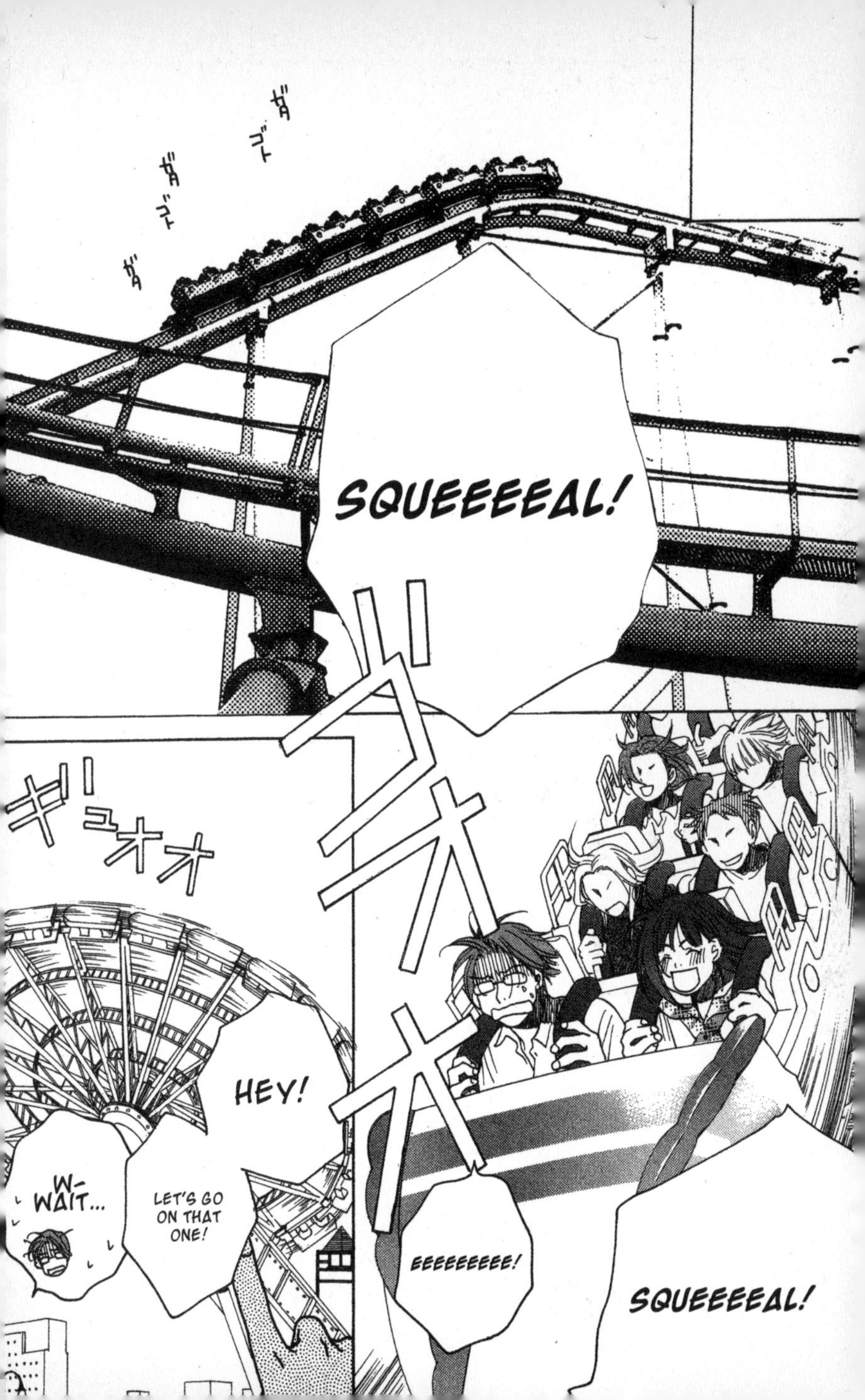
ガタ
ゴト
ガタ
ゴト
ガタ
SQUEEEEAL!
ゴオオ
SQUEEEEAL!
EEEEEEEEE!
キュオオ
HEY!
LET'S GO ON THAT ONE!
W-WAIT...

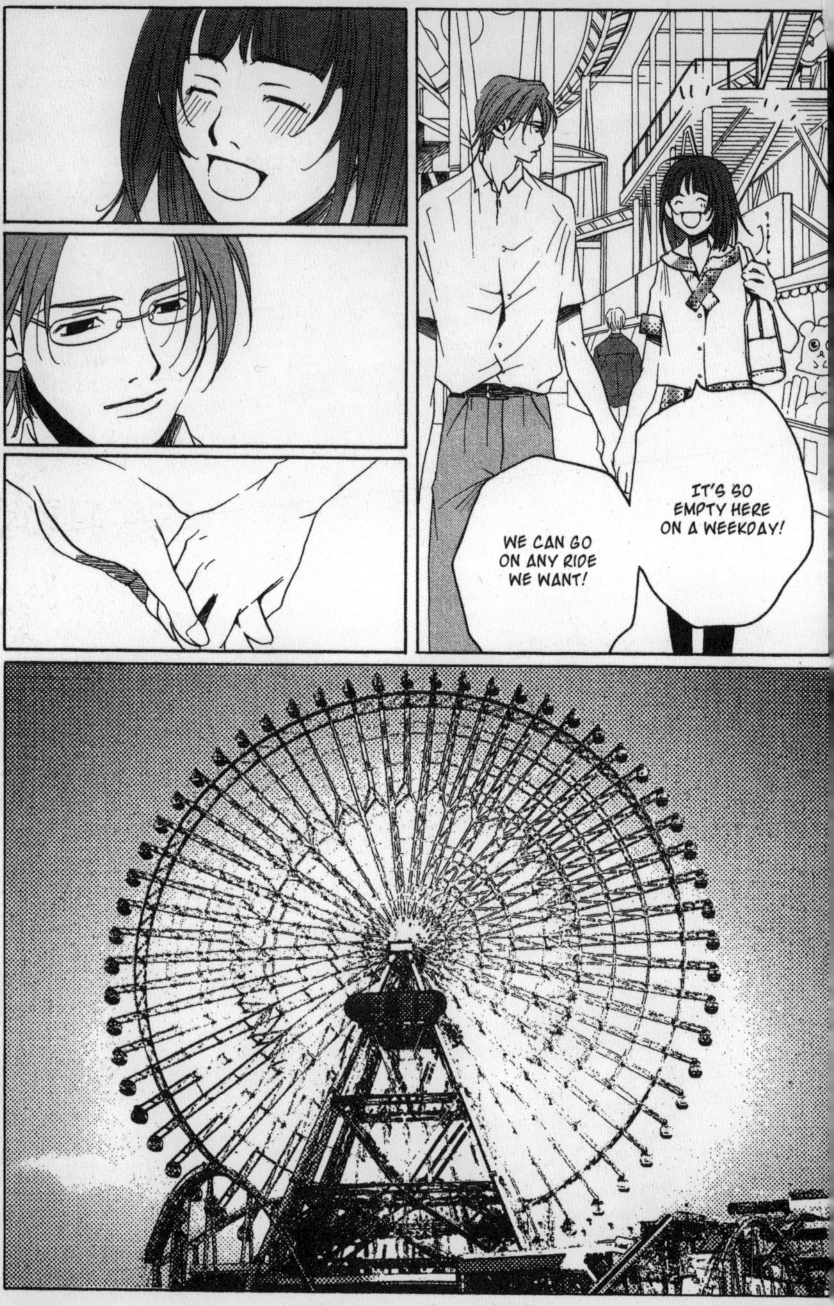
IT'S SO
EMPTY HERE
ON A WEEKDAY!
WE CAN GO
ON ANY RIDE
WE WANT!

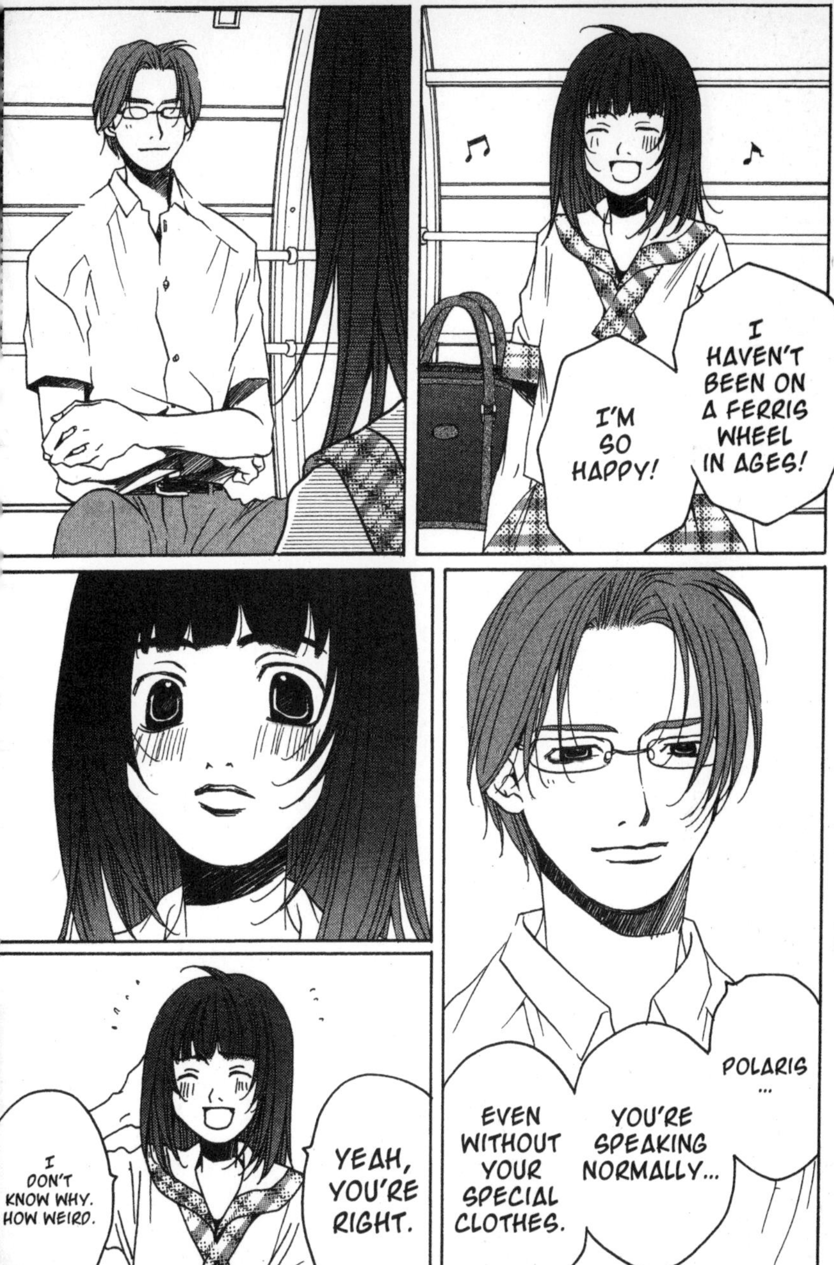
I HAVEN'T BEEN ON A FERRIS WHEEL IN AGES!
I'M SO HAPPY!
POLARIS ...
YOU'RE SPEAKING NORMALLY...
EVEN WITHOUT YOUR SPECIAL CLOTHES.
YEAH, YOU'RE RIGHT.
I DON'T KNOW WHY. HOW WEIRD.

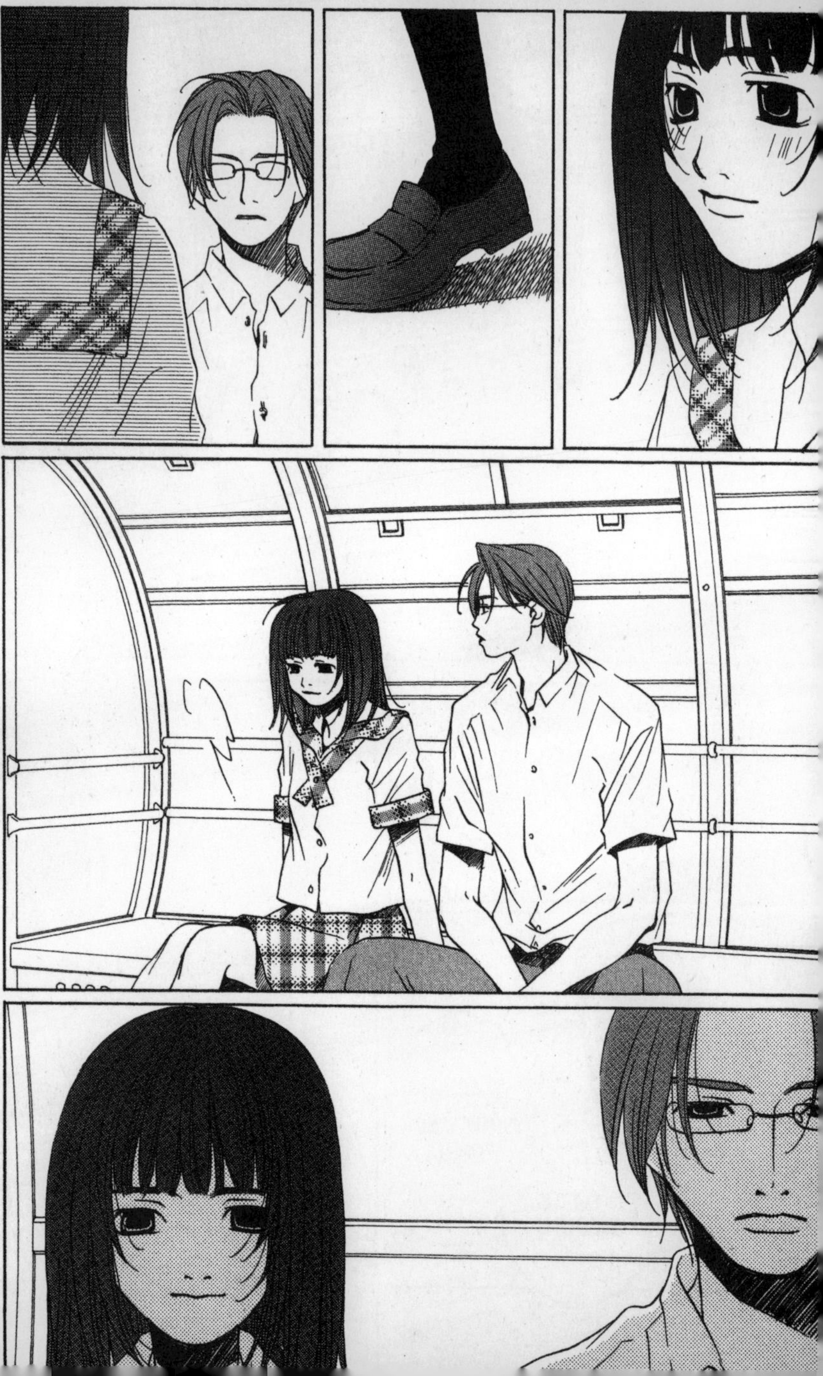

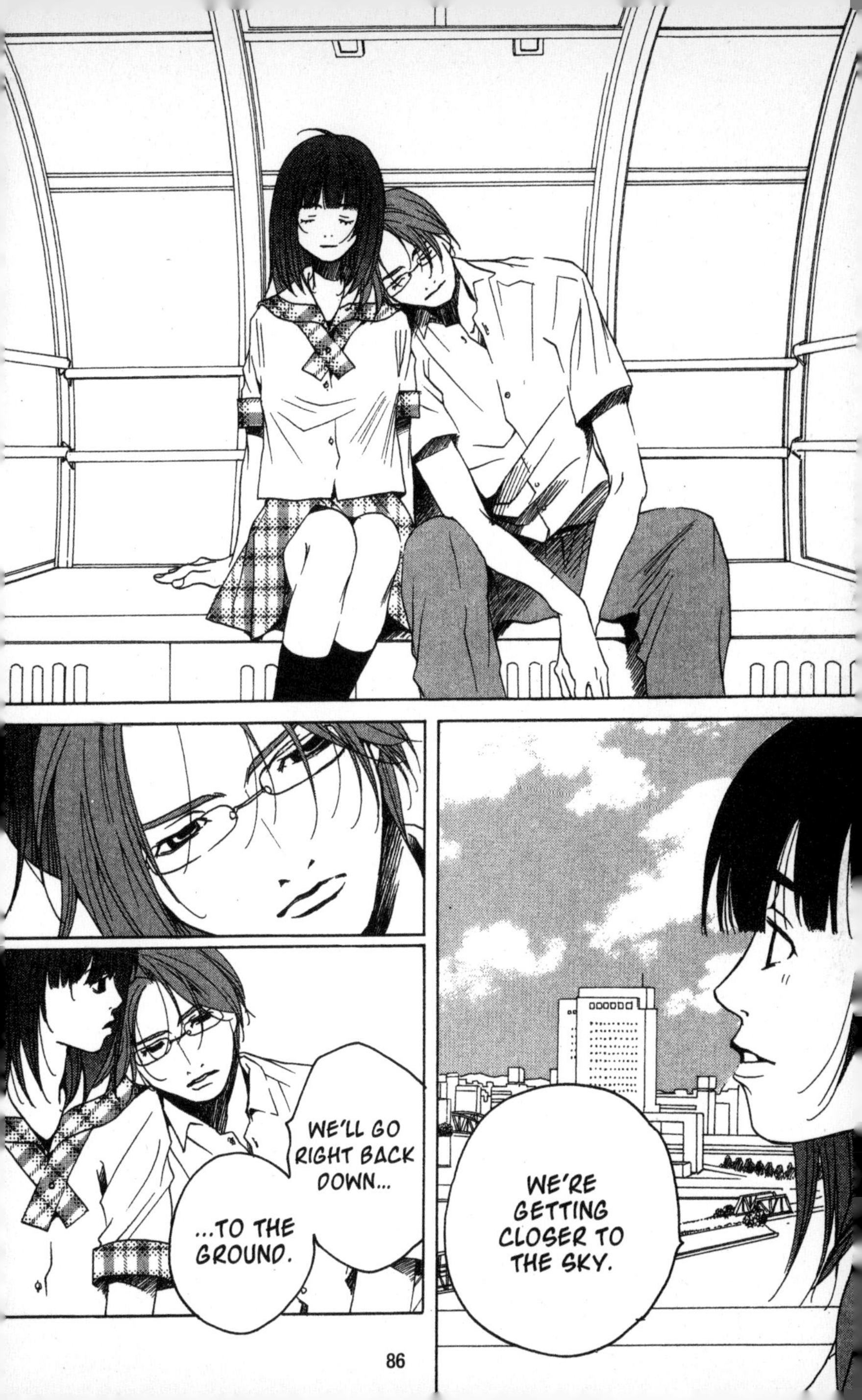
WE'RE GETTING CLOSER TO THE SKY.
WE'LL GO RIGHT BACK DOWN...
...TO THE GROUND.

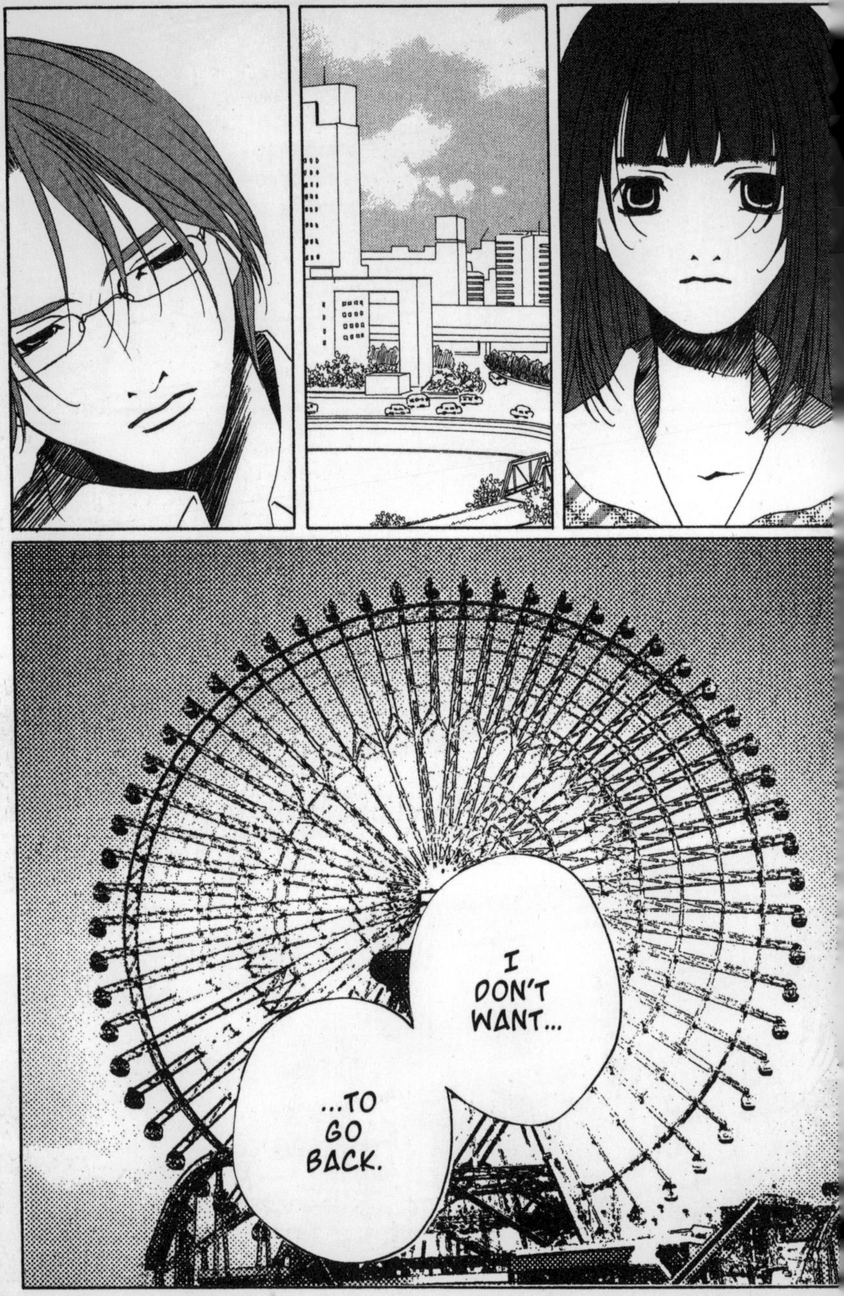
I DON'T WANT...
...TO GO BACK.

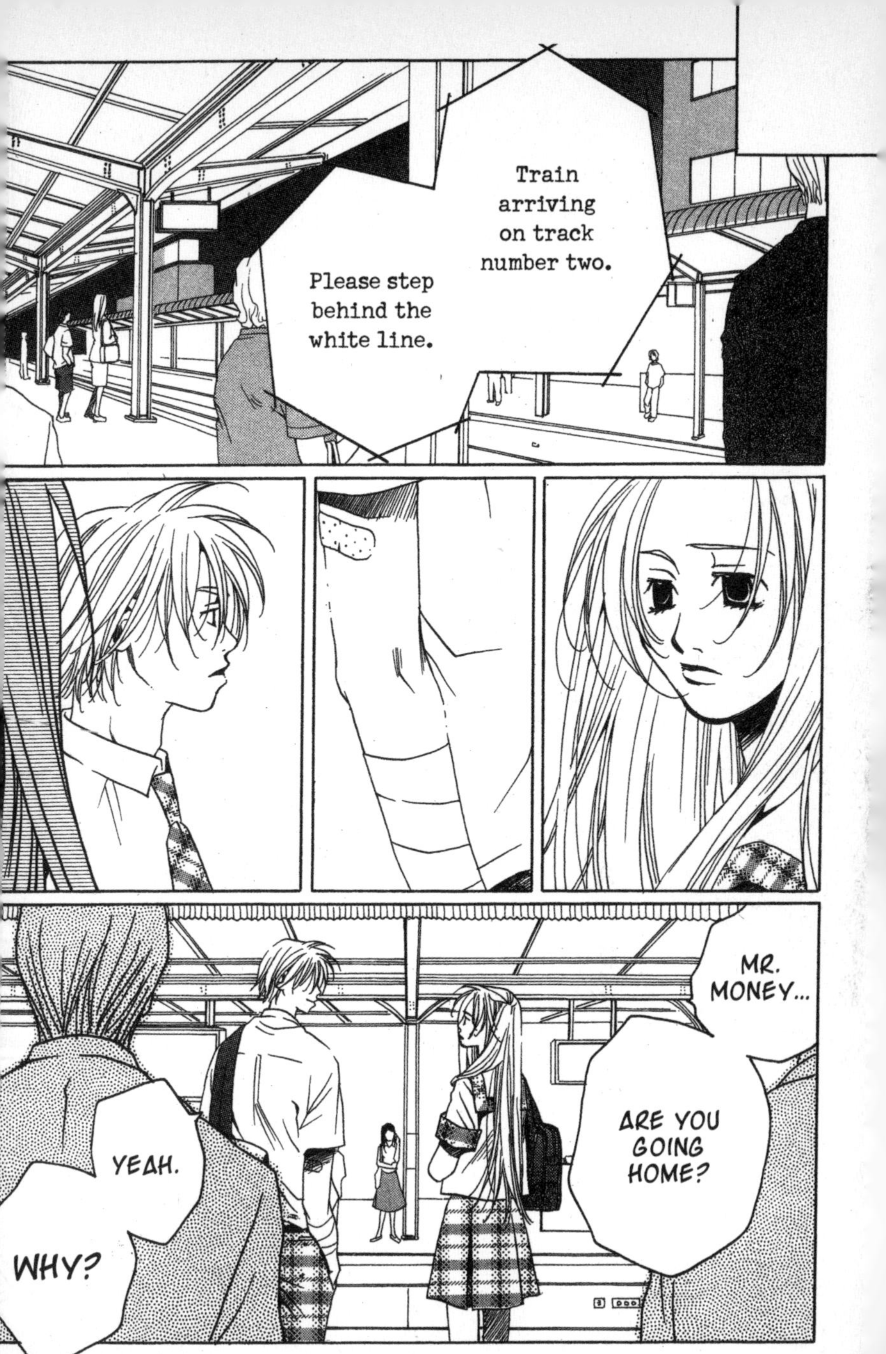
Train arriving on track number two.
Please step behind the white line.
MR. MONEY...
ARE YOU GOING HOME?
YEAH.
WHY?

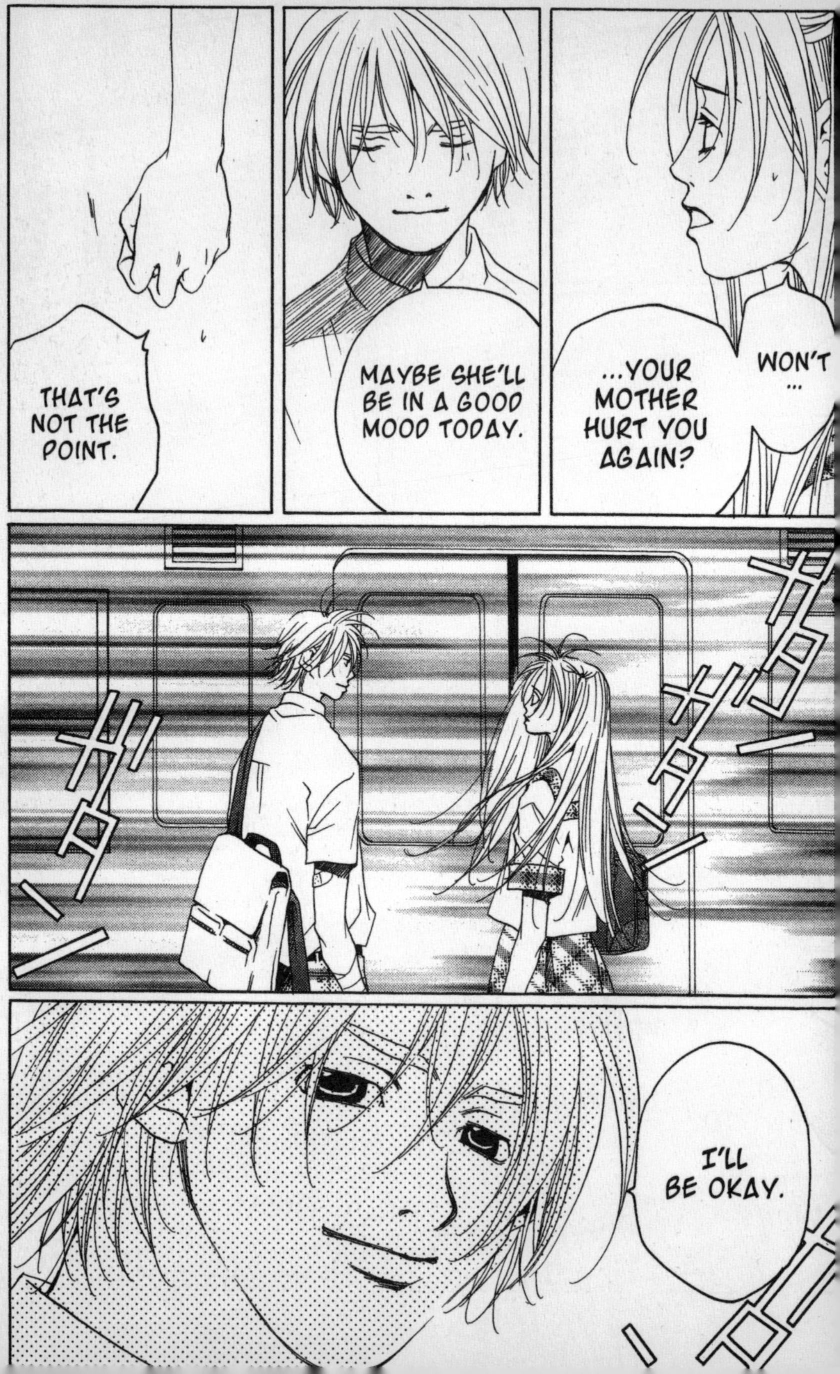
WON'T ...
...YOUR MOTHER HURT YOU AGAIN?
MAYBE SHE'LL BE IN A GOOD MOOD TODAY.
THAT'S NOT THE POINT.
I'LL BE OKAY.

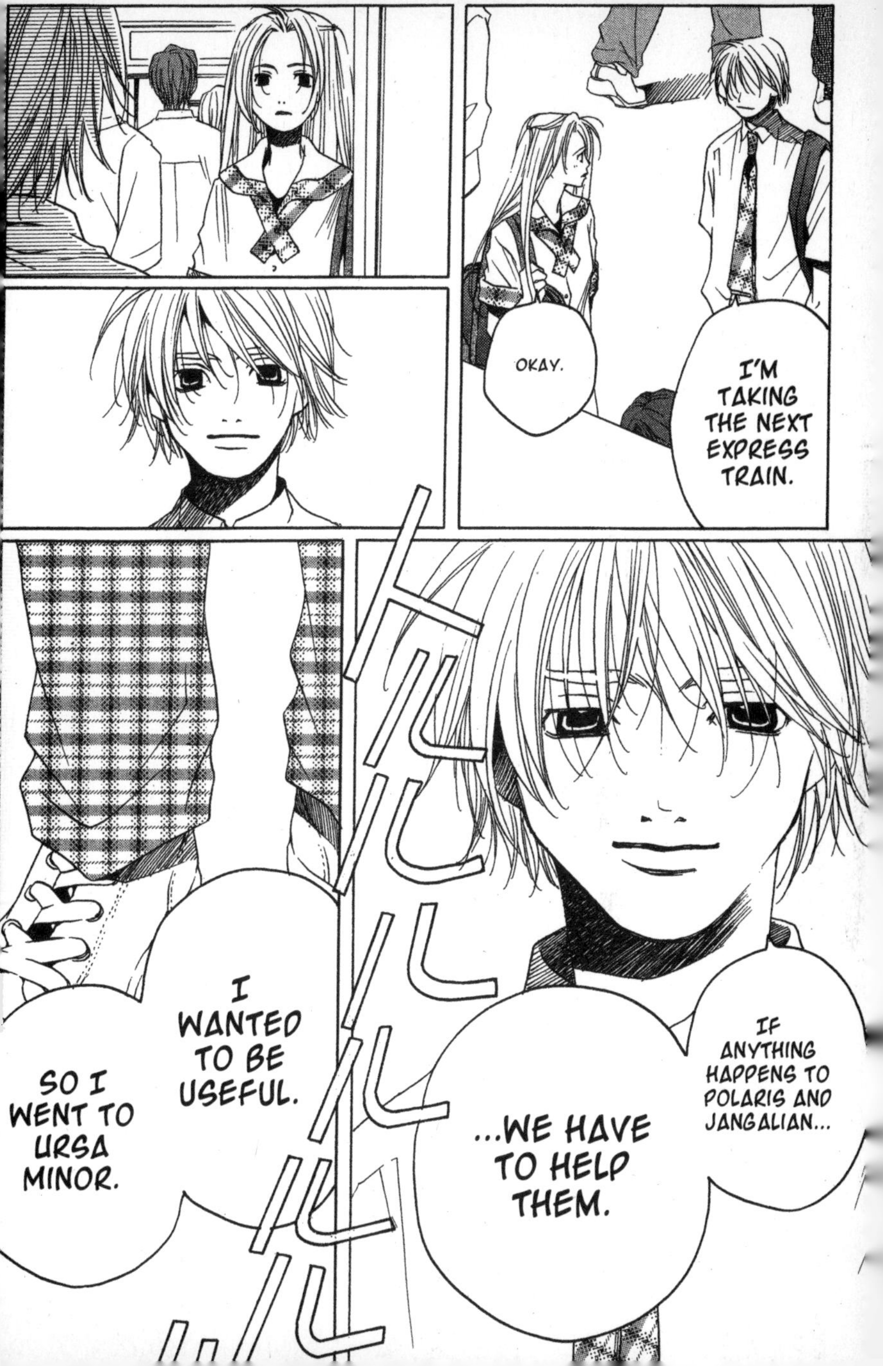
I'M TAKING THE NEXT EXPRESS TRAIN.
OKAY.
IF ANYTHING HAPPENS TO POLARIS AND JANGALIAN...
...WE HAVE TO HELP THEM.
I WANTED TO BE USEFUL.
SO I WENT TO URSA MINOR.

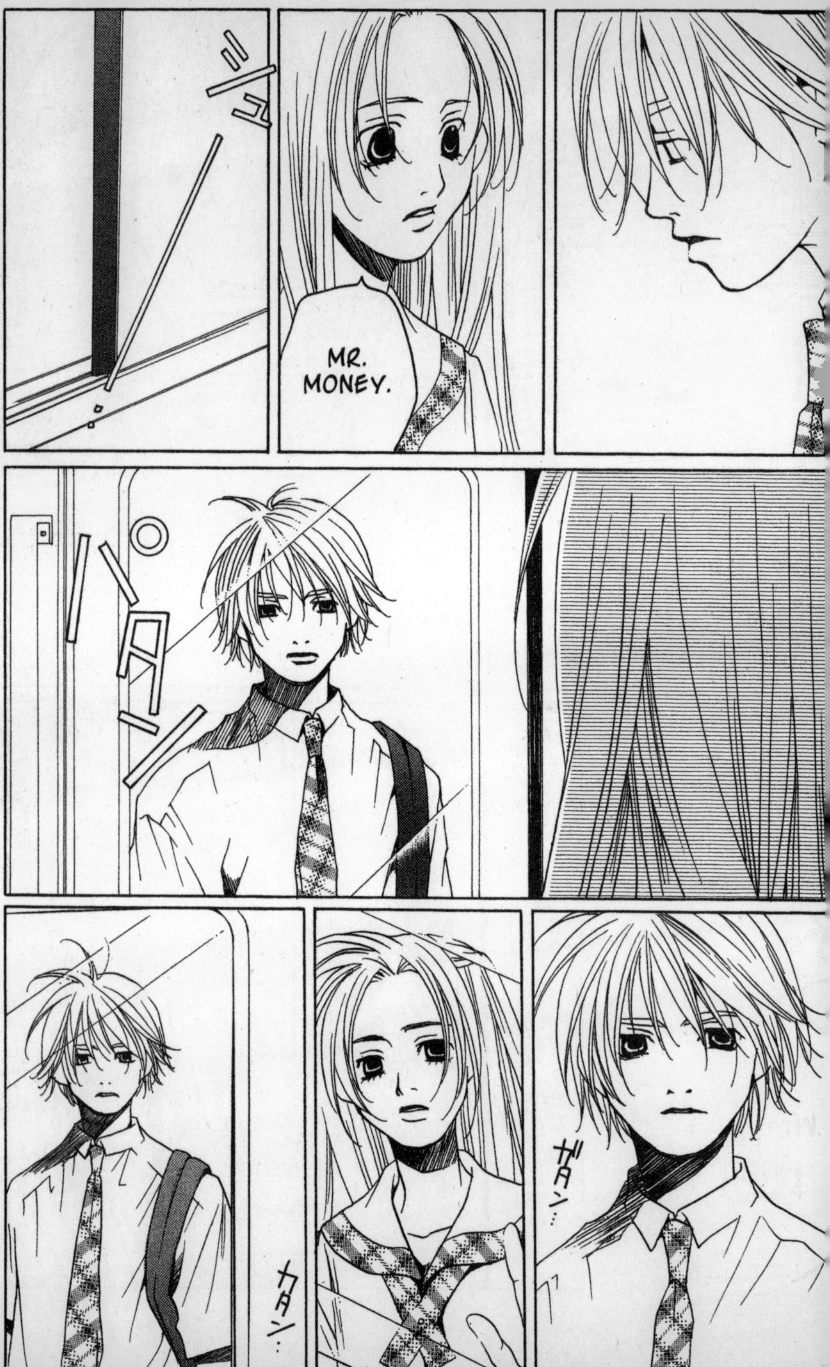
MR. MONEY.
シュ
パタン
ガタン…
カタン…

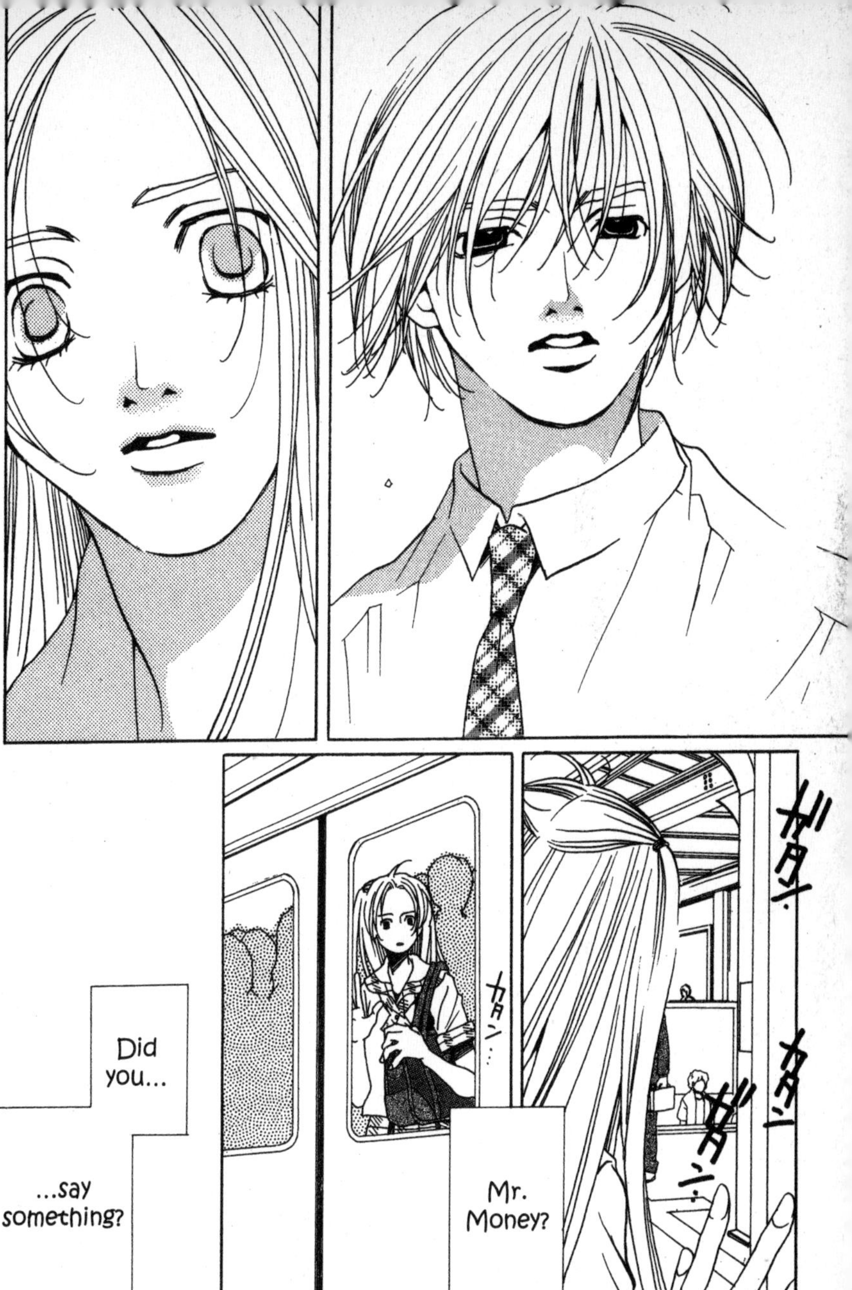
ガタン!
ガタン
ガタン…
カタン…
Mr. Money?
Did you...
...say something?

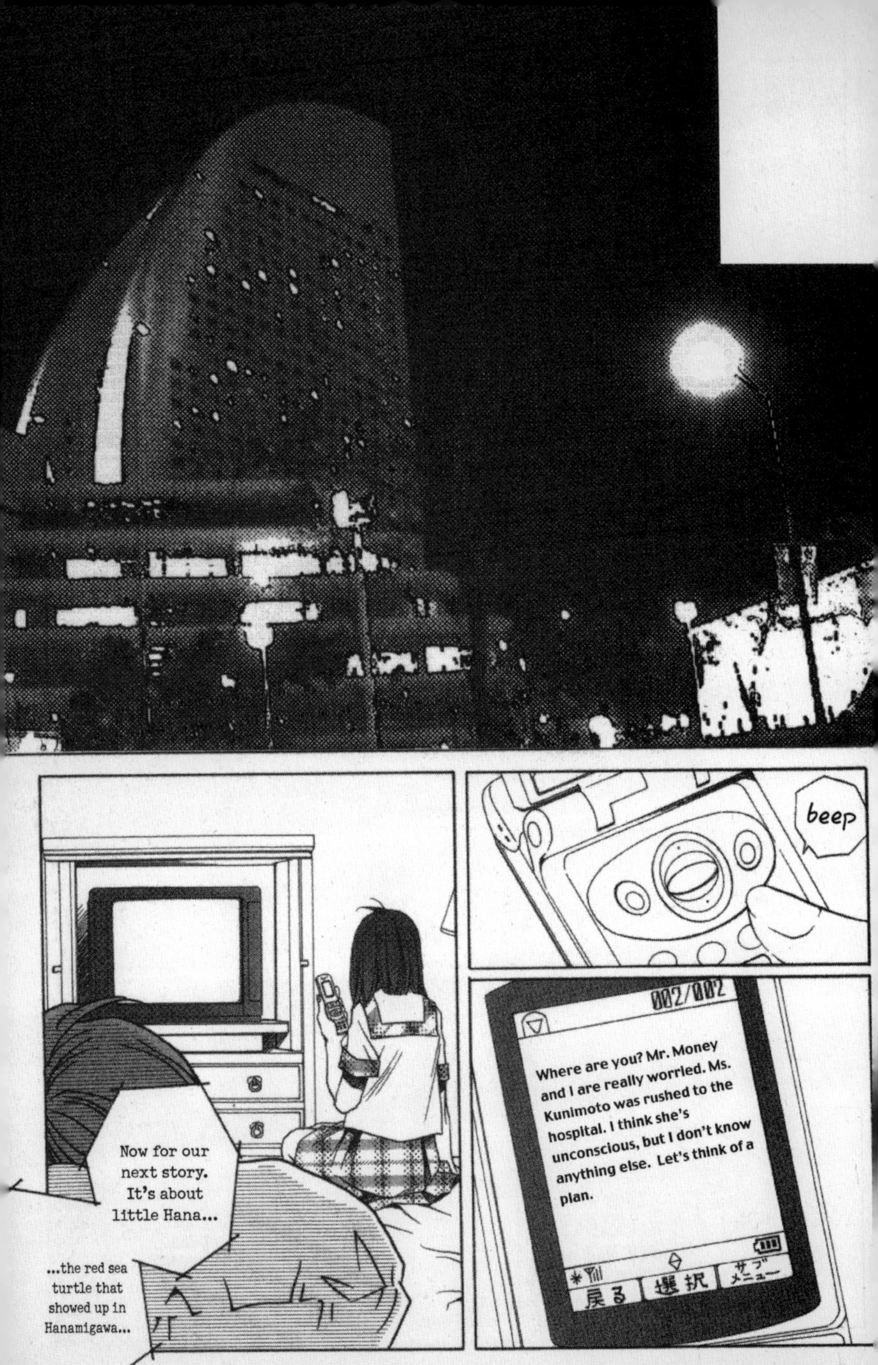
beep
002/002
Where are you? Mr. Money and I are really worried. Ms. Kunimoto was rushed to the hospital. I think she's unconscious, but I don't know anything else. Let's think of a plan.
戻る
選択
サブメニュー
Now for our next story. It's about little Hana...
...the red sea turtle that showed up in Hanamigawa...

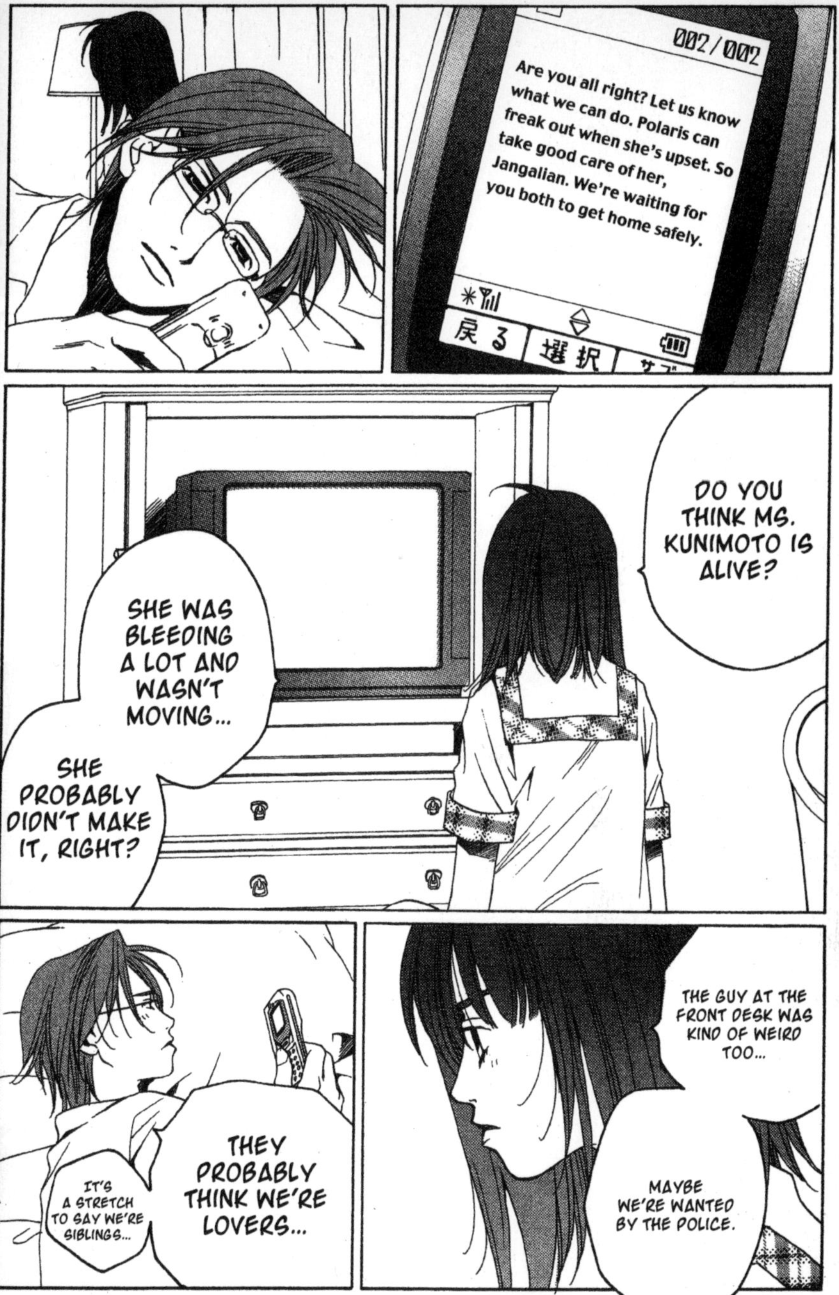
002/002
Are you all right? Let us know what we can do. Polaris can freak out when she's upset. So take good care of her, Jangalian. We're waiting for you both to get home safely.
戻る
選択
DO YOU THINK MS. KUNIMOTO IS ALIVE?
SHE WAS BLEEDING A LOT AND WASN'T MOVING...
SHE PROBABLY DIDN'T MAKE IT, RIGHT?
THE GUY AT THE FRONT DESK WAS KIND OF WEIRD TOO...
MAYBE WE'RE WANTED BY THE POLICE.
THEY PROBABLY THINK WE'RE LOVERS...
IT'S A STRETCH TO SAY WE'RE SIBLINGS...

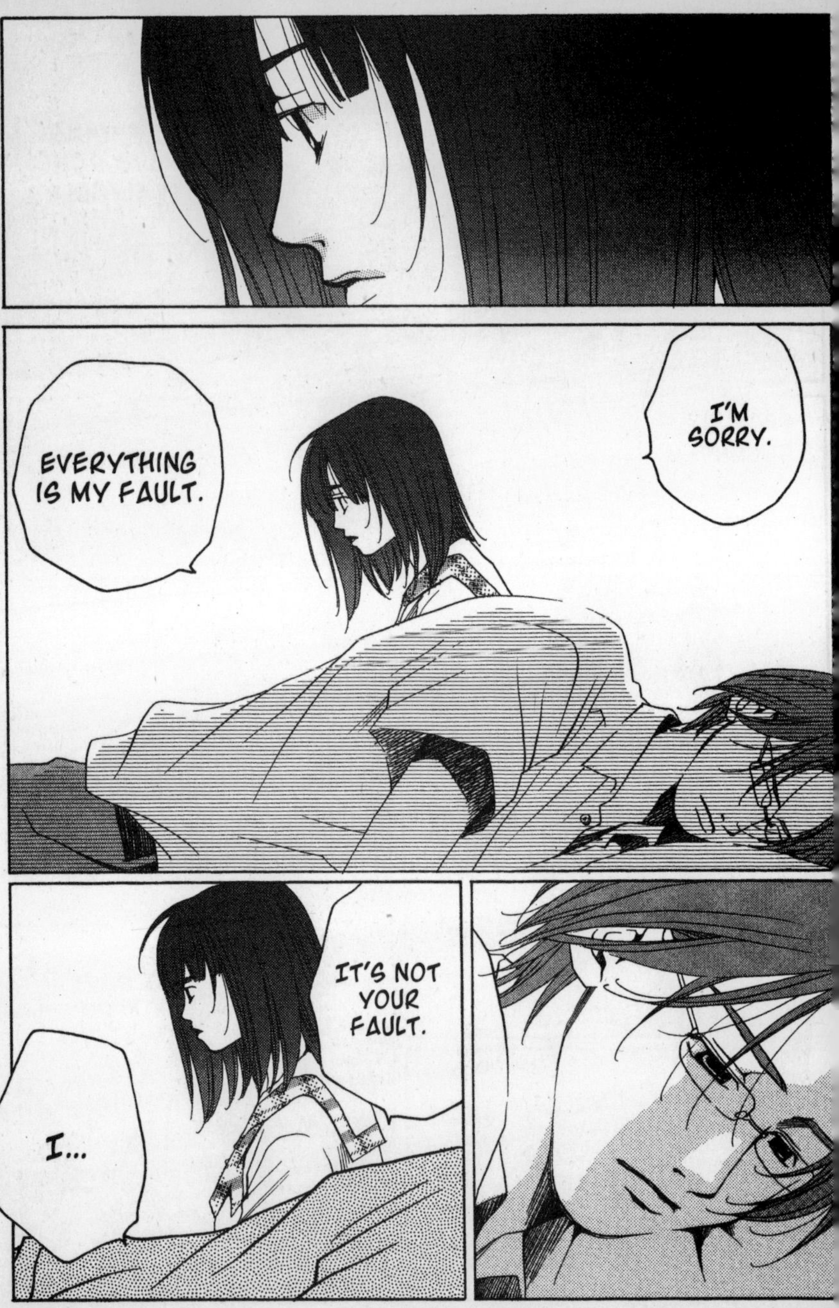
I'M SORRY.
EVERYTHING IS MY FAULT.
IT'S NOT YOUR FAULT.
I...

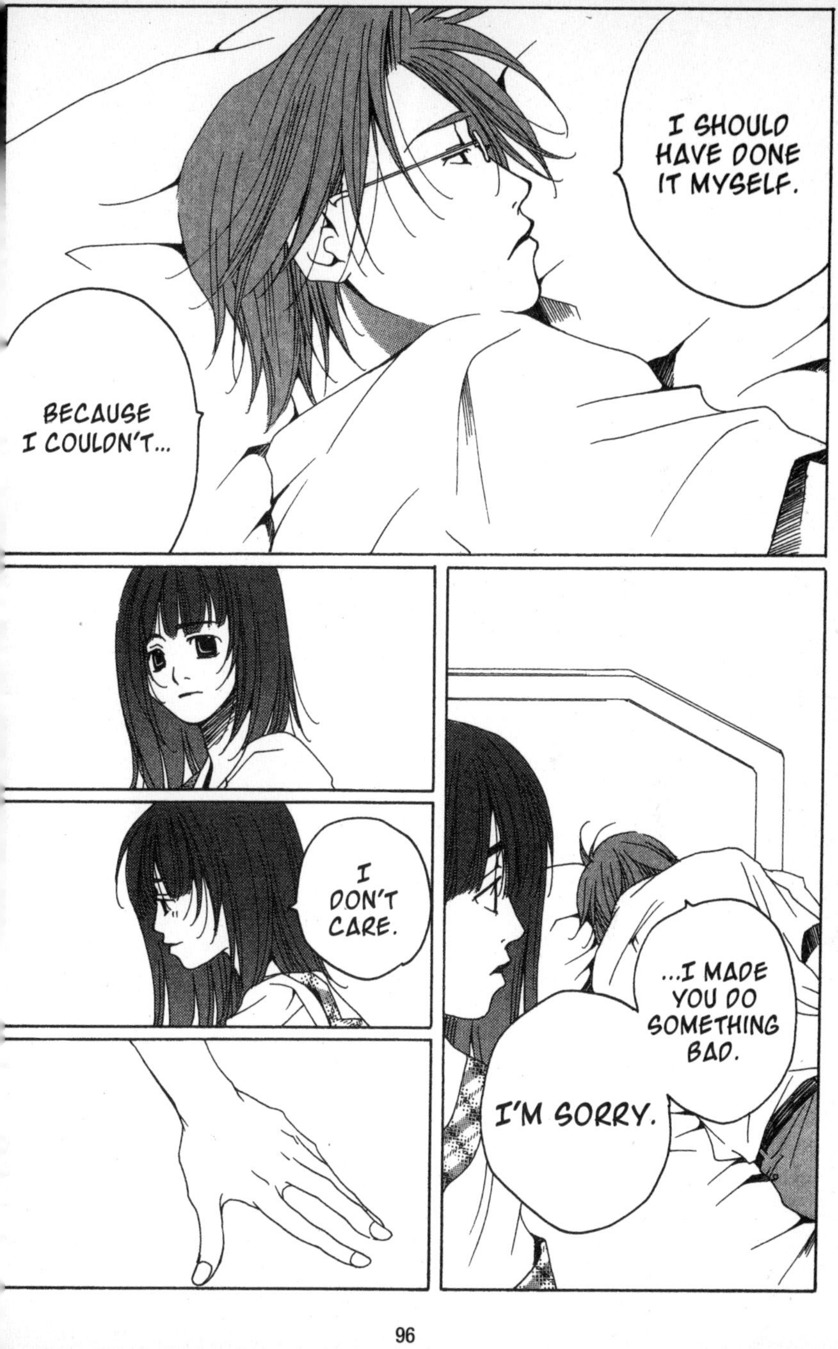
I SHOULD HAVE DONE IT MYSELF.
BECAUSE I COULDN'T...
...I MADE YOU DO SOMETHING BAD.
I'M SORRY.
I DON'T CARE.

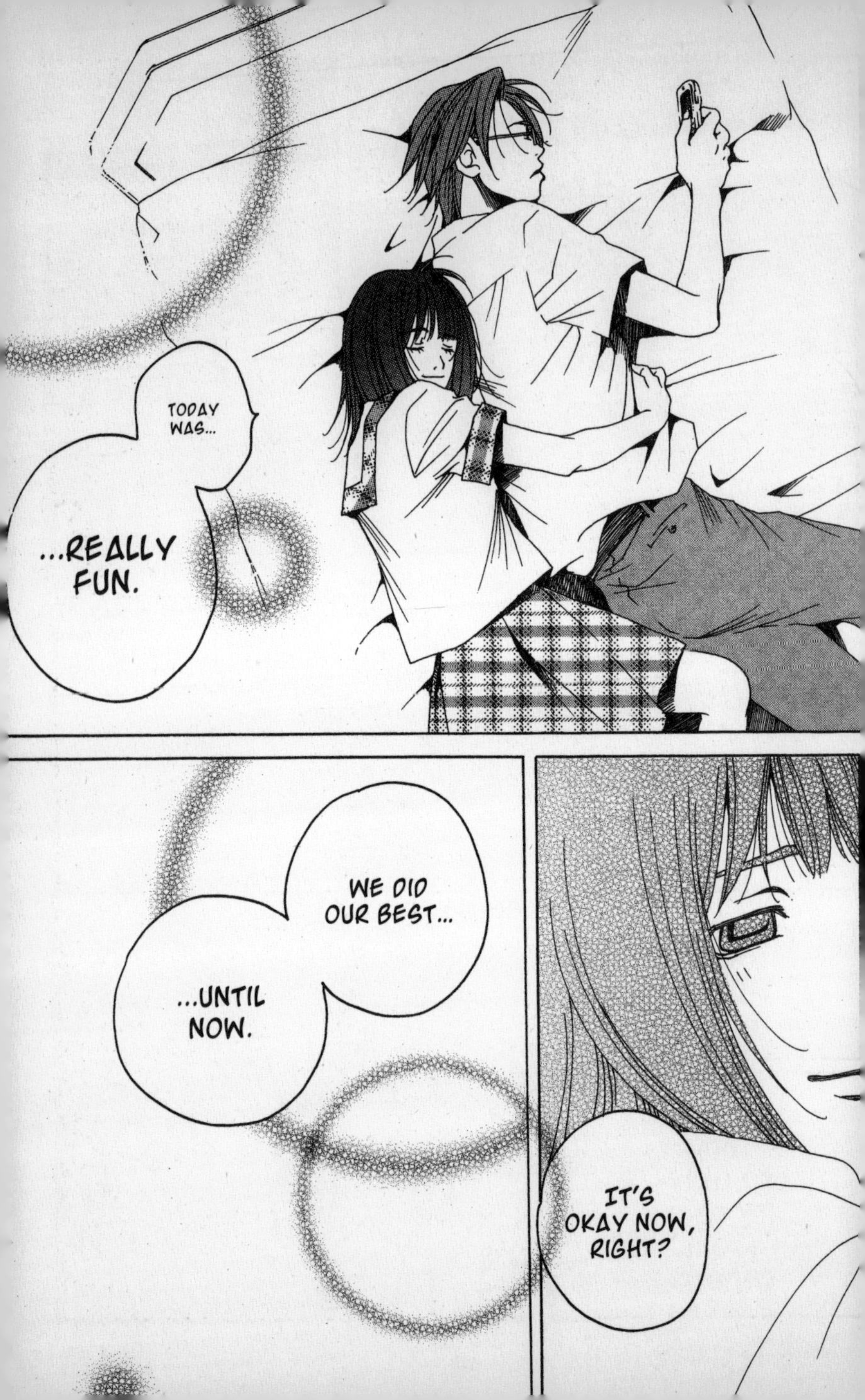
TODAY WAS...
...REALLY FUN.
IT'S OKAY NOW, RIGHT?
WE DID OUR BEST...
...UNTIL NOW.

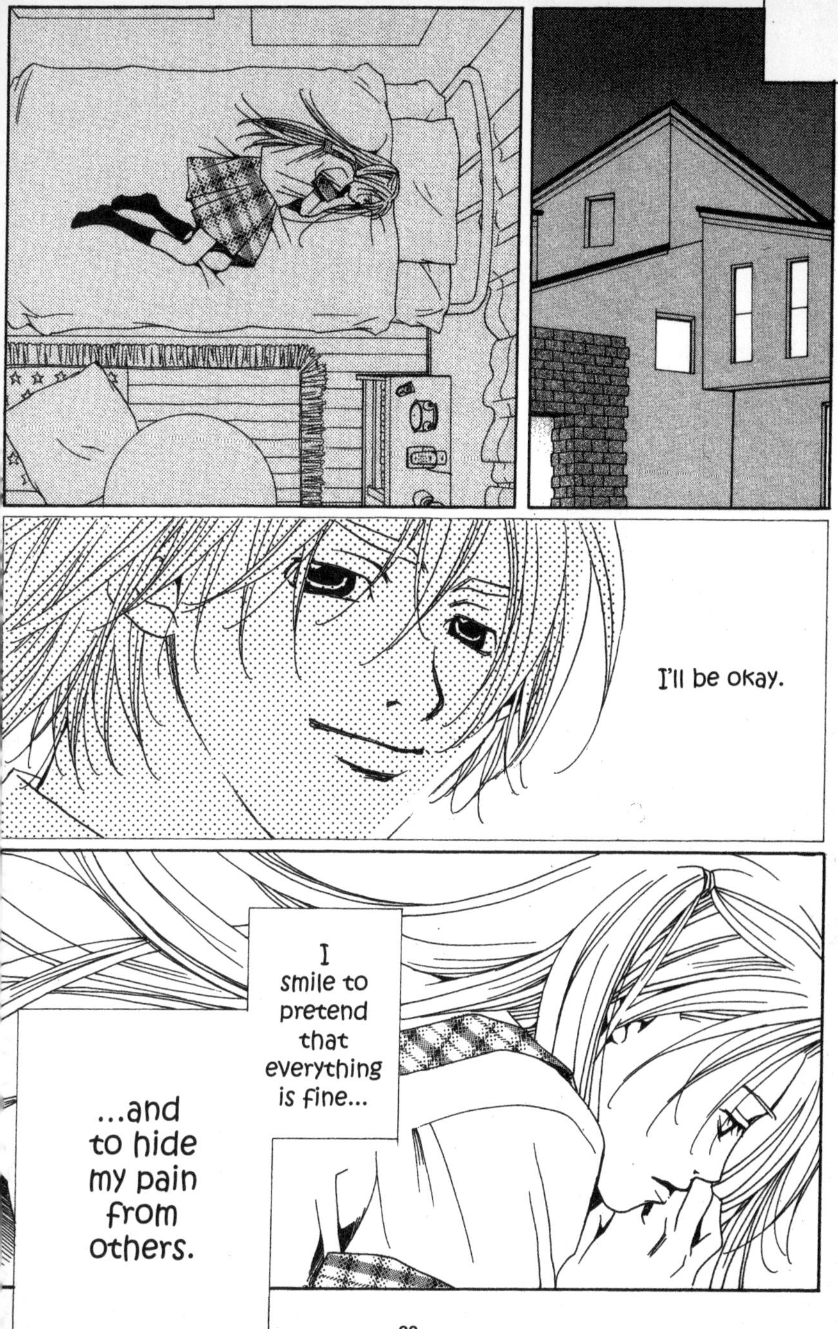
I'll be okay.
I smile to pretend that everything is fine...
...and to hide my pain from others.

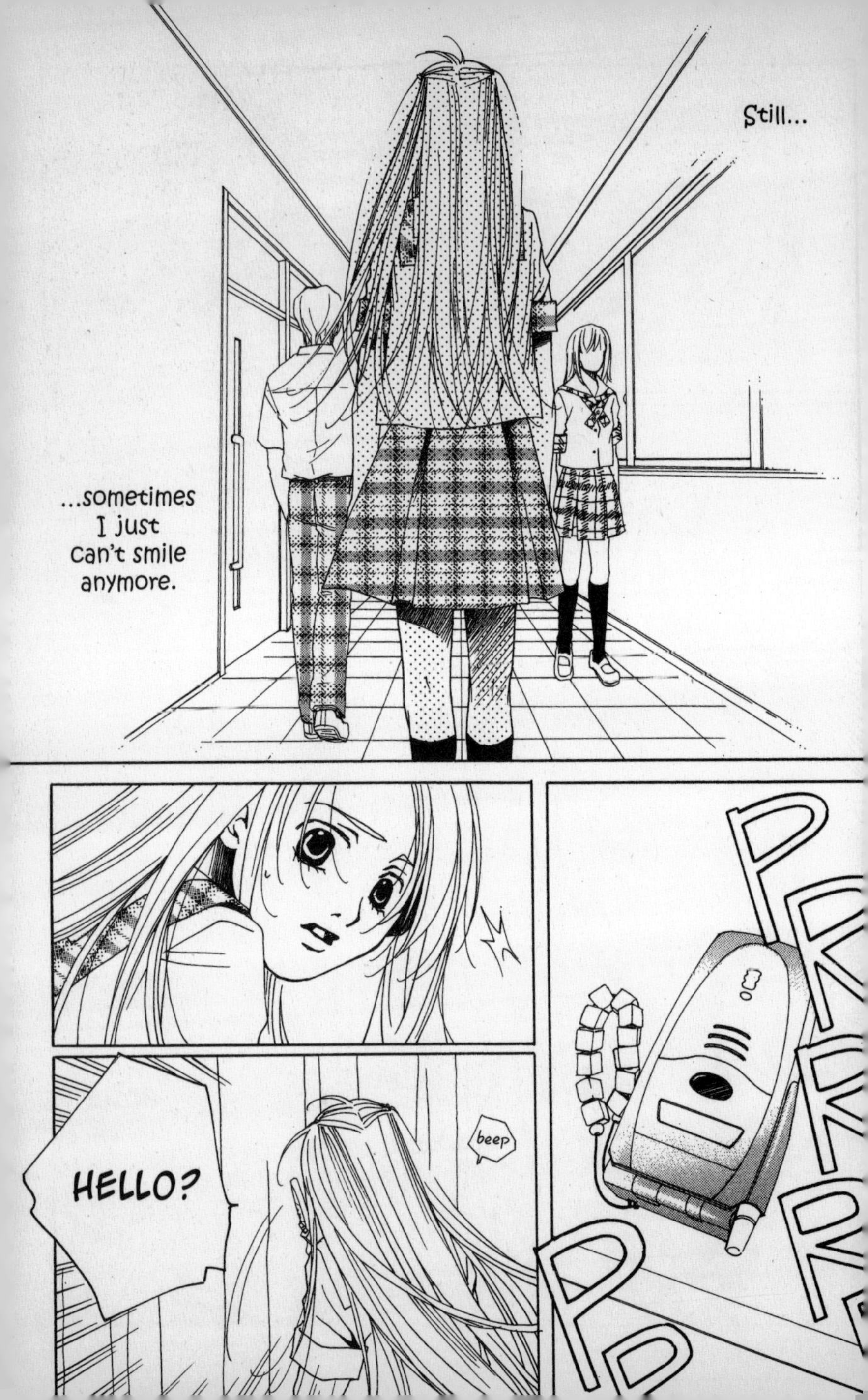

Still...
...sometimes I just can't smile anymore.
PRRR
PRRR
beep
HELLO?

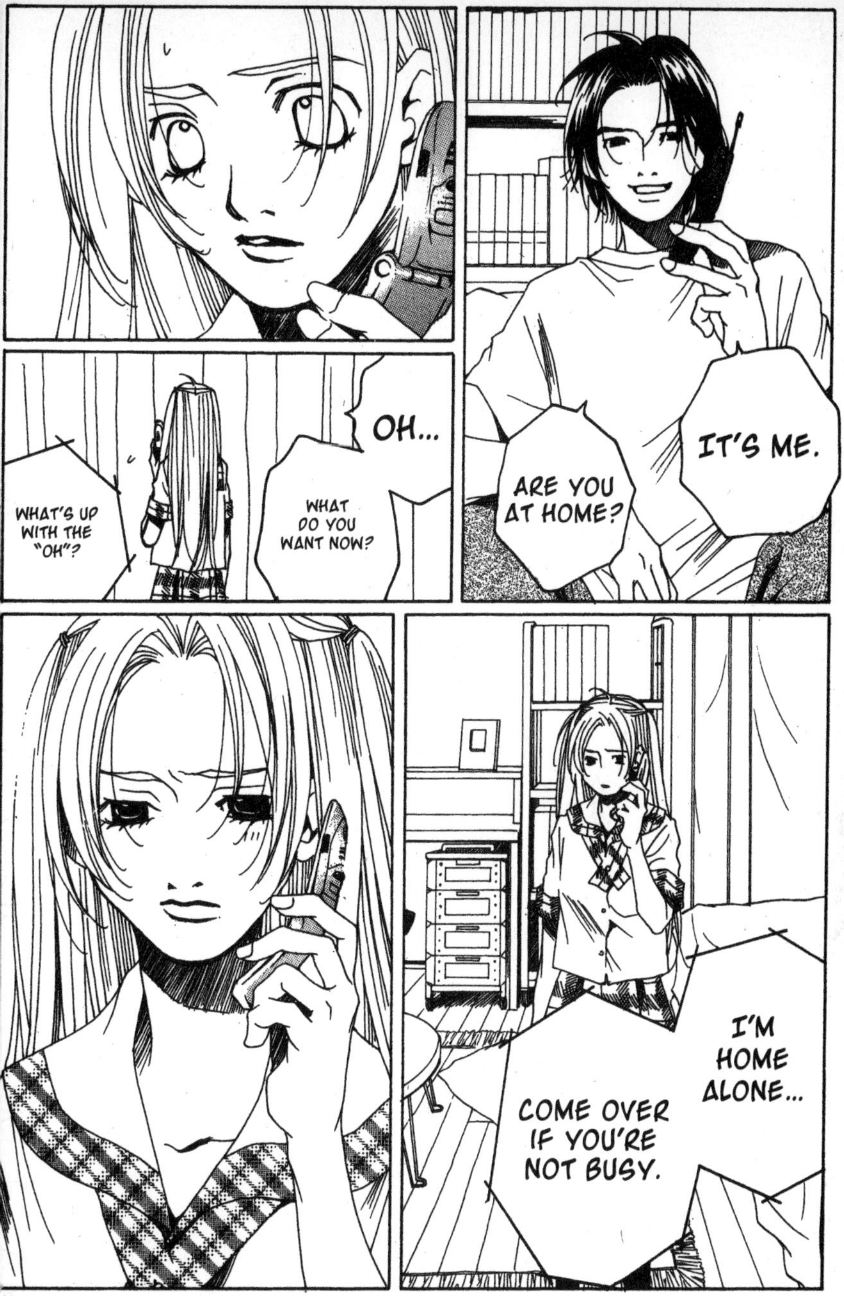
IT'S ME.
ARE YOU AT HOME?
OH...
WHAT DO YOU WANT NOW?
WHAT'S UP WITH THE "OH"?
I'M HOME ALONE...
COME OVER IF YOU'RE NOT BUSY.

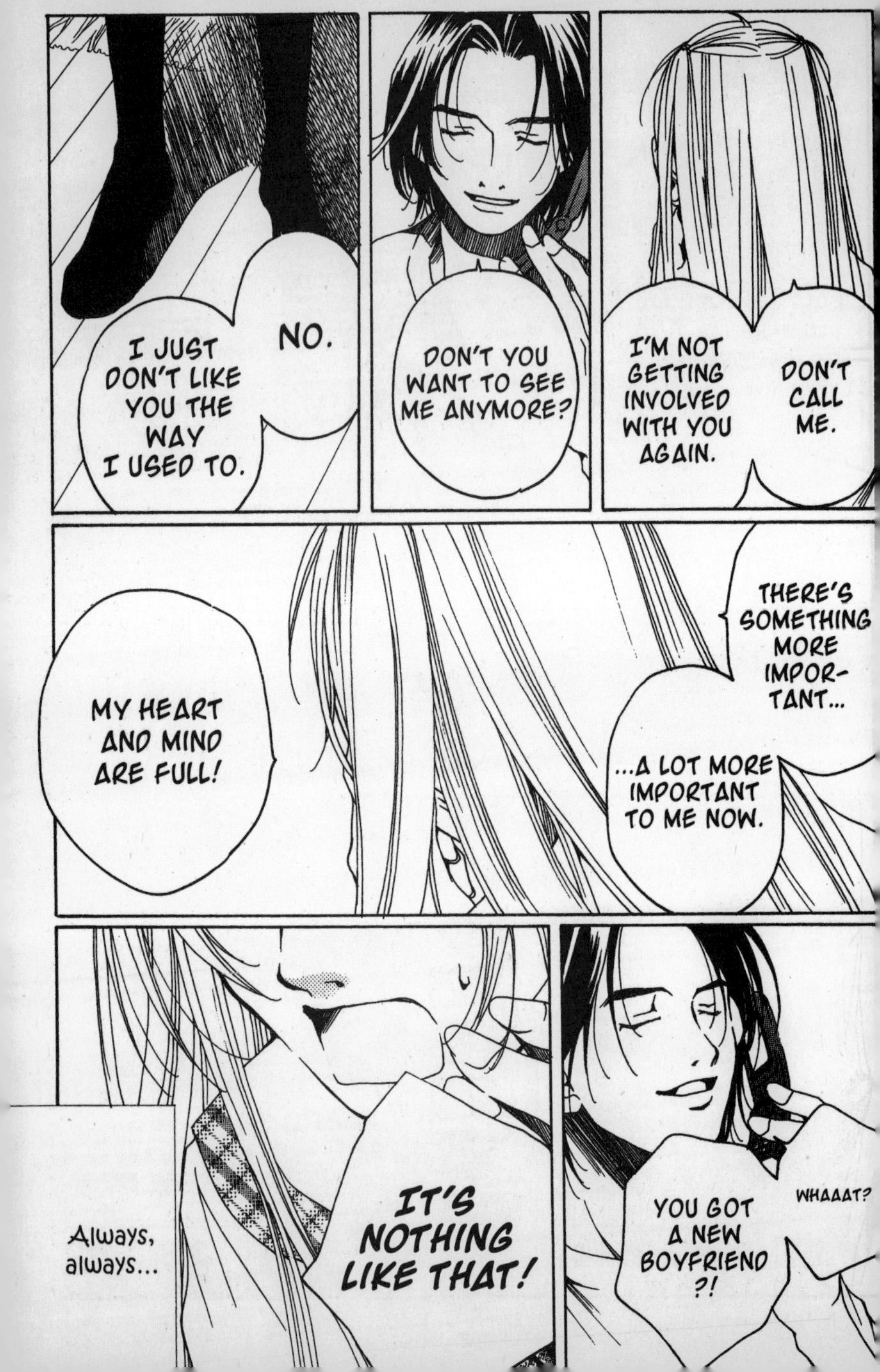
DON'T CALL ME.
I'M NOT GETTING INVOLVED WITH YOU AGAIN.
DON'T YOU WANT TO SEE ME ANYMORE?
NO.
I JUST DON'T LIKE YOU THE WAY I USED TO.
THERE'S SOMETHING MORE IMPOR-TANT...
...A LOT MORE IMPORTANT TO ME NOW.
MY HEART AND MIND ARE FULL!
WHAAAT?
YOU GOT A NEW BOYFRIEND?!
IT'S NOTHING LIKE THAT!
Always, always...

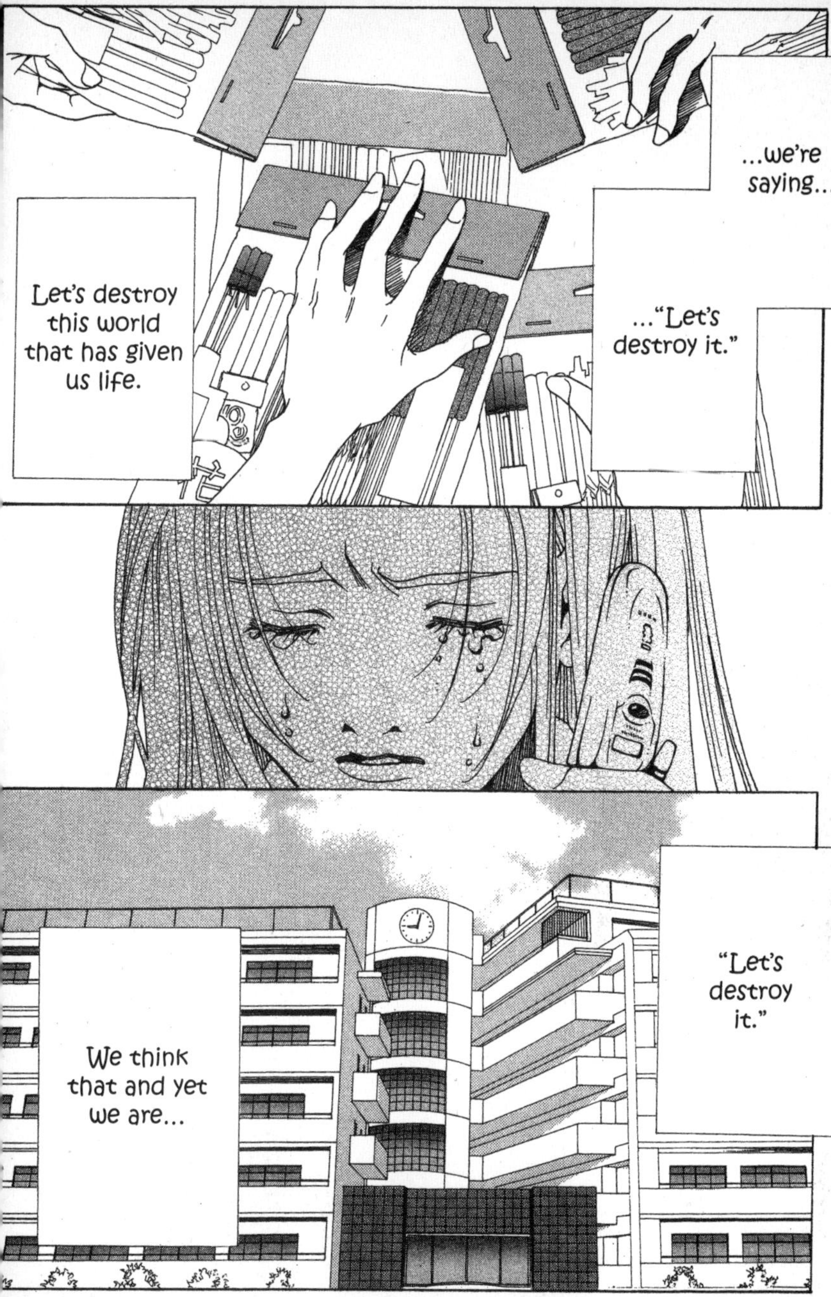
...we're saying...
..."Let's destroy it."
Let's destroy this world that has given us life.
"Let's destroy it."
We think that and yet we are...

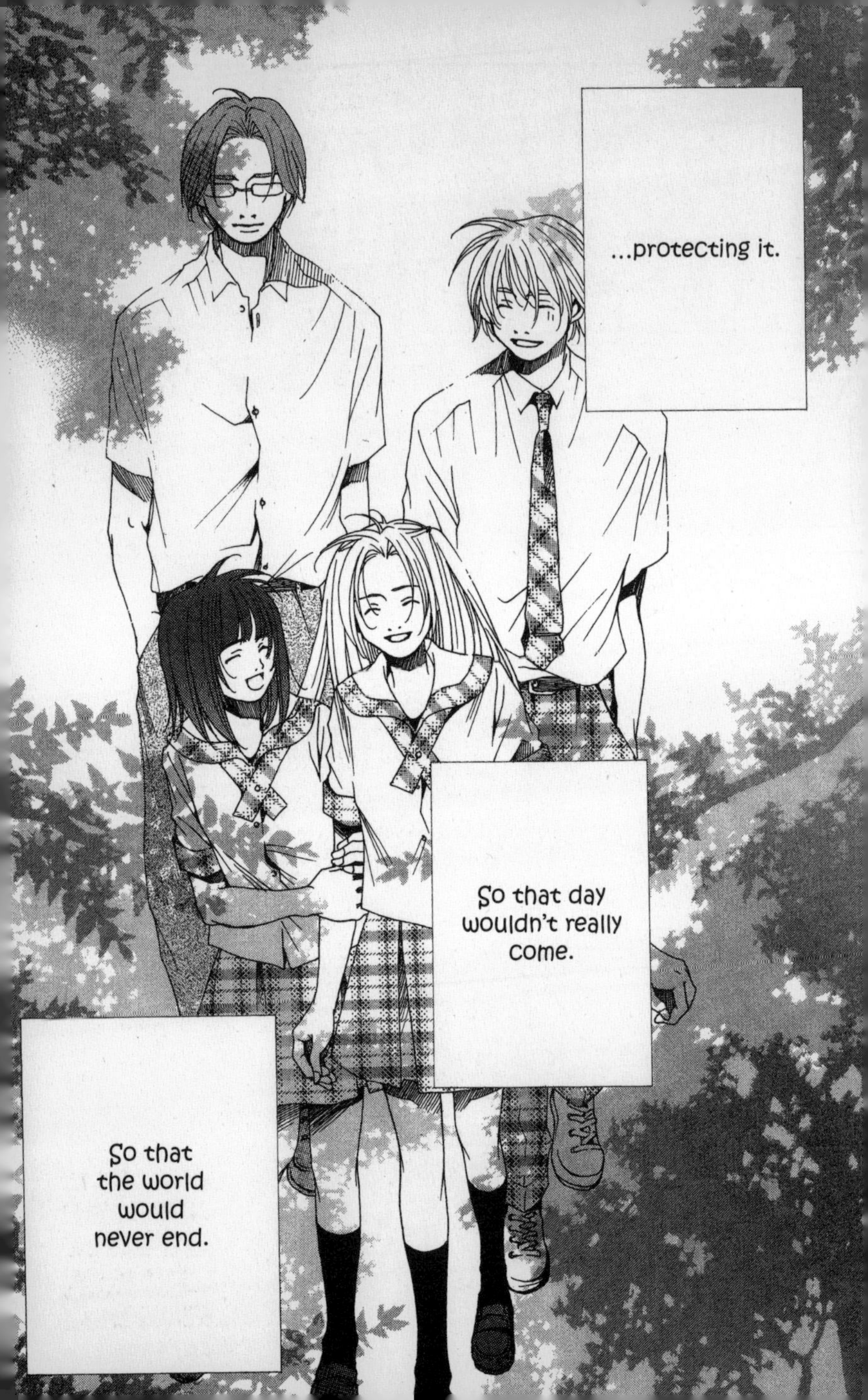
...protecting it.
So that day wouldn't really come.
So that the world would never end.

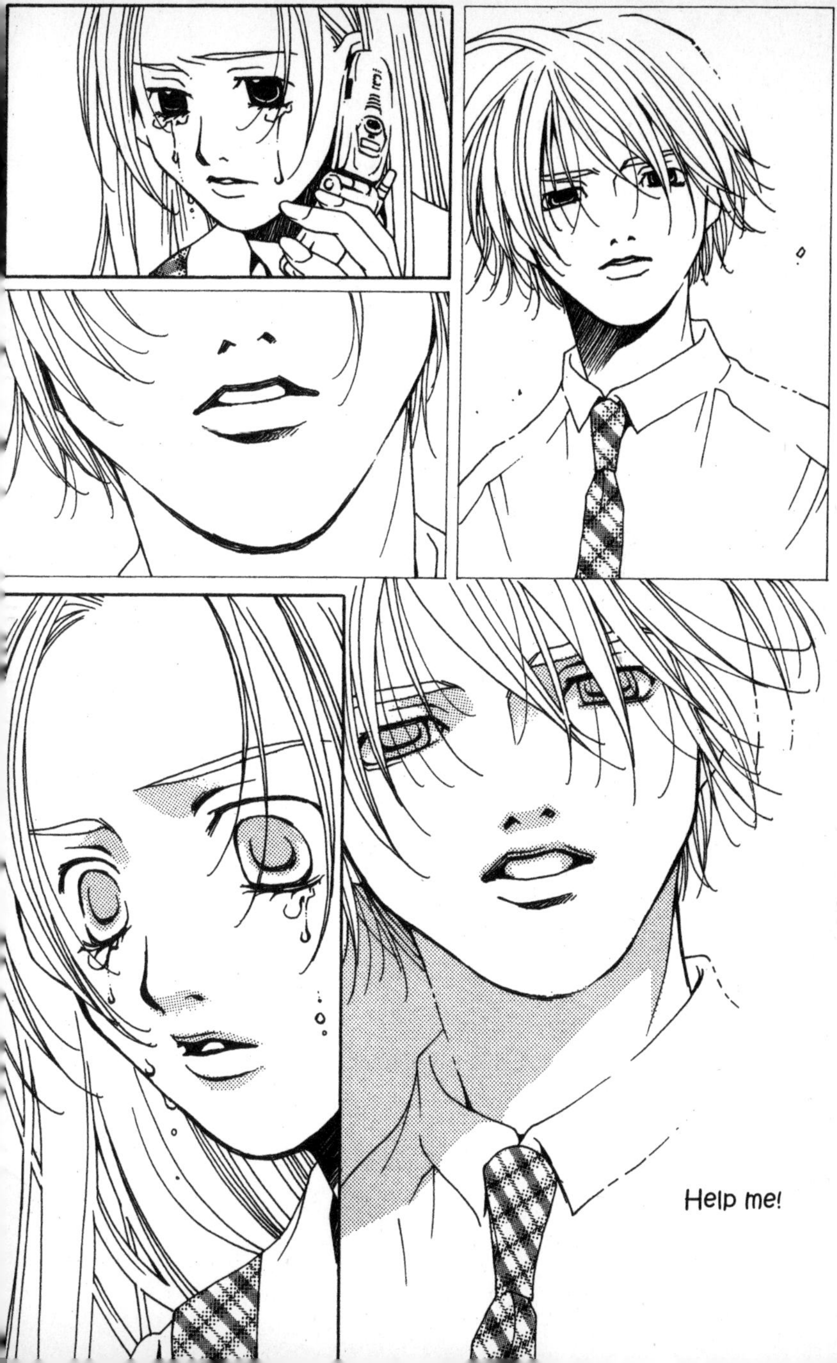
Help me!

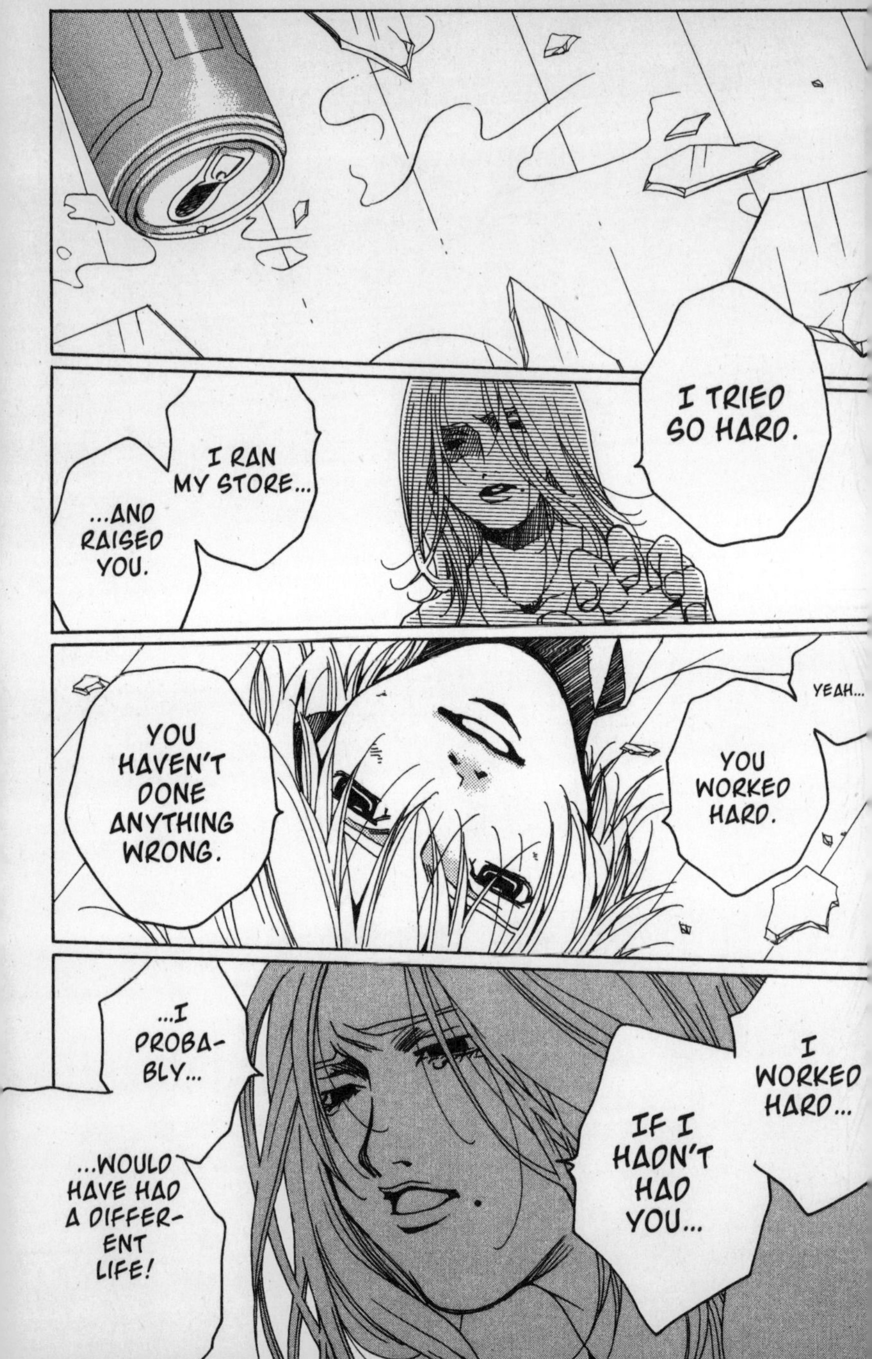
I TRIED SO HARD.
I RAN MY STORE...
...AND RAISED YOU.
YEAH...
YOU WORKED HARD.
YOU HAVEN'T DONE ANYTHING WRONG.
I WORKED HARD...
IF I HADN'T HAD YOU...
...I PROBABLY...
...WOULD HAVE HAD A DIFFERENT LIFE!

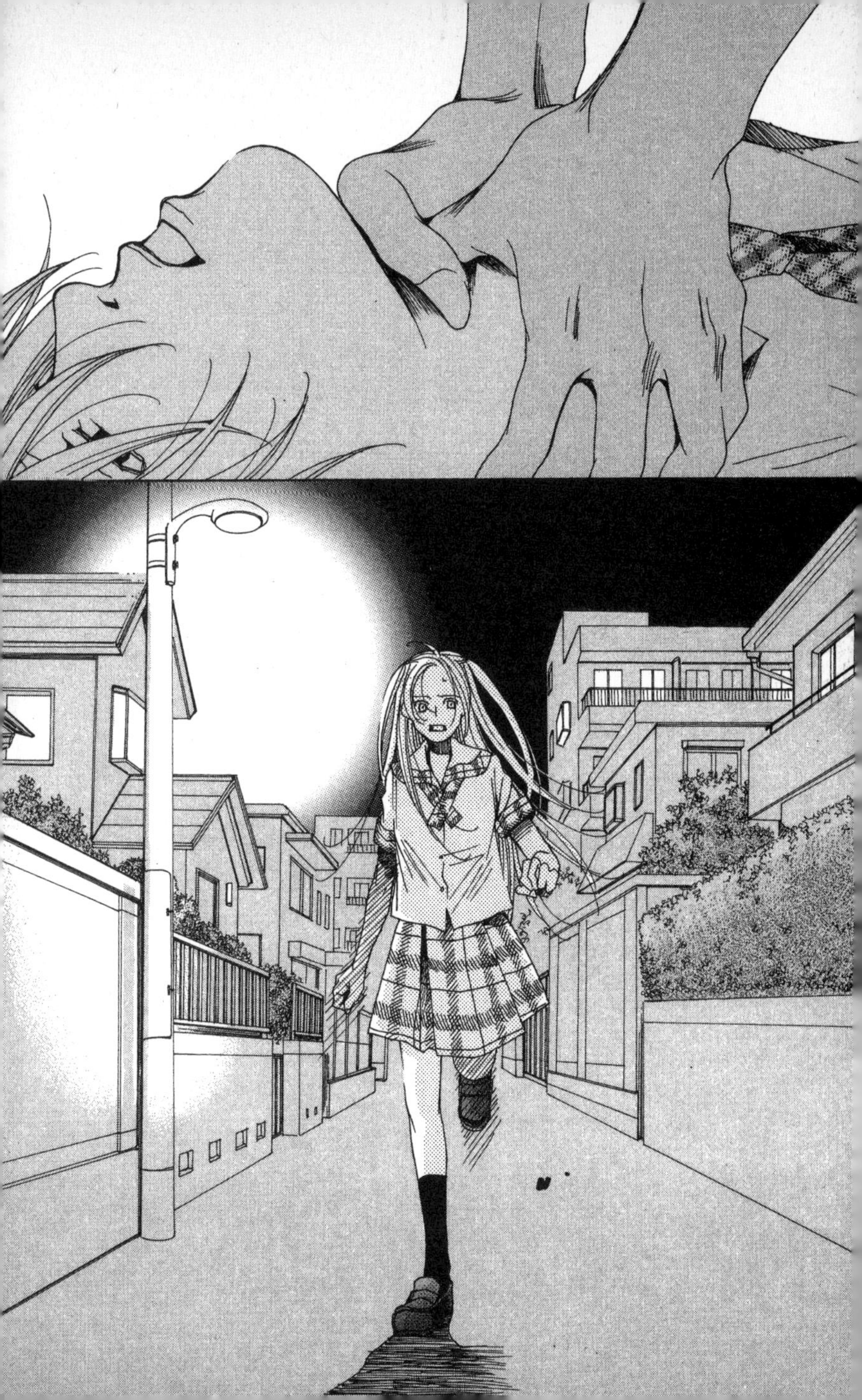

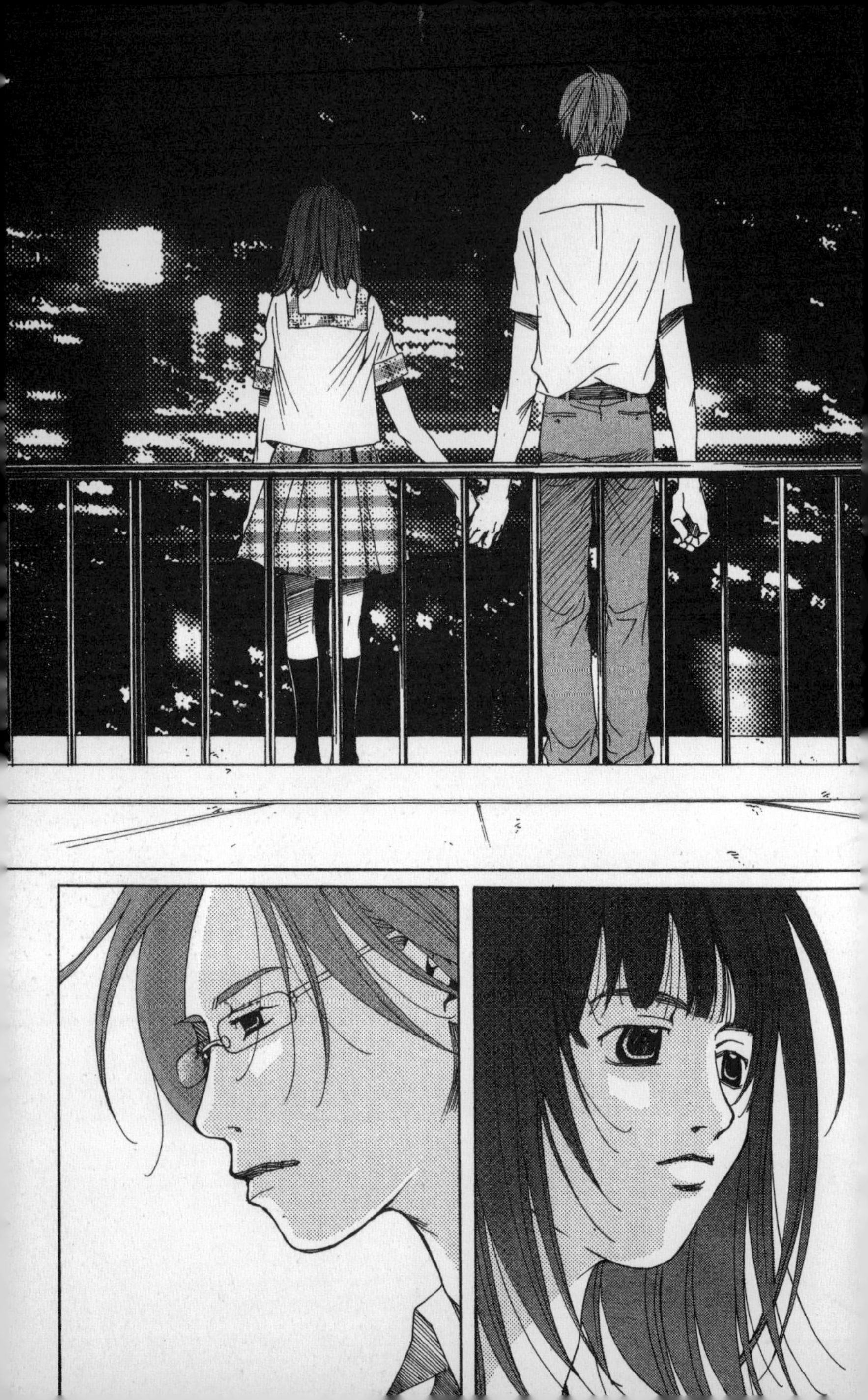

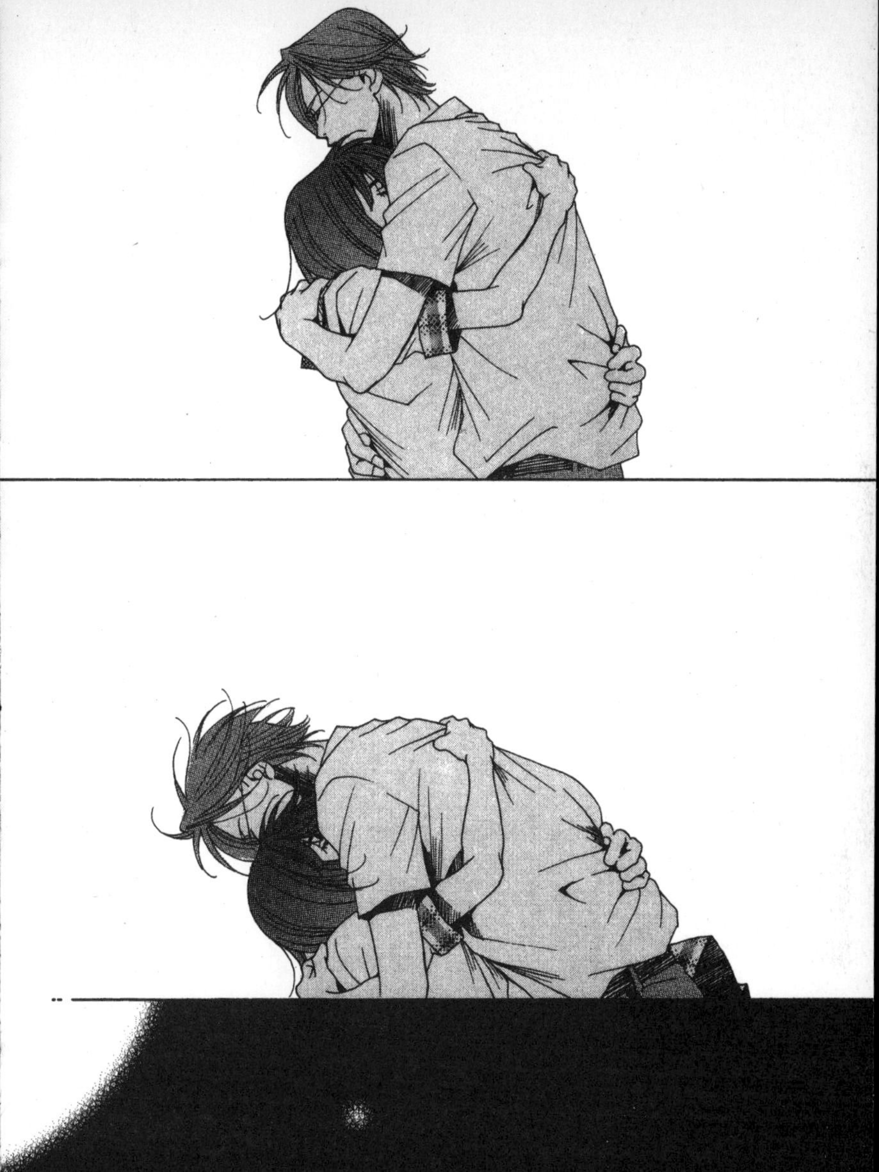

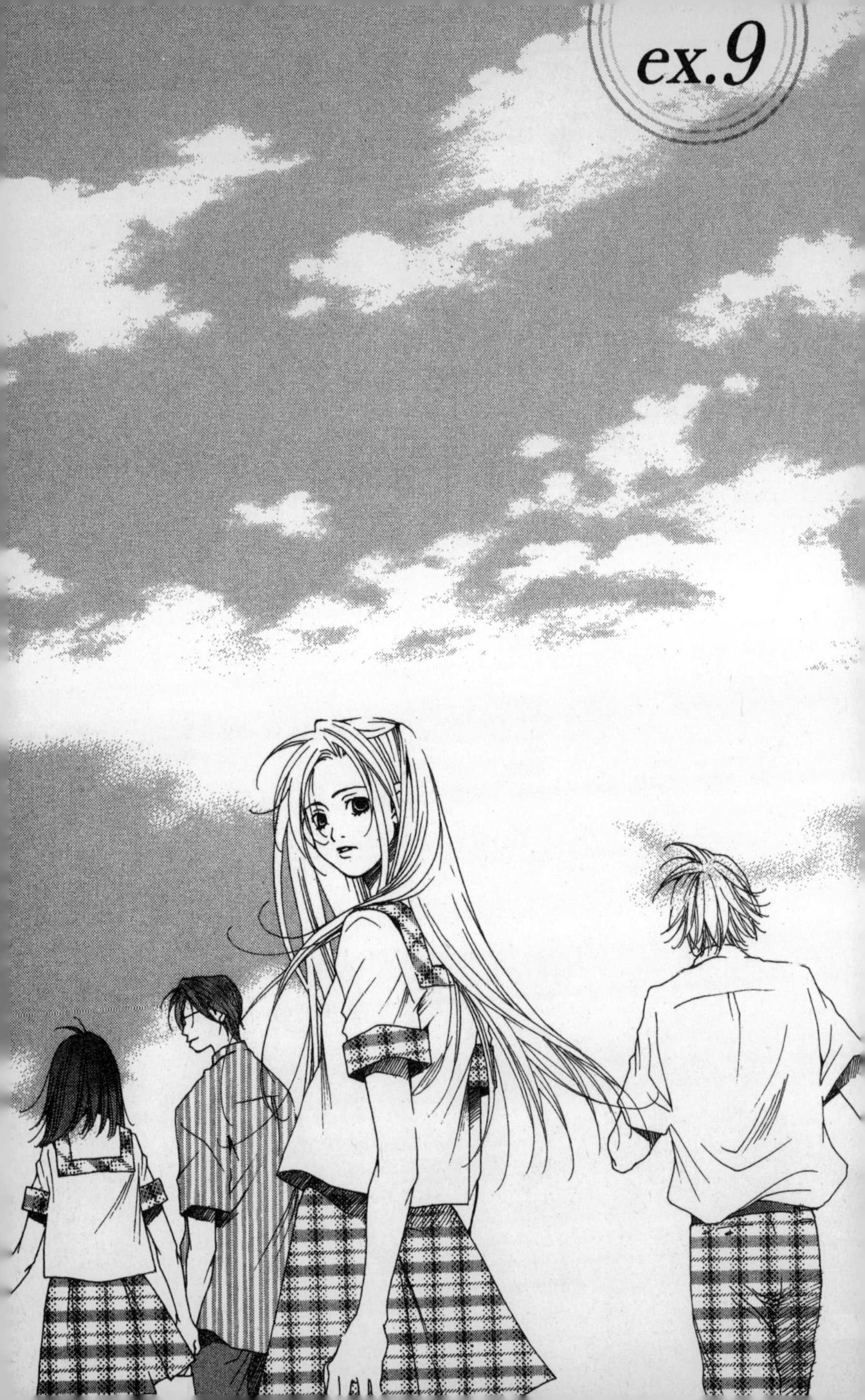
ex.9

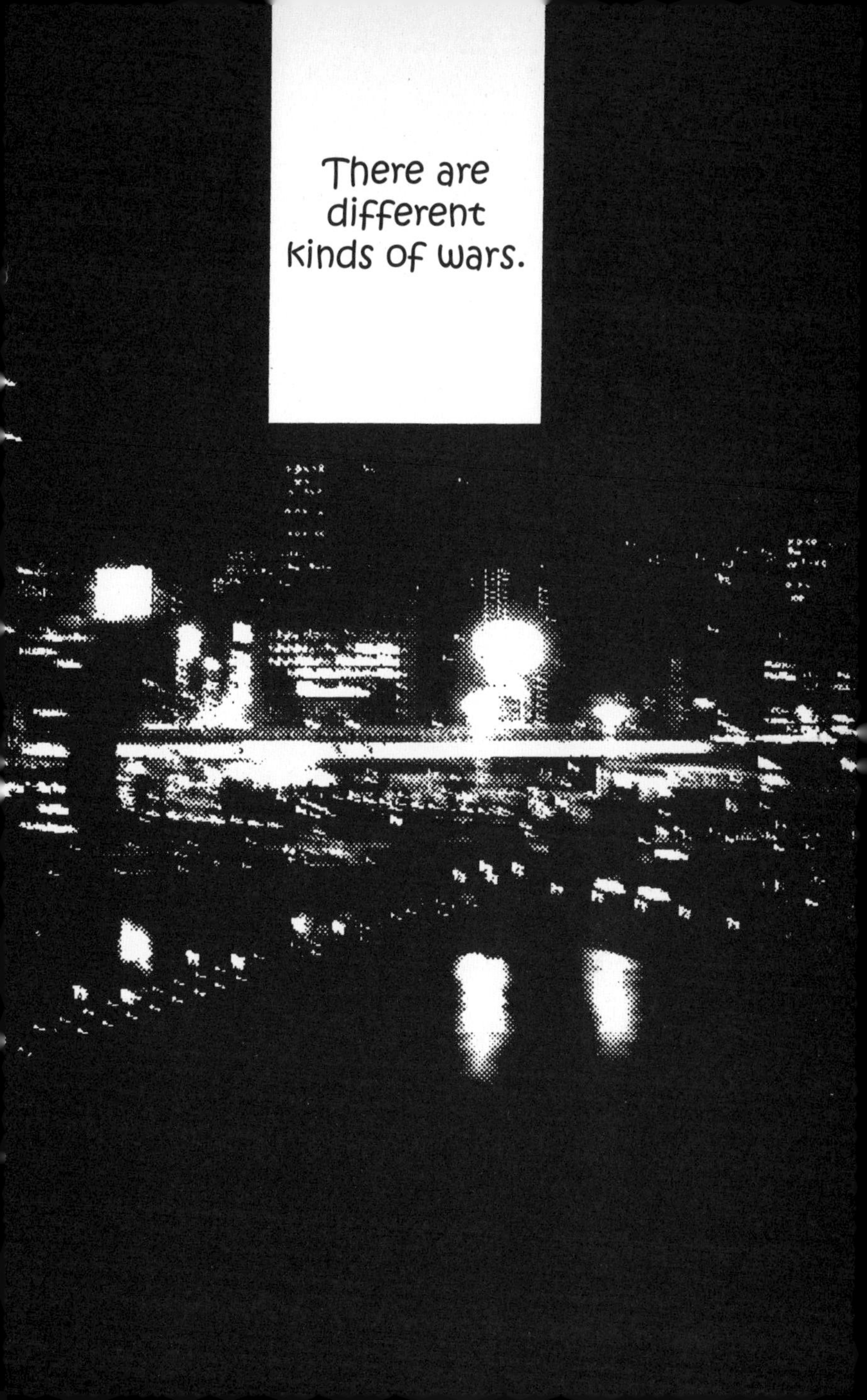
There are different kinds of wars.

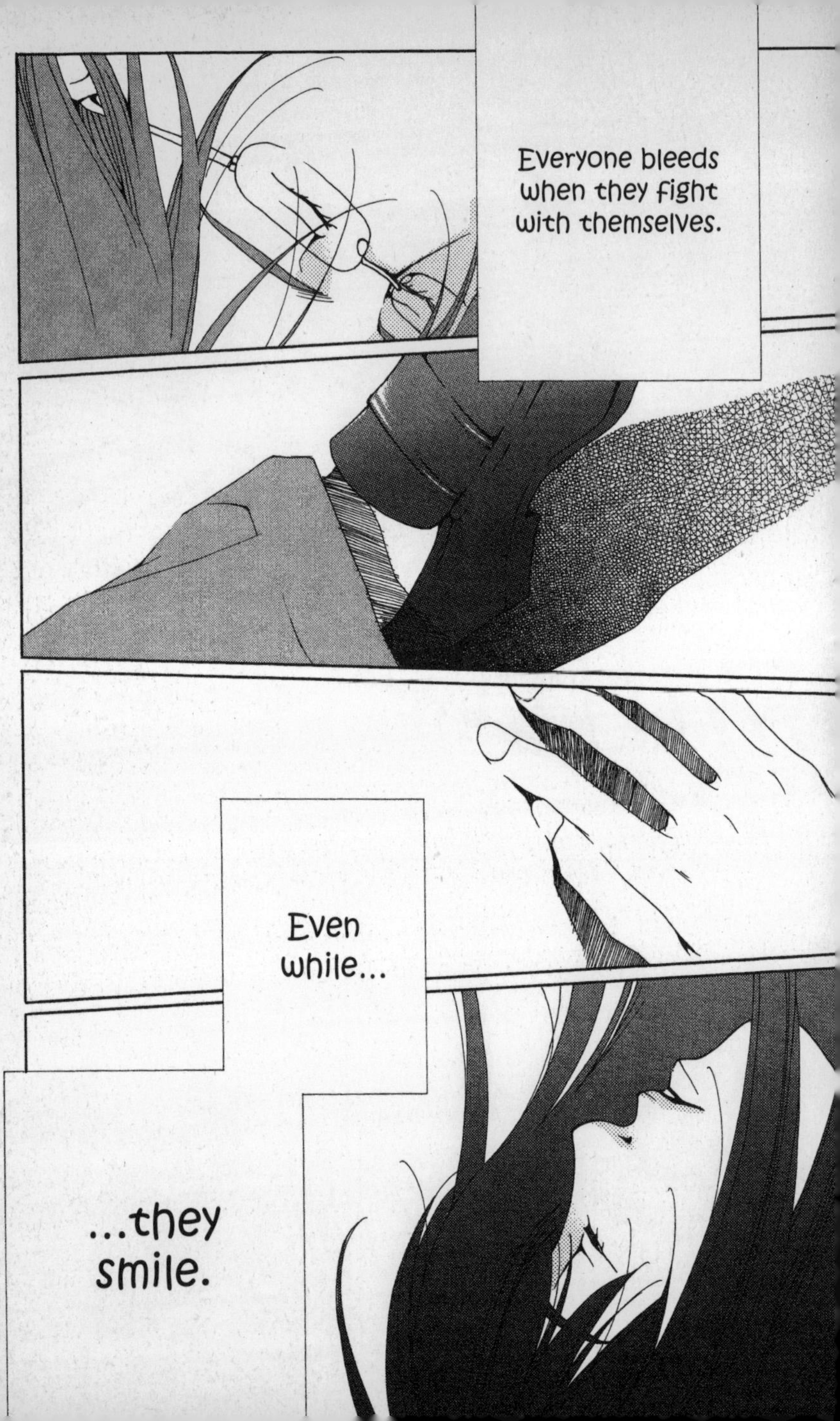
Everyone bleeds when they fight with themselves.
Even while...
...they smile.

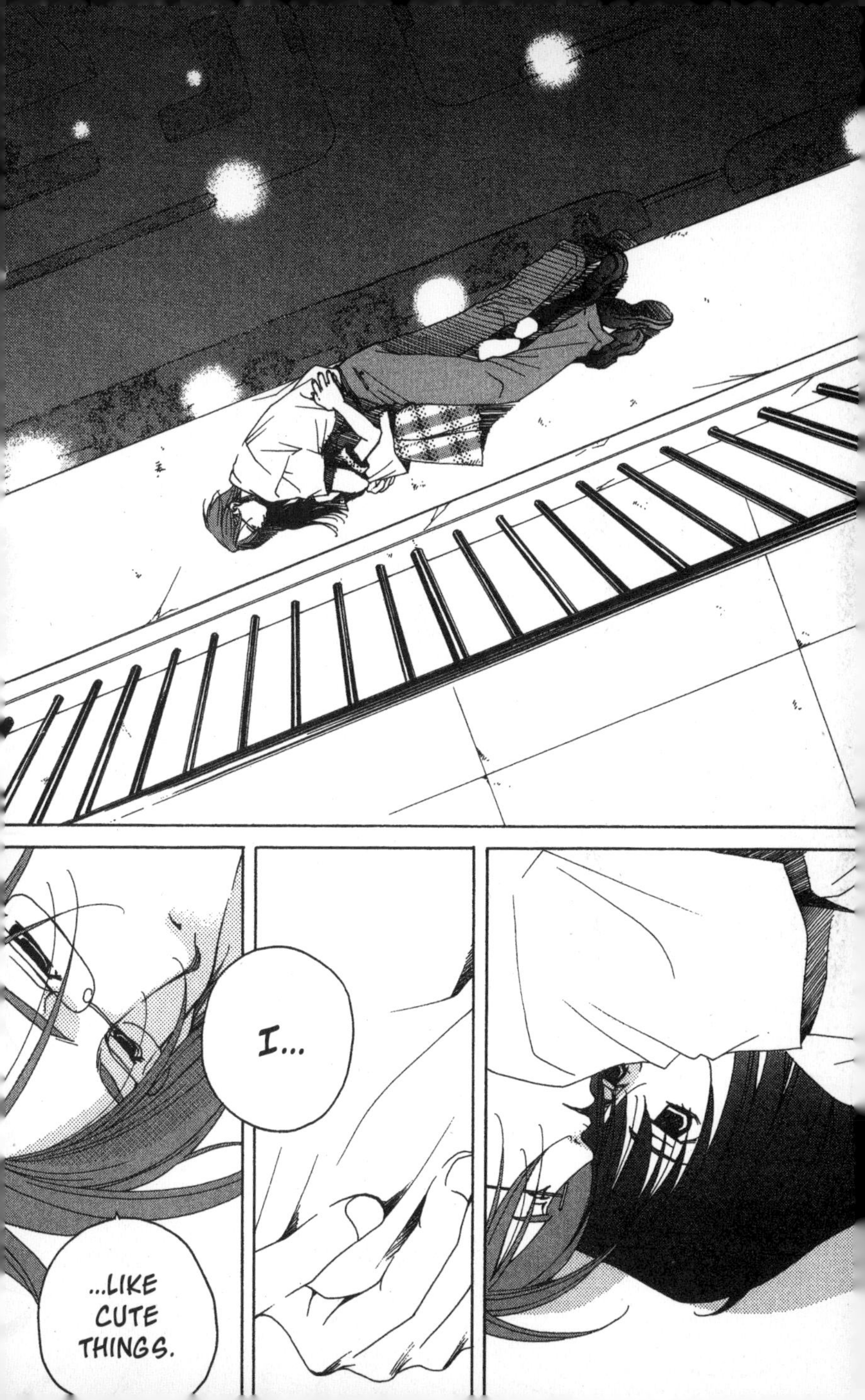
I...
...LIKE CUTE THINGS.

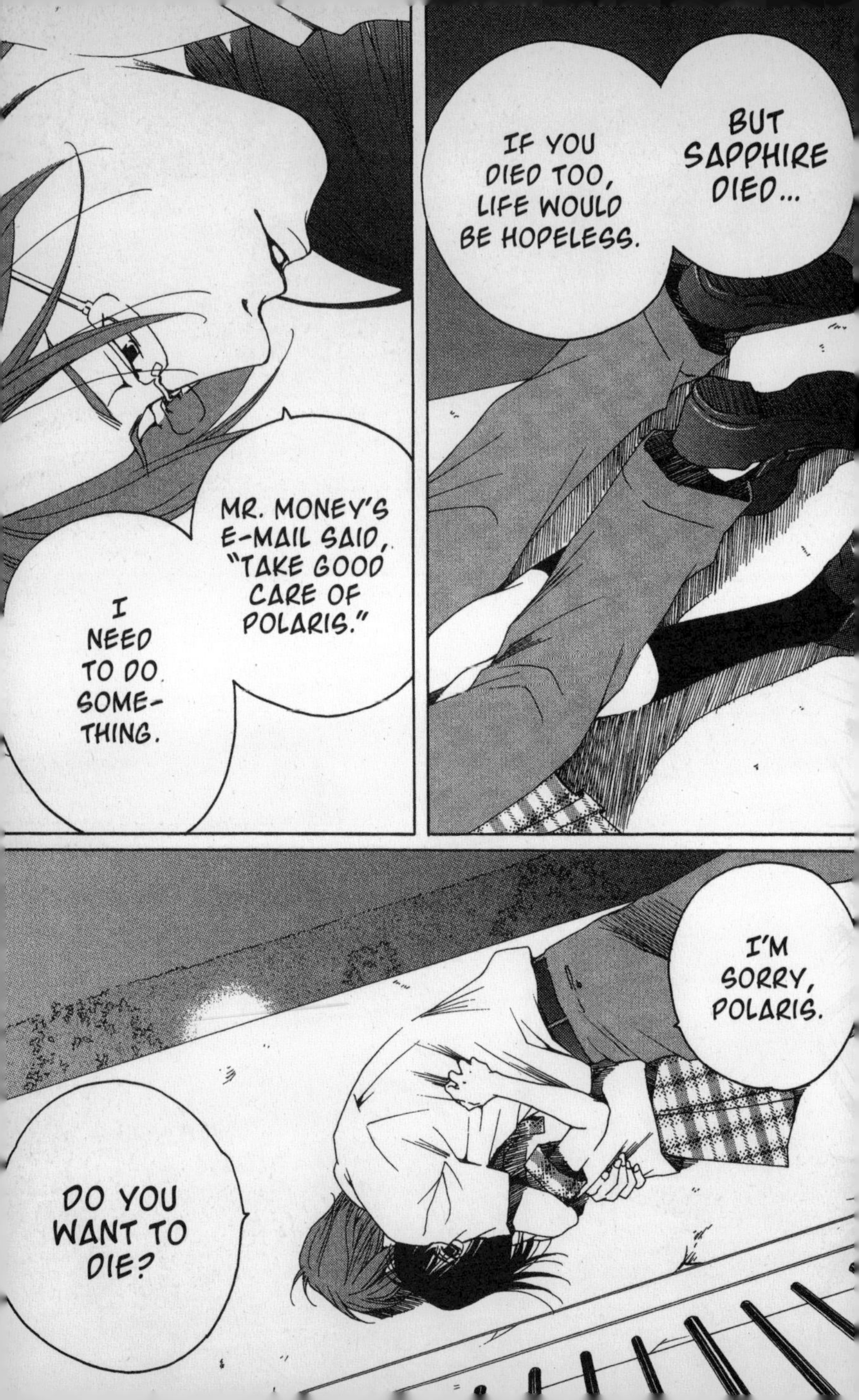
BUT SAPPHIRE DIED...
IF YOU DIED TOO, LIFE WOULD BE HOPELESS.
MR. MONEY'S E-MAIL SAID, "TAKE GOOD CARE OF POLARIS."
I NEED TO DO SOMETHING.
I'M SORRY, POLARIS.
DO YOU WANT TO DIE?

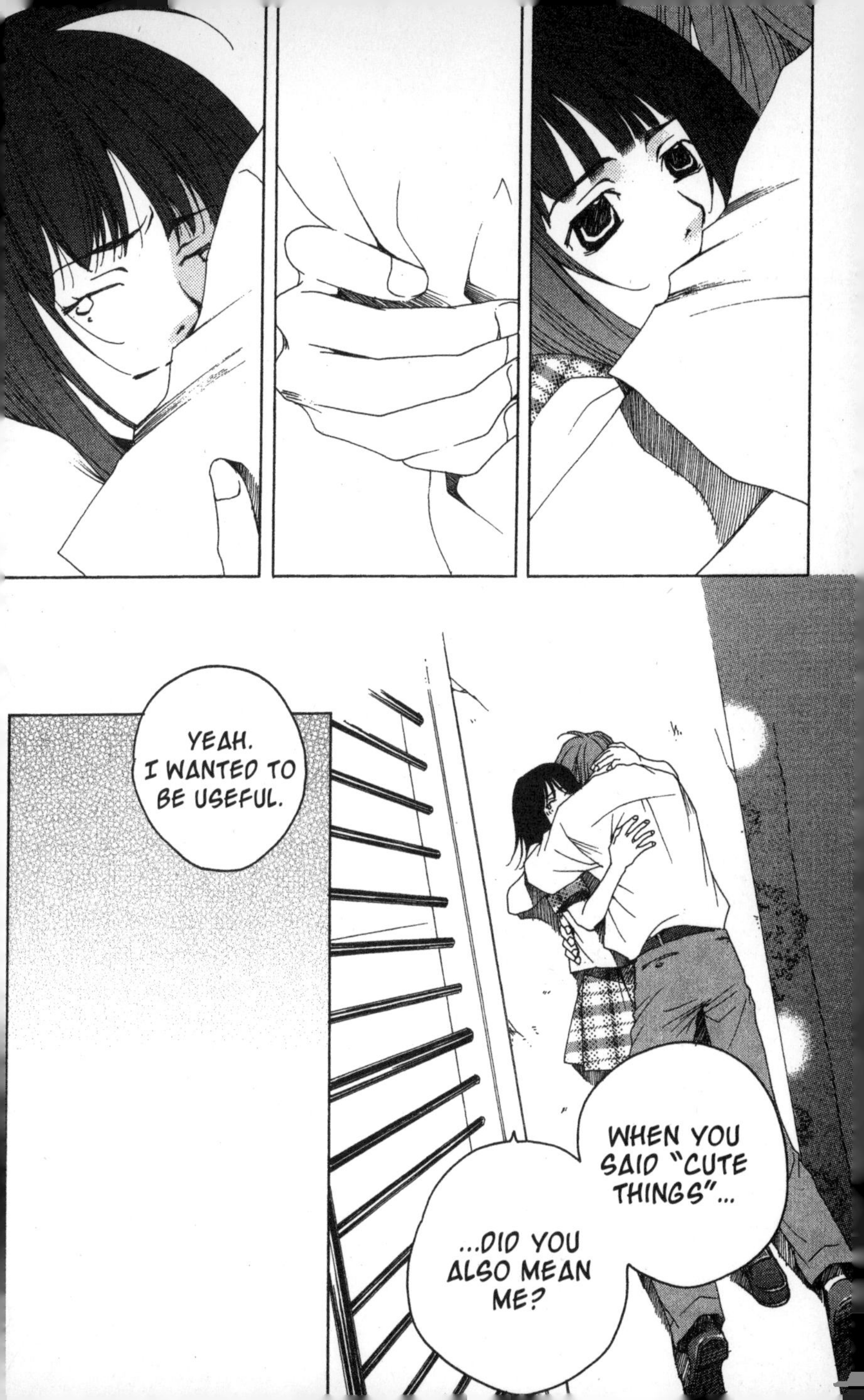
WHEN YOU SAID "CUTE THINGS"...
...DID YOU ALSO MEAN ME?
YEAH. I WANTED TO BE USEFUL.

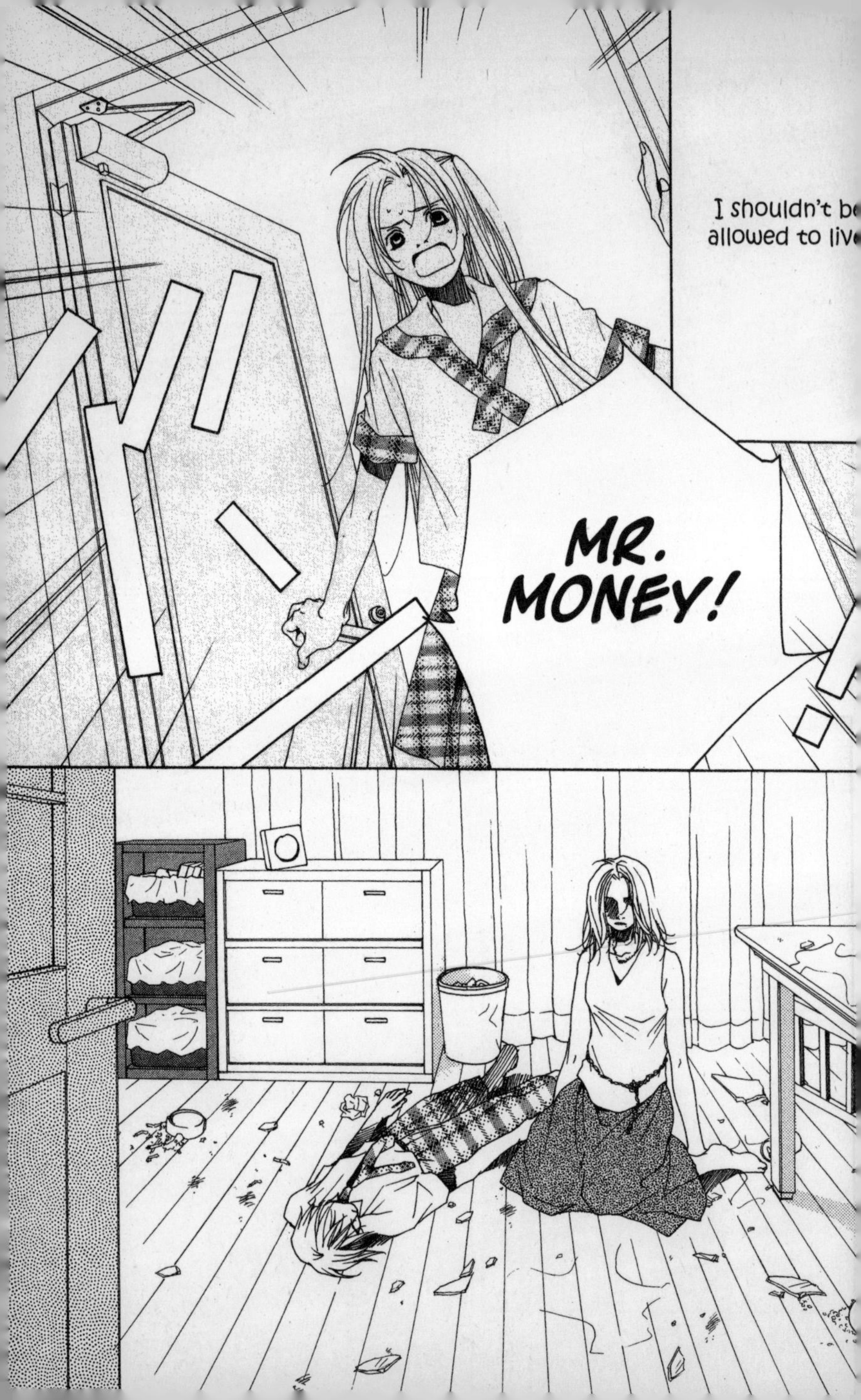
I shouldn't b
allowed to liv
MR. MONEY!

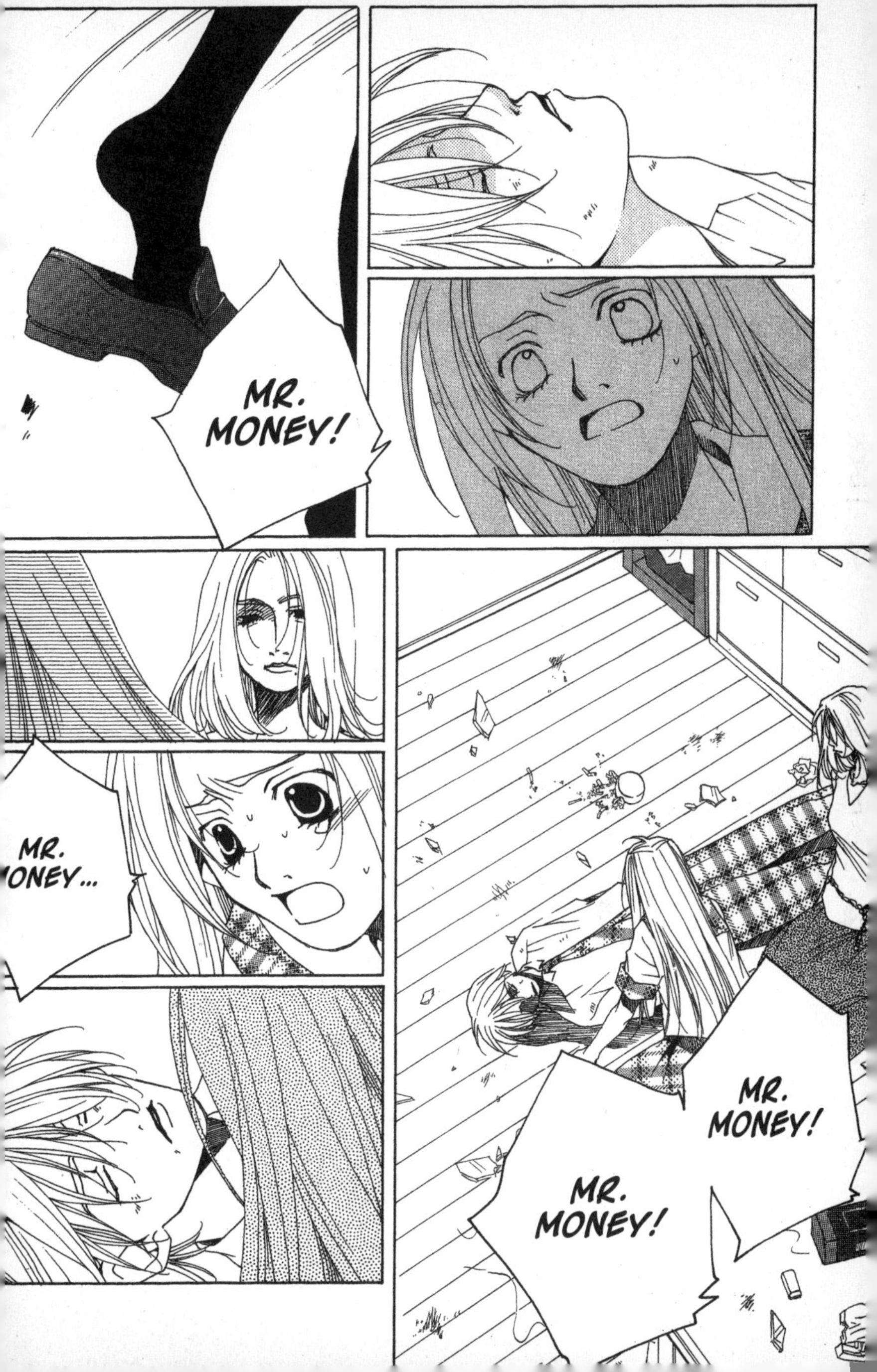
MR. MONEY!
MR. MONEY!
MR. MONEY!
MR. ONEY...

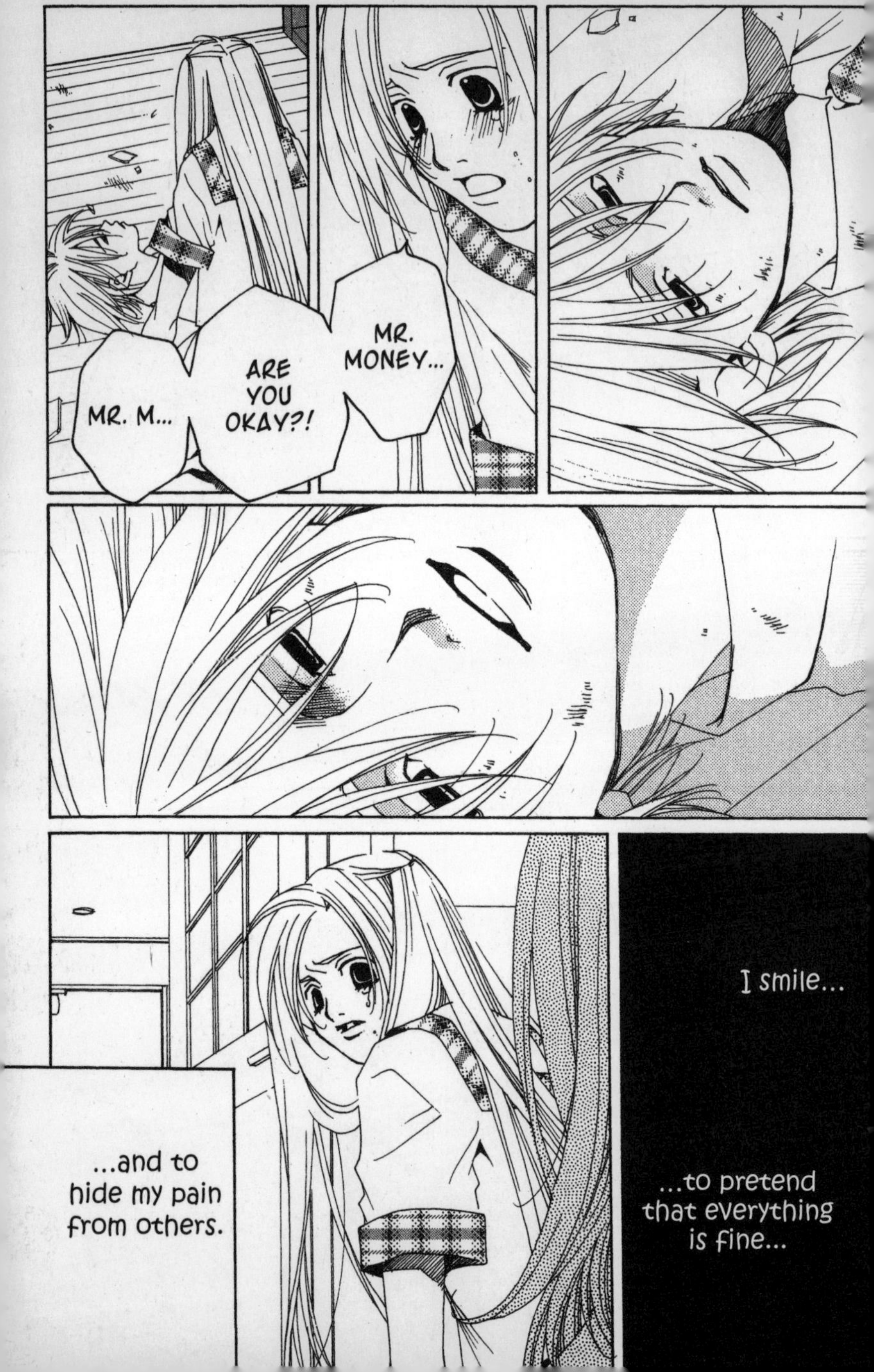
MR. MONEY...
ARE YOU OKAY?!
MR. M...
I smile...
...to pretend that everything is fine...
...and to hide my pain from others.

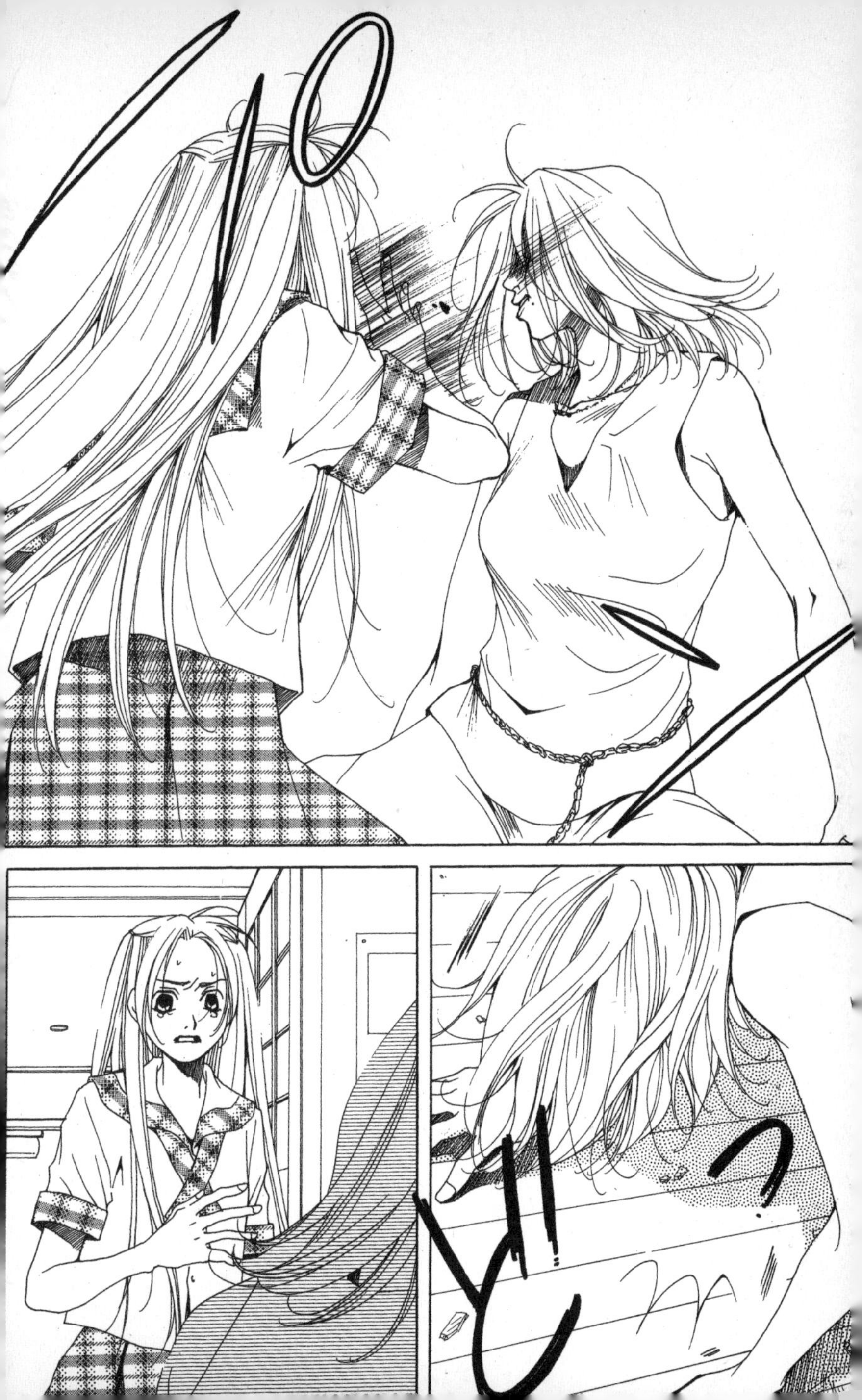

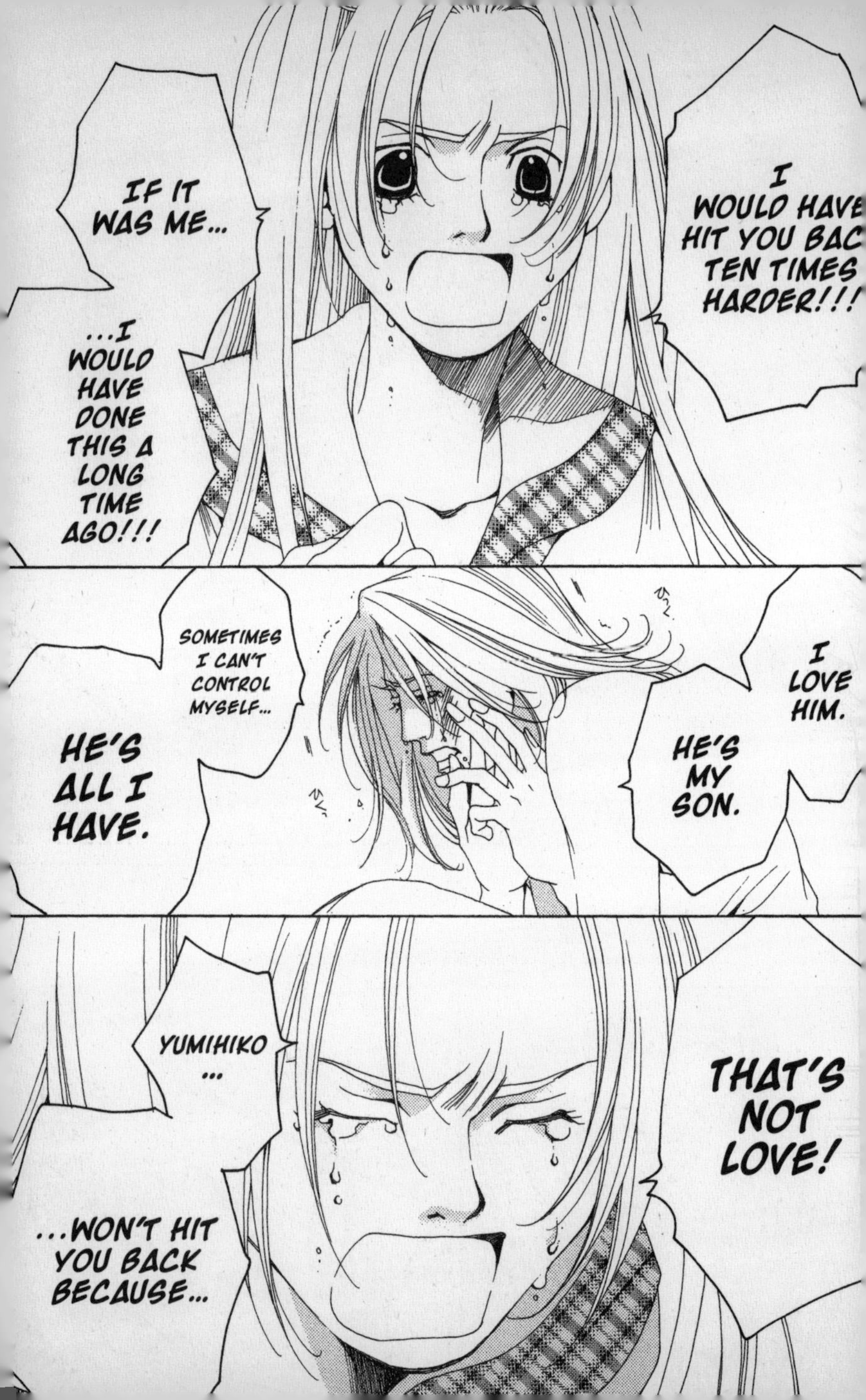
I WOULD HAVE HIT YOU BAC TEN TIMES HARDER!!!
IF IT WAS ME...
...I WOULD HAVE DONE THIS A LONG TIME AGO!!!
I LOVE HIM.
HE'S MY SON.
SOMETIMES I CAN'T CONTROL MYSELF...
HE'S ALL I HAVE.
THAT'S NOT LOVE!
YUMIHIKO...
...WON'T HIT YOU BACK BECAUSE...

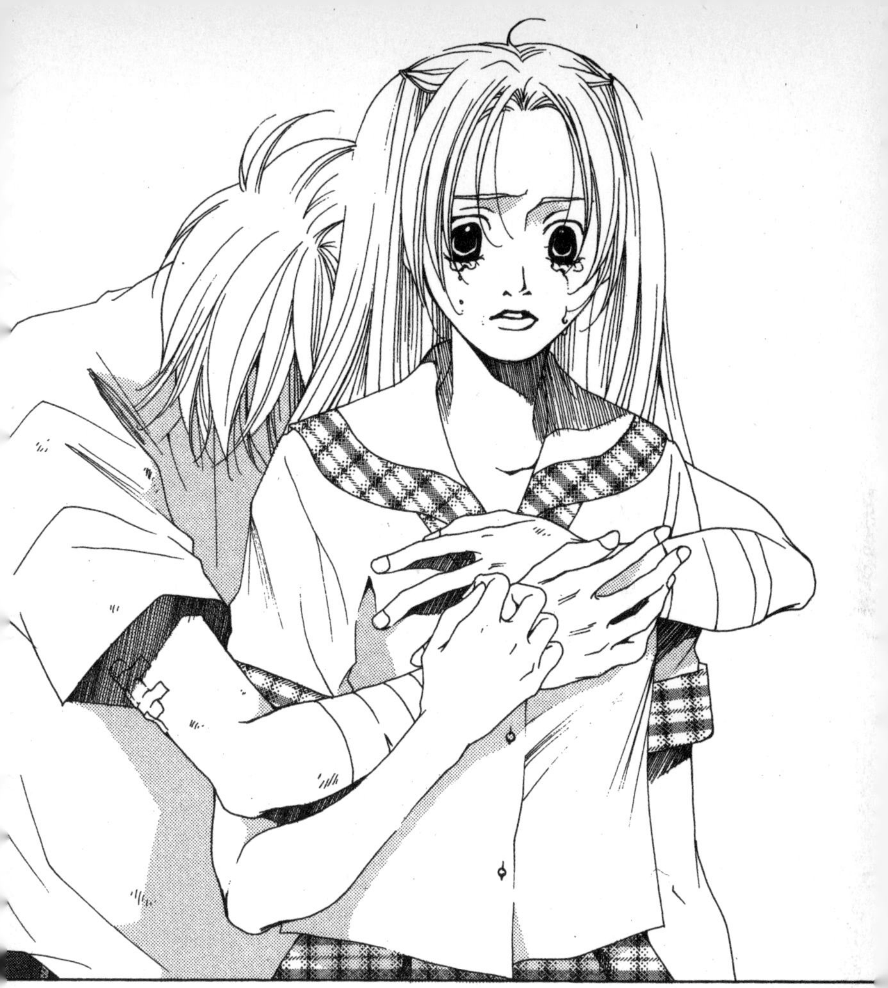
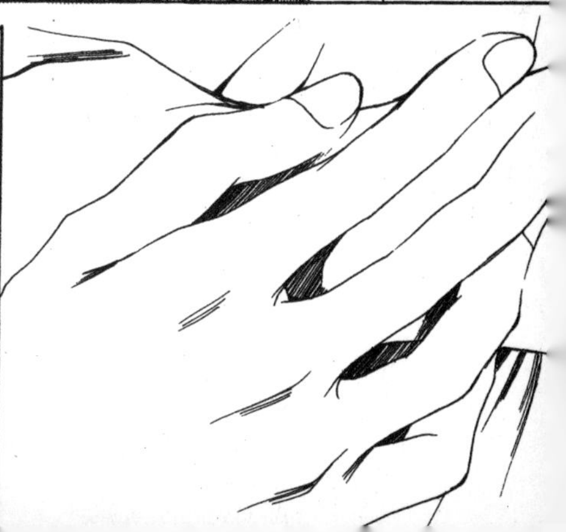
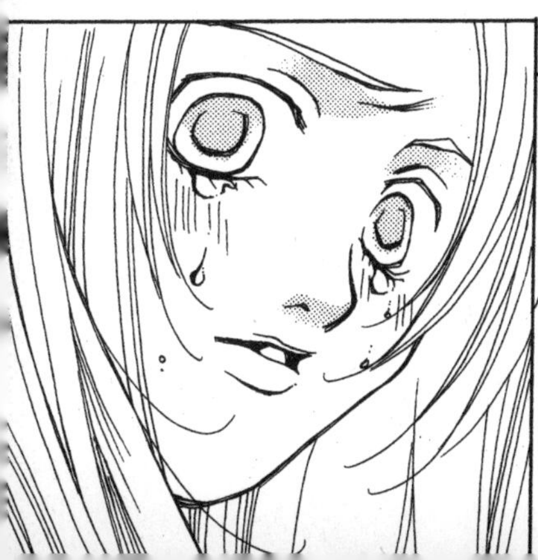

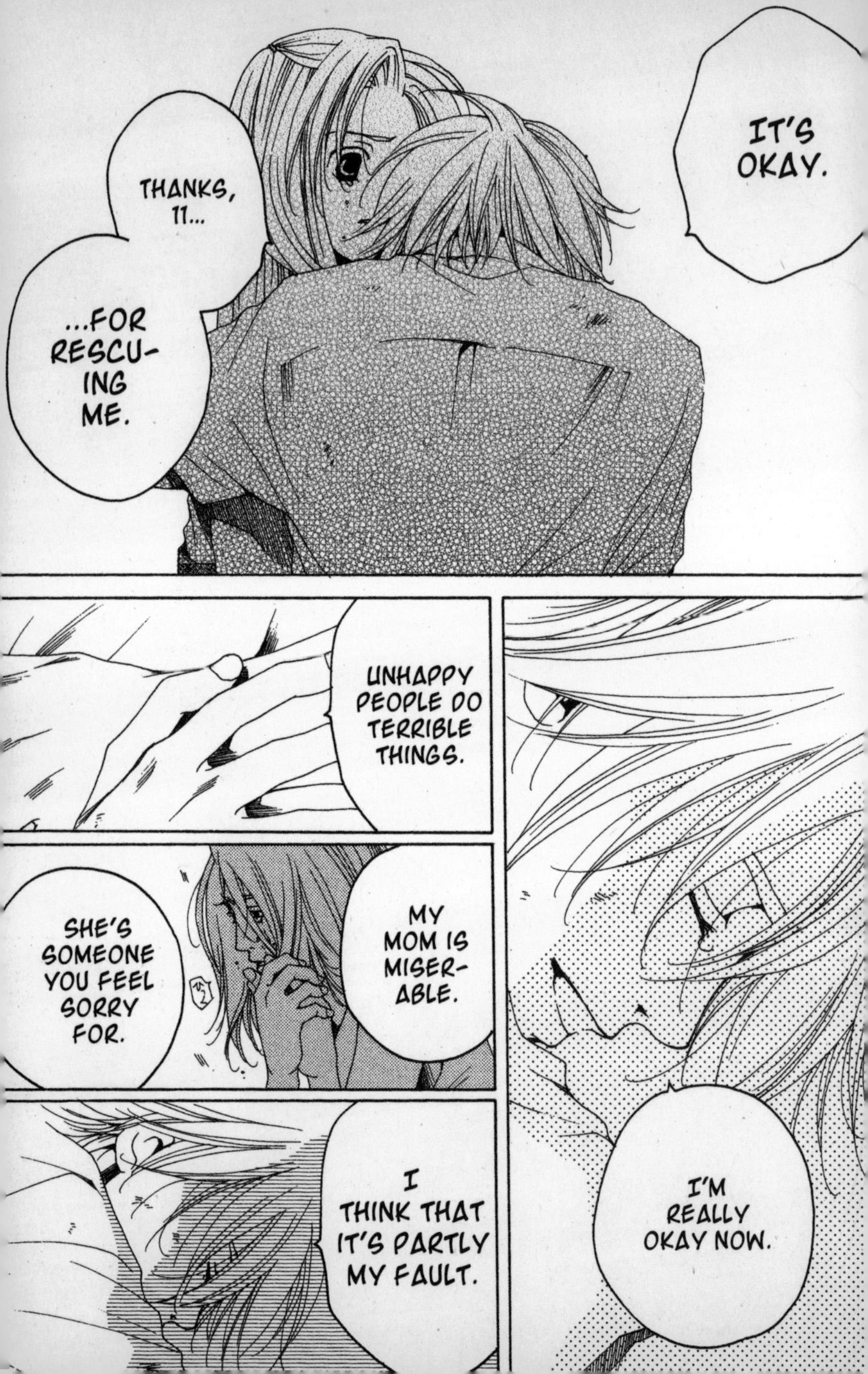
IT'S OKAY.
THANKS, 11...
...FOR RESCU-ING ME.
I'M REALLY OKAY NOW.
UNHAPPY PEOPLE DO TERRIBLE THINGS.
MY MOM IS MISER-ABLE.
SHE'S SOMEONE YOU FEEL SORRY FOR.
I THINK THAT IT'S PARTLY MY FAULT.

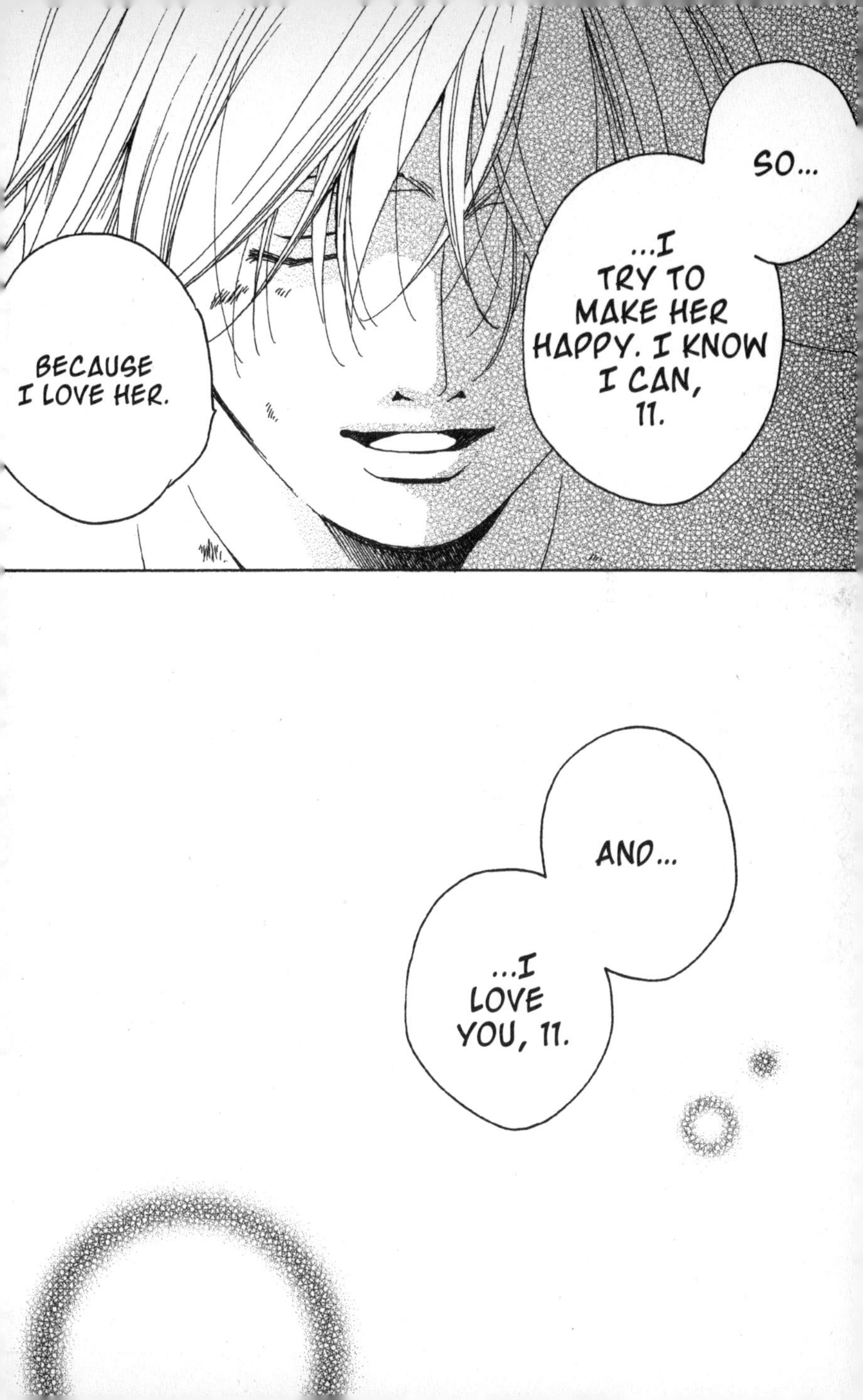
SO...
...I TRY TO MAKE HER HAPPY. I KNOW I CAN, 11.
BECAUSE I LOVE HER.
AND...
...I LOVE YOU, 11.

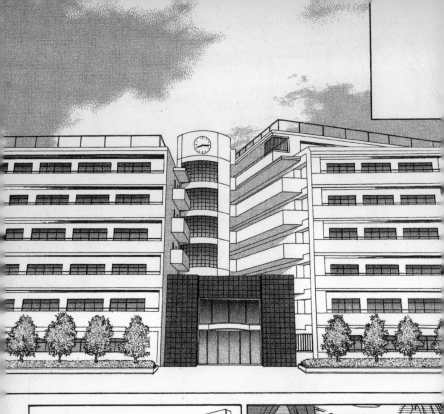

CHANCELLOR'S OFFICE

FORTUNATELY, MY DAUGHTER JUST HAD A MILD CONCUSSION...

...BUT SHE NEEDED THREE STITCHES.

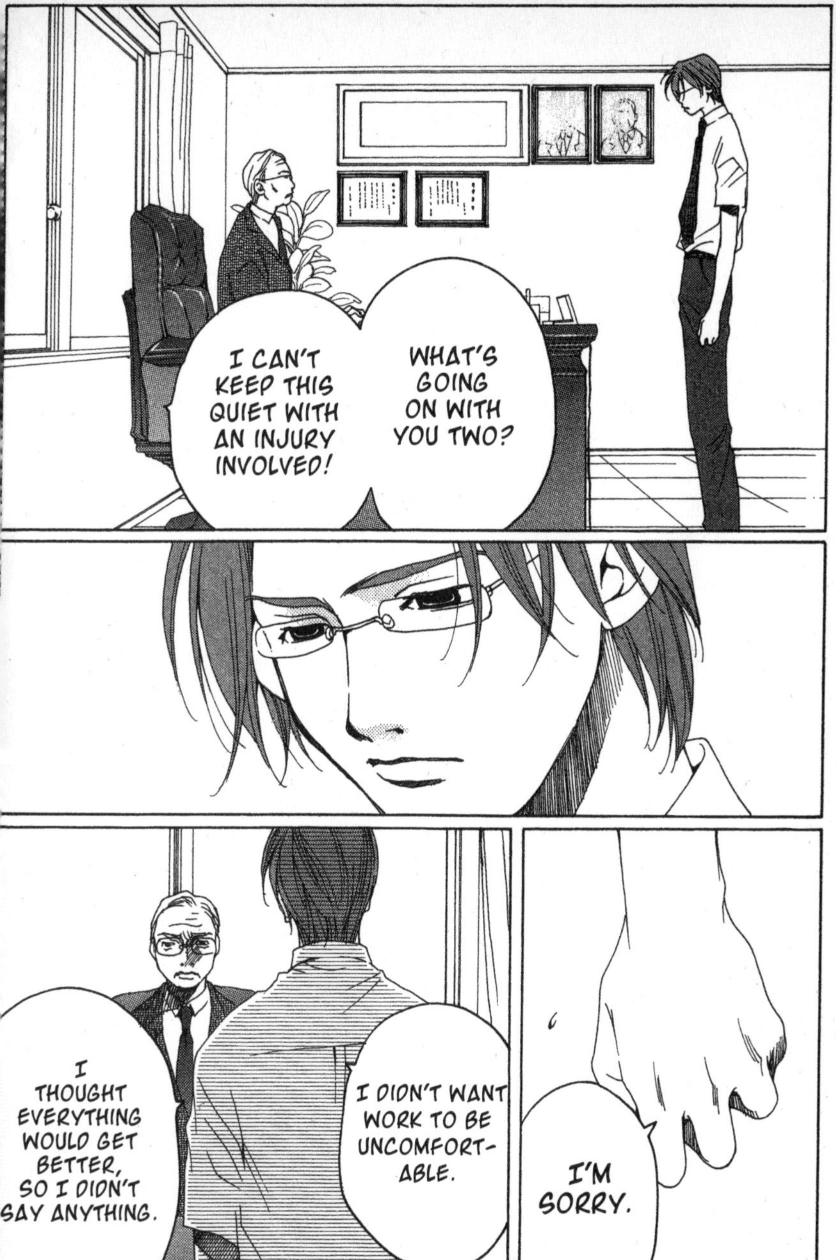
WHAT'S GOING ON WITH YOU TWO?
I CAN'T KEEP THIS QUIET WITH AN INJURY INVOLVED!
I'M SORRY.
I DIDN'T WANT WORK TO BE UNCOMFORT-ABLE.
I THOUGHT EVERYTHING WOULD GET BETTER, SO I DIDN'T SAY ANYTHING.

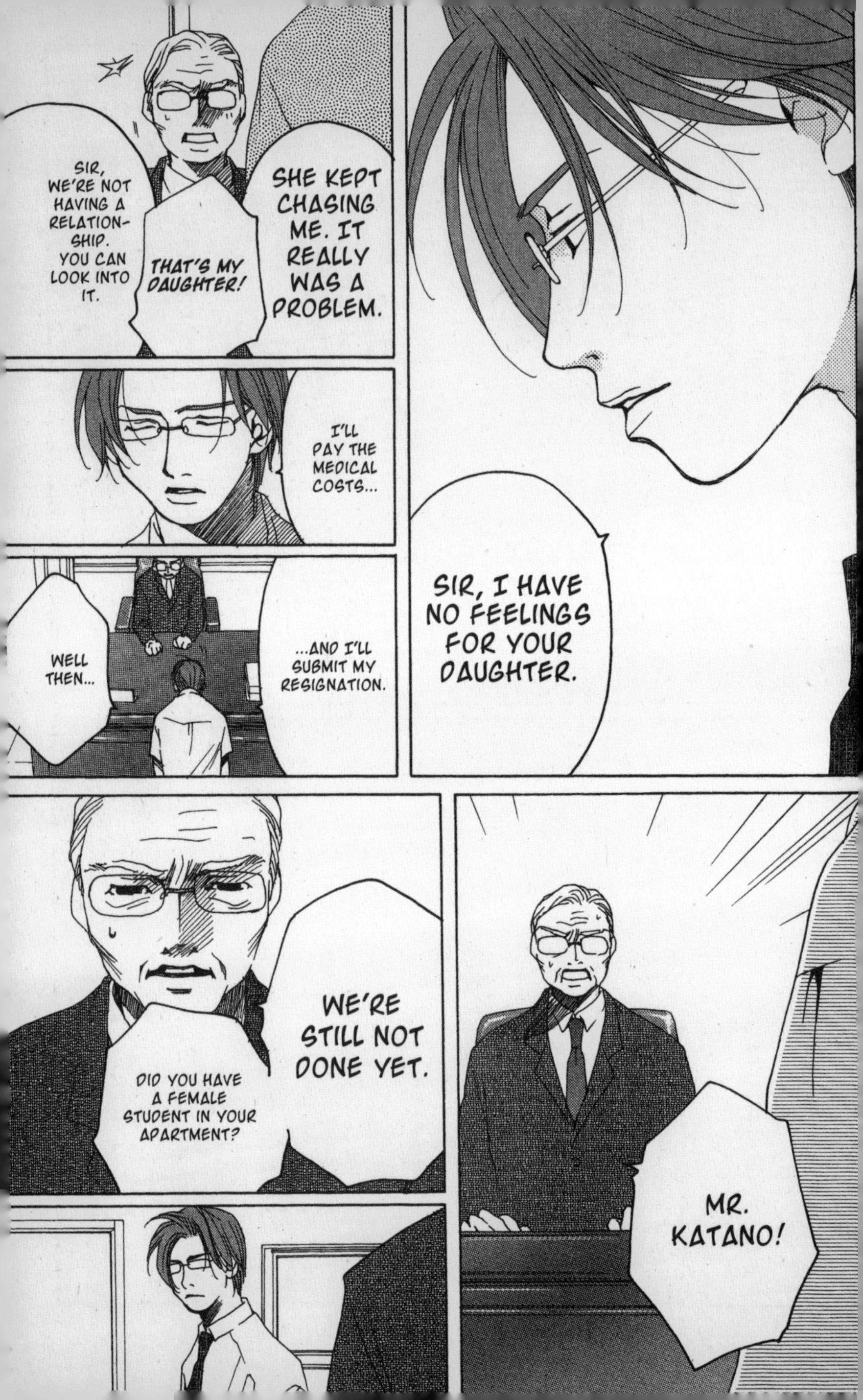
SIR, I HAVE NO FEELINGS FOR YOUR DAUGHTER.
SHE KEPT CHASING ME. IT REALLY WAS A PROBLEM.
THAT'S MY DAUGHTER!
SIR, WE'RE NOT HAVING A RELATIONSHIP. YOU CAN LOOK INTO IT.
I'LL PAY THE MEDICAL COSTS...
...AND I'LL SUBMIT MY RESIGNATION.
WELL THEN...
MR. KATANO!
WE'RE STILL NOT DONE YET.
DID YOU HAVE A FEMALE STUDENT IN YOUR APARTMENT?

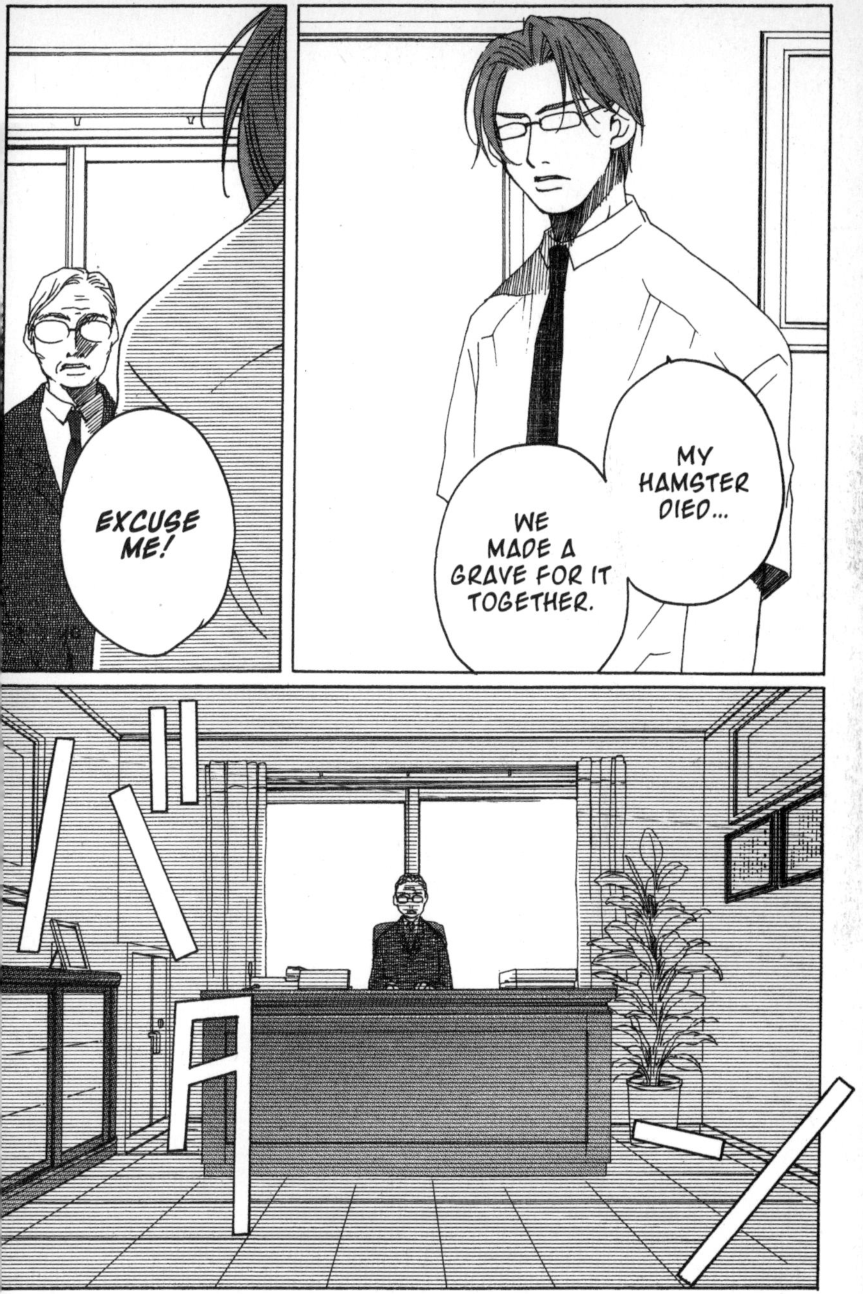
MY HAMSTER DIED...
WE MADE A GRAVE FOR IT TOGETHER.
EXCUSE ME!

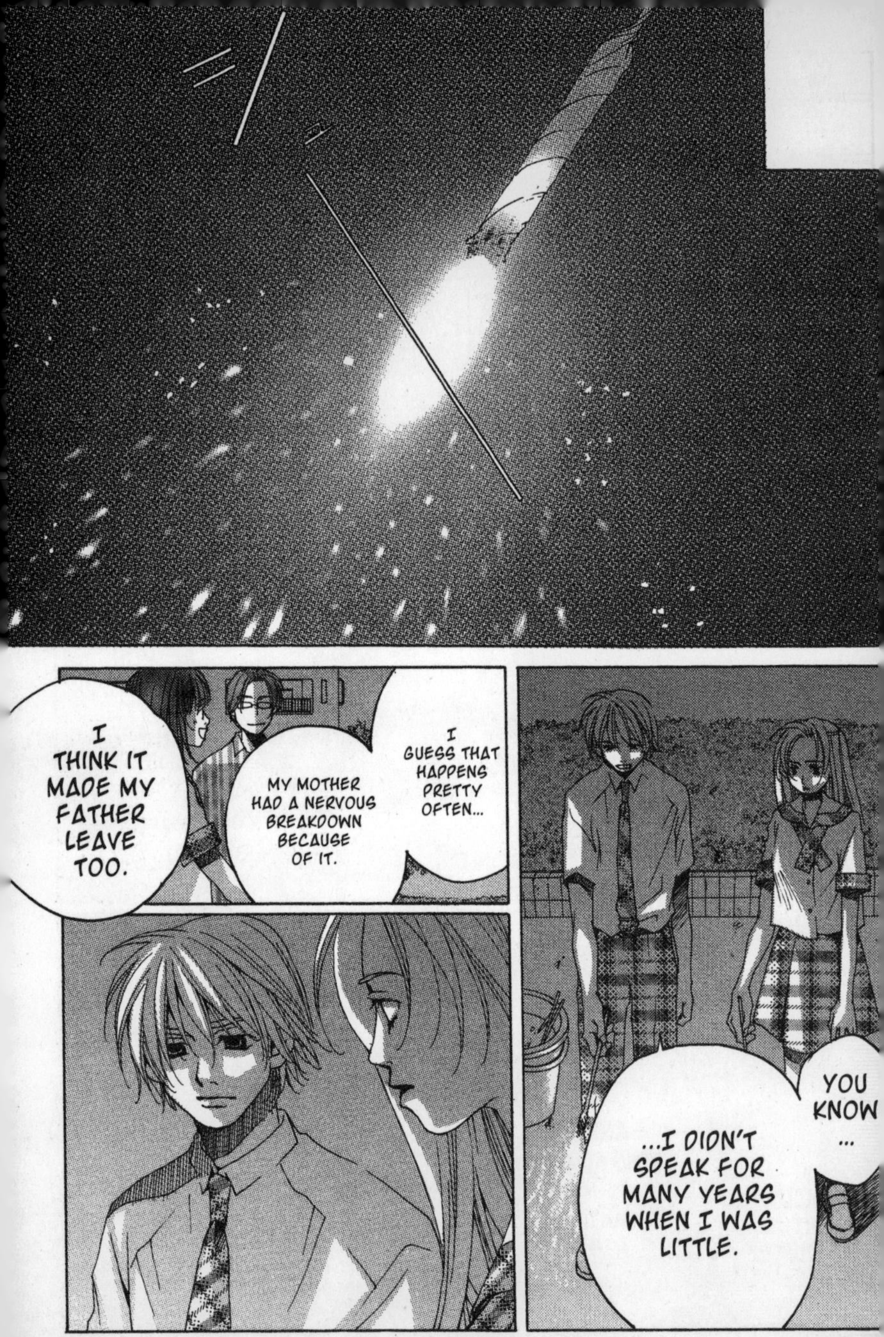
YOU KNOW ...
...I DIDN'T SPEAK FOR MANY YEARS WHEN I WAS LITTLE.
I GUESS THAT HAPPENS PRETTY OFTEN...
MY MOTHER HAD A NERVOUS BREAKDOWN BECAUSE OF IT.
I THINK IT MADE MY FATHER LEAVE TOO.

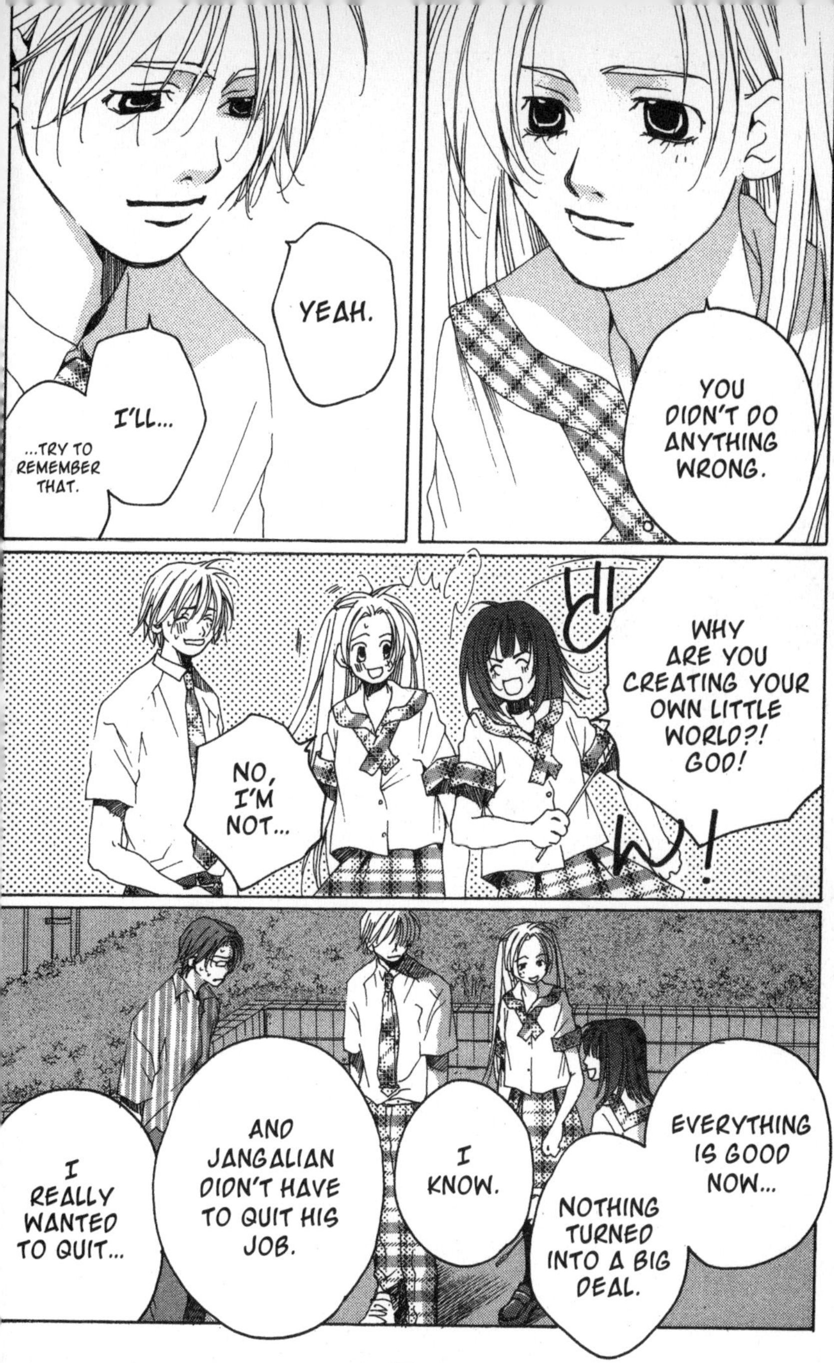
YOU DIDN'T DO ANYTHING WRONG.
YEAH.
I'LL...
...TRY TO REMEMBER THAT.
WHY ARE YOU CREATING YOUR OWN LITTLE WORLD?! GOD!
NO, I'M NOT...
EVERYTHING IS GOOD NOW...
NOTHING TURNED INTO A BIG DEAL.
I KNOW.
AND JANGALIAN DIDN'T HAVE TO QUIT HIS JOB.
I REALLY WANTED TO QUIT...

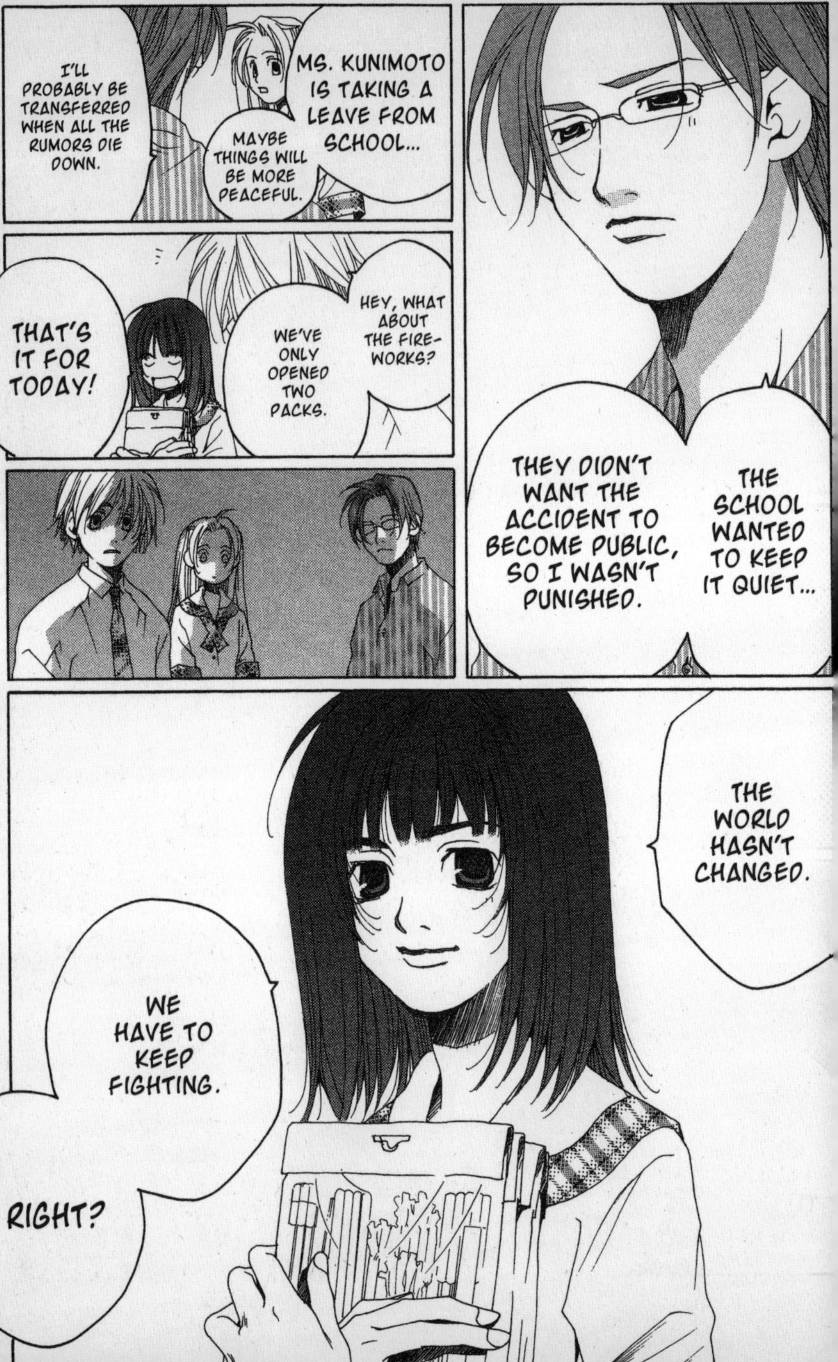
THE SCHOOL WANTED TO KEEP IT QUIET...
THEY DIDN'T WANT THE ACCIDENT TO BECOME PUBLIC, SO I WASN'T PUNISHED.
MS. KUNIMOTO IS TAKING A LEAVE FROM SCHOOL...
I'LL PROBABLY BE TRANSFERRED WHEN ALL THE RUMORS DIE DOWN.
MAYBE THINGS WILL BE MORE PEACEFUL.
HEY, WHAT ABOUT THE FIRE-WORKS?
WE'VE ONLY OPENED TWO PACKS.
THAT'S IT FOR TODAY!
THE WORLD HASN'T CHANGED.
WE HAVE TO KEEP FIGHTING.
RIGHT?

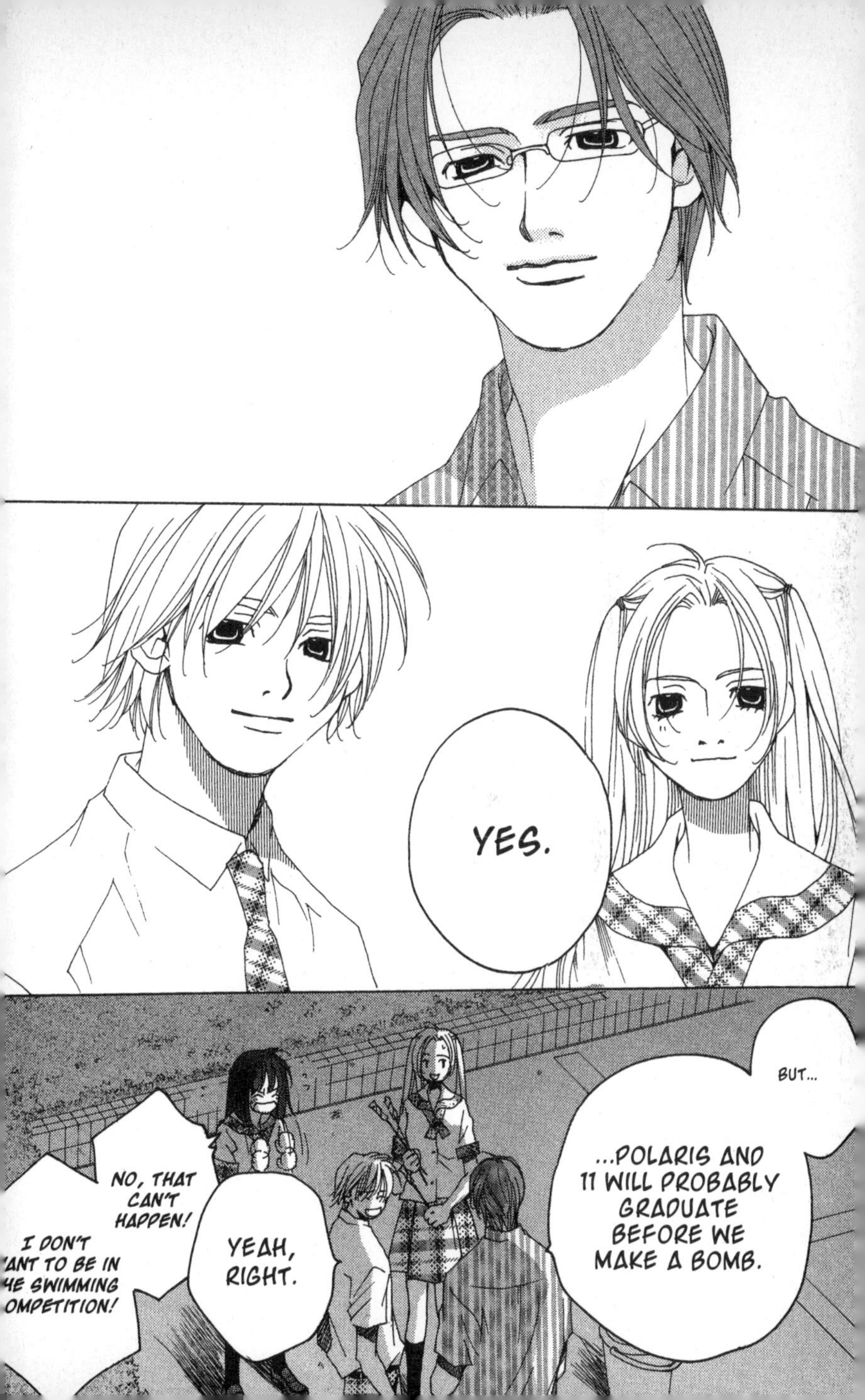
YES.
BUT...
...POLARIS AND 11 WILL PROBABLY GRADUATE BEFORE WE MAKE A BOMB.
YEAH, RIGHT.
NO, THAT CAN'T HAPPEN!
I DON'T 'ANT TO BE IN HE SWIMMING OMPETITION!

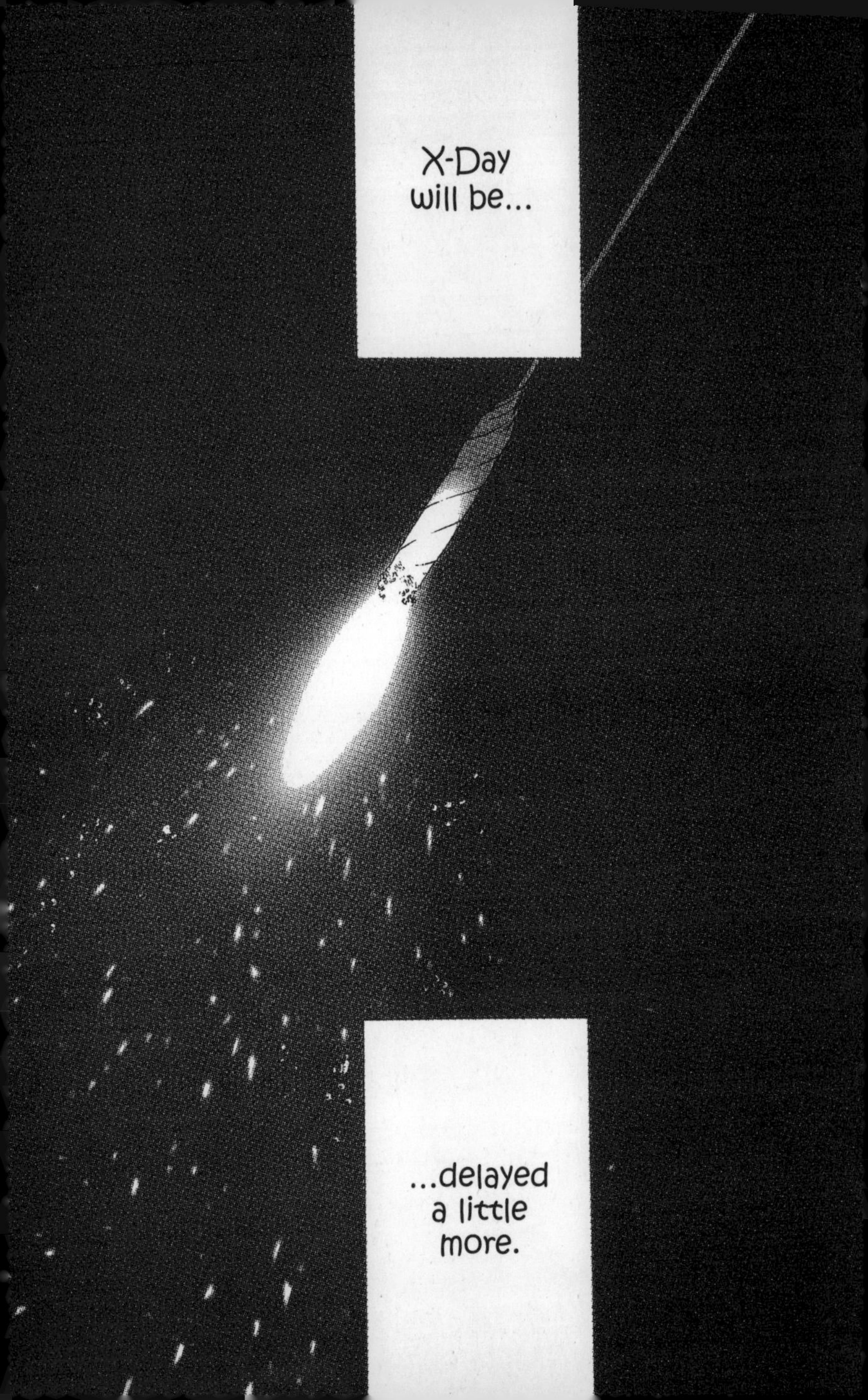
X-Day will be...
...delayed a little more.

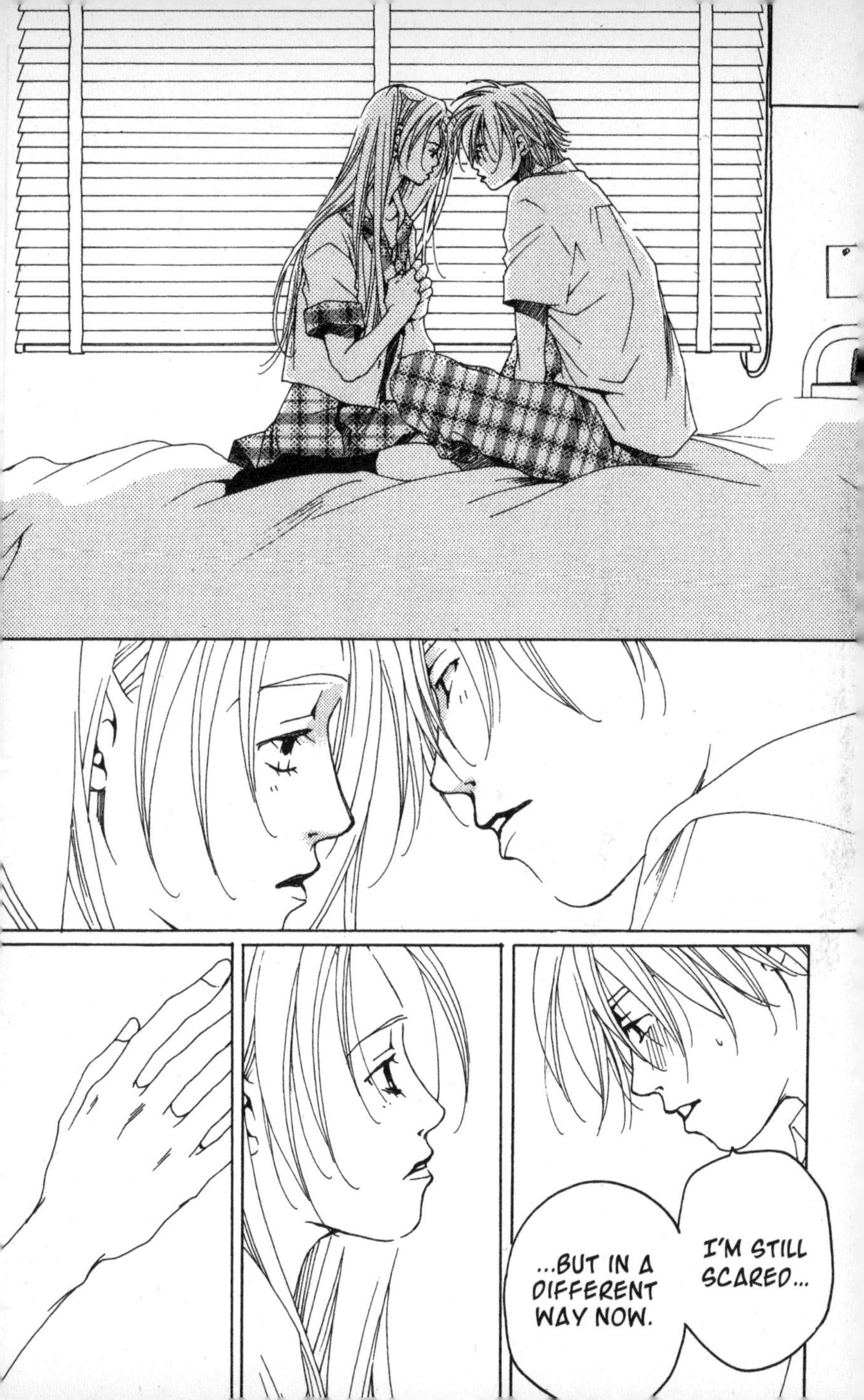
I'M STILL SCARED...
...BUT IN A DIFFERENT WAY NOW.

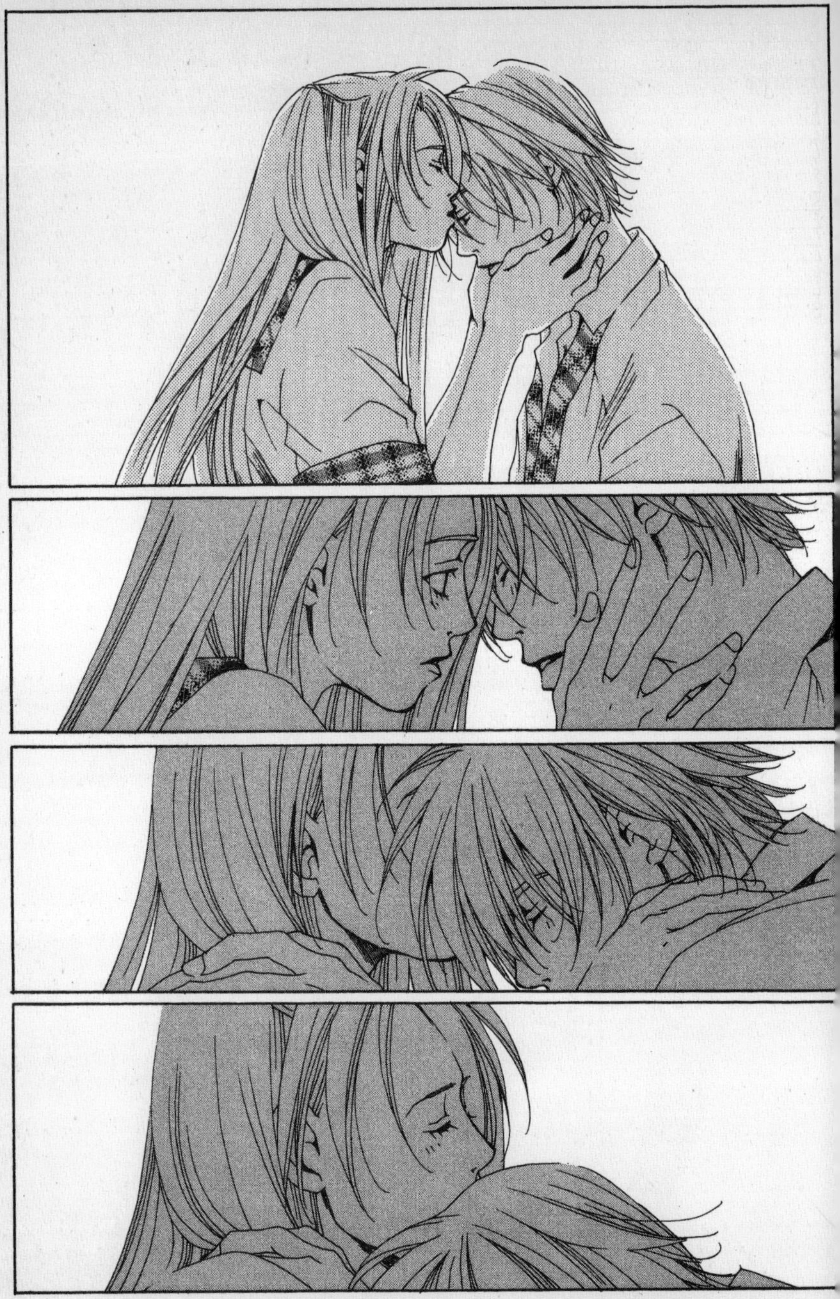

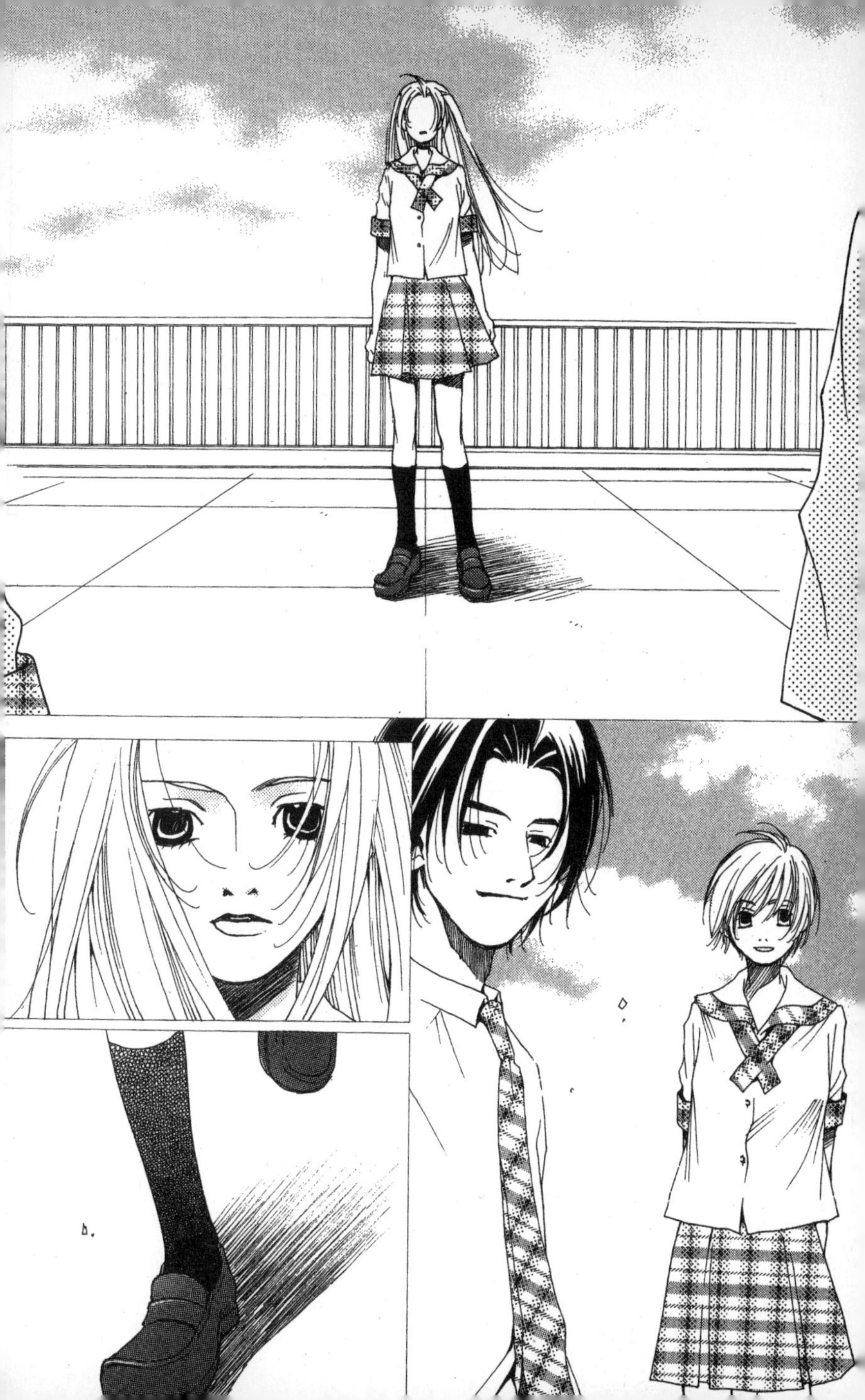

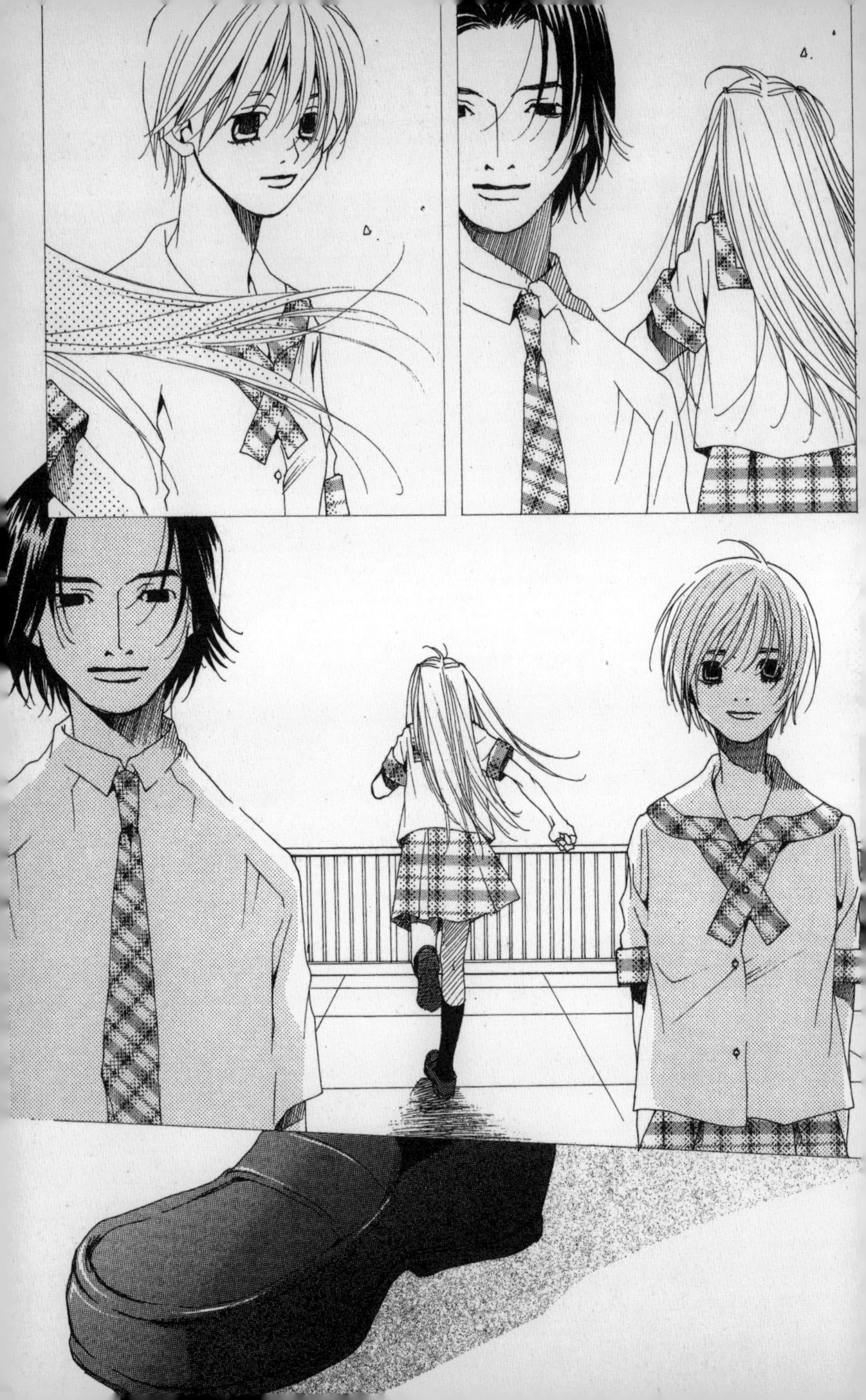

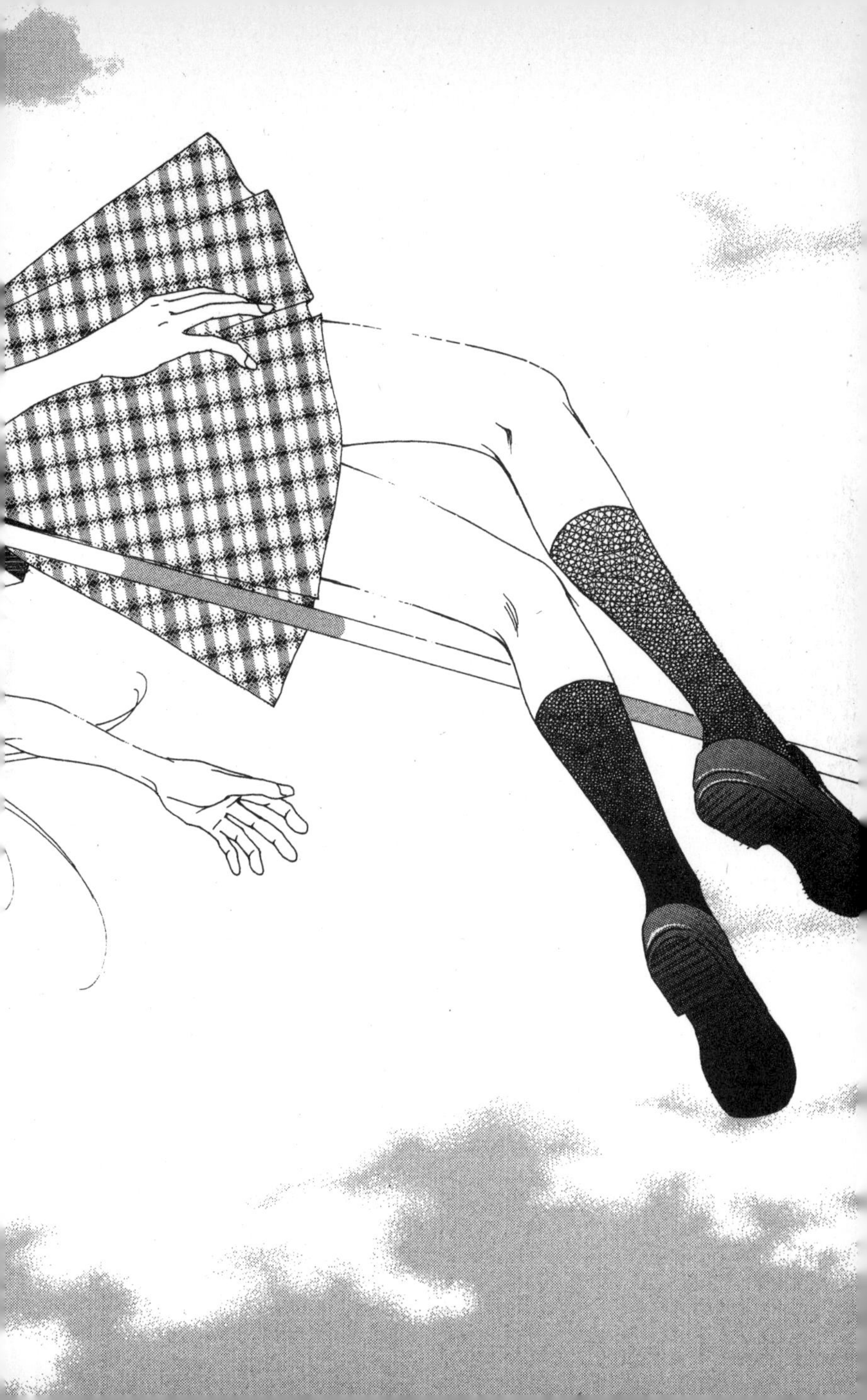

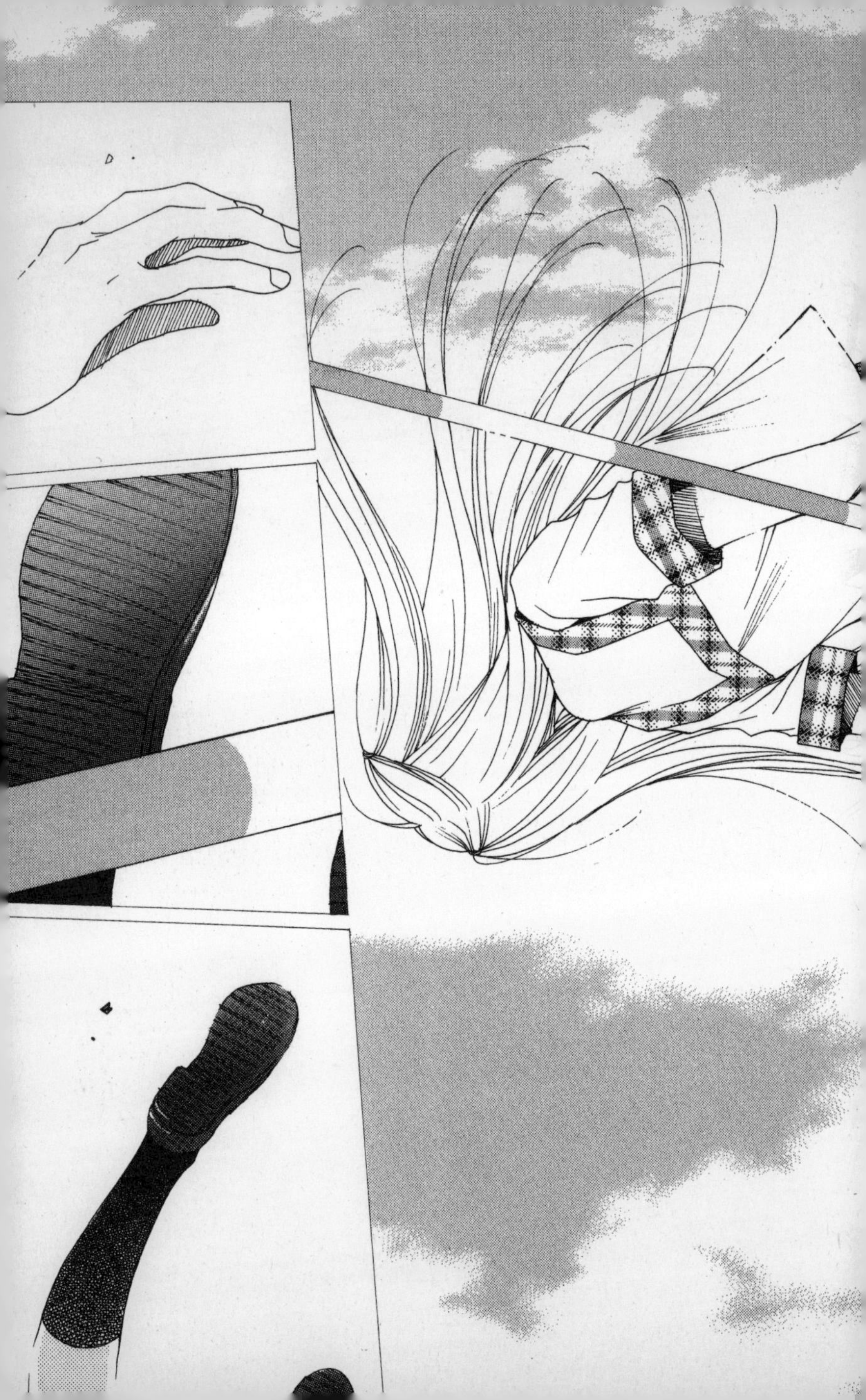

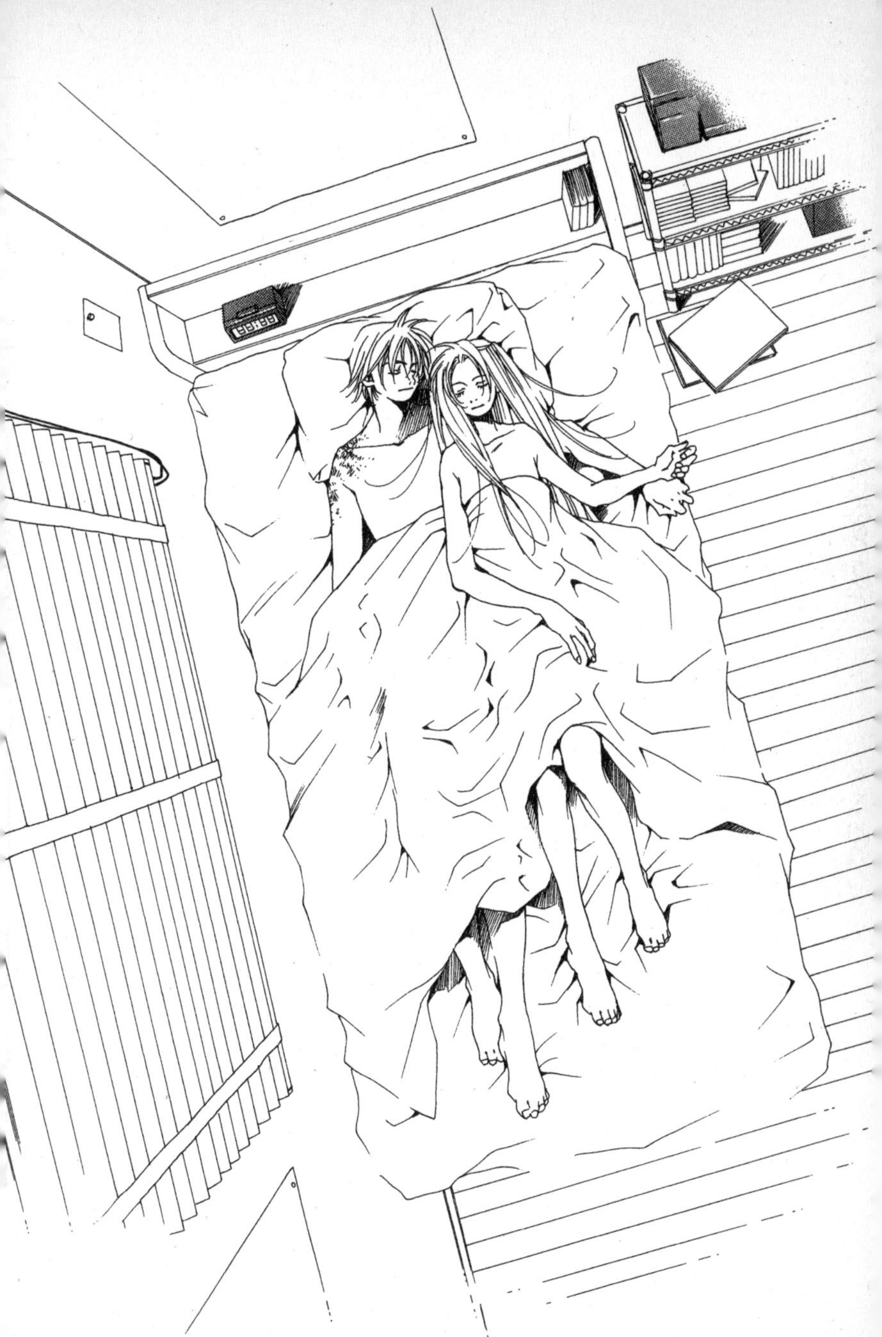

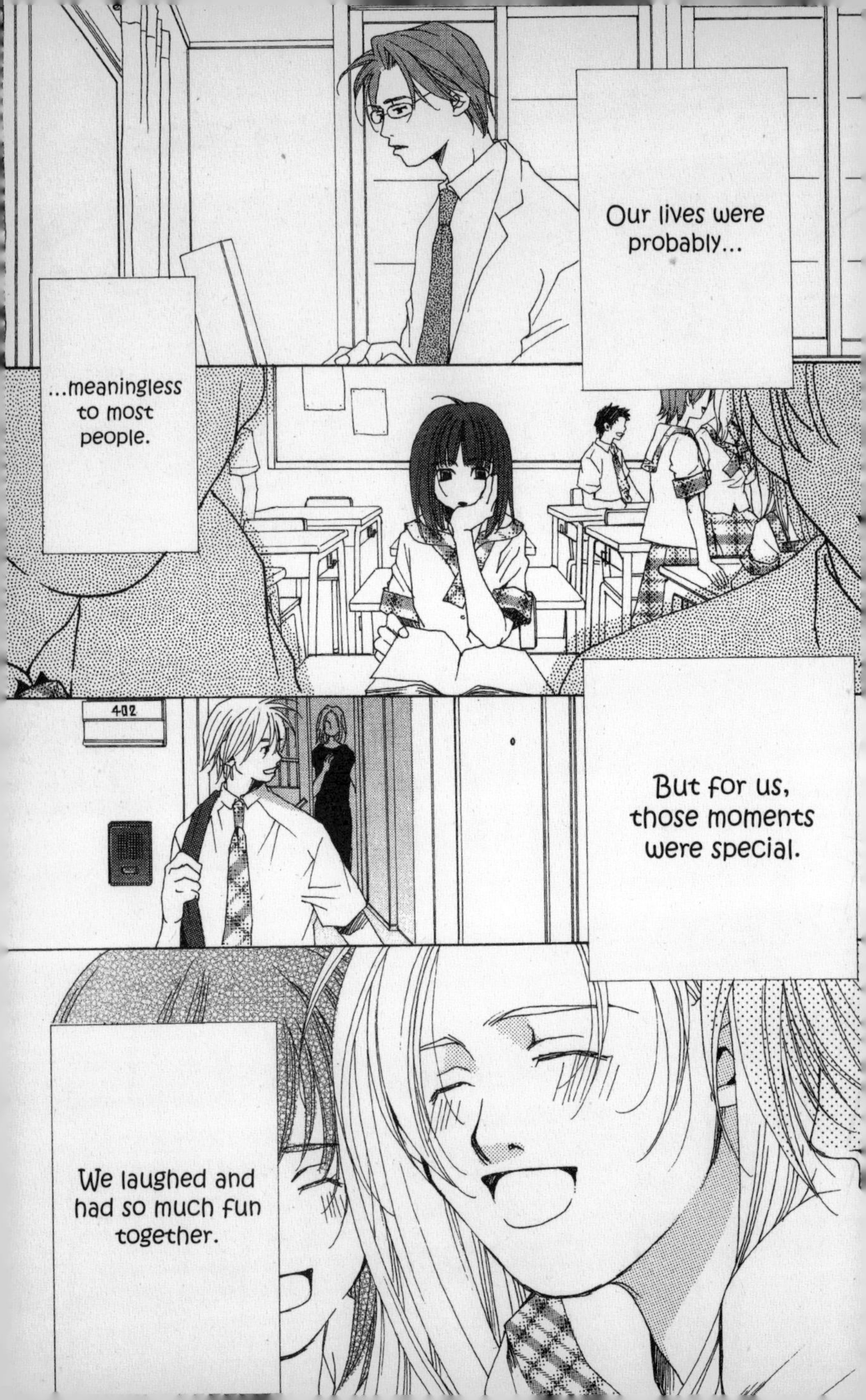
Our lives were probably...
...meaningless to most people.
402
But for us, those moments were special.
We laughed and had so much fun together.

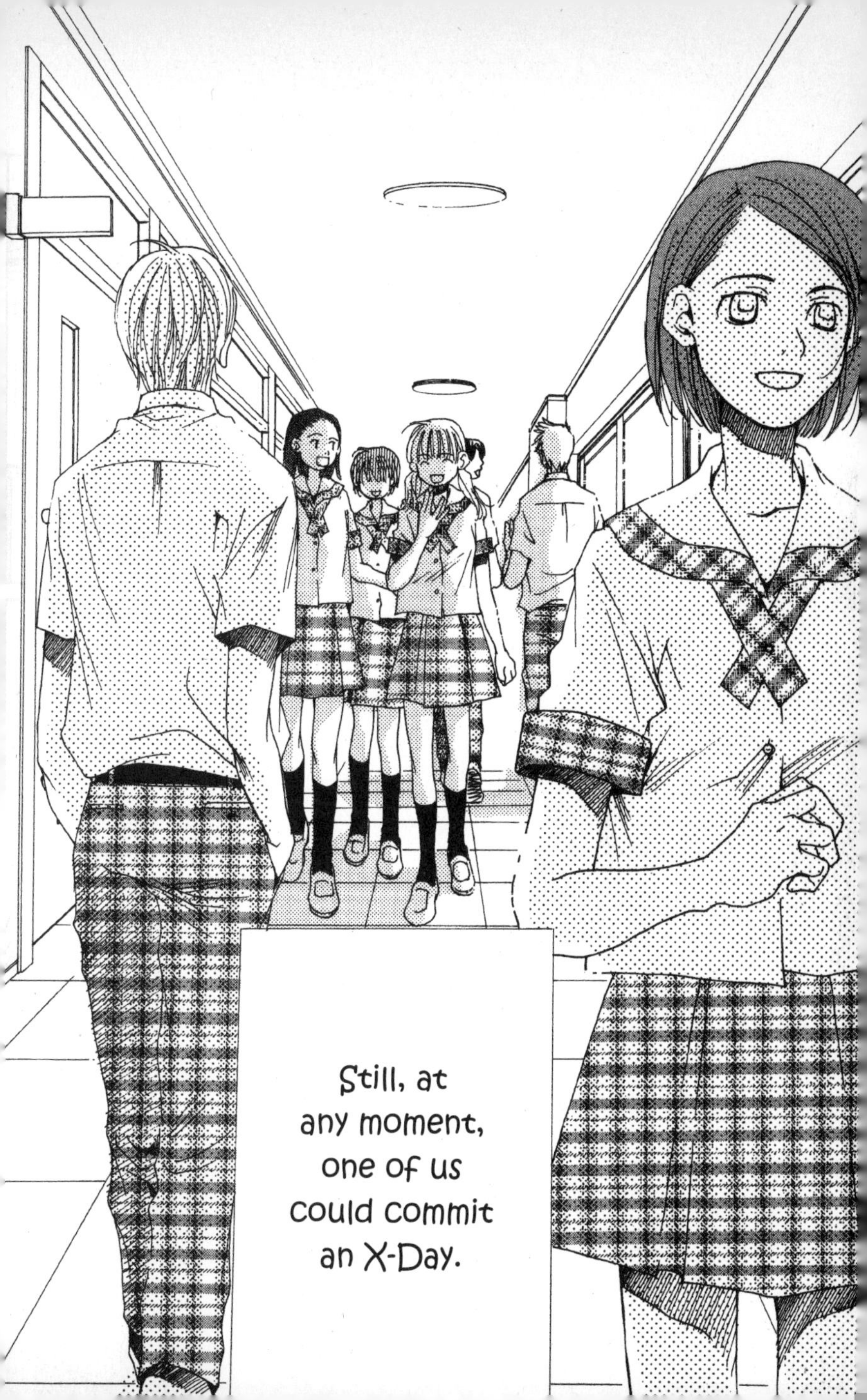
Still, at any moment, one of us could commit an X-Day.

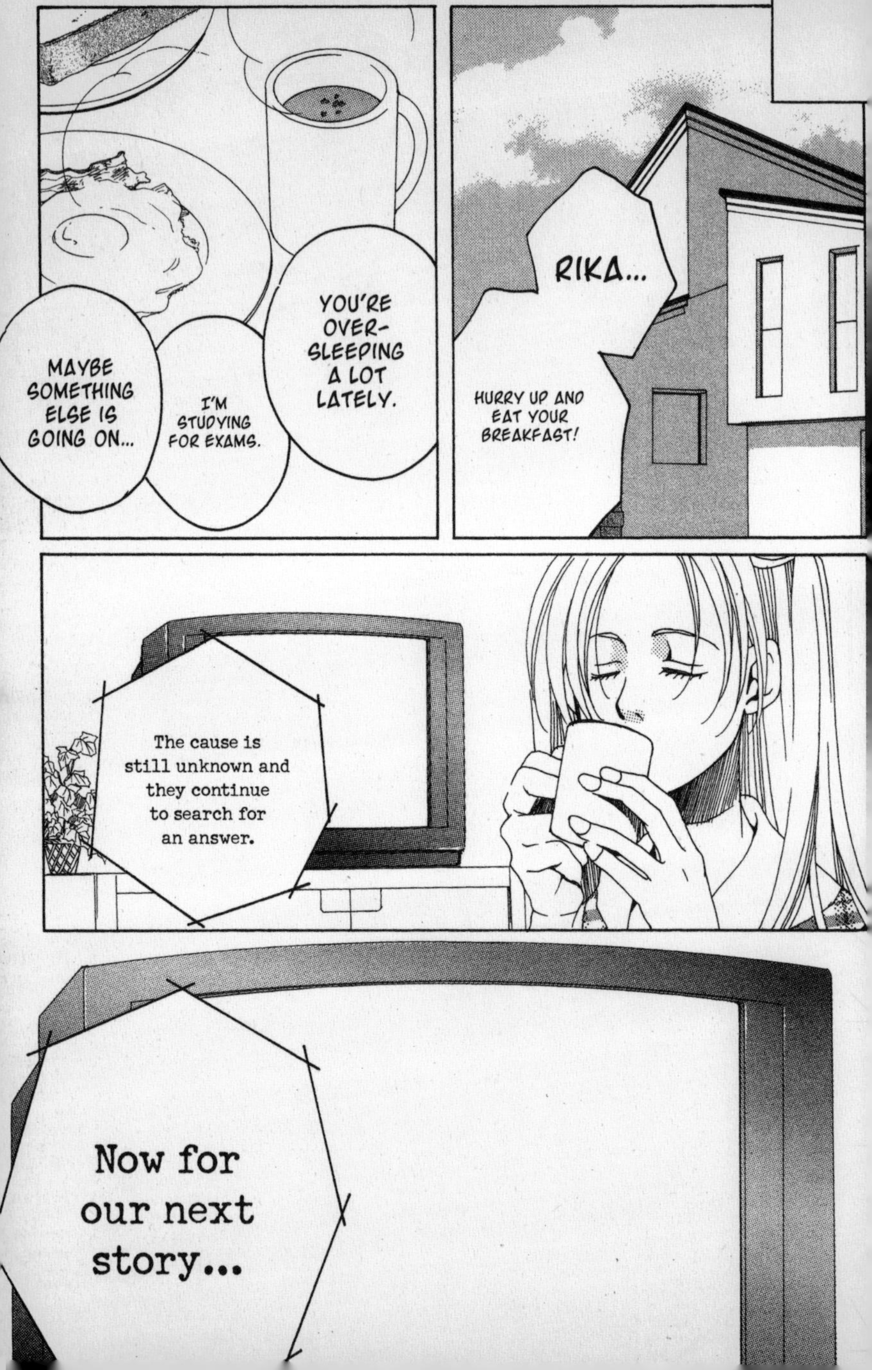
RIKA...
HURRY UP AND EAT YOUR BREAKFAST!
YOU'RE OVER-SLEEPING A LOT LATELY.
I'M STUDYING FOR EXAMS.
MAYBE SOMETHING ELSE IS GOING ON...
The cause is still unknown and they continue to search for an answer.
Now for our next story...

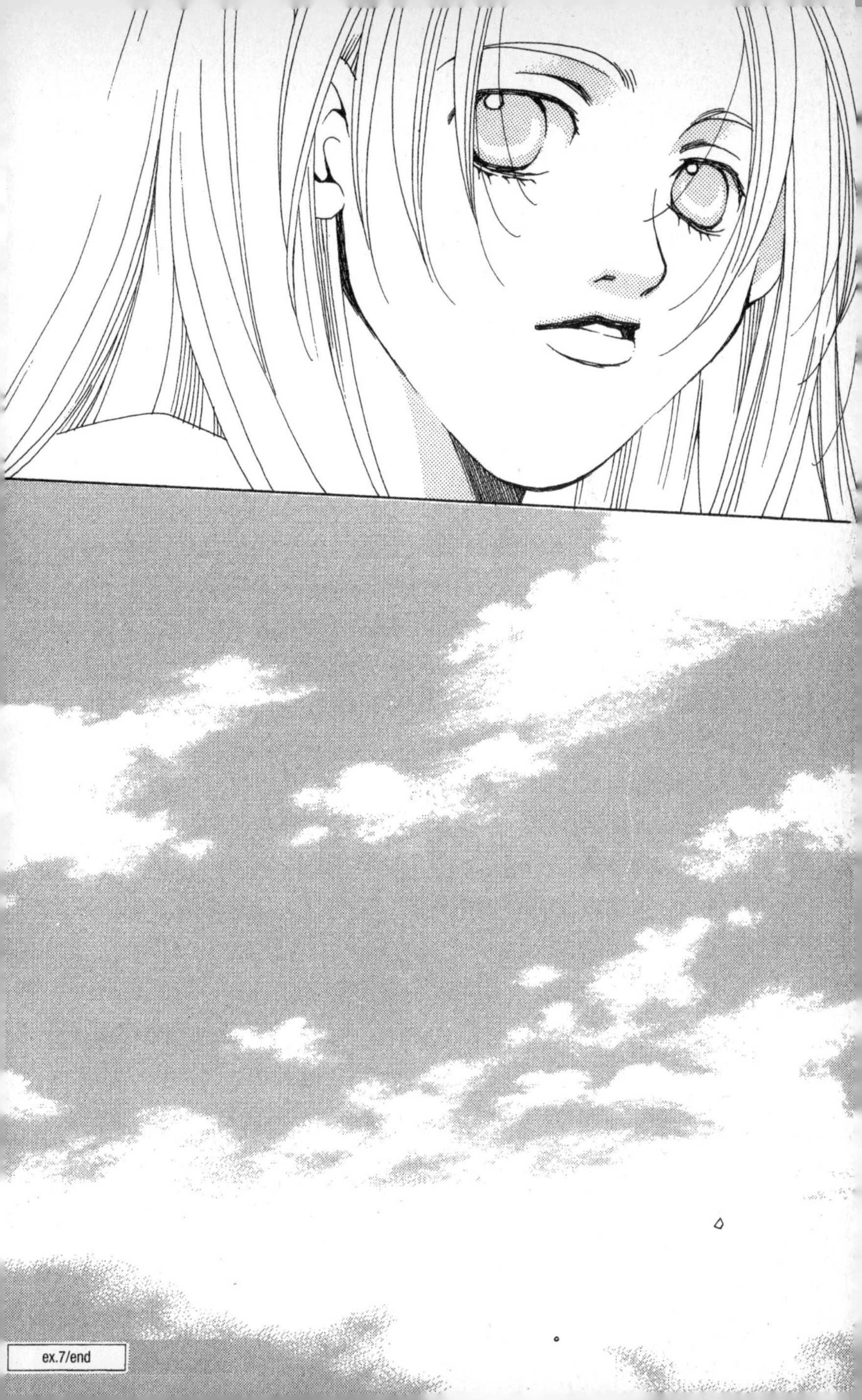
ex.7/end

THE LAST SUPPER

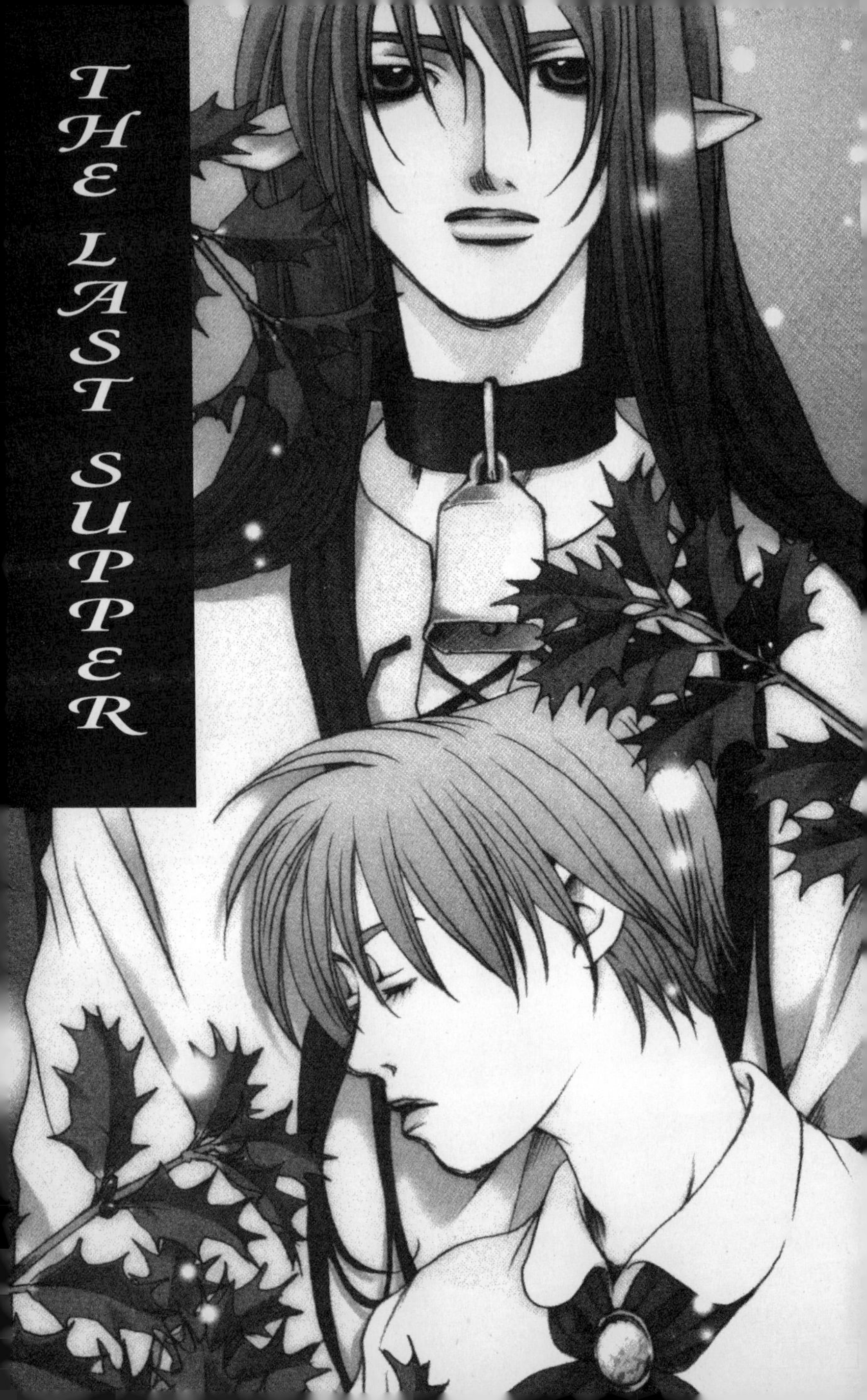

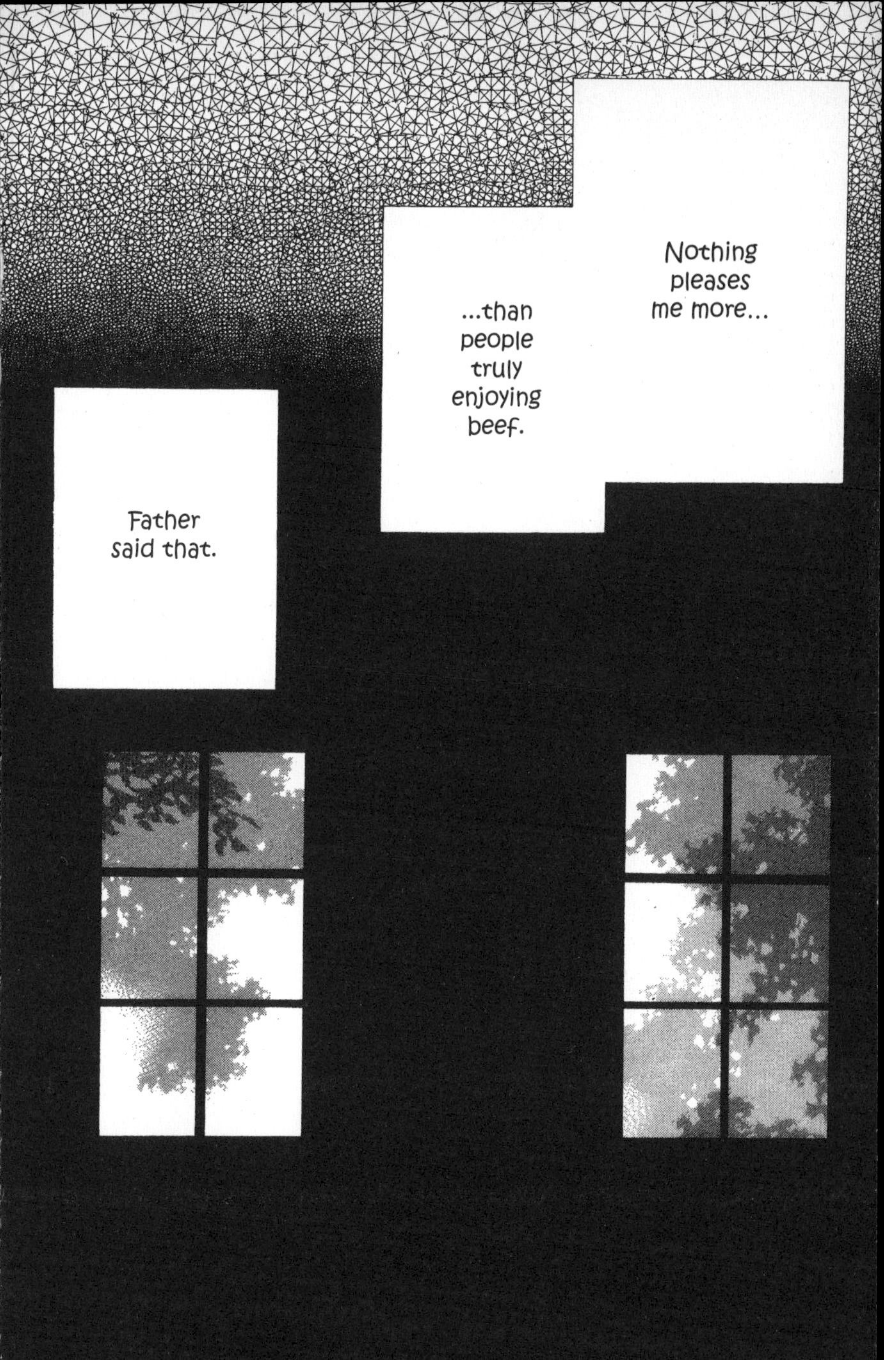
Nothing pleases me more...
...than people truly enjoying beef.
Father said that.

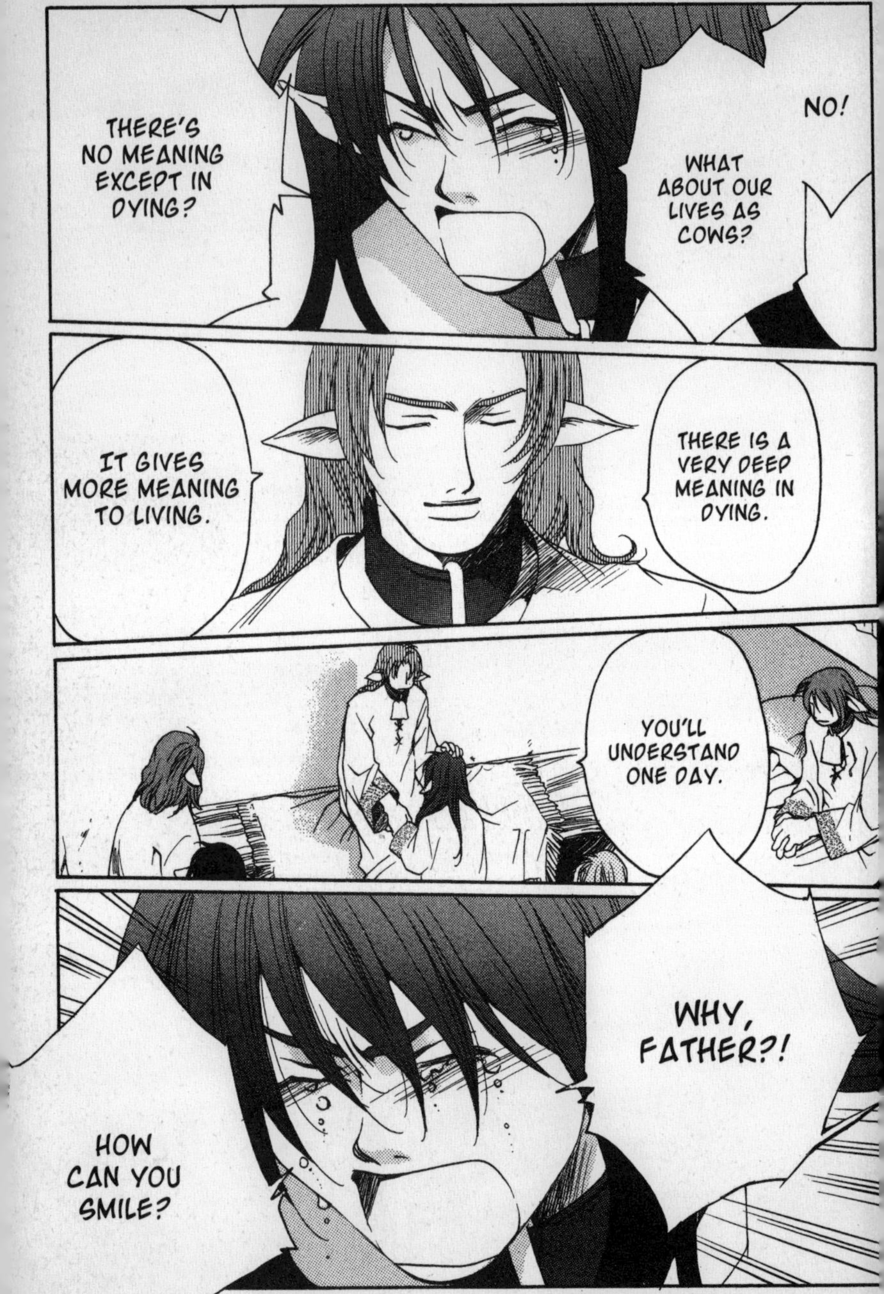
NO!
WHAT ABOUT OUR LIVES AS COWS?
THERE'S NO MEANING EXCEPT IN DYING?
THERE IS A VERY DEEP MEANING IN DYING.
IT GIVES MORE MEANING TO LIVING.
YOU'LL UNDERSTAND ONE DAY.
WHY, FATHER?!
HOW CAN YOU SMILE?

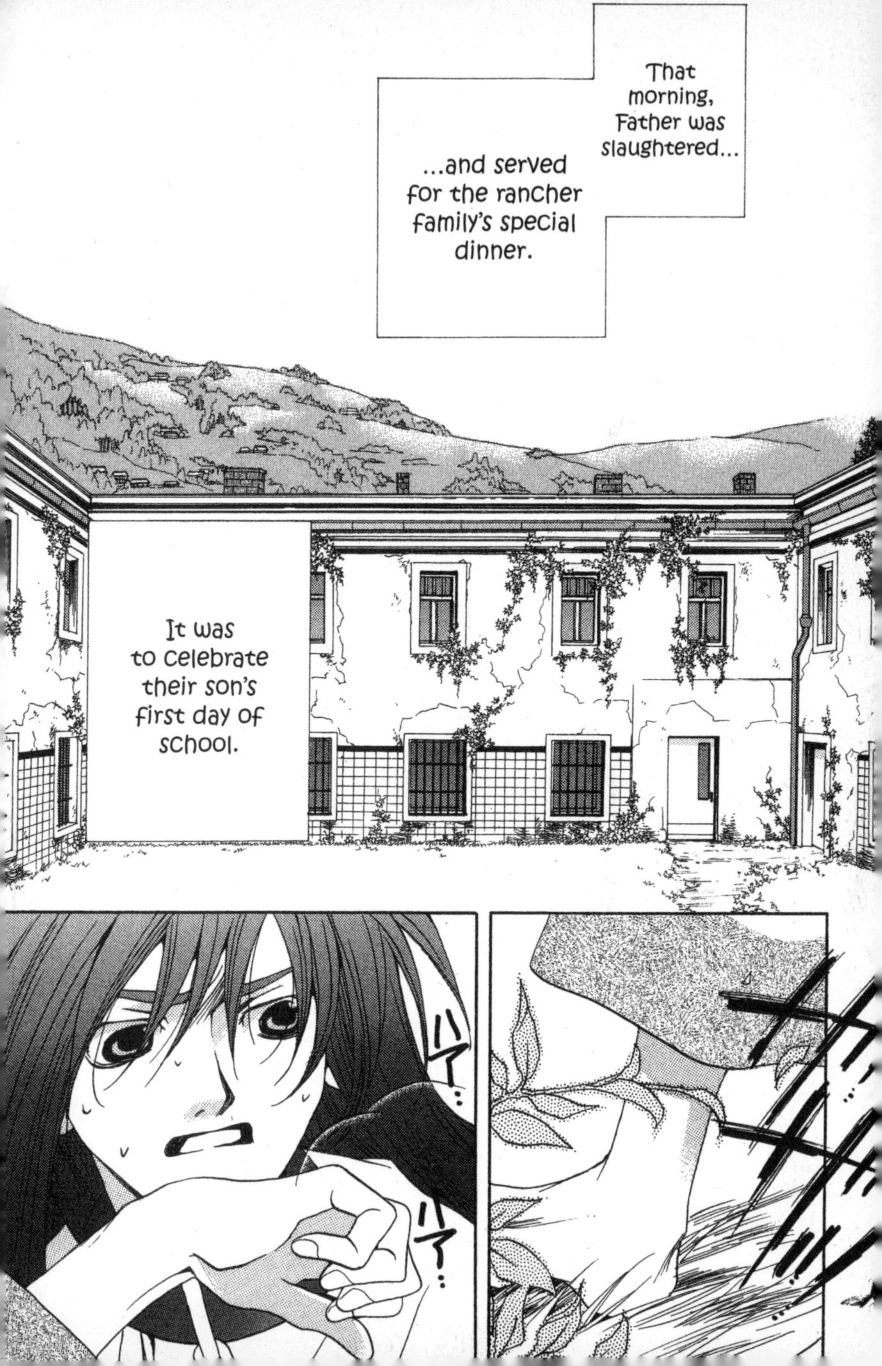
That morning, Father was slaughtered...
...and served for the rancher family's special dinner.
It was to celebrate their son's first day of school.
ハア…
ハア…

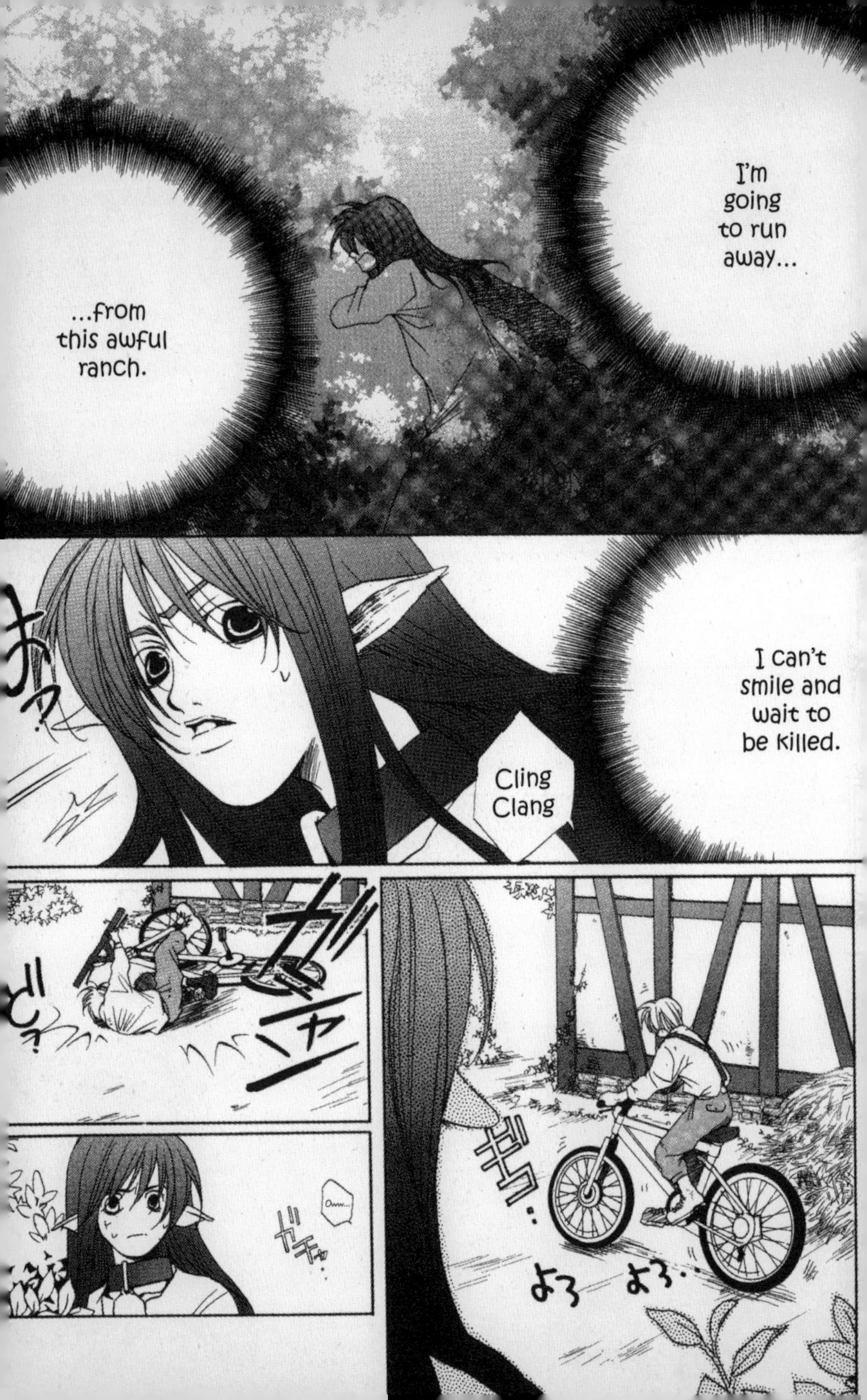
I'm going to run away...
...from this awful ranch.
I can't smile and wait to be killed.
Cling Clang
おっ?
ギコ..
よろ よろ
ガシャーン
Oww...
ガチャ

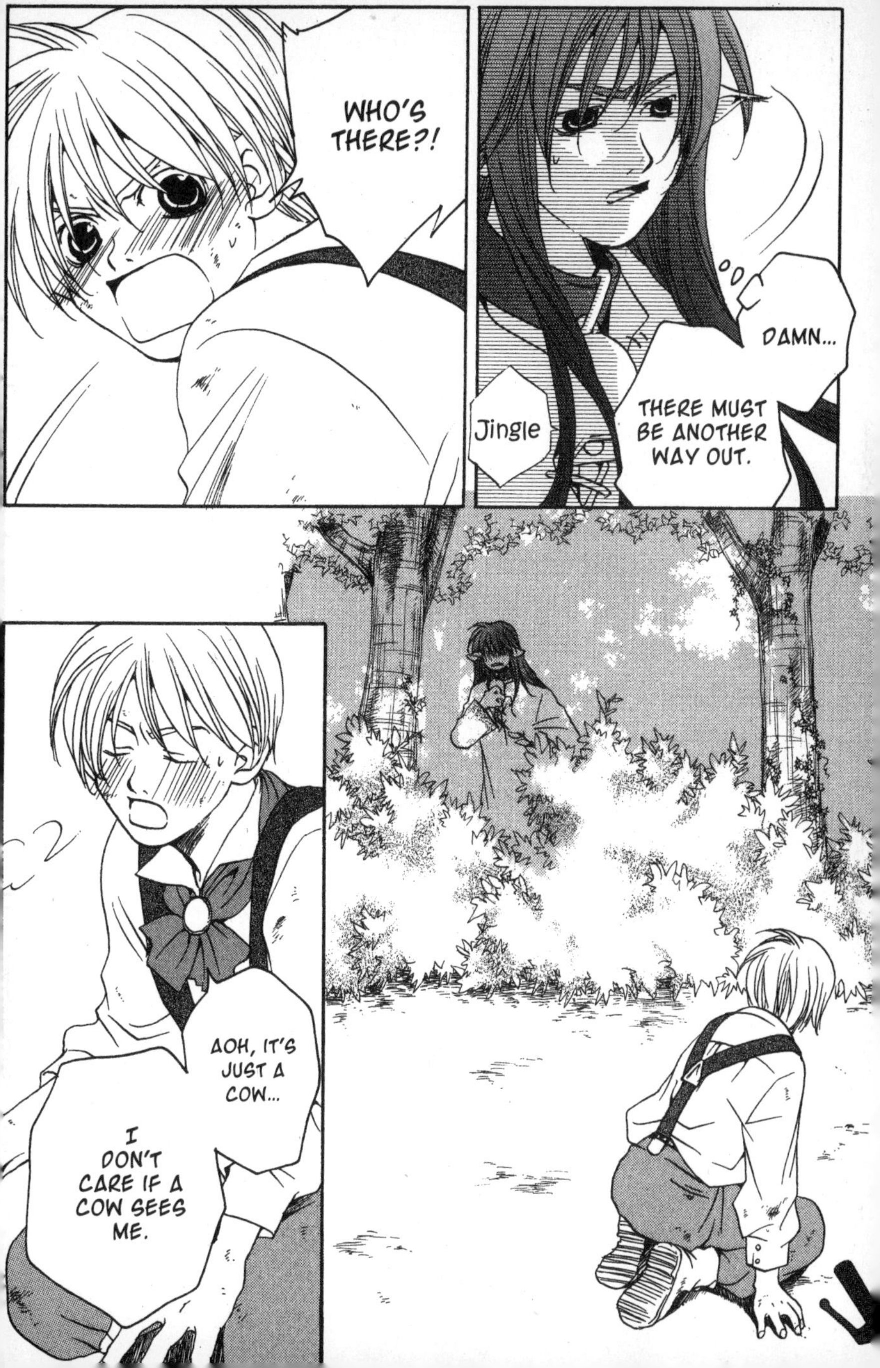
DAMN...
THERE MUST BE ANOTHER WAY OUT.
Jingle
WHO'S THERE?!
AOH, IT'S JUST A COW...
I DON'T CARE IF A COW SEES ME.

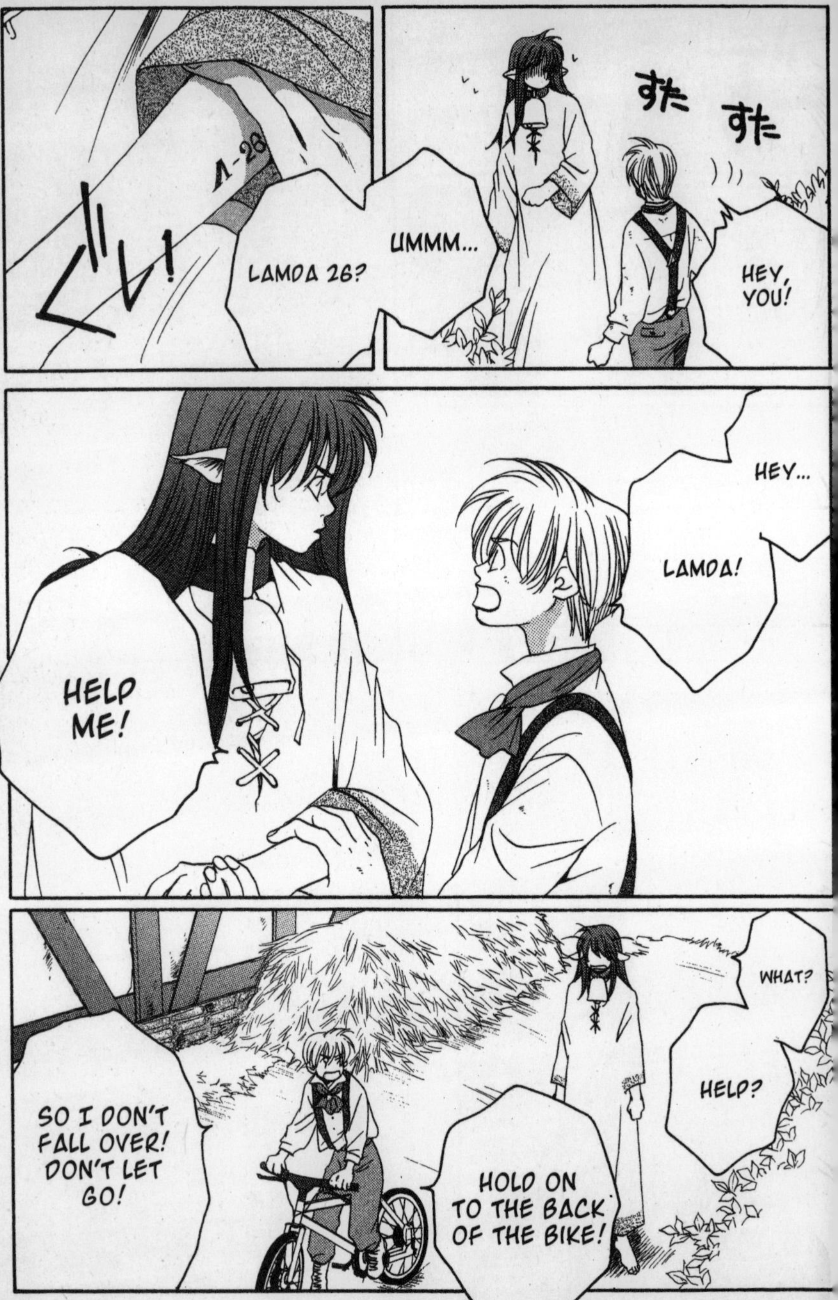
すた すた
HEY, YOU!
UMMM...
LAMDA 26?
ぐい!
HEY...
LAMDA!
HELP ME!
WHAT?
HELP?
HOLD ON TO THE BACK OF THE BIKE!
SO I DON'T FALL OVER! DON'T LET GO!

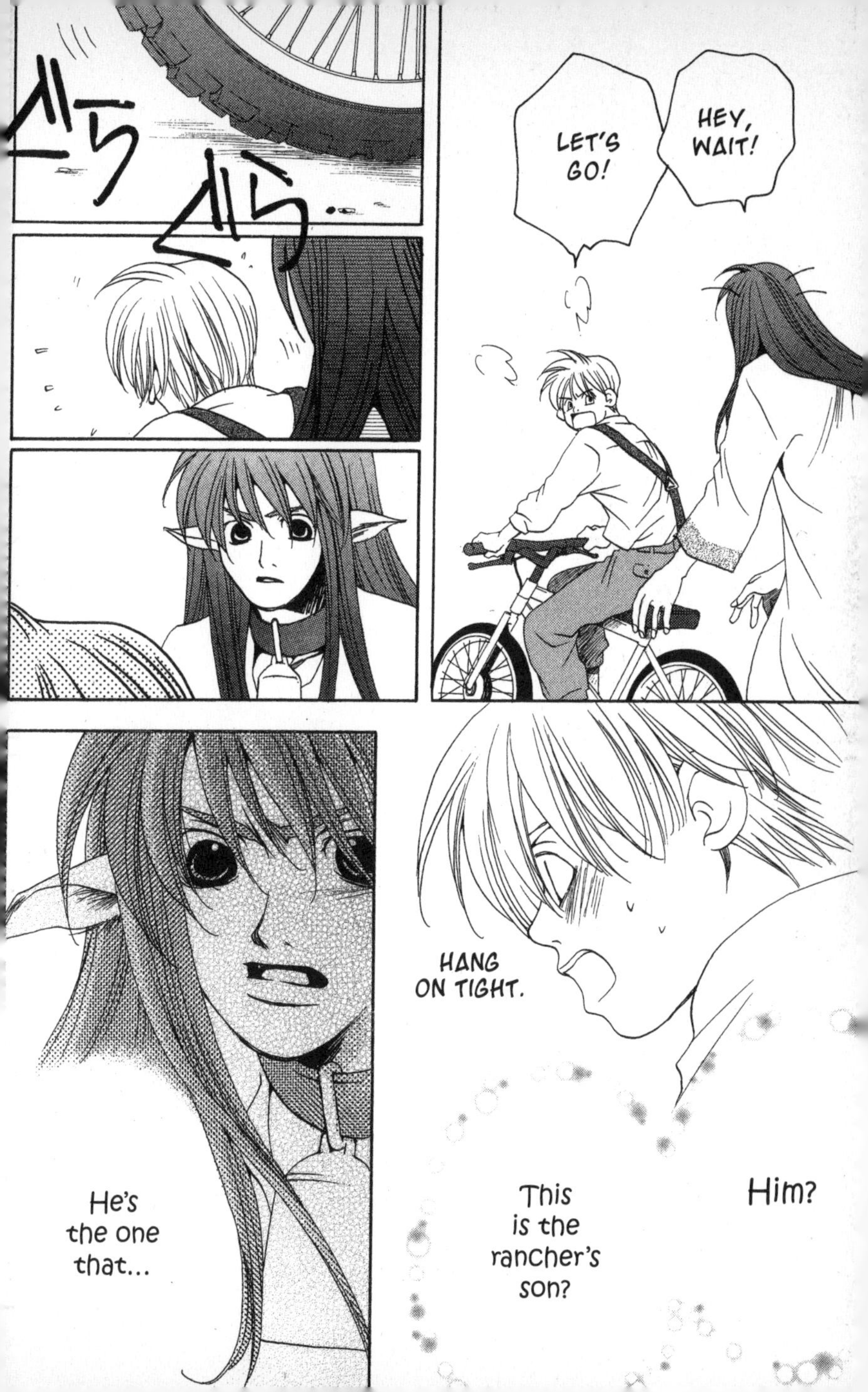
HEY, WAIT!
LET'S GO!
HANG ON TIGHT.
Him?
This is the rancher's son?
He's the one that...

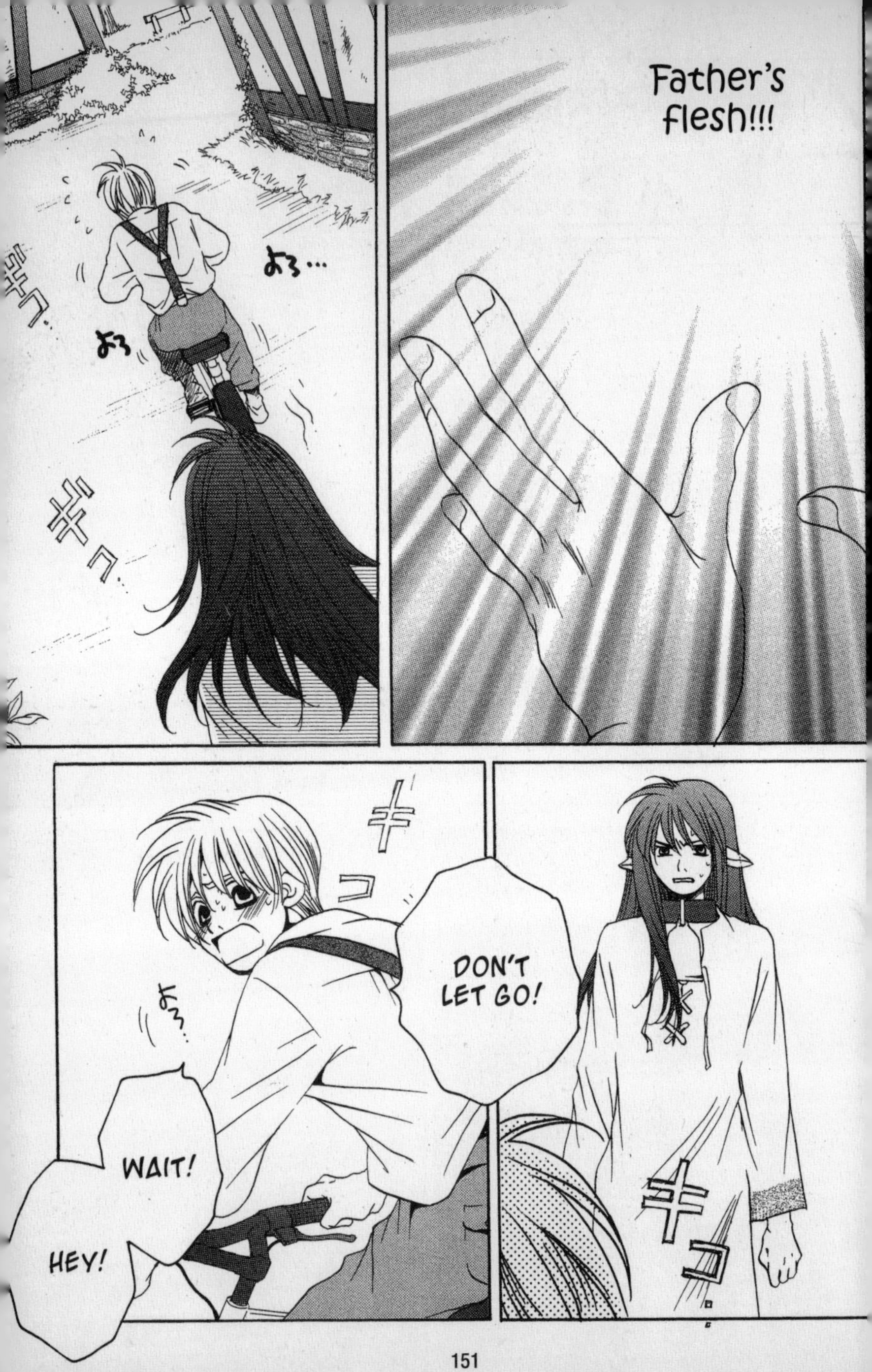
Father's flesh!!!
よろ…
ギク…
よろ
ギク…
キュ
DON'T LET GO!
よろ…
キュ
WAIT!
HEY!

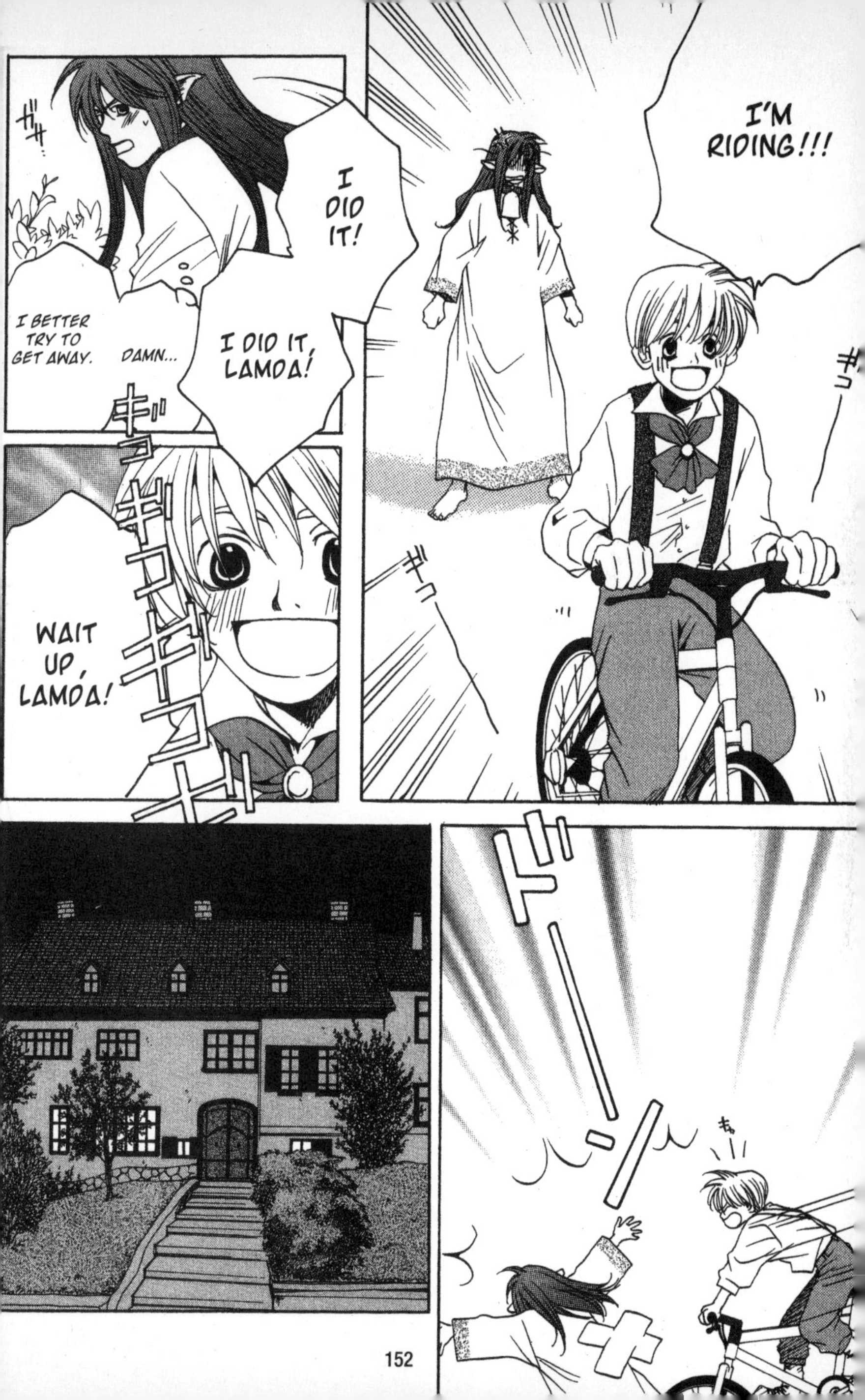
I'M RIDING!!!
I DID IT!
I DID IT, LAMDA!
DAMN...
I BETTER TRY TO GET AWAY.
WAIT UP, LAMDA!

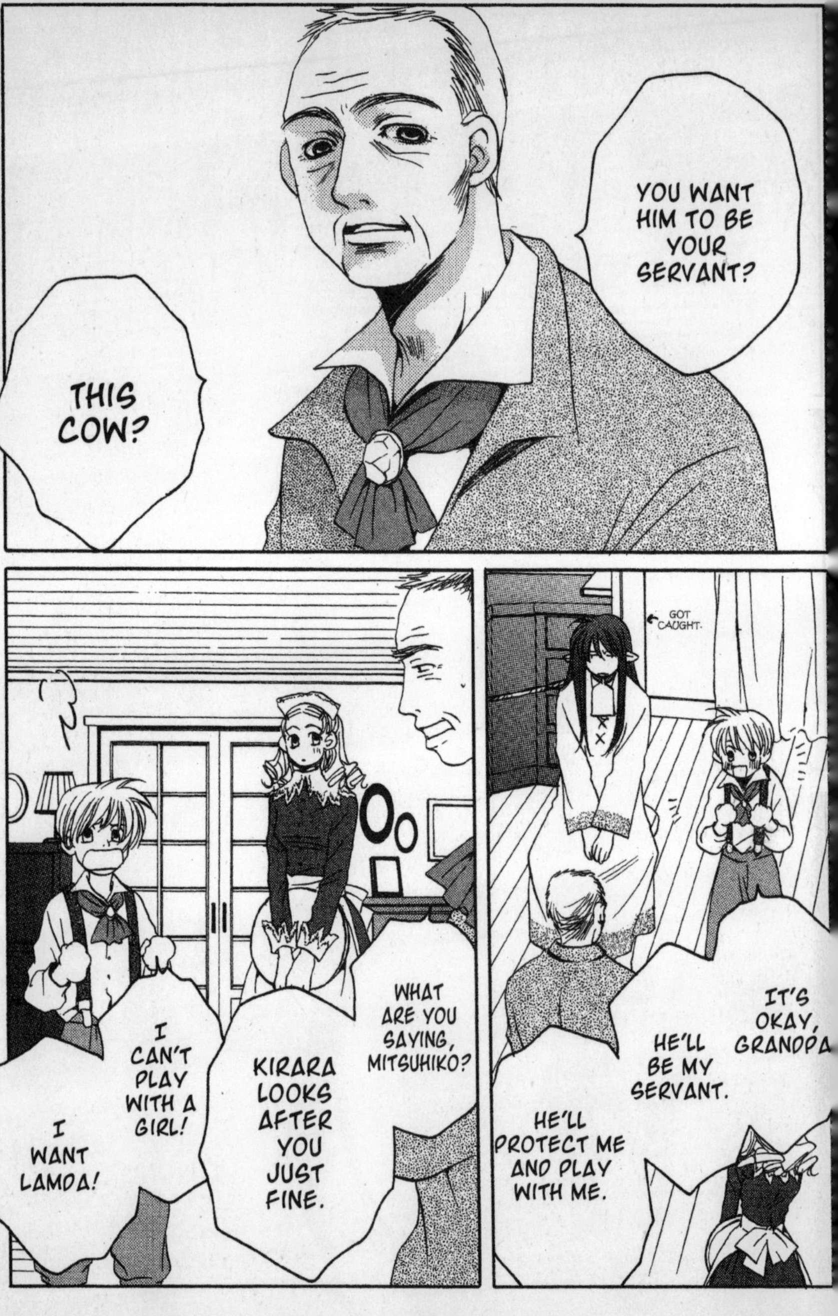
YOU WANT HIM TO BE YOUR SERVANT?
THIS COW?
GOT CAUGHT.
IT'S OKAY, GRANDPA
HE'LL BE MY SERVANT.
HE'LL PROTECT ME AND PLAY WITH ME.
WHAT ARE YOU SAYING, MITSUHIKO?
KIRARA LOOKS AFTER YOU JUST FINE.
I CAN'T PLAY WITH A GIRL!
I WANT LAMDA!

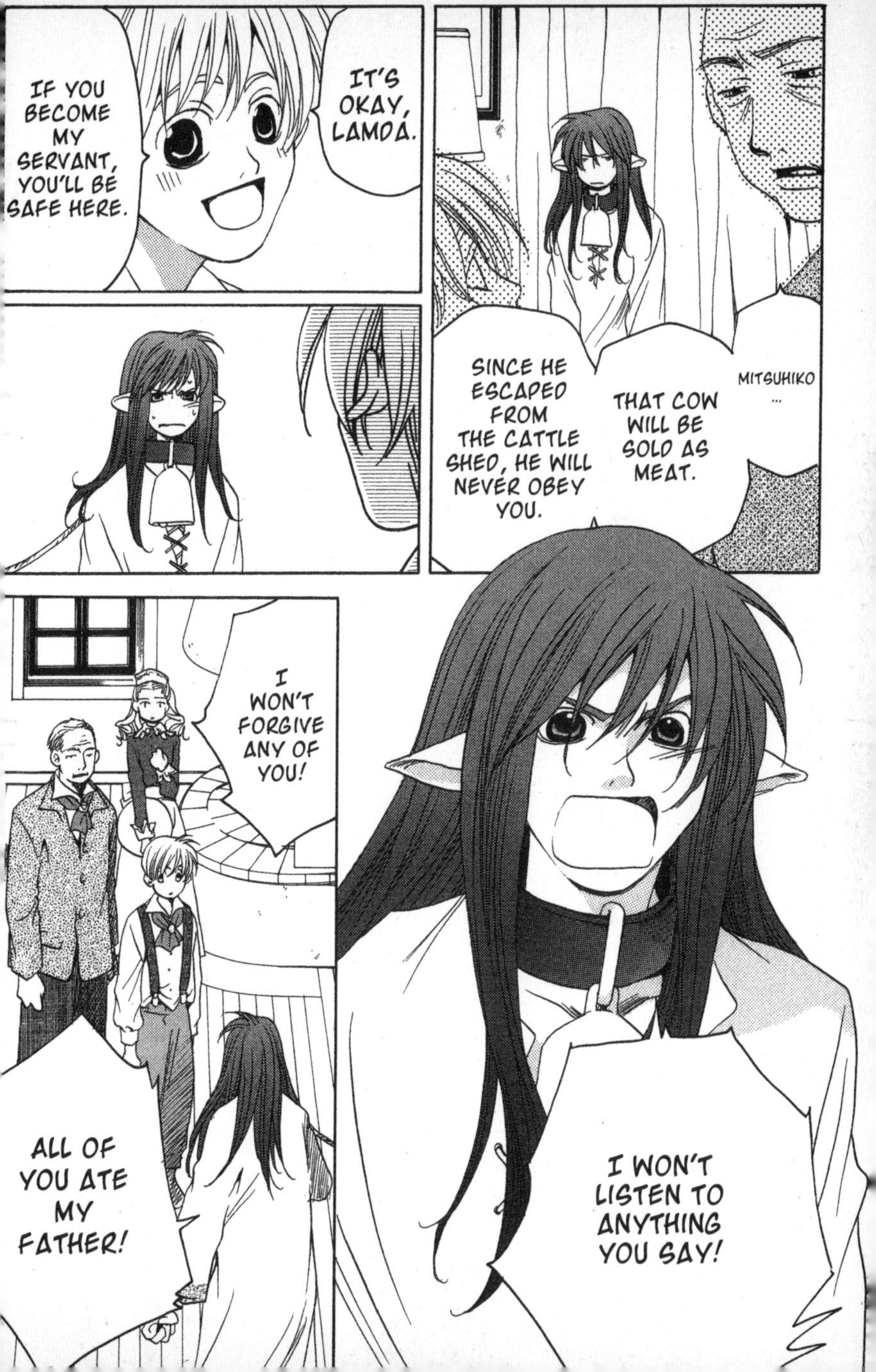
MITSUHIKO ...
THAT COW WILL BE SOLD AS MEAT.
SINCE HE ESCAPED FROM THE CATTLE SHED, HE WILL NEVER OBEY YOU.
IT'S OKAY, LAMDA.
IF YOU BECOME MY SERVANT, YOU'LL BE SAFE HERE.
I WON'T LISTEN TO ANYTHING YOU SAY!
I WON'T FORGIVE ANY OF YOU!
ALL OF YOU ATE MY FATHER!

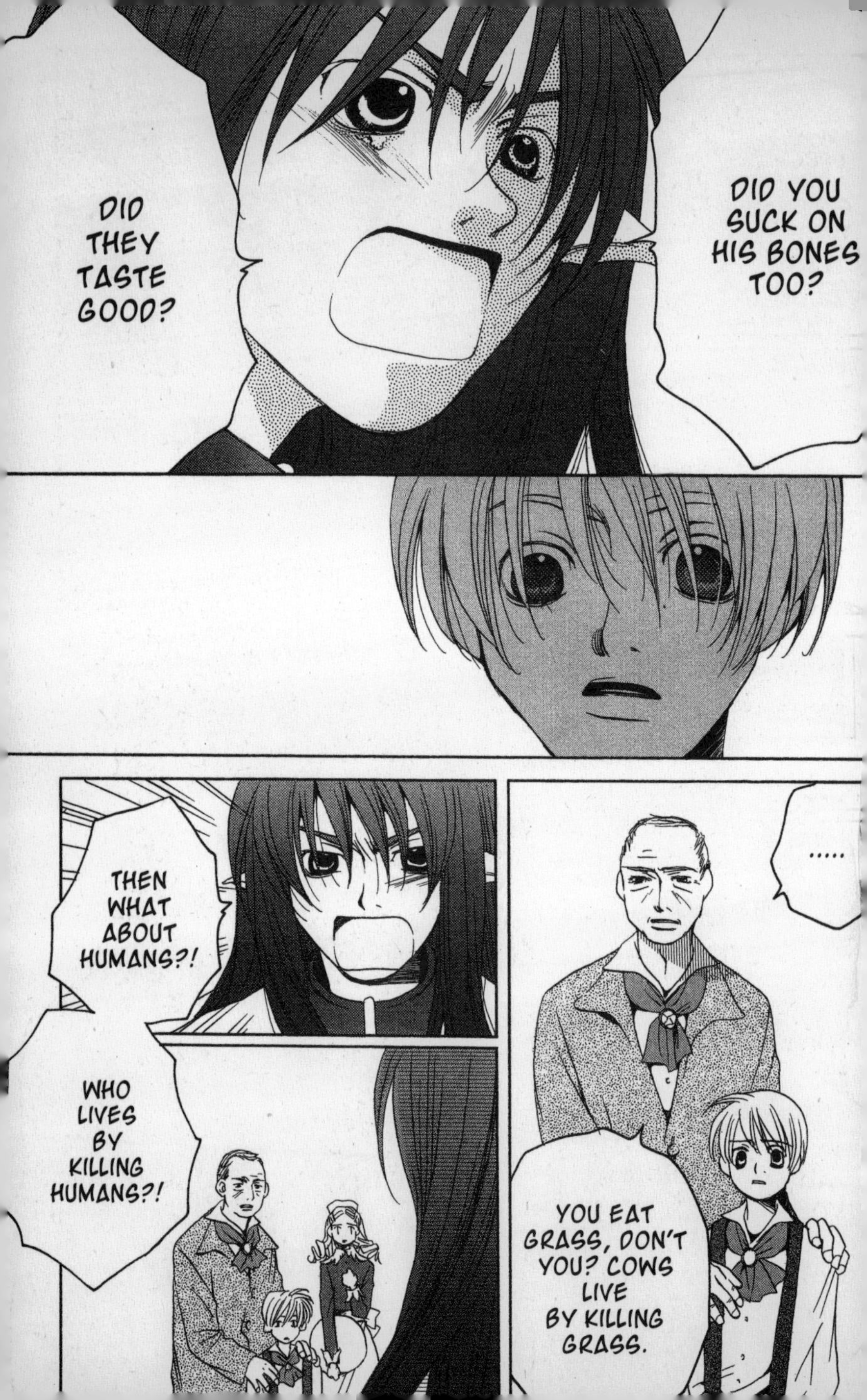
DID YOU SUCK ON HIS BONES TOO?
DID THEY TASTE GOOD?
.....
YOU EAT GRASS, DON'T YOU? COWS LIVE BY KILLING GRASS.
THEN WHAT ABOUT HUMANS?!
WHO LIVES BY KILLING HUMANS?!

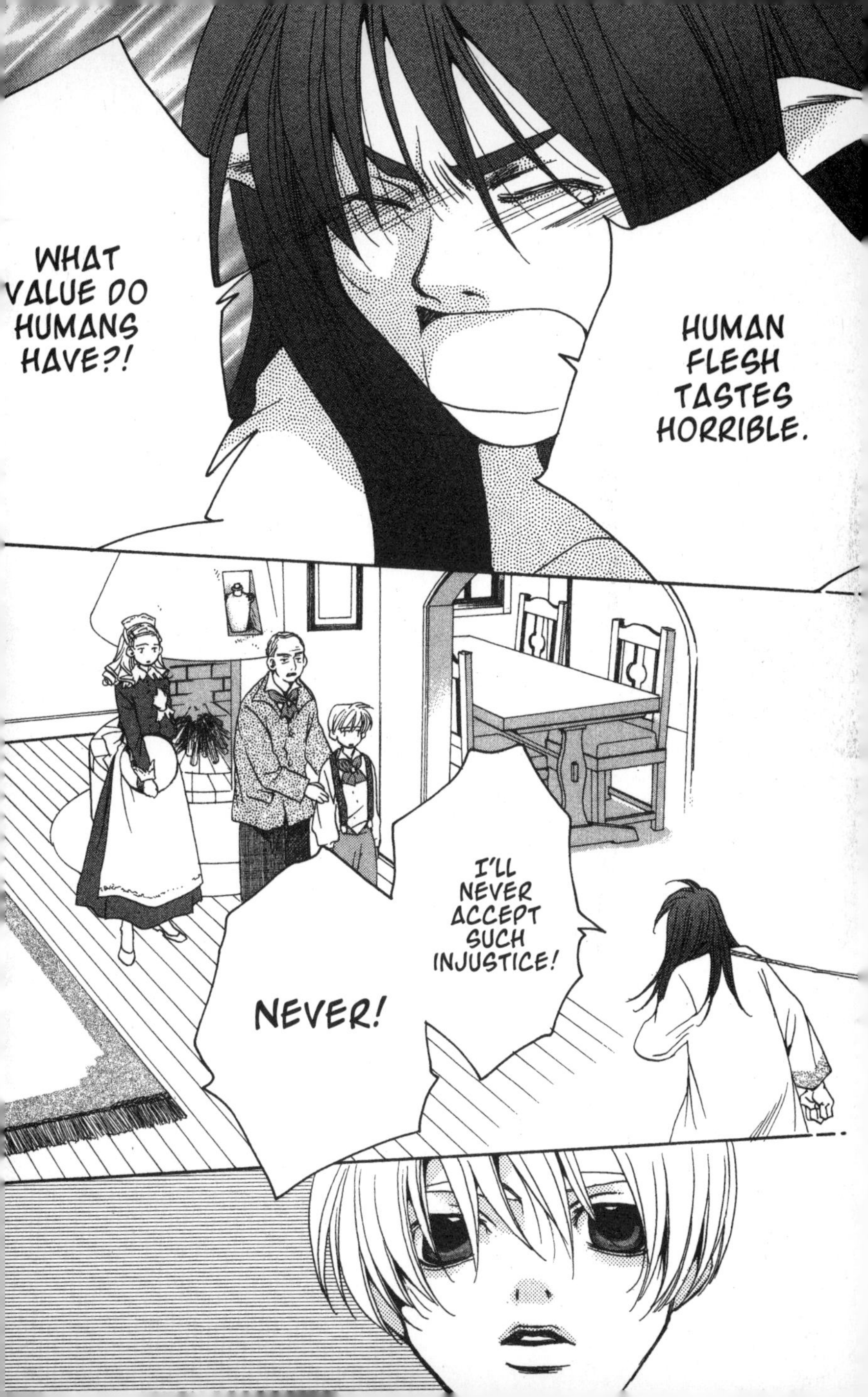
HUMAN FLESH TASTES HORRIBLE.
WHAT VALUE DO HUMANS HAVE?!
I'LL NEVER ACCEPT SUCH INJUSTICE!
NEVER!

HAVE
YOU EVER
HEARD
OF THE
BLACK
PLAGUE?

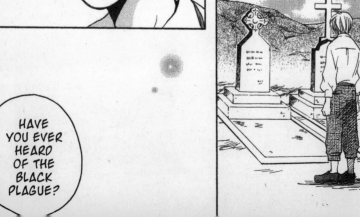

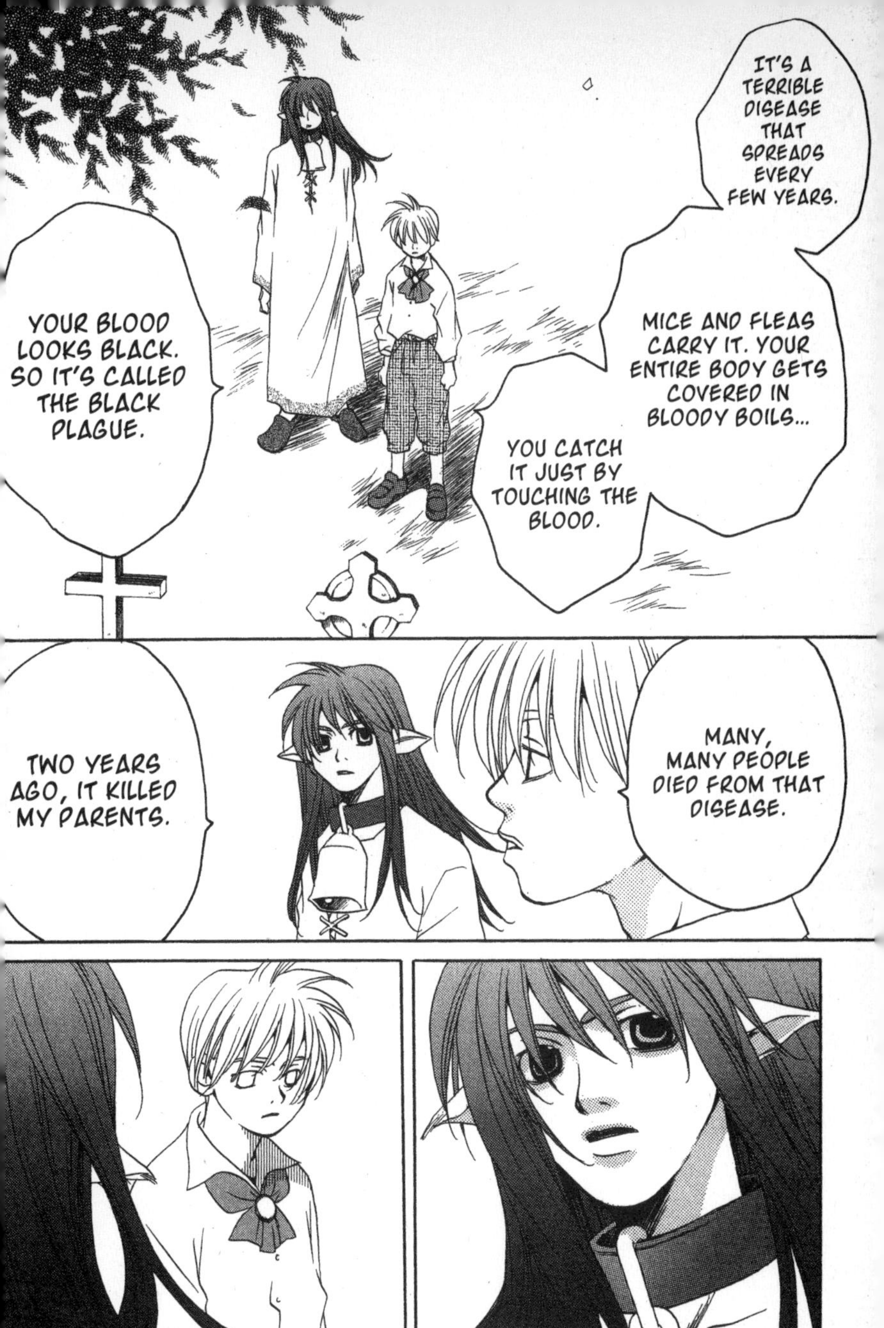
IT'S A TERRIBLE DISEASE THAT SPREADS EVERY FEW YEARS.
MICE AND FLEAS CARRY IT. YOUR ENTIRE BODY GETS COVERED IN BLOODY BOILS...
YOU CATCH IT JUST BY TOUCHING THE BLOOD.
YOUR BLOOD LOOKS BLACK. SO IT'S CALLED THE BLACK PLAGUE.
MANY, MANY PEOPLE DIED FROM THAT DISEASE.
TWO YEARS AGO, IT KILLED MY PARENTS.

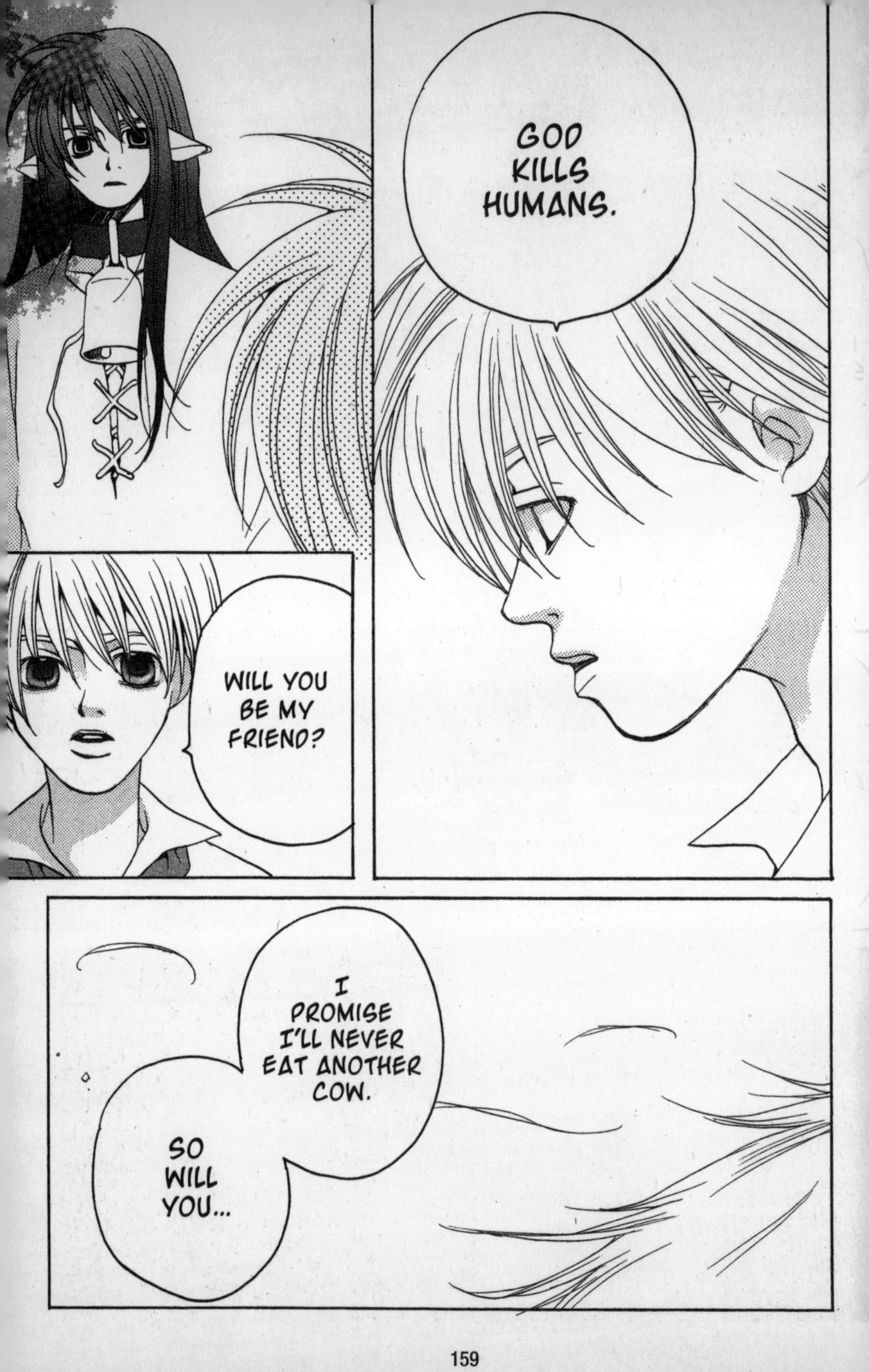
GOD KILLS HUMANS.
WILL YOU BE MY FRIEND?
I PROMISE I'LL NEVER EAT ANOTHER COW.
SO WILL YOU...

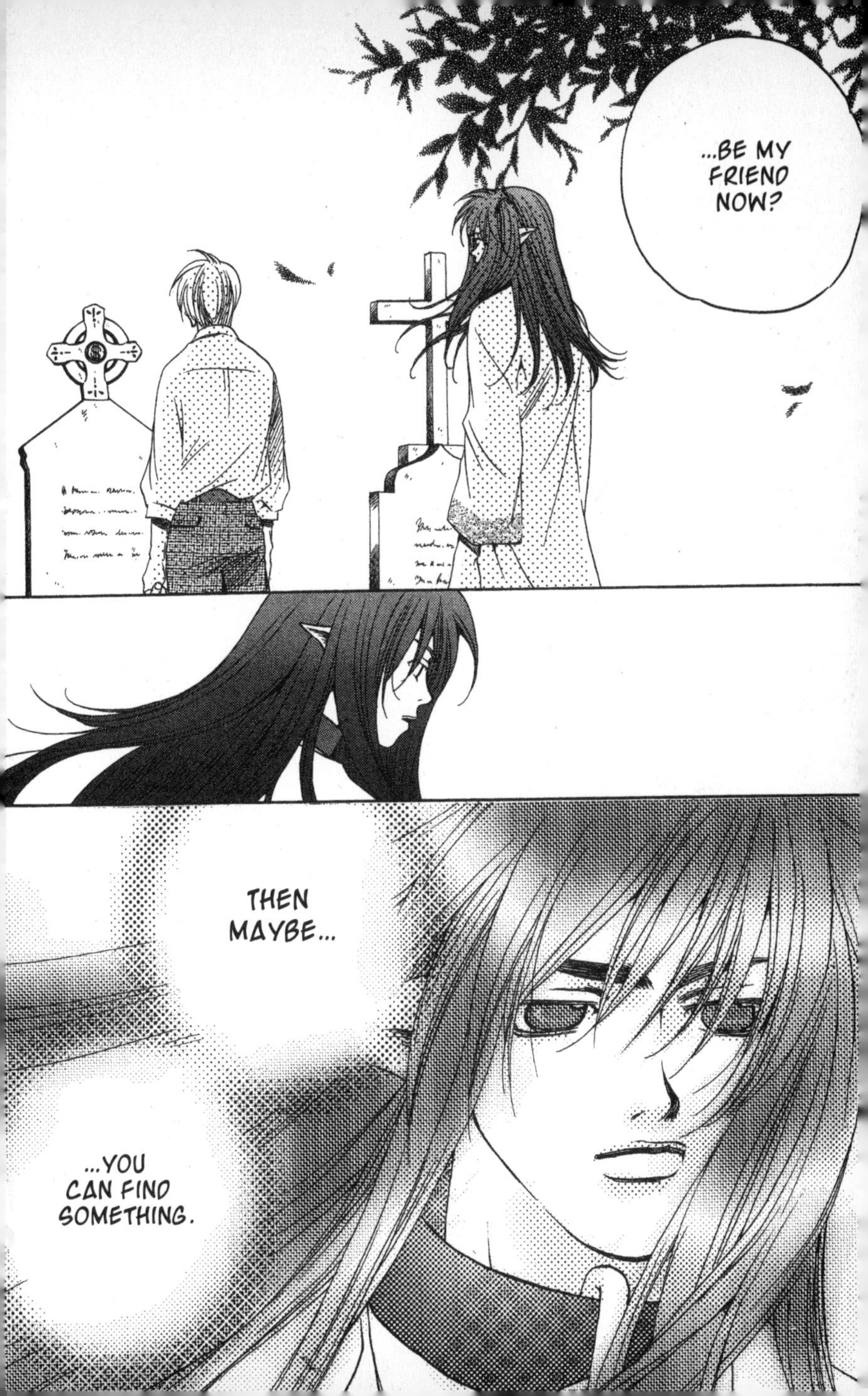
...BE MY FRIEND NOW?
THEN MAYBE...
...YOU CAN FIND SOMETHING.

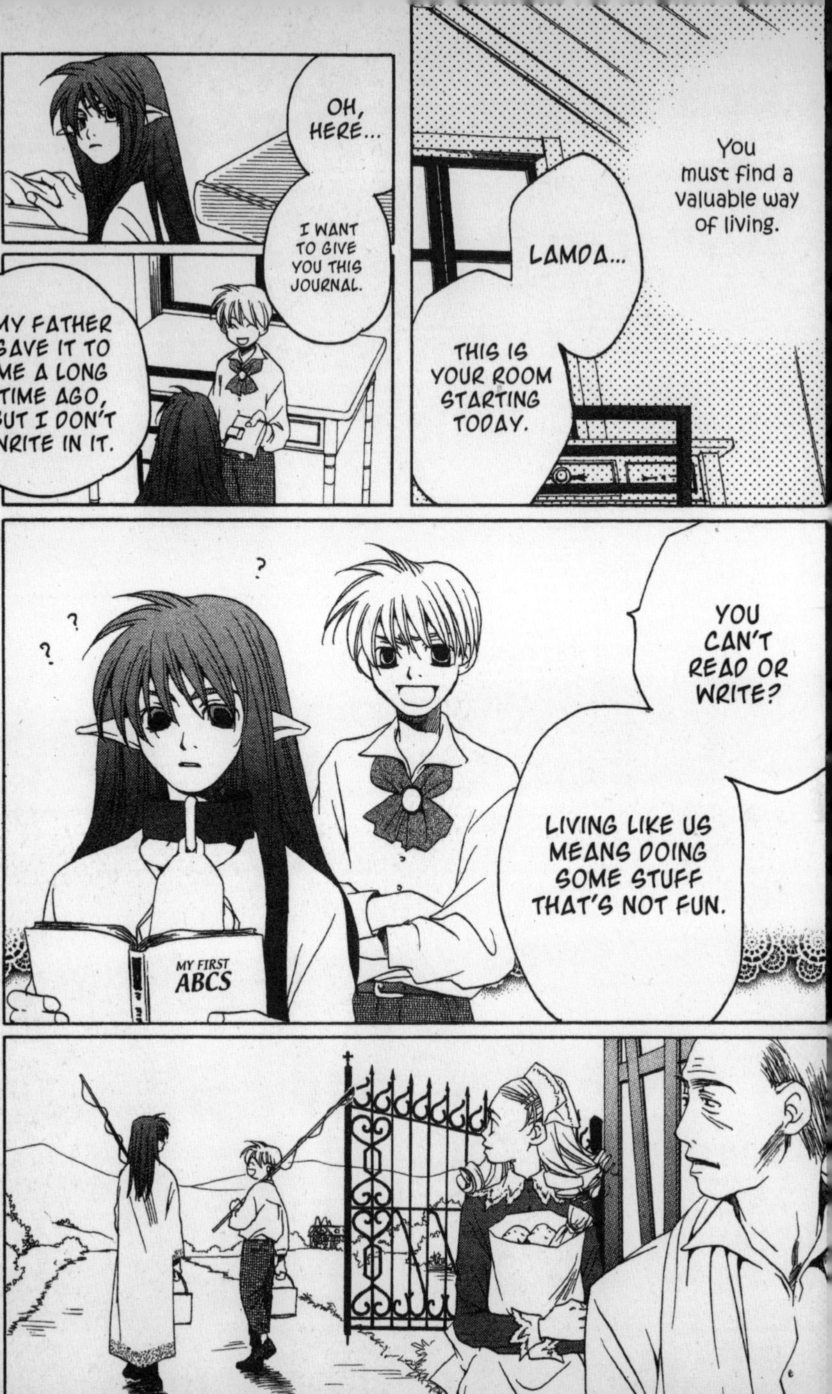
You must find a valuable way of living.
LAMDA...
THIS IS YOUR ROOM STARTING TODAY.
OH, HERE...
I WANT TO GIVE YOU THIS JOURNAL.
MY FATHER GAVE IT TO ME A LONG TIME AGO, BUT I DON'T WRITE IN IT.
YOU CAN'T READ OR WRITE?
LIVING LIKE US MEANS DOING SOME STUFF THAT'S NOT FUN.
?
?
?
MY FIRST ABCS

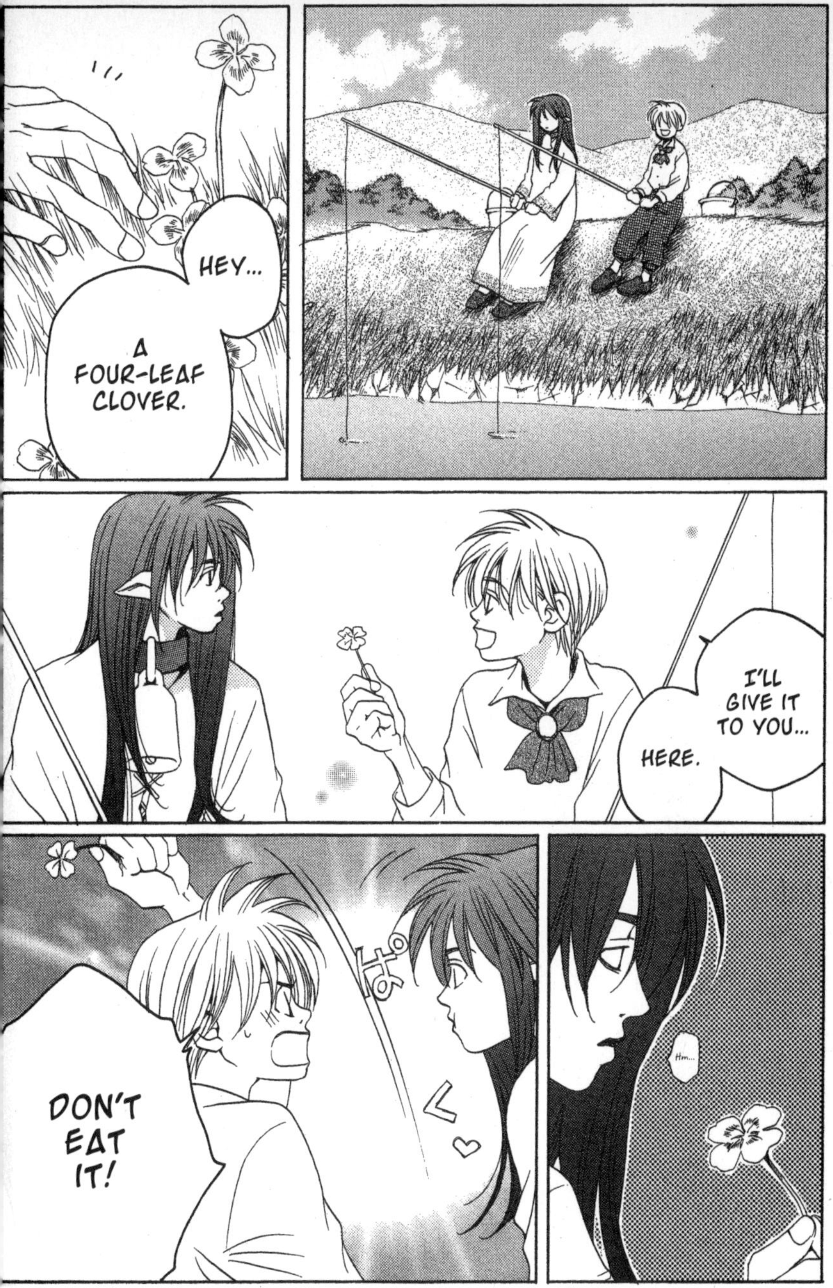
HEY...
A FOUR-LEAF CLOVER.
I'LL GIVE IT TO YOU...
HERE.
Hm...
ぱ
く
DON'T EAT IT!

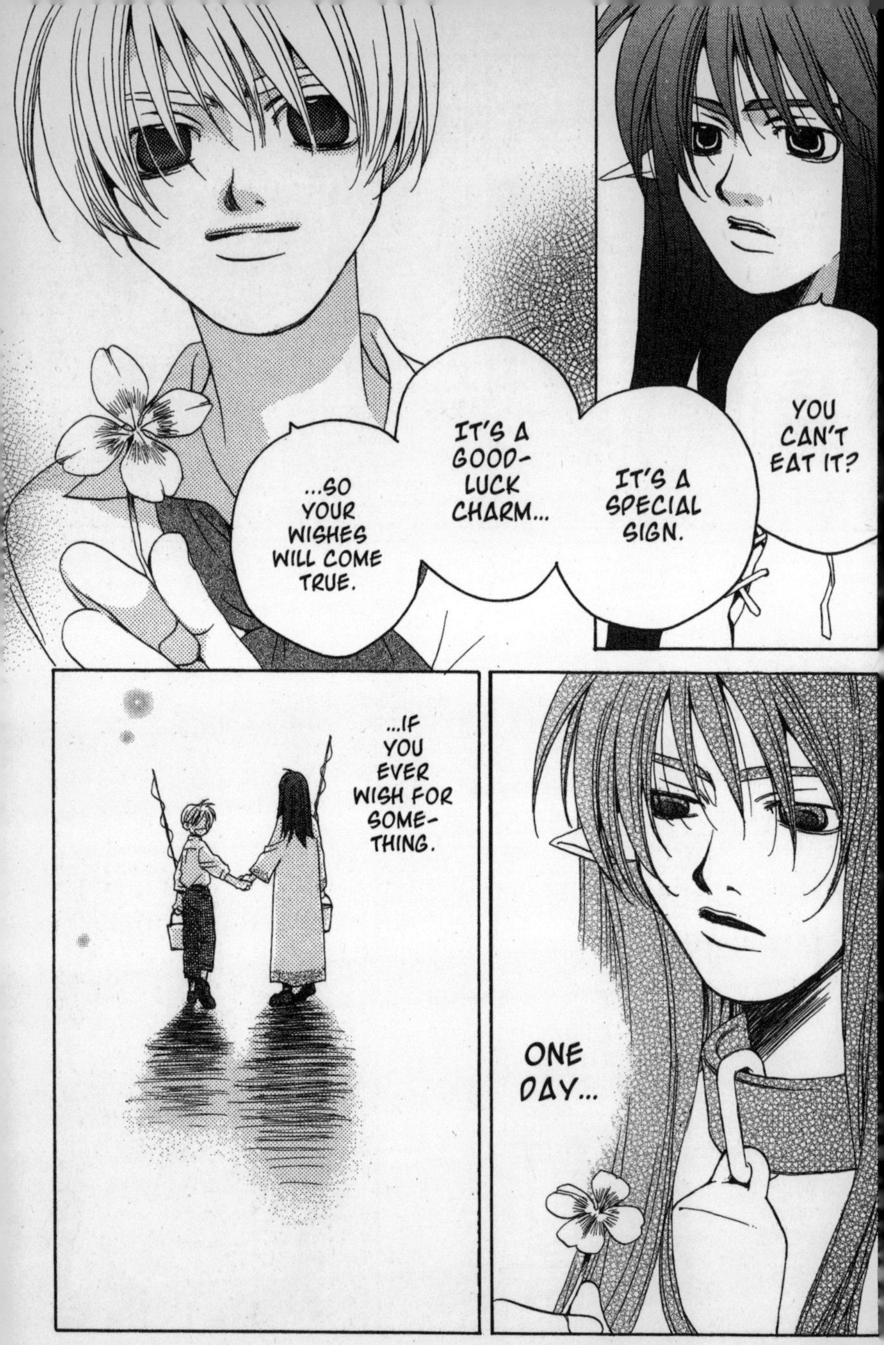
YOU CAN'T EAT IT?
IT'S A SPECIAL SIGN.
IT'S A GOOD-LUCK CHARM...
...SO YOUR WISHES WILL COME TRUE.
ONE DAY...
...IF YOU EVER WISH FOR SOMETHING.

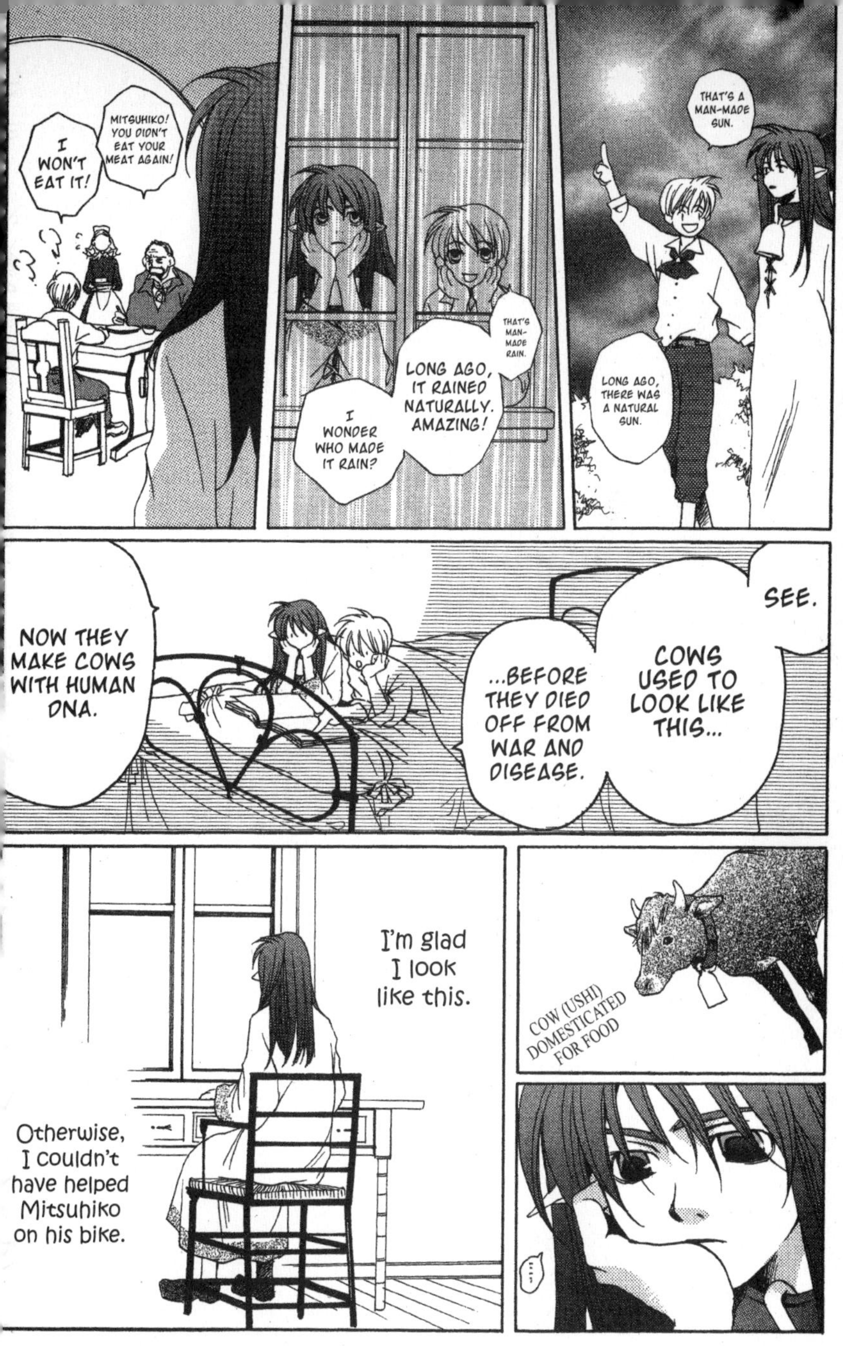
THAT'S A MAN-MADE SUN.
LONG AGO, THERE WAS A NATURAL SUN.
THAT'S MAN-MADE RAIN.
LONG AGO, IT RAINED NATURALLY. AMAZING!
I WONDER WHO MADE IT RAIN?
MITSUHIKO! YOU DIDN'T EAT YOUR MEAT AGAIN!
I WON'T EAT IT!
SEE.
COWS USED TO LOOK LIKE THIS...
...BEFORE THEY DIED OFF FROM WAR AND DISEASE.
NOW THEY MAKE COWS WITH HUMAN DNA.
COW (USHI) DOMESTICATED FOR FOOD
...
I'm glad I look like this.
Otherwise, I couldn't have helped Mitsuhiko on his bike.

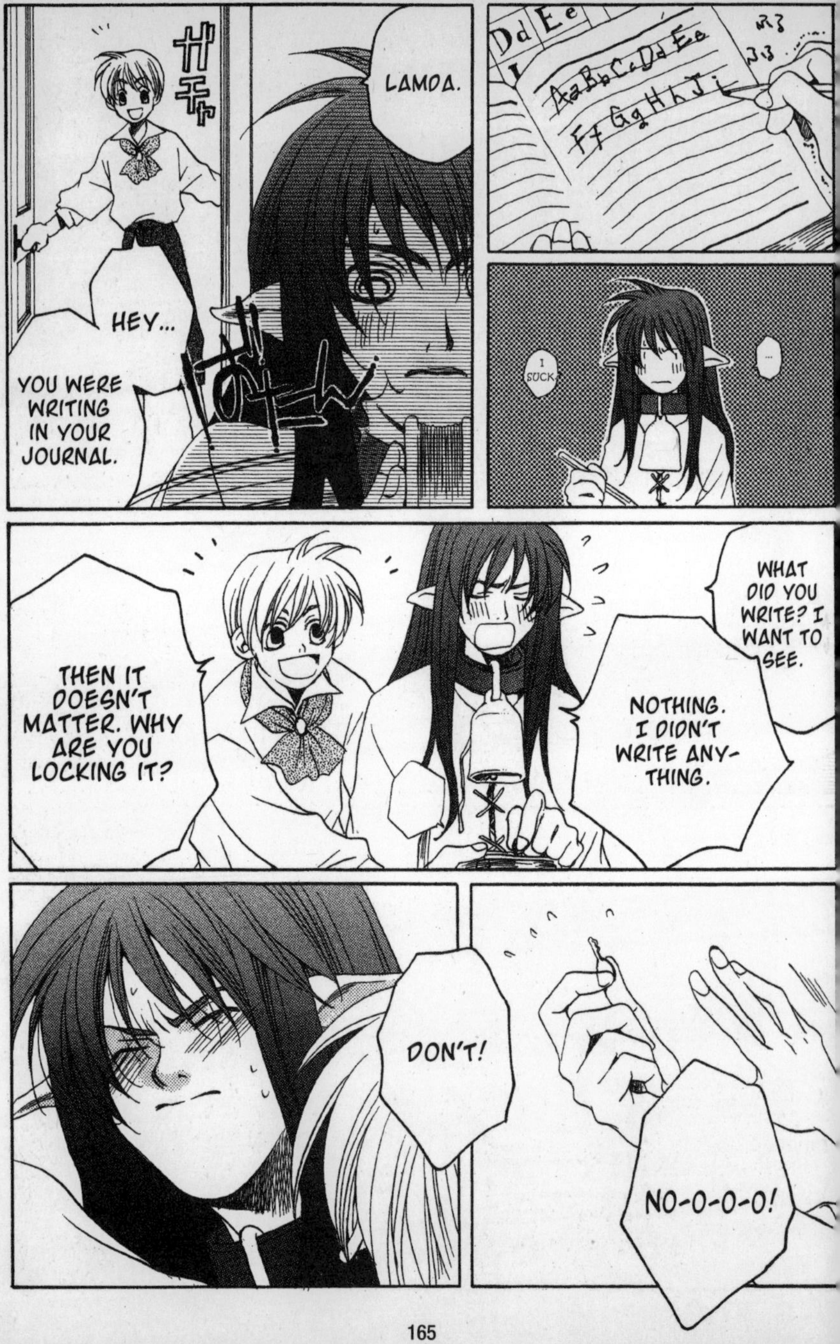
...
I SUCK
LAMDA.
ガチャ
HEY...
YOU WERE WRITING IN YOUR JOURNAL.
WHAT DID YOU WRITE? I WANT TO SEE.
NOTHING. I DIDN'T WRITE ANYTHING.
THEN IT DOESN'T MATTER. WHY ARE YOU LOCKING IT?
NO-O-O-O!
DON'T!

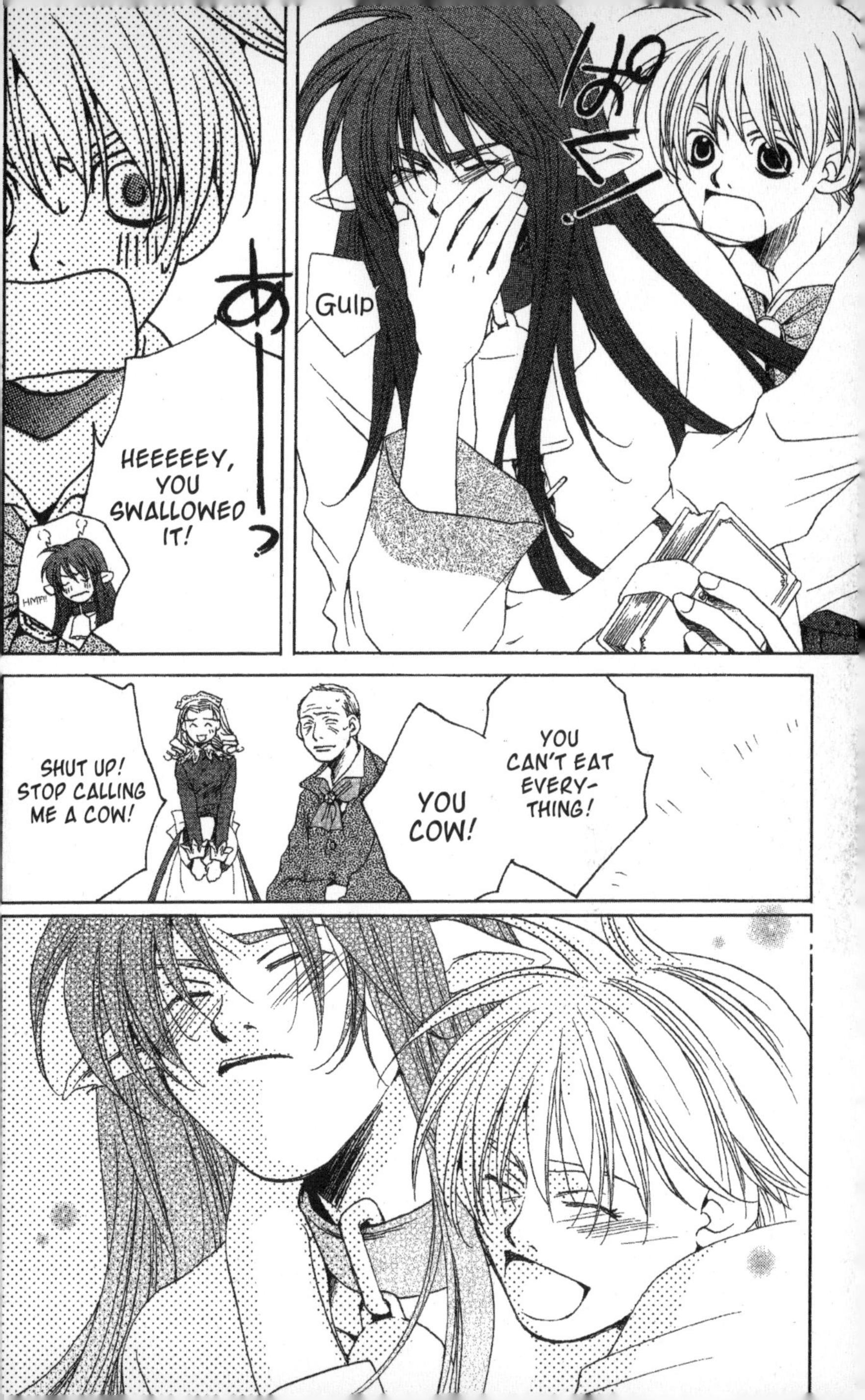
Gulp
あー!?
HEEEEEY, YOU SWALLOWED IT!
HMF!!
YOU CAN'T EAT EVERY-THING!
YOU COW!
SHUT UP! STOP CALLING ME A COW!

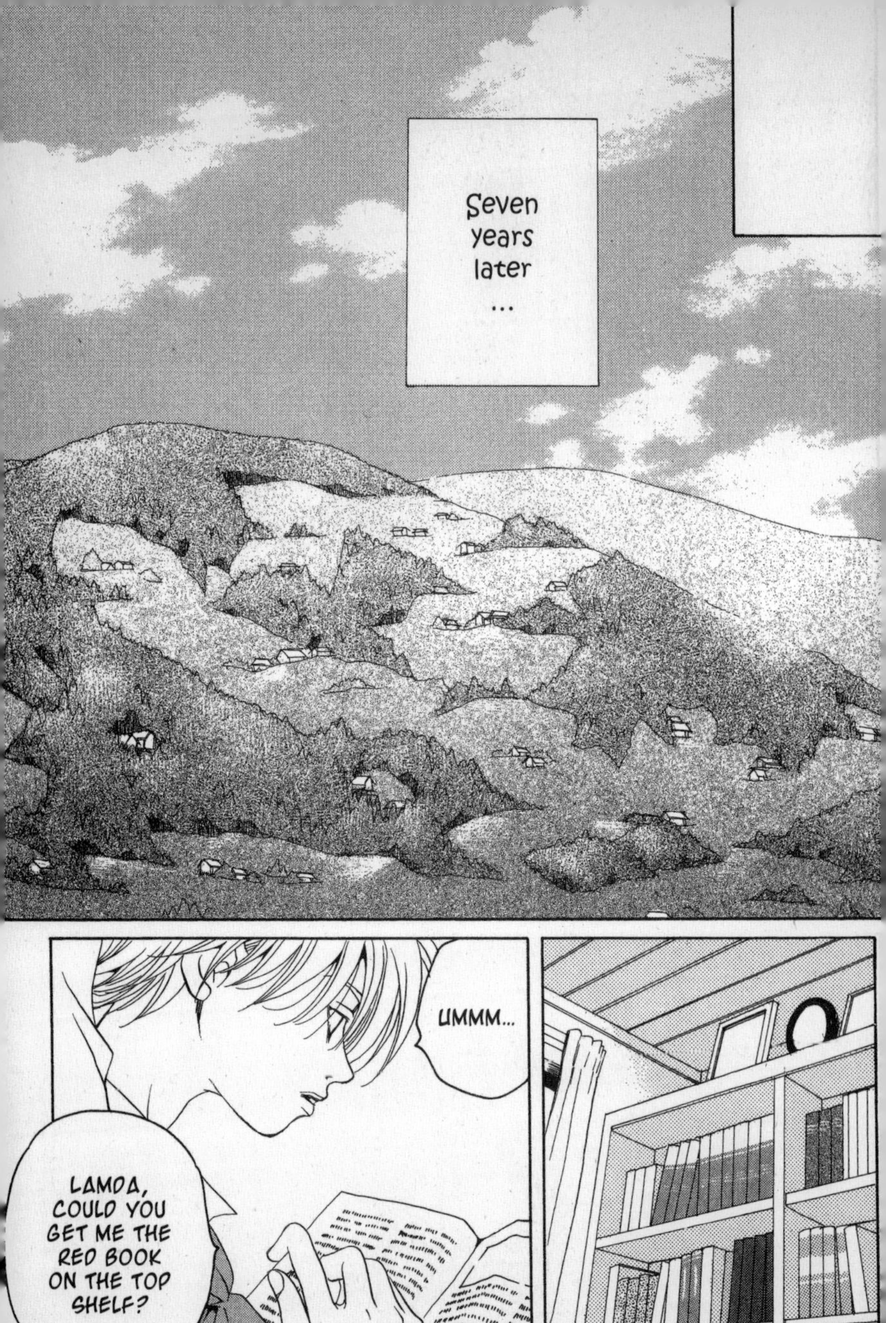
Seven years later ...
UMMM...
LAMDA, COULD YOU GET ME THE RED BOOK ON THE TOP SHELF?

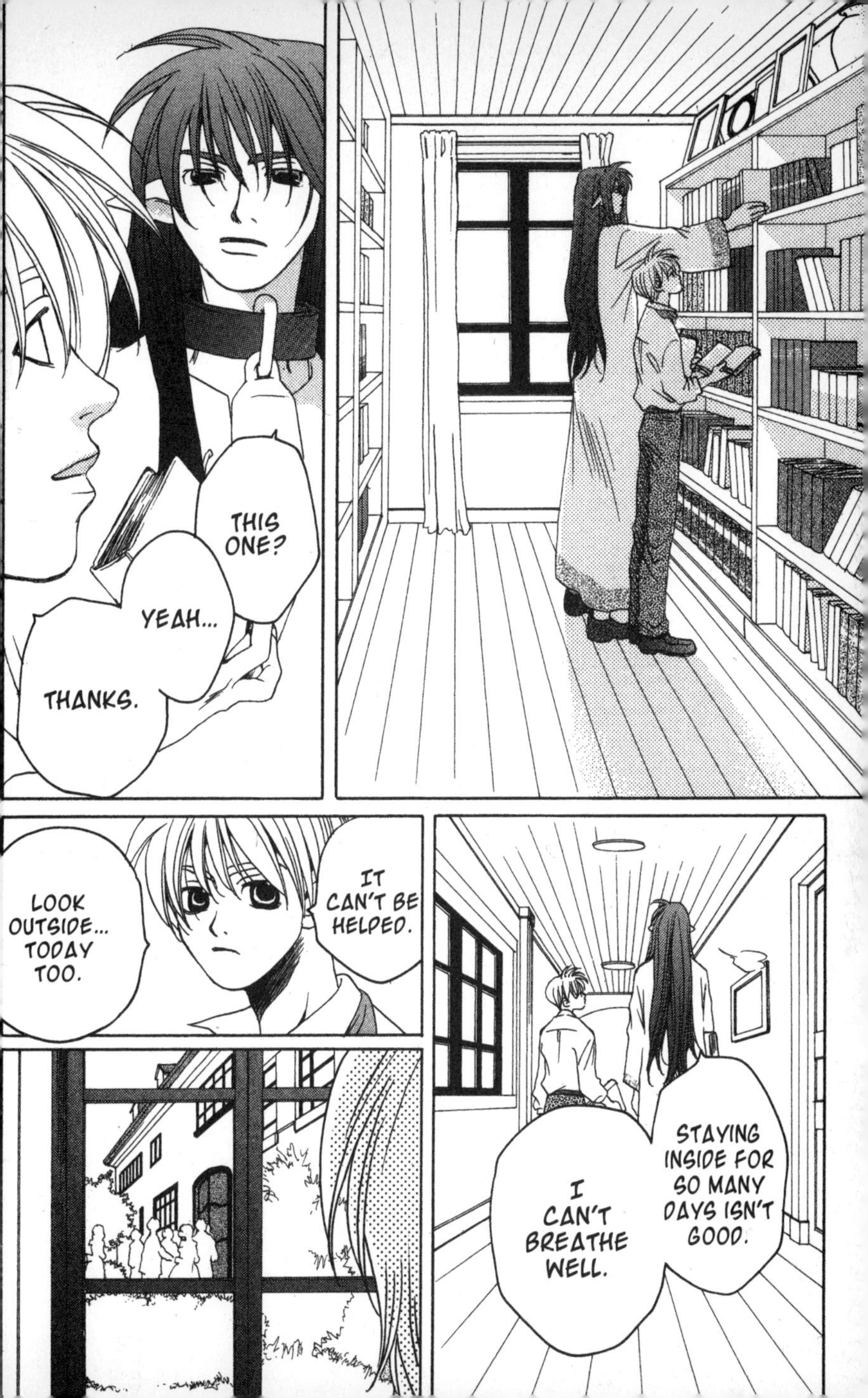
THIS ONE?
YEAH...
THANKS.
STAYING INSIDE FOR SO MANY DAYS ISN'T GOOD.
I CAN'T BREATHE WELL.
IT CAN'T BE HELPED.
LOOK OUTSIDE... TODAY TOO.

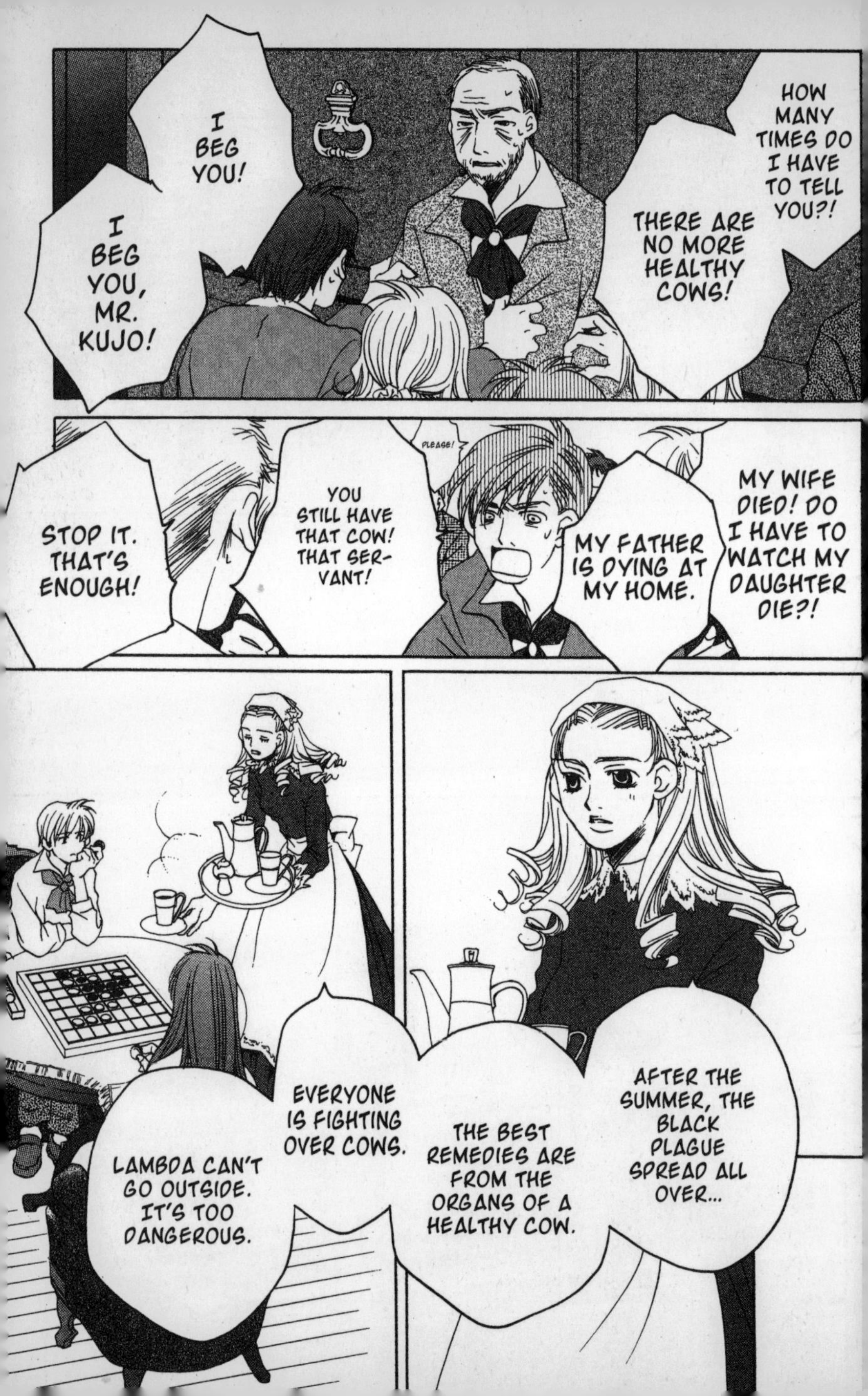
HOW MANY TIMES DO I HAVE TO TELL YOU?!
THERE ARE NO MORE HEALTHY COWS!
I BEG YOU!
I BEG YOU, MR. KUJO!
MY WIFE DIED! DO I HAVE TO WATCH MY DAUGHTER DIE?!
MY FATHER IS DYING AT MY HOME.
PLEASE!
YOU STILL HAVE THAT COW! THAT SER-VANT!
STOP IT. THAT'S ENOUGH!
AFTER THE SUMMER, THE BLACK PLAGUE SPREAD ALL OVER...
THE BEST REMEDIES ARE FROM THE ORGANS OF A HEALTHY COW.
EVERYONE IS FIGHTING OVER COWS.
LAMBDA CAN'T GO OUTSIDE. IT'S TOO DANGEROUS.

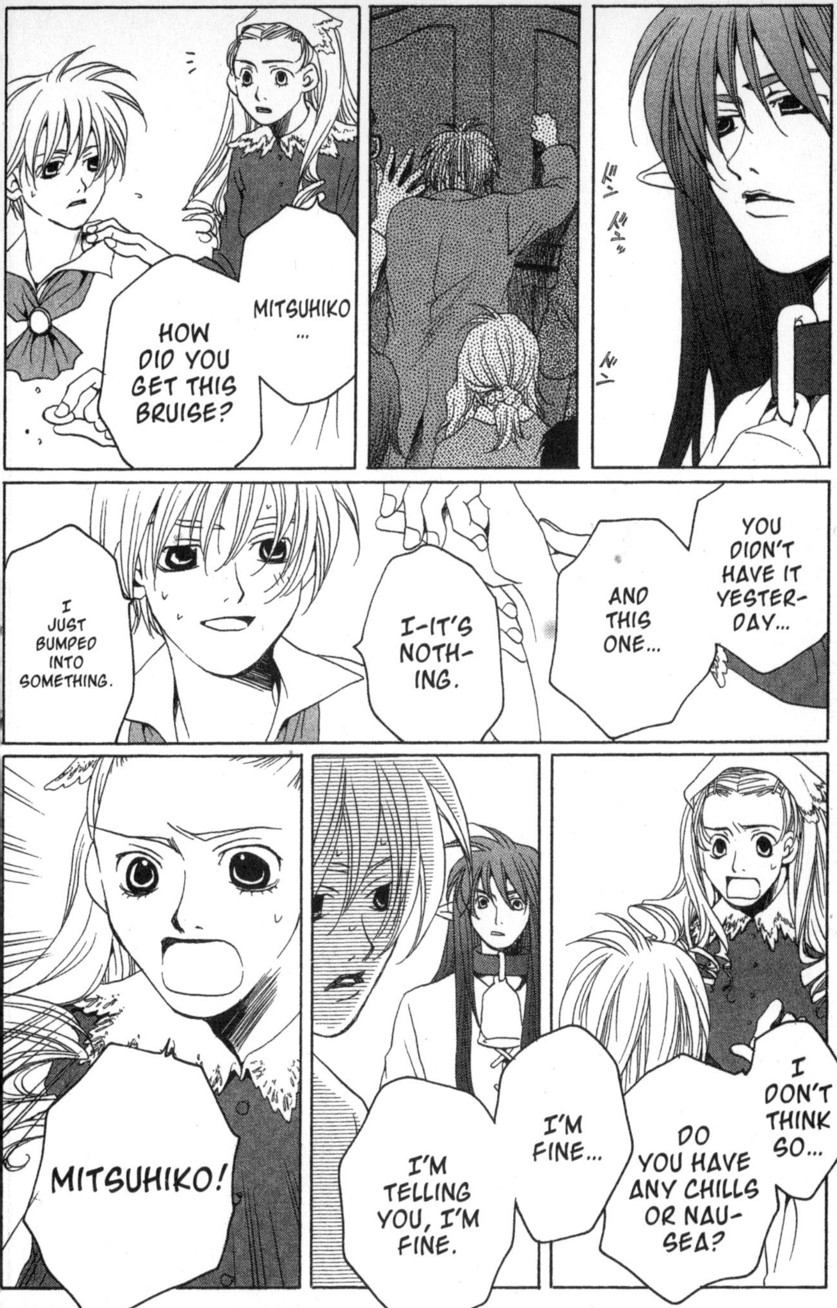
MITSUHIKO ...
HOW DID YOU GET THIS BRUISE?
YOU DIDN'T HAVE IT YESTERDAY...
AND THIS ONE...
I-IT'S NOTHING.
I JUST BUMPED INTO SOMETHING.
I DON'T THINK SO...
DO YOU HAVE ANY CHILLS OR NAUSEA?
I'M FINE...
I'M TELLING YOU, I'M FINE.
MITSUHIKO!

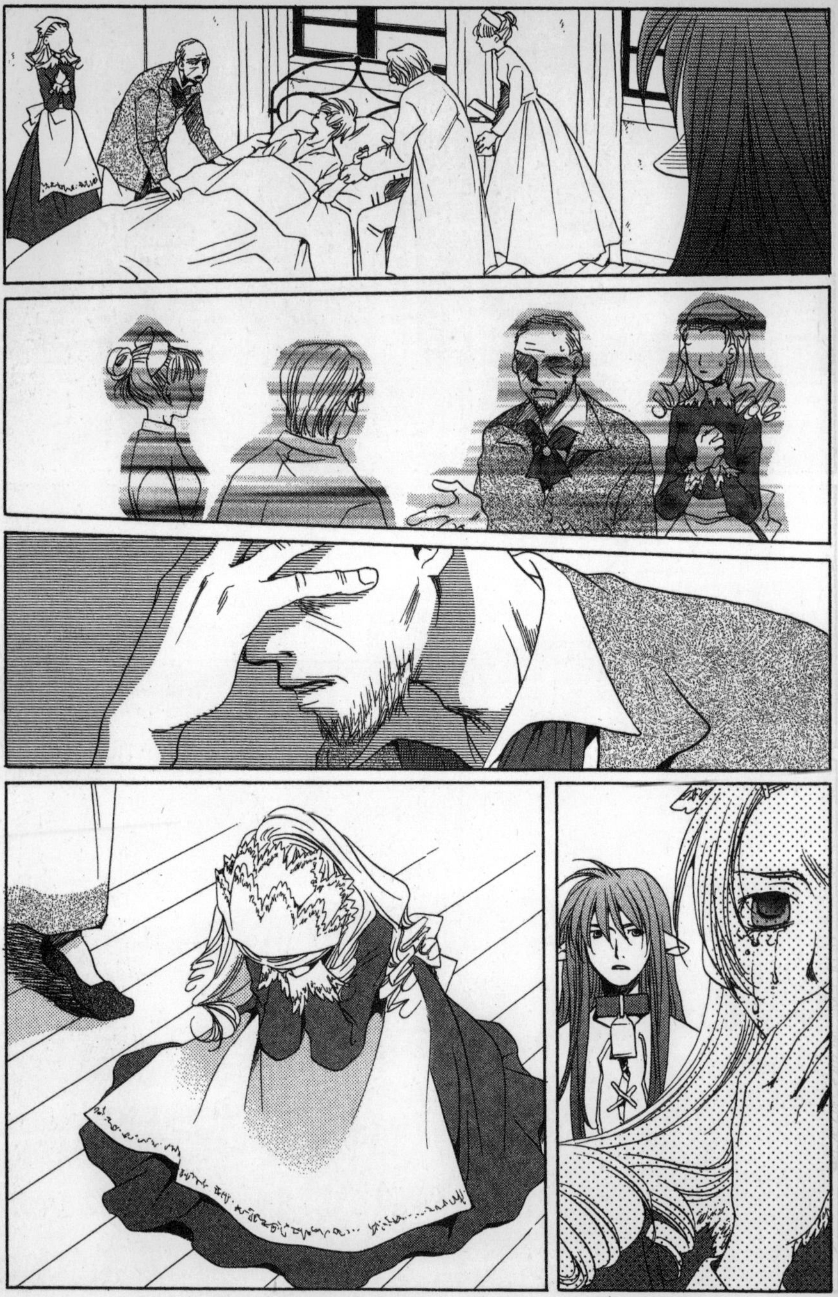

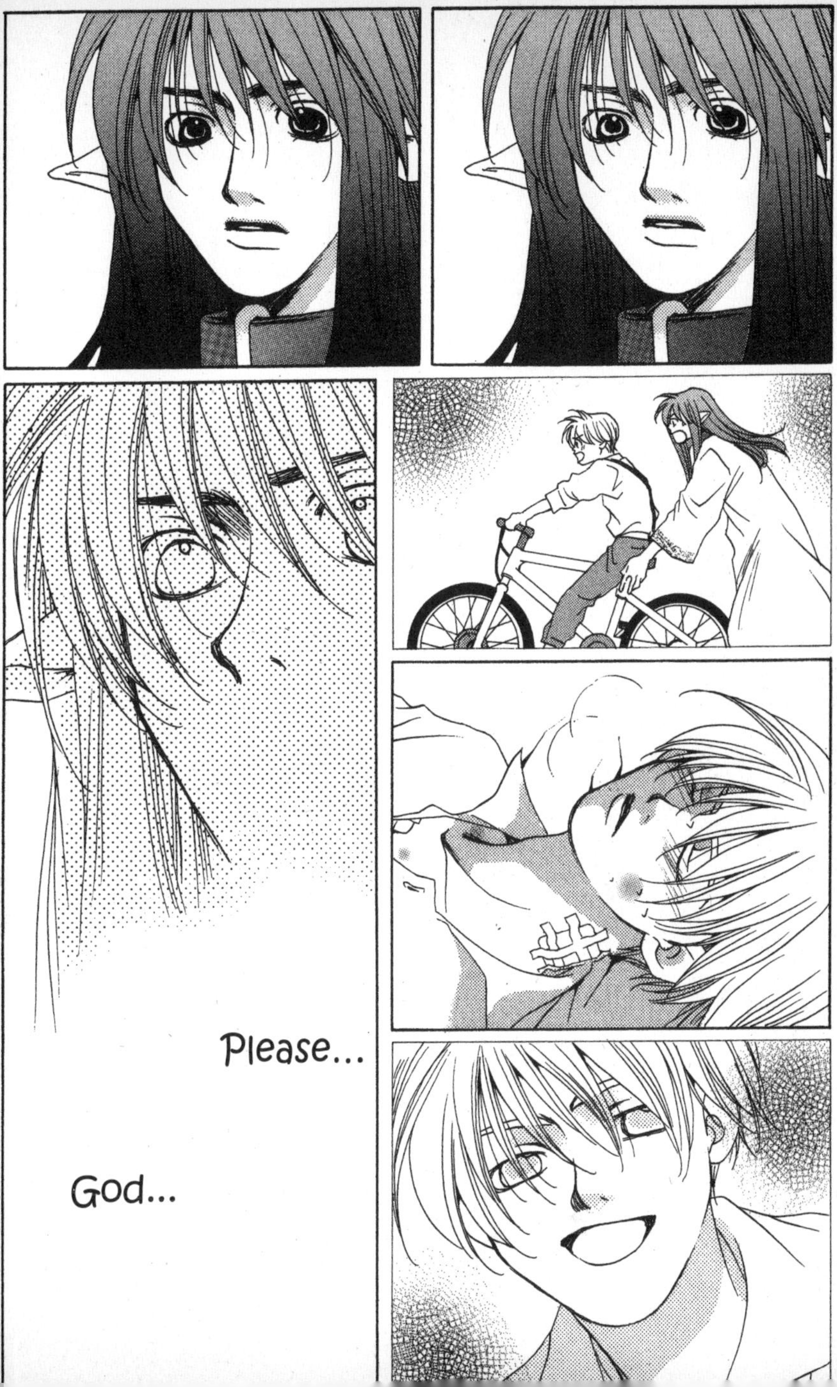
Please...
God...

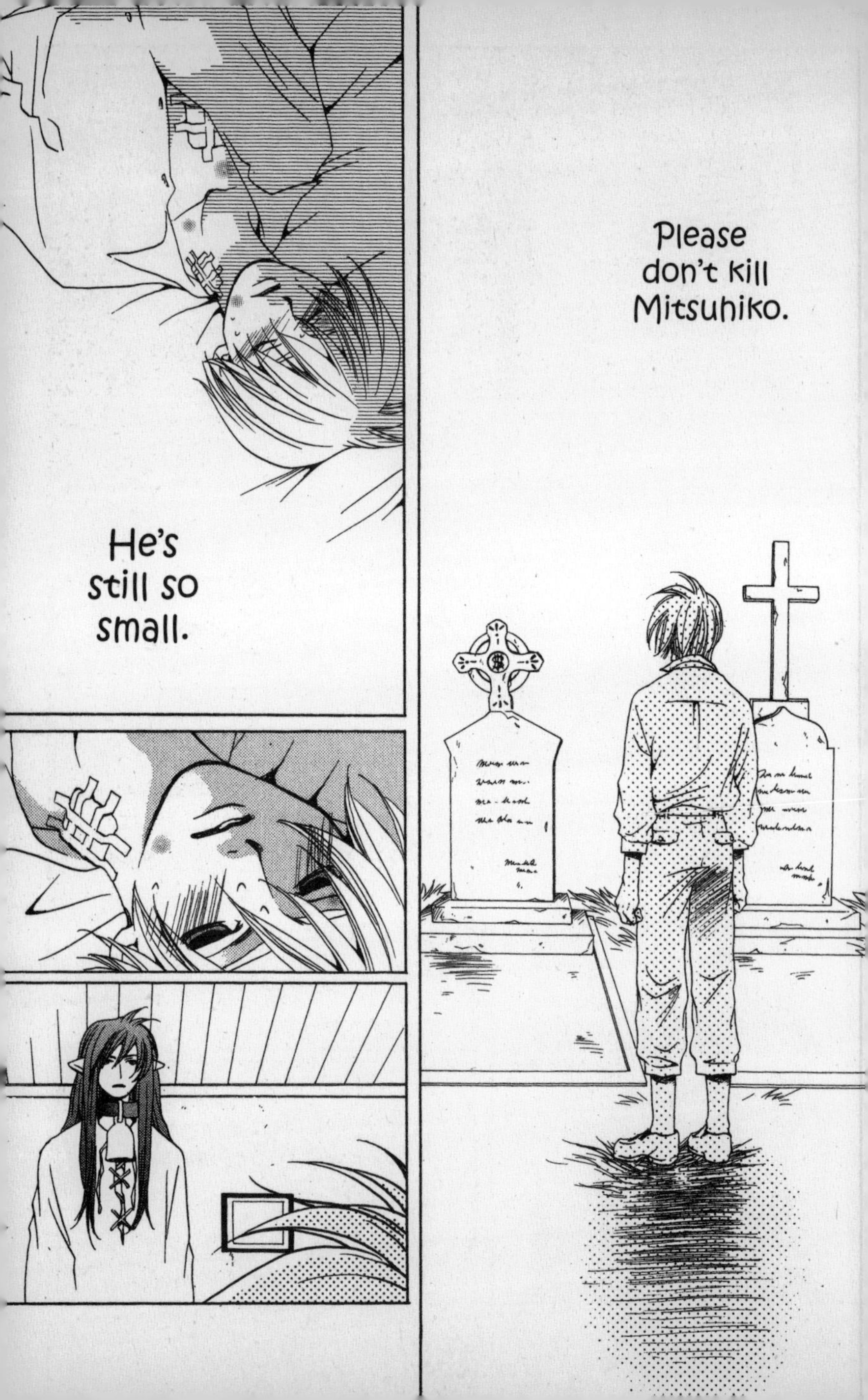
Please don't kill Mitsuhiko.
He's still so small.

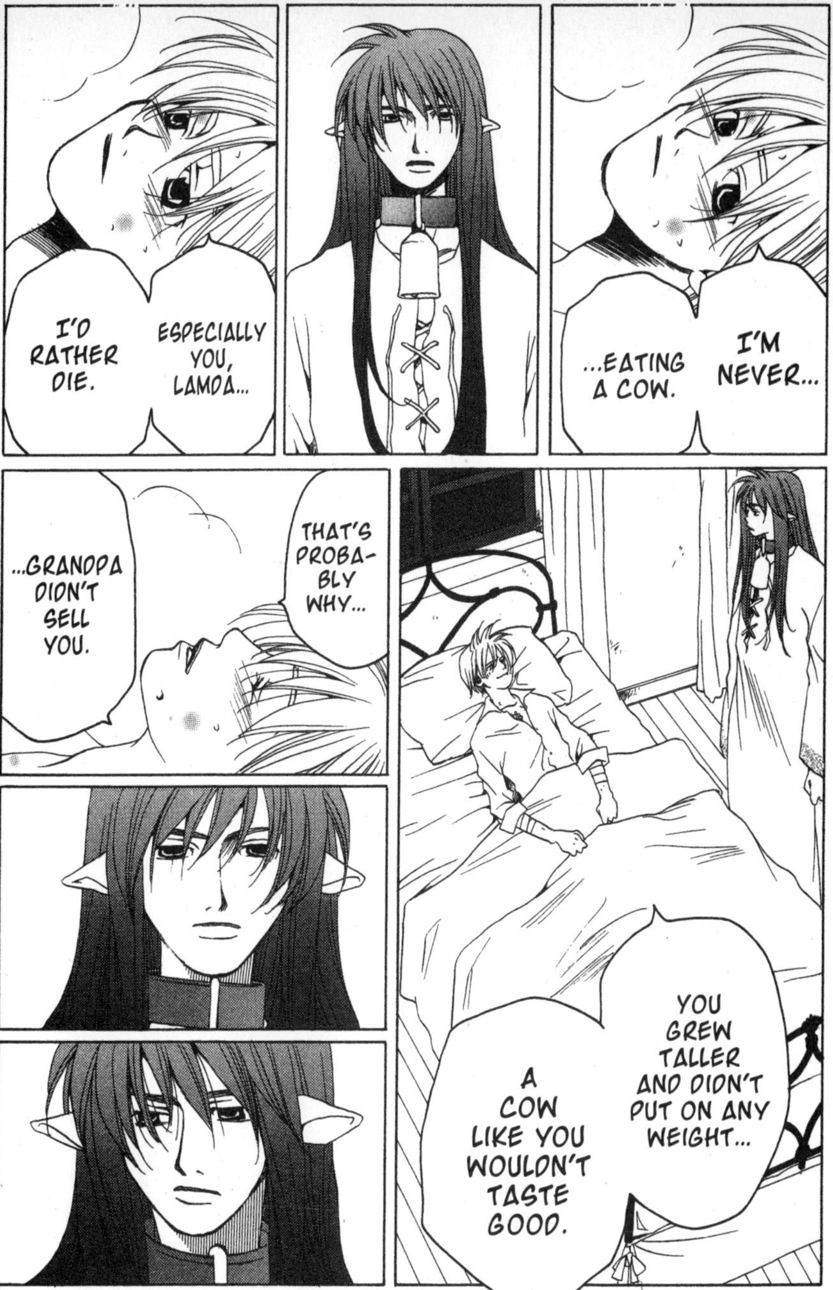
I'M NEVER...
...EATING A COW.
ESPECIALLY YOU, LAMDA...
I'D RATHER DIE.
YOU GREW TALLER AND DIDN'T PUT ON ANY WEIGHT...
A COW LIKE YOU WOULDN'T TASTE GOOD.
THAT'S PROBA-BLY WHY...
...GRANDPA DIDN'T SELL YOU.

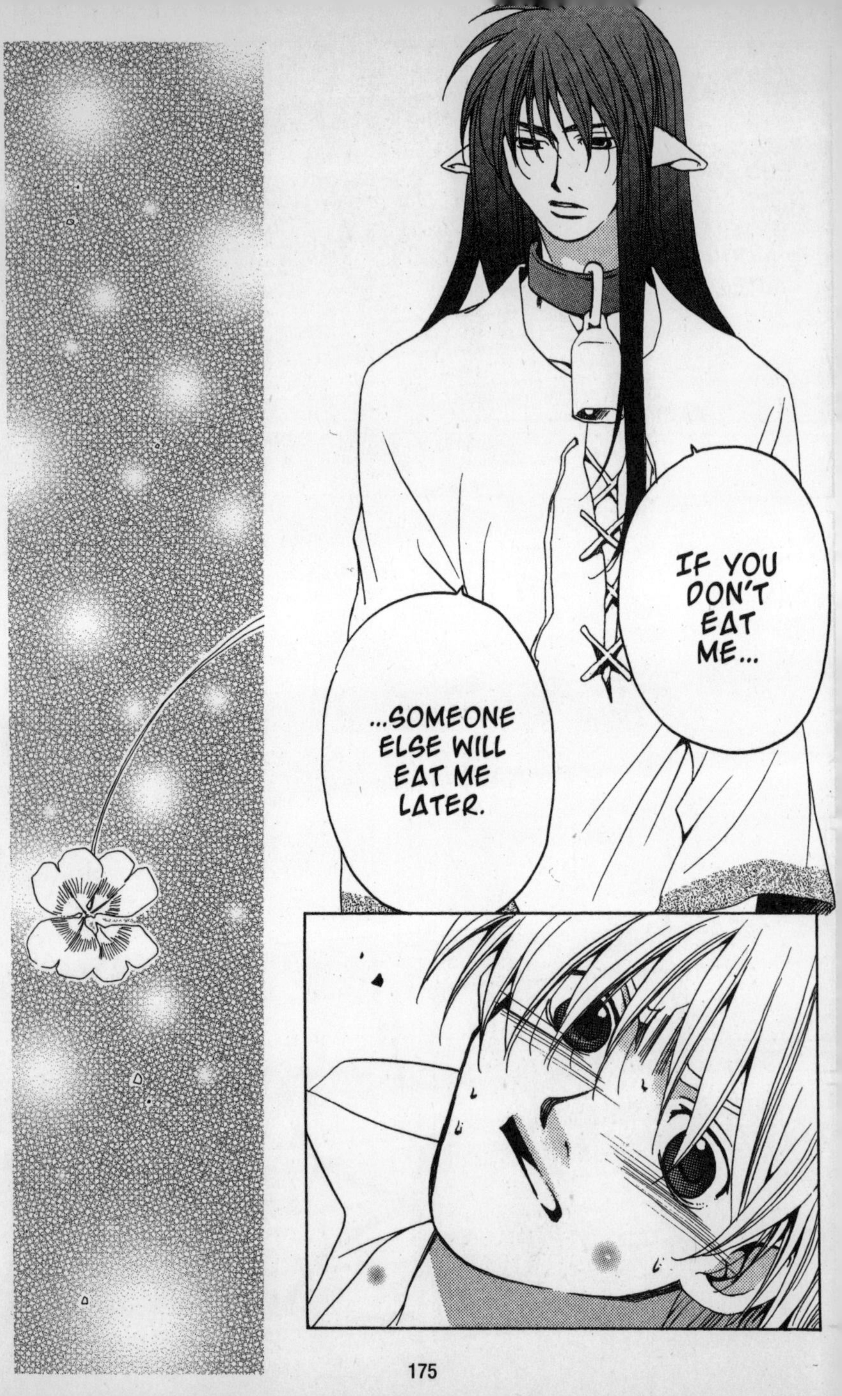
IF YOU DON'T EAT ME...
...SOMEONE ELSE WILL EAT ME LATER.

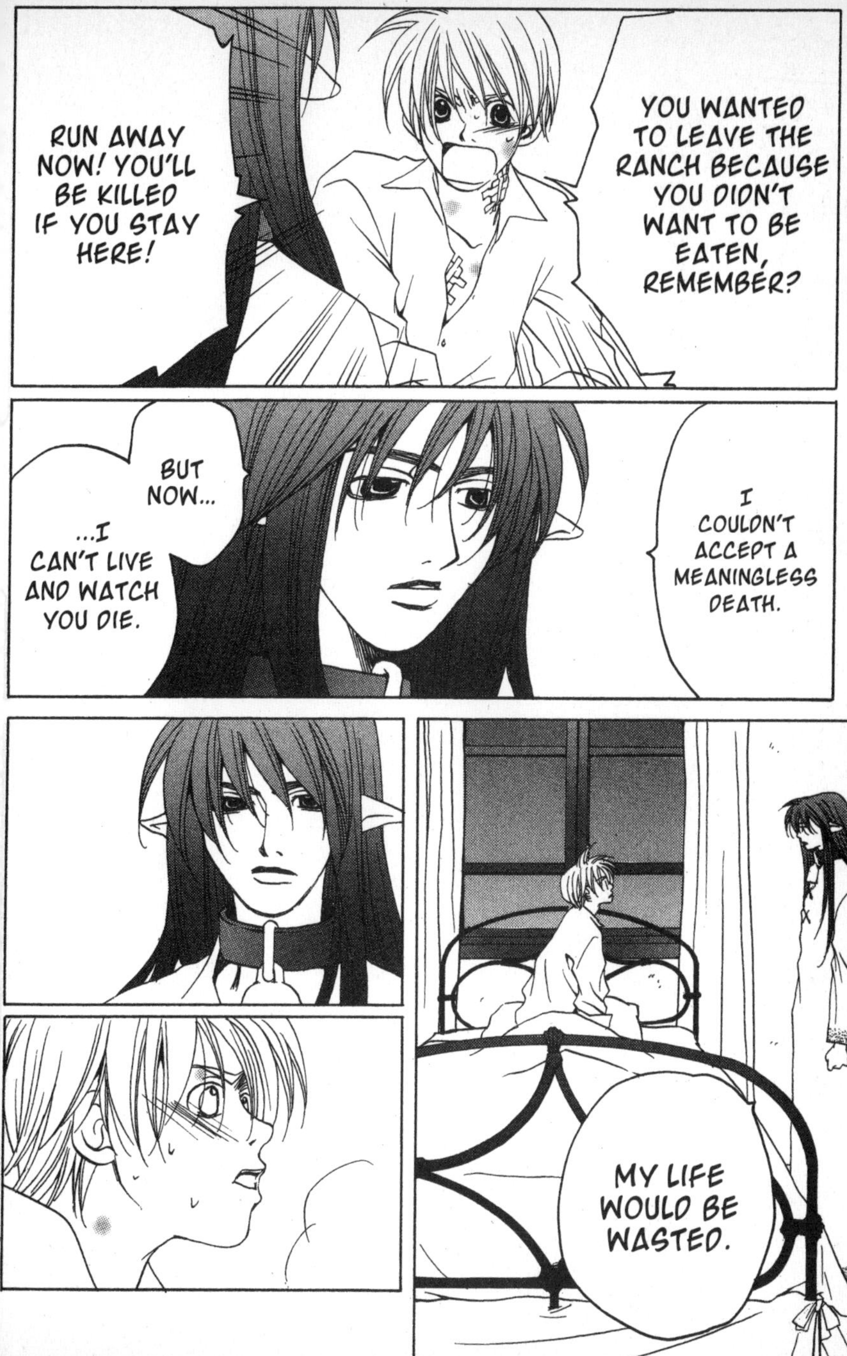
YOU WANTED TO LEAVE THE RANCH BECAUSE YOU DIDN'T WANT TO BE EATEN, REMEMBER?
RUN AWAY NOW! YOU'LL BE KILLED IF YOU STAY HERE!
I COULDN'T ACCEPT A MEANINGLESS DEATH.
BUT NOW...
...I CAN'T LIVE AND WATCH YOU DIE.
MY LIFE WOULD BE WASTED.

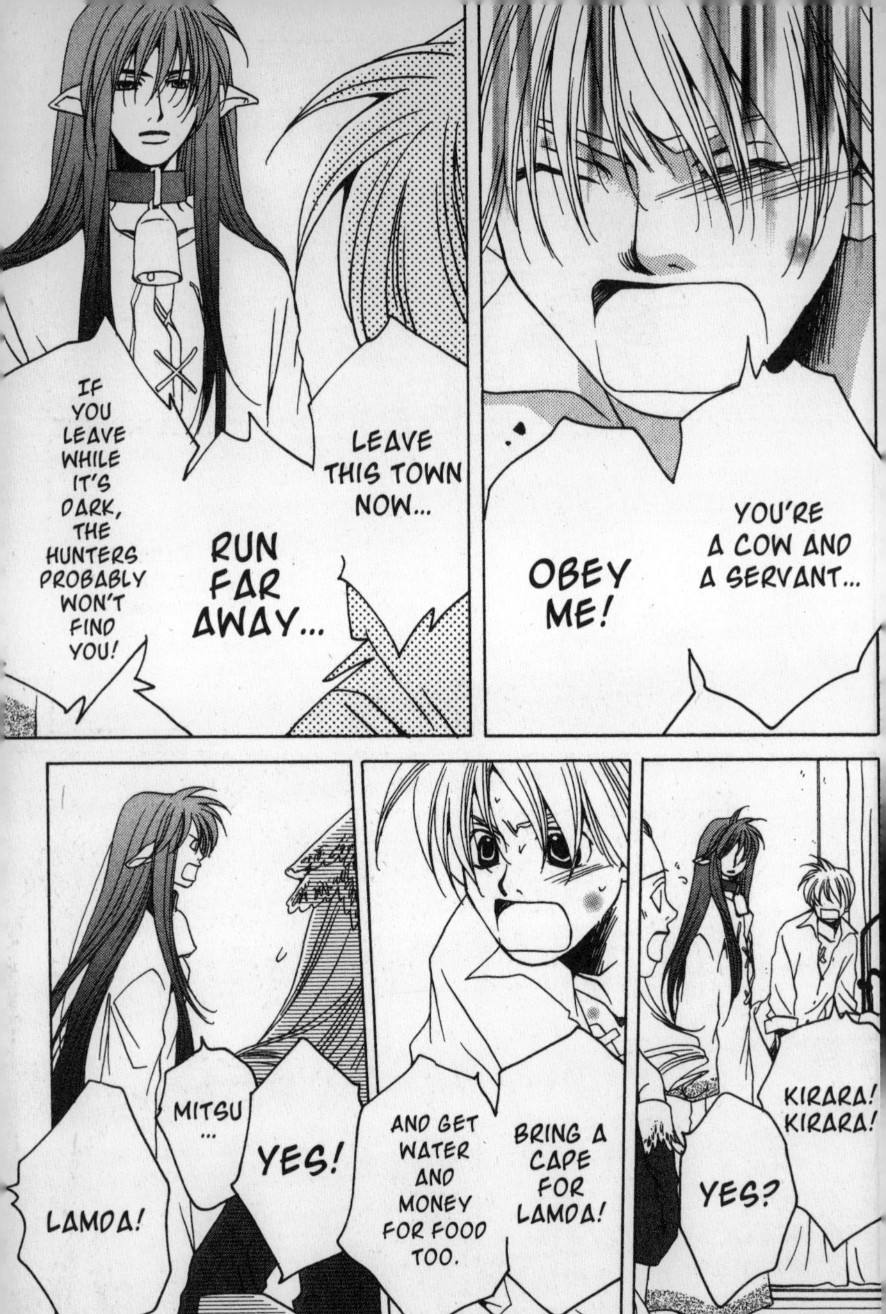
YOU'RE A COW AND A SERVANT...
OBEY ME!
LEAVE THIS TOWN NOW...
RUN FAR AWAY...
IF YOU LEAVE WHILE IT'S DARK, THE HUNTERS PROBABLY WON'T FIND YOU!
KIRARA! KIRARA!
YES?
BRING A CAPE FOR LAMDA!
AND GET WATER AND MONEY FOR FOOD TOO.
YES!
MITSU...
LAMDA!

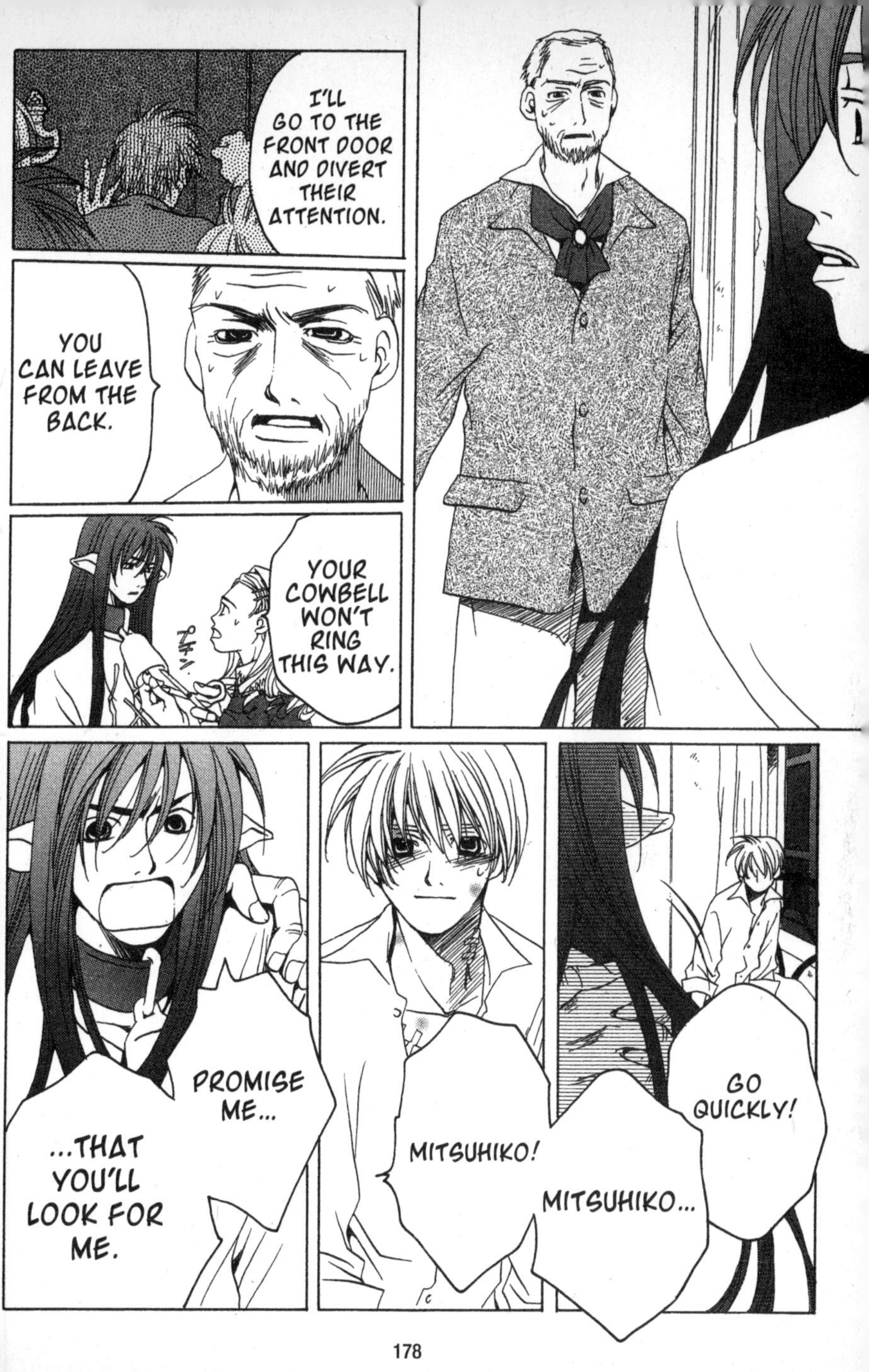
I'LL GO TO THE FRONT DOOR AND DIVERT THEIR ATTENTION.
YOU CAN LEAVE FROM THE BACK.
YOUR COWBELL WON'T RING THIS WAY.
GO QUICKLY!
MITSUHIKO...
MITSUHIKO!
PROMISE ME...
...THAT YOU'LL LOOK FOR ME.

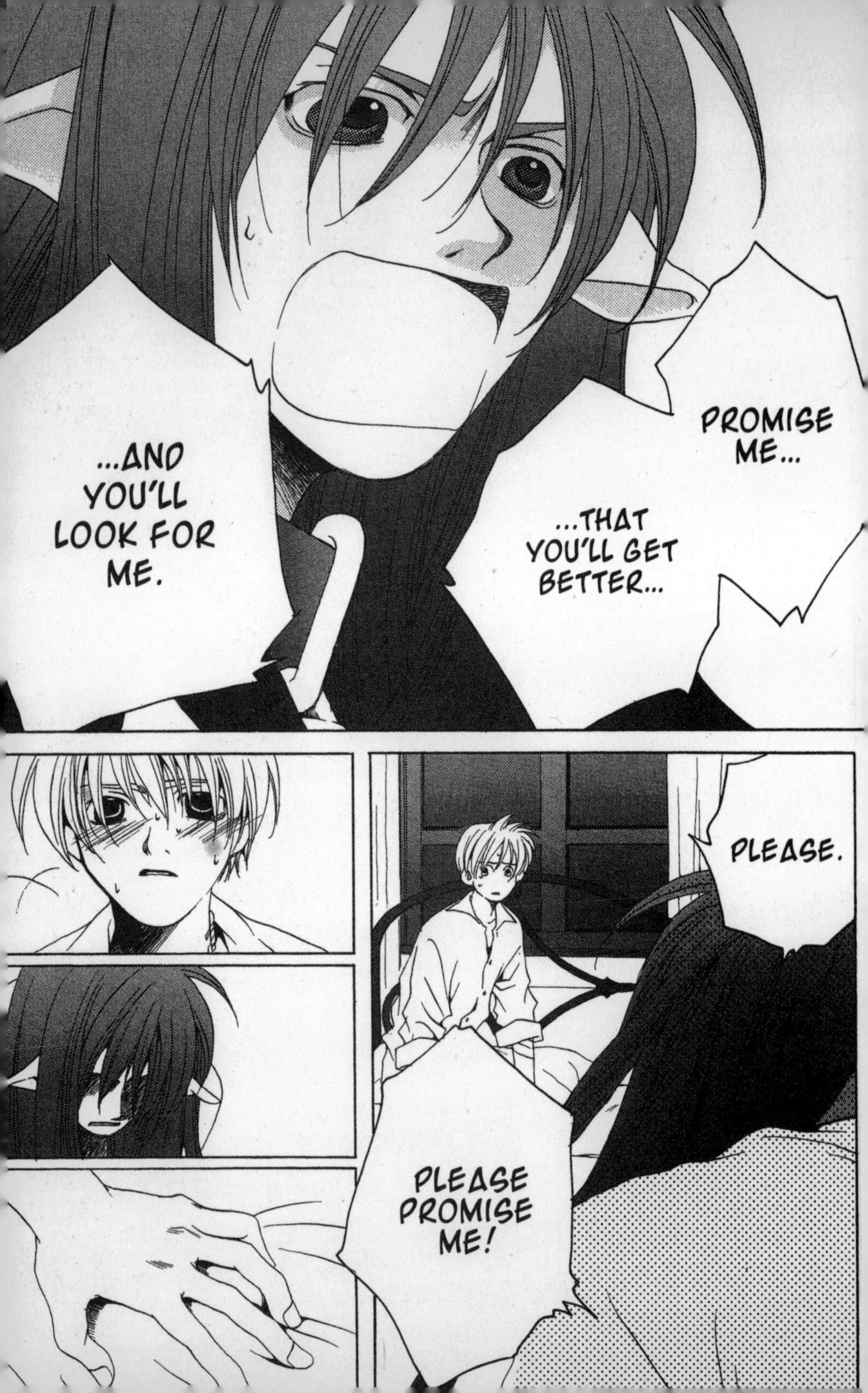
PROMISE ME...
...THAT YOU'LL GET BETTER...
...AND YOU'LL LOOK FOR ME.
PLEASE.
PLEASE PROMISE ME!

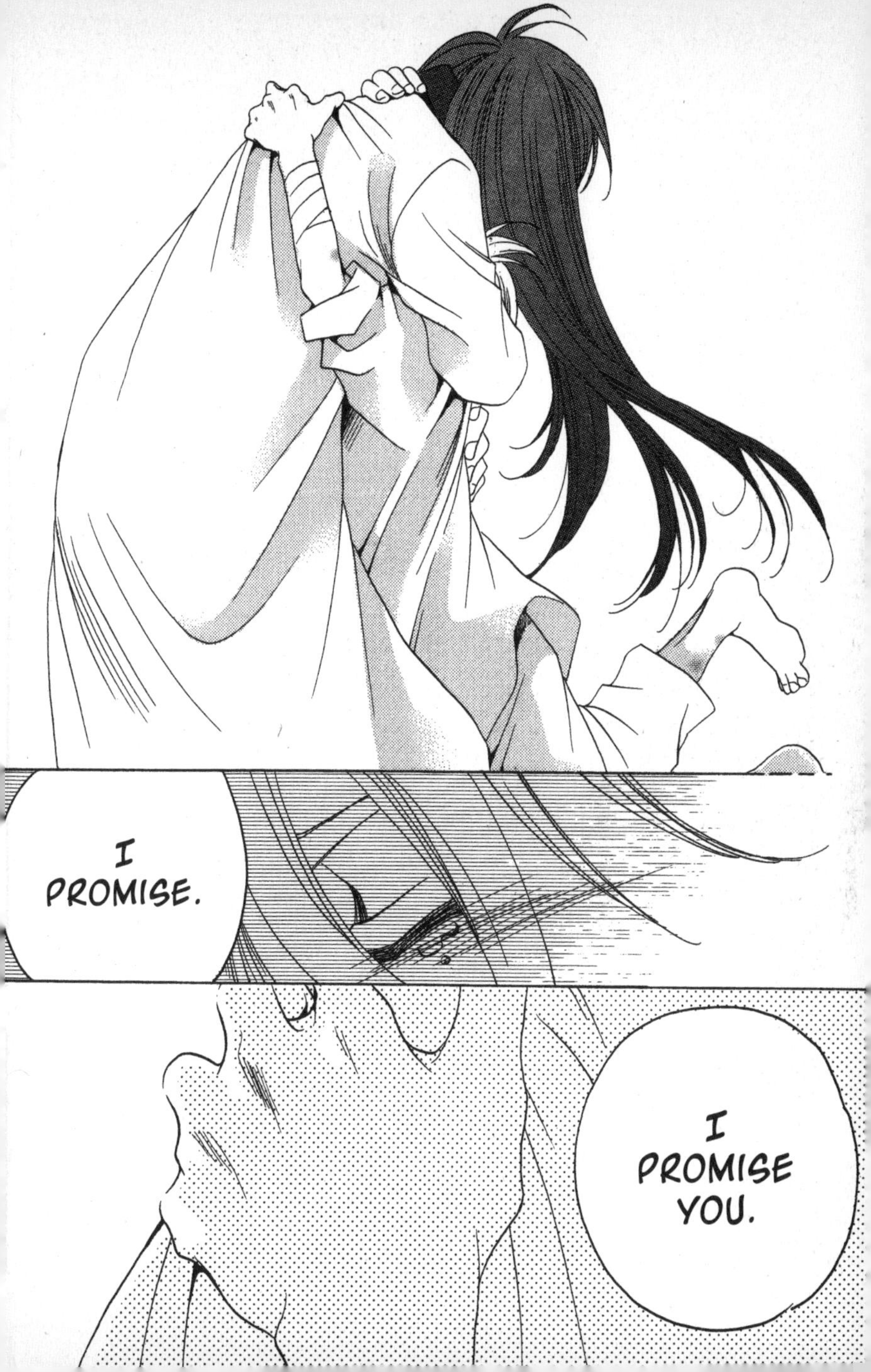
I PROMISE.
I PROMISE YOU.

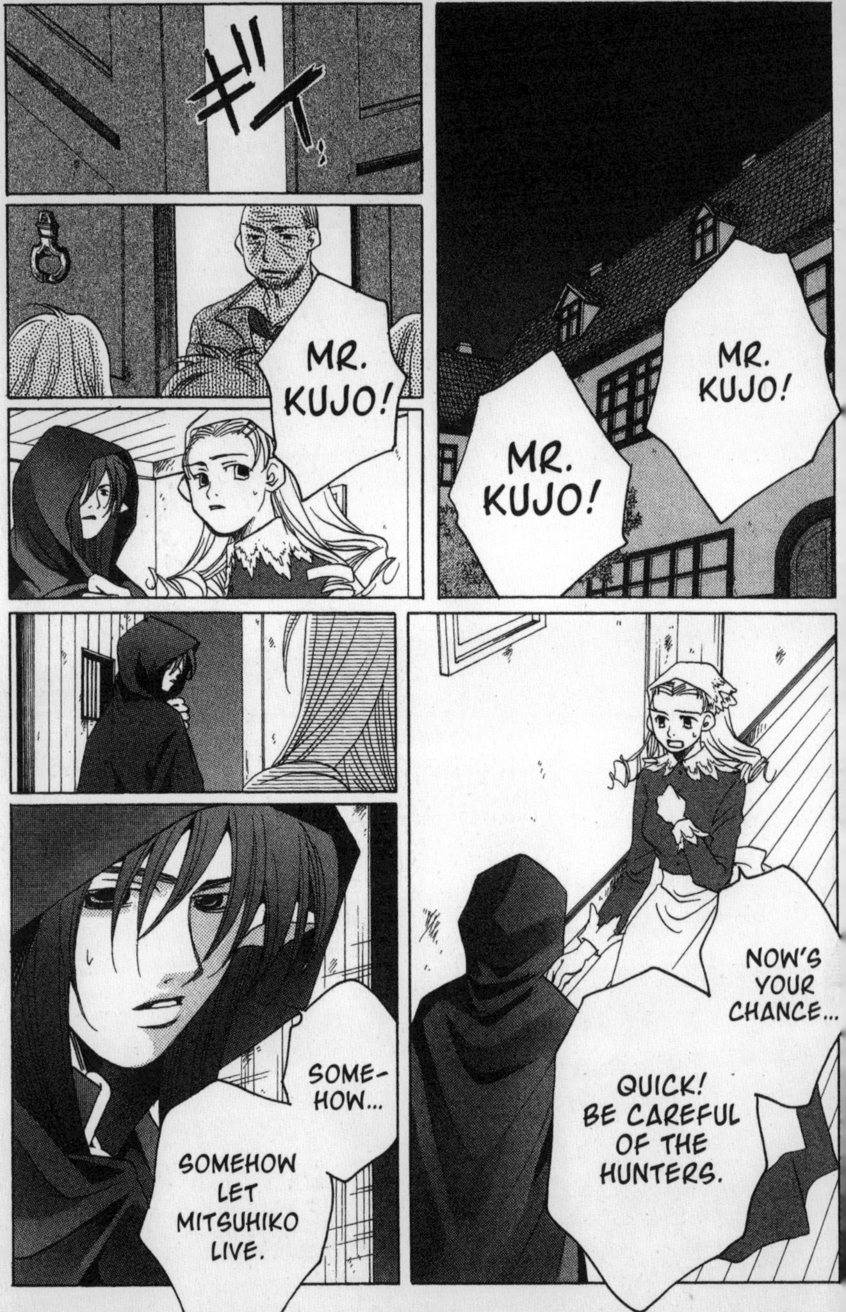
MR. KUJO!
MR. KUJO!
ギイ
MR. KUJO!
NOW'S YOUR CHANCE...
QUICK! BE CAREFUL OF THE HUNTERS.
SOME-HOW...
SOMEHOW LET MITSUHIKO LIVE.

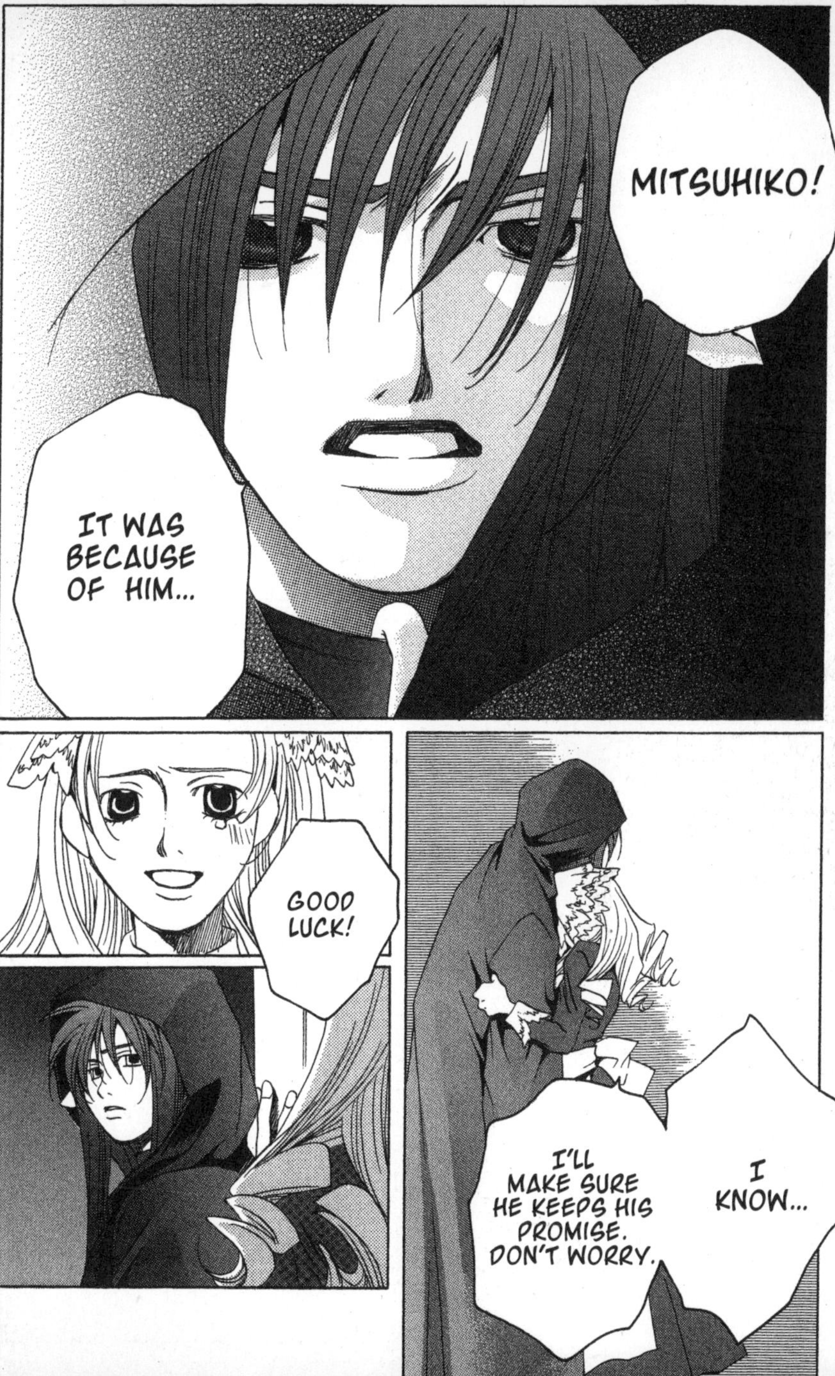
MITSUHIKO!
IT WAS BECAUSE OF HIM...
I KNOW...
I'LL MAKE SURE HE KEEPS HIS PROMISE. DON'T WORRY.
GOOD LUCK!

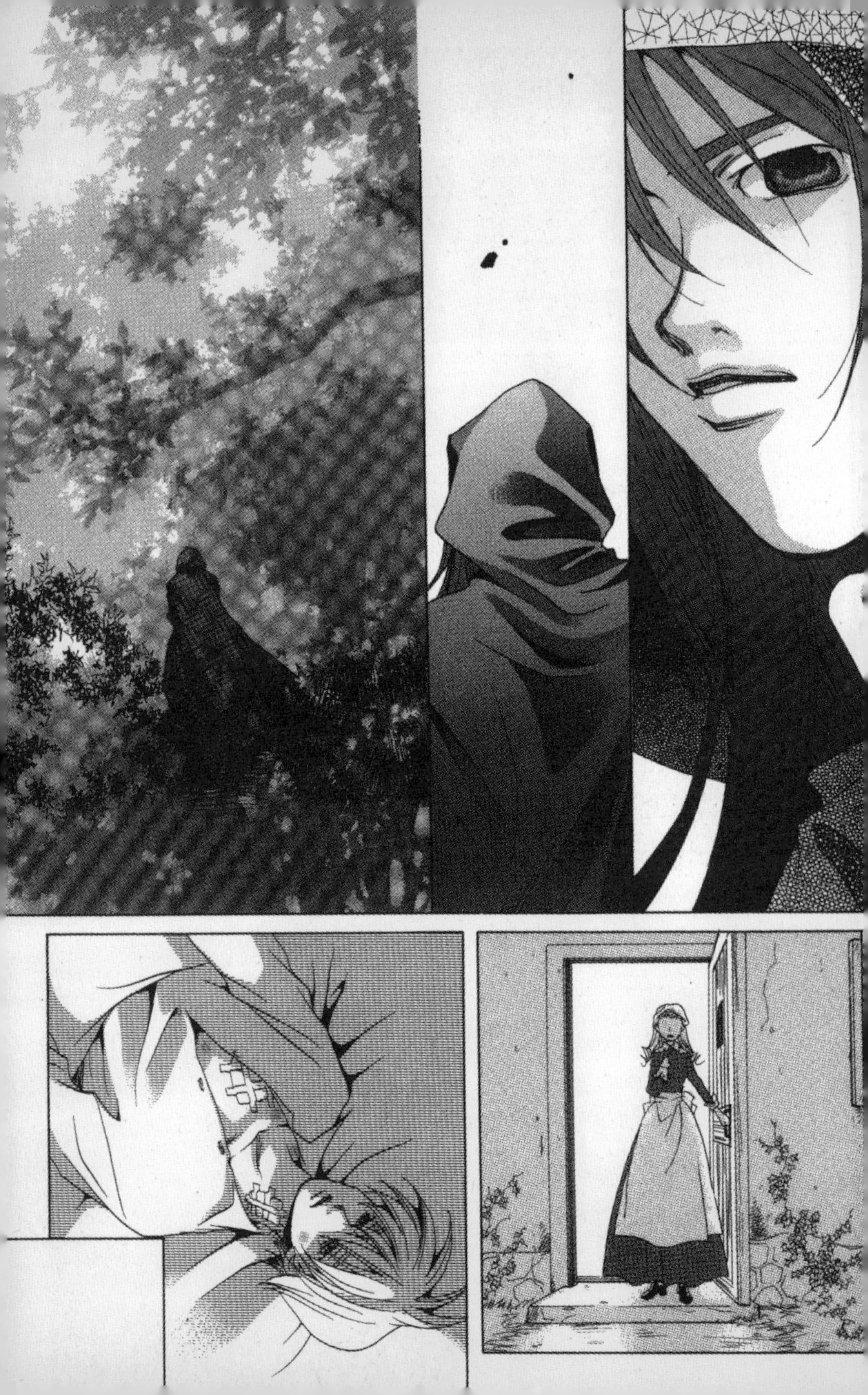

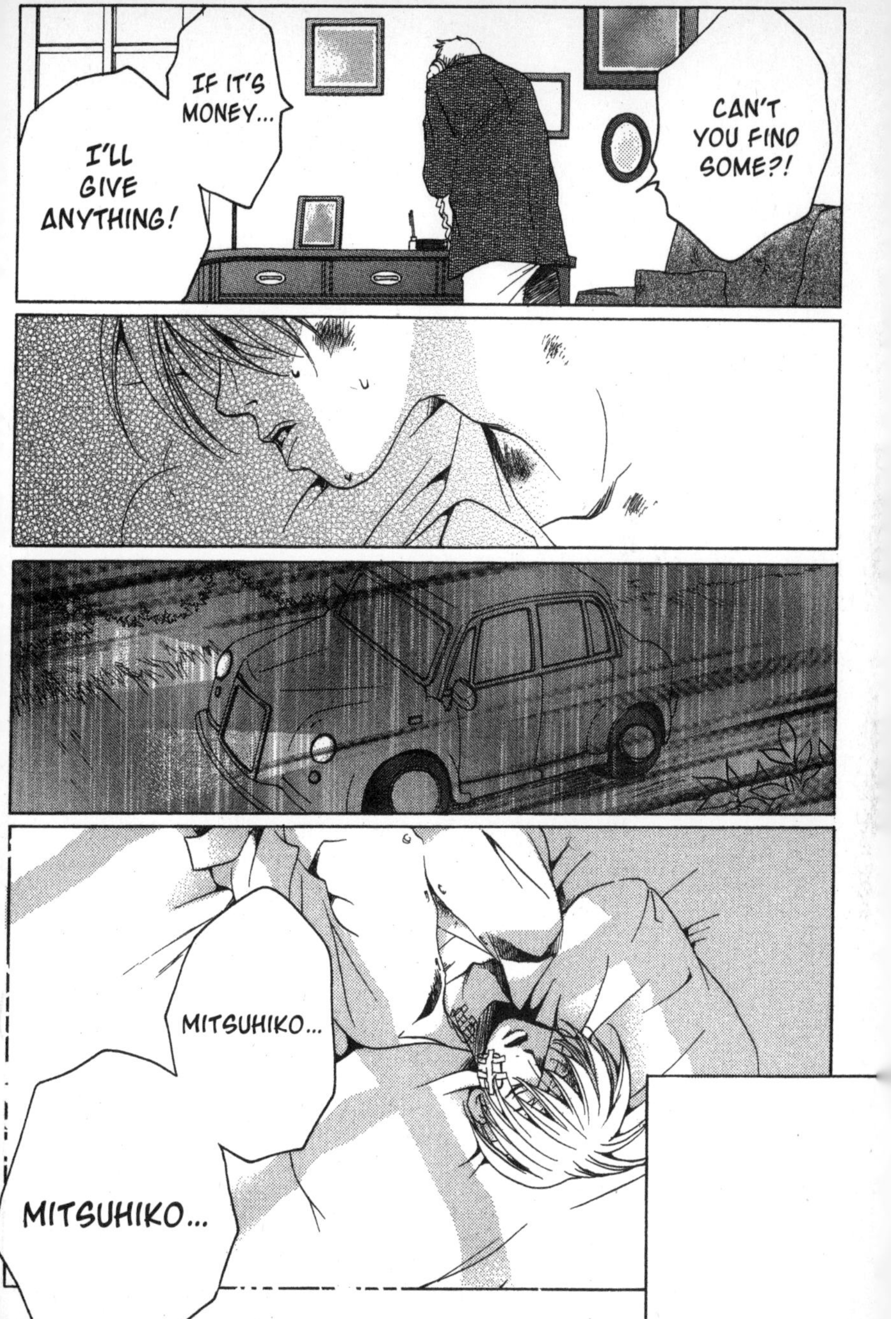
CAN'T YOU FIND SOME?!
IF IT'S MONEY...
I'LL GIVE ANYTHING!
MITSUHIKO...
MITSUHIKO...

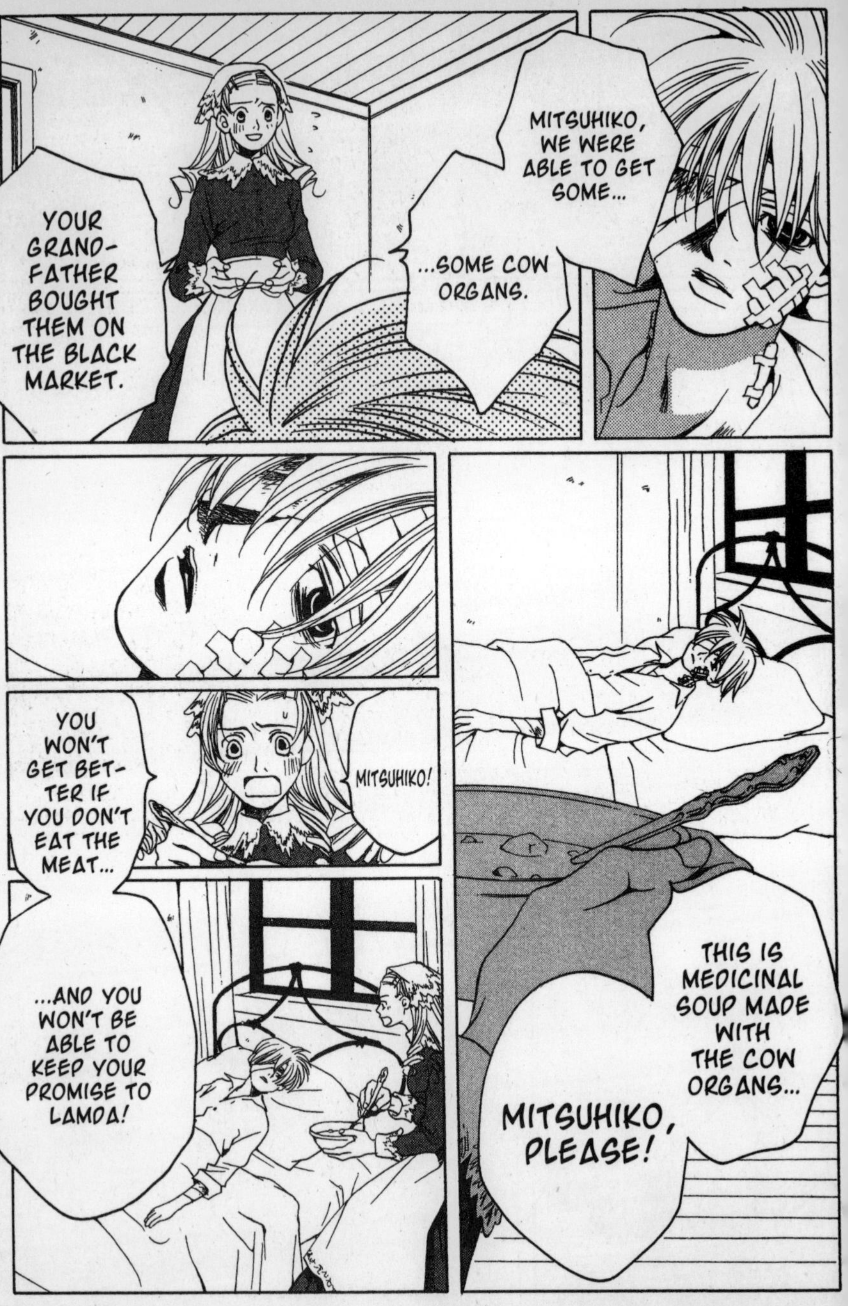
MITSUHIKO, WE WERE ABLE TO GET SOME...
...SOME COW ORGANS.
YOUR GRAND-FATHER BOUGHT THEM ON THE BLACK MARKET.
THIS IS MEDICINAL SOUP MADE WITH THE COW ORGANS...
MITSUHIKO, PLEASE!
MITSUHIKO!
YOU WON'T GET BET-TER IF YOU DON'T EAT THE MEAT...
...AND YOU WON'T BE ABLE TO KEEP YOUR PROMISE TO LAMDA!

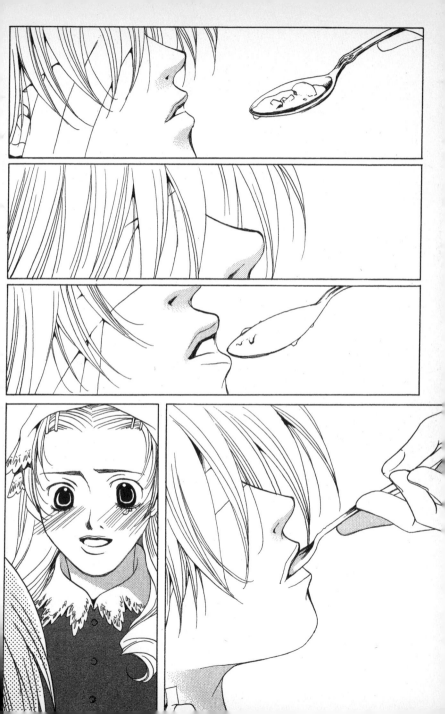

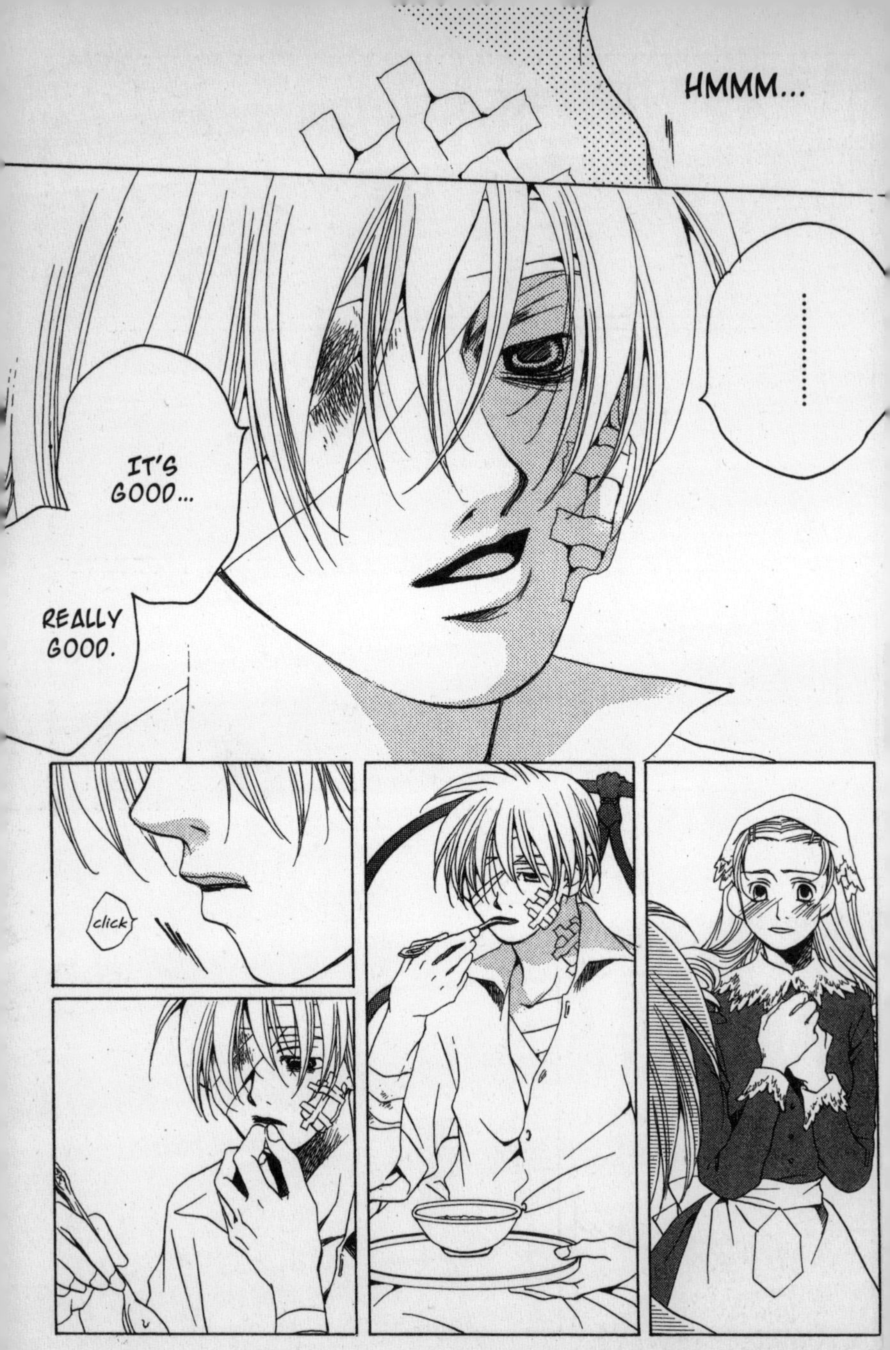
HMMM...
......
IT'S GOOD...
REALLY GOOD.
click

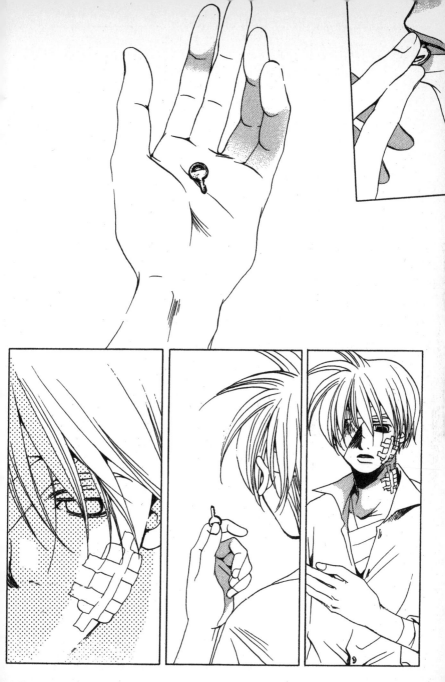

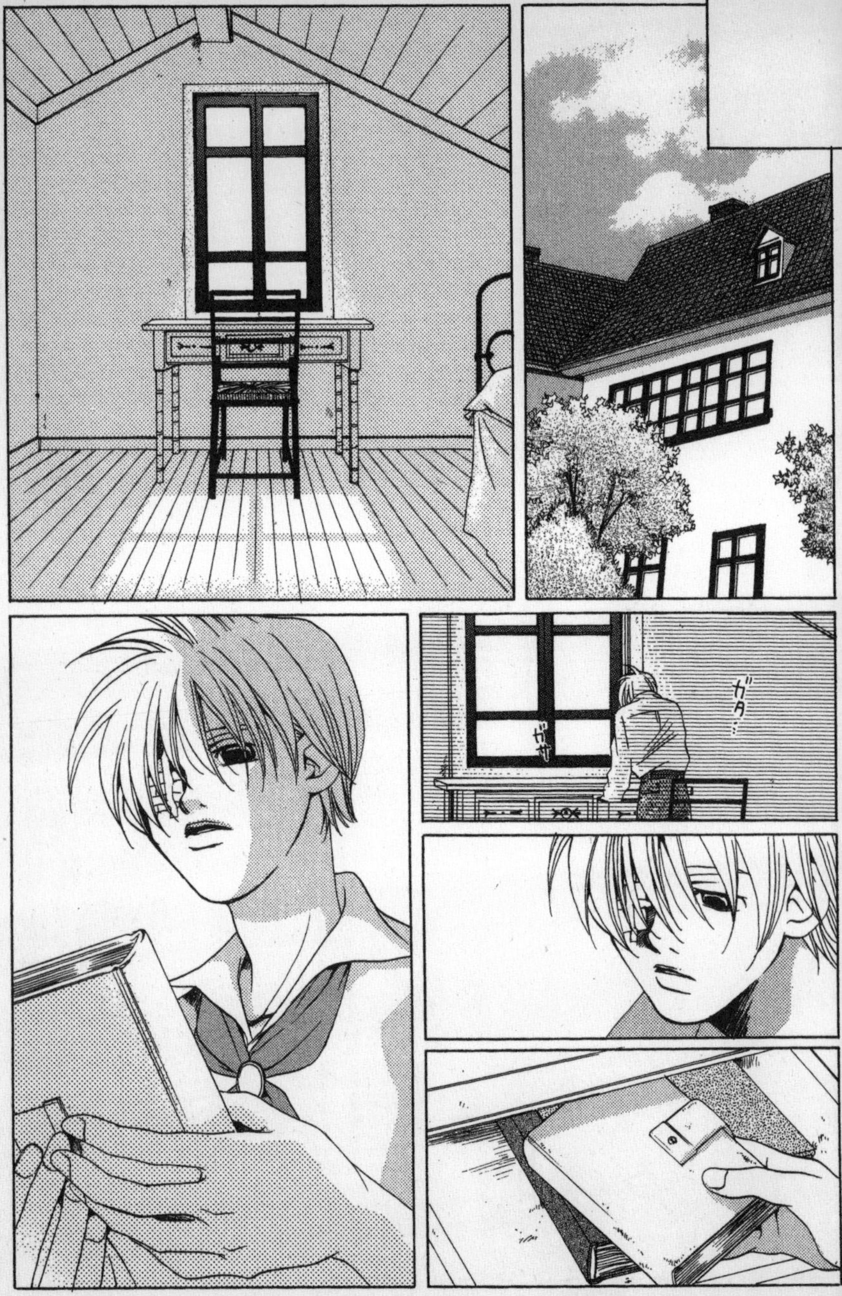
ガタ…
ガサ

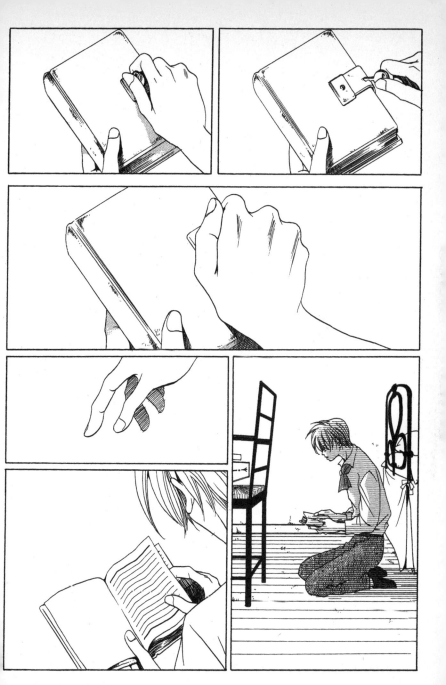

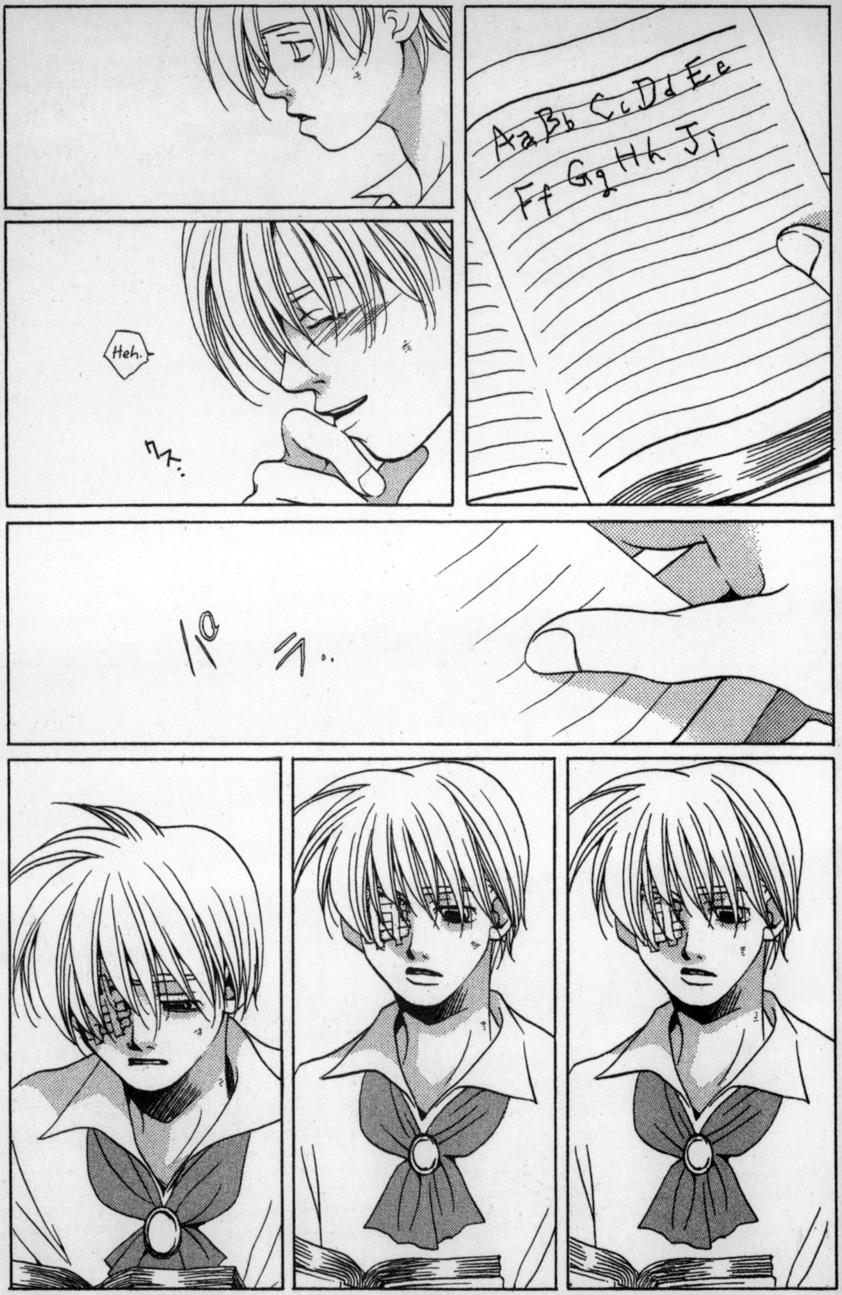
AaBb CcDdEe
Ff Gg Hh Ji
Heh.
パ ラ..

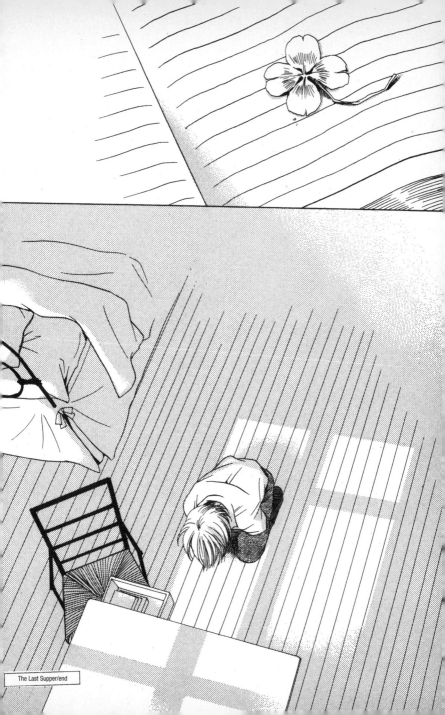

The Last Supper/end

Thank you for staying with me.
And thank you to everyone who sent e-mails and letters. I've been using them as inspiration and encouragement. I'd be very happy to hear more of your ideas. I hope that we'll meet again.

-Setona Mizushiro

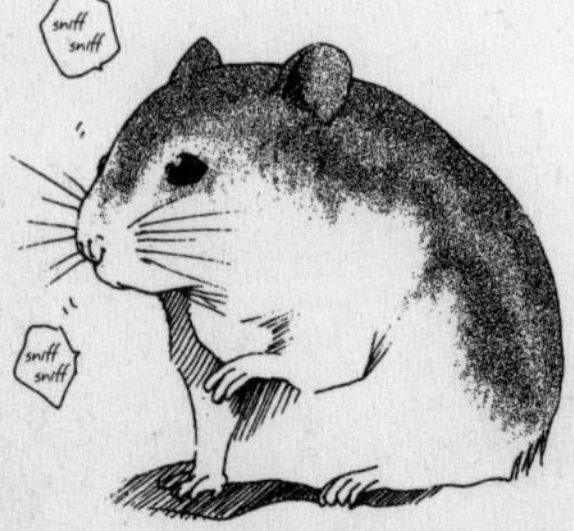
sniff sniff
sniff sniff

MARS

A Bad Boy Can Change
A Good Girl Forever.

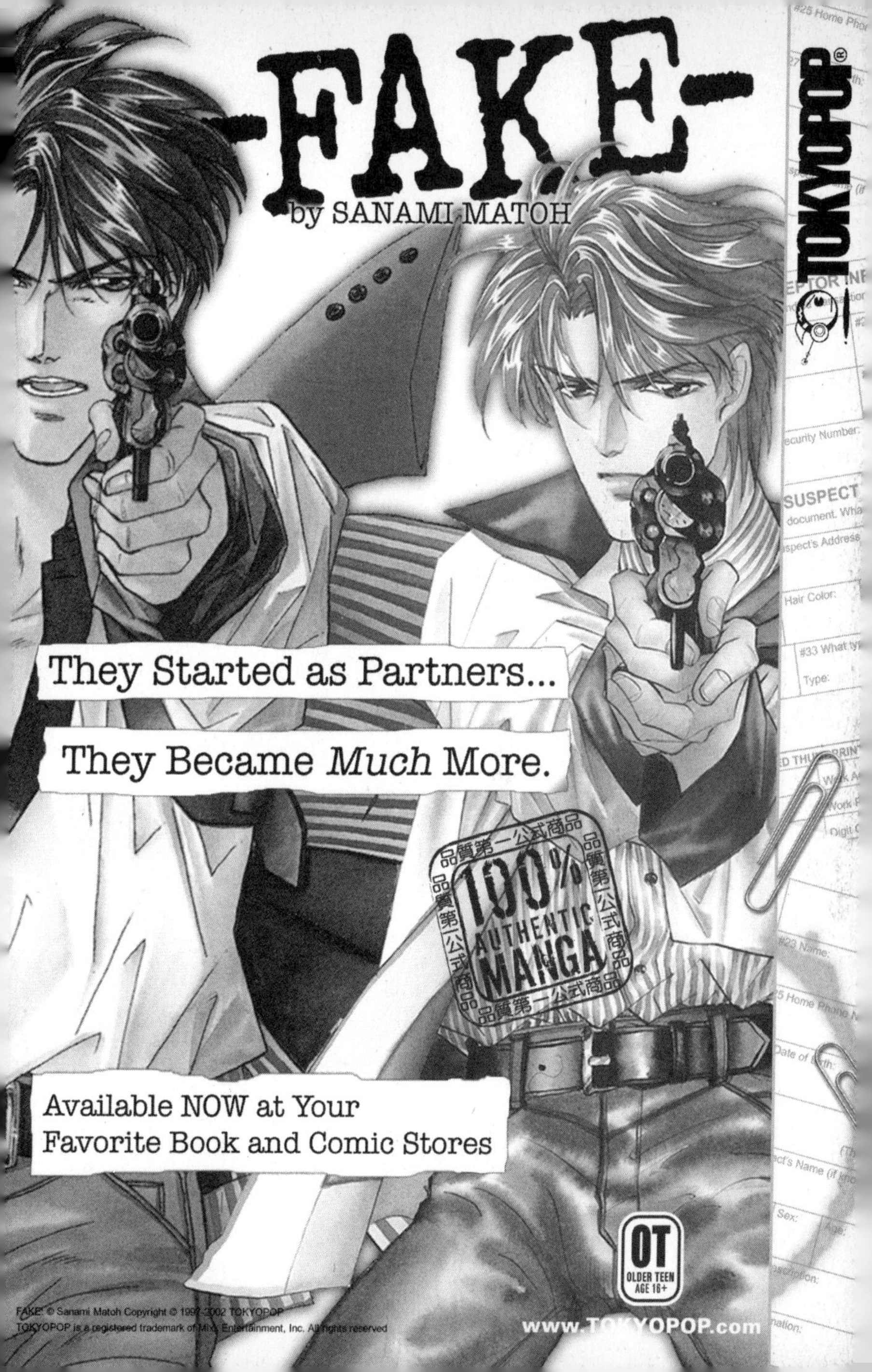

-FAKE-
by SANAMI MATOH
TOKYOPOP
They Started as Partners...
They Became *Much* More.
100% AUTHENTIC MANGA
品質第一公式商品
Available NOW at Your
Favorite Book and Comic Stores
OT
OLDER TEEN AGE 16+
FAKE © Sanami Matoh Copyright © 1997-2002 TOKYOPOP
TOKYOPOP is a registered trademark of Mixx Entertainment, Inc. All rights reserved
www.TOKYOPOP.com

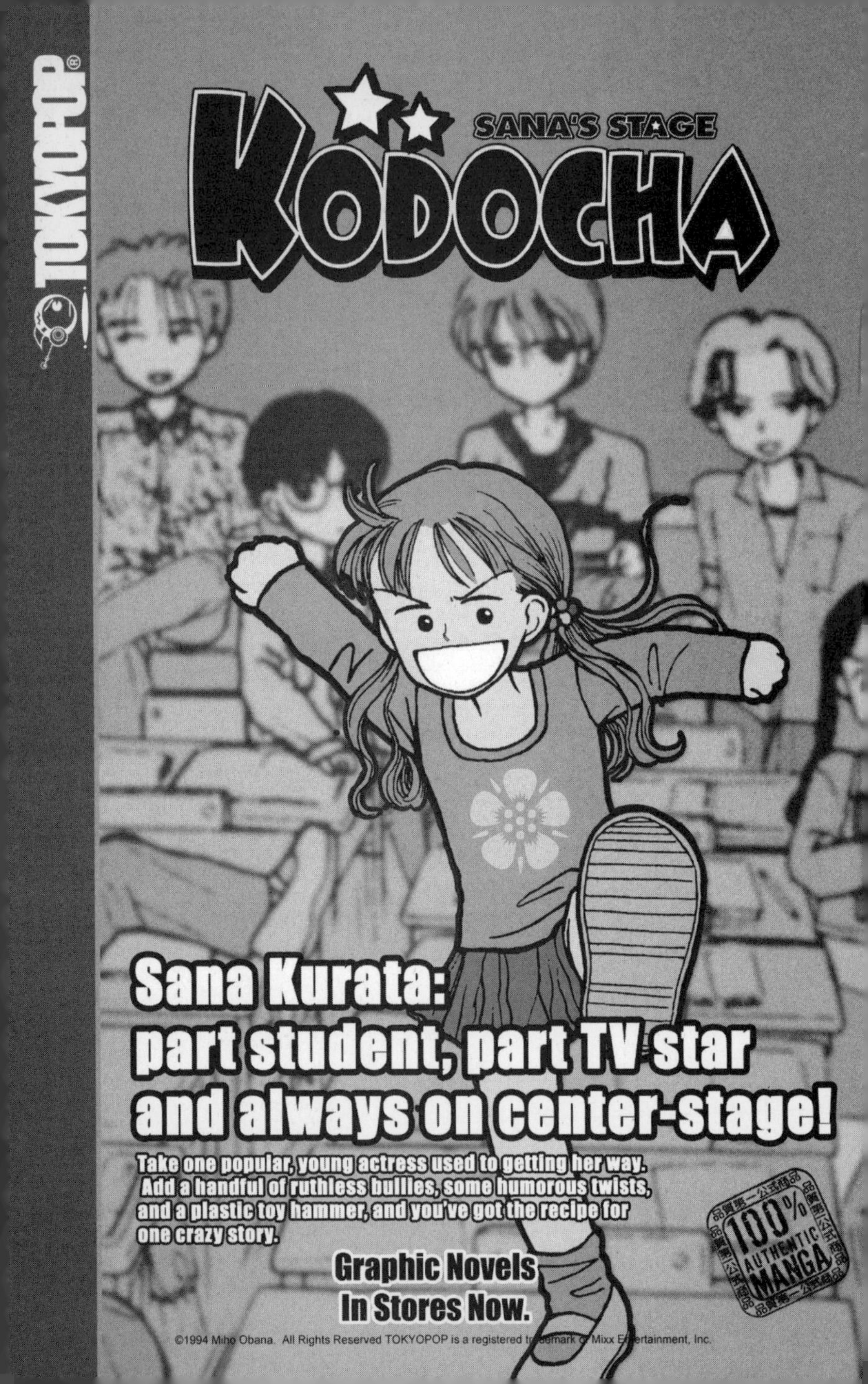
TOKYOPOP
KODOCHA
SANA'S STAGE
Sana Kurata:
part student, part TV star
and always on center-stage!
Take one popular, young actress used to getting her way. Add a handful of ruthless bullies, some humorous twists, and a plastic toy hammer, and you've got the recipe for one crazy story.
100% AUTHENTIC MANGA
Graphic Novels
In Stores Now.
©1994 Miho Obana. All Rights Reserved TOKYOPOP is a registered trademark of Mixx Entertainment, Inc.

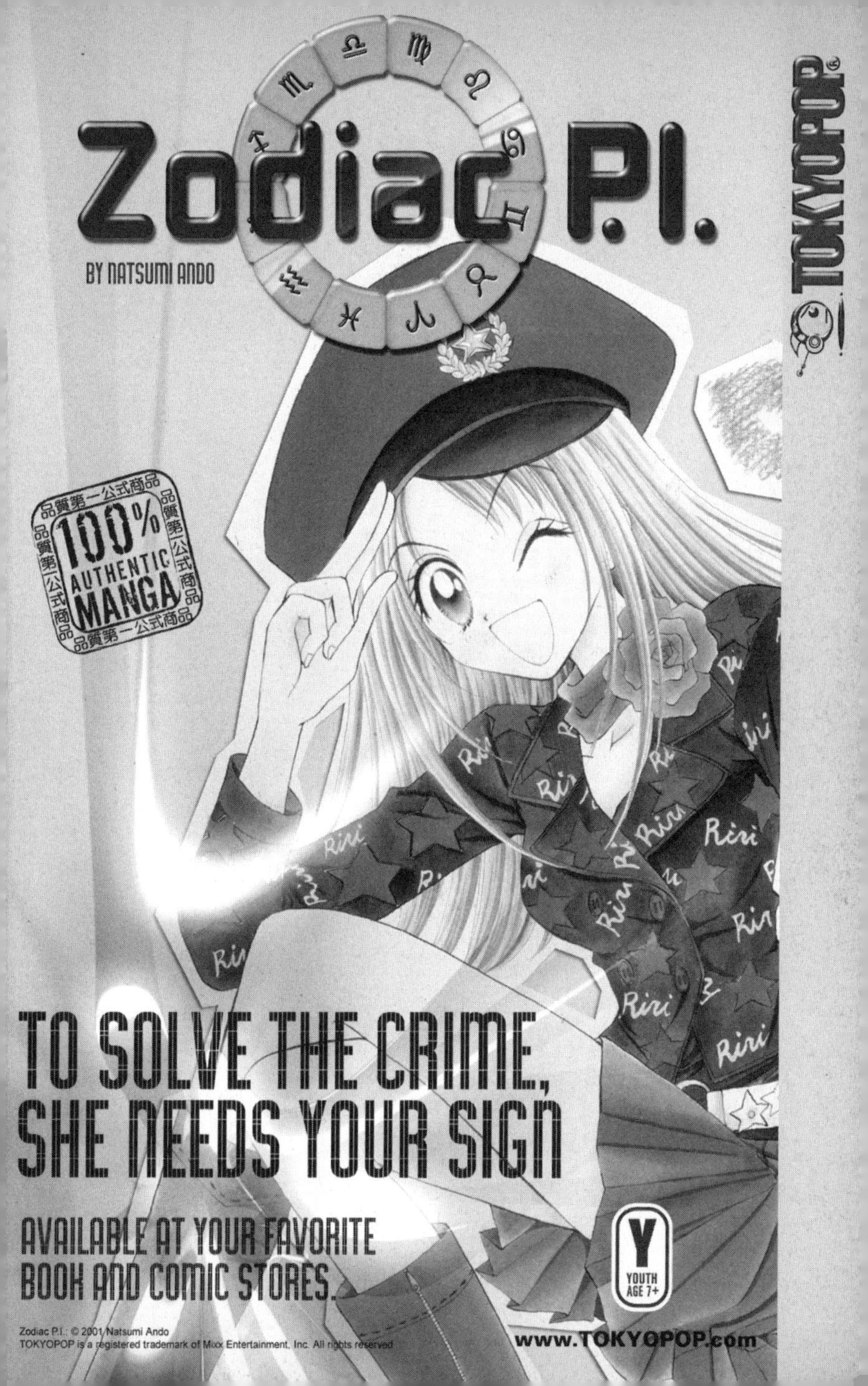
Zodiac P.I.
BY NATSUMI ANDO
TOKYOPOP
100% AUTHENTIC MANGA
TO SOLVE THE CRIME, SHE NEEDS YOUR SIGN
AVAILABLE AT YOUR FAVORITE BOOK AND COMIC STORES.
Y YOUTH AGE 7+
Zodiac P.I.: © 2001 Natsumi Ando
TOKYOPOP is a registered trademark of Mixx Entertainment, Inc. All rights reserved
www.TOKYOPOP.com

STOP!

This is the back of the book.
You wouldn't want to spoil a great ending!

This book is printed "manga-style," in the authentic Japanese right-to-left format. Since none of the artwork has been flipped or altered, readers get to experience the story just as the creator intended. You've been asking for it, so TOKYOPOP® delivered: authentic, hot-off-the-press, and far more fun!

DIRECTIONS

If this is your first time reading manga-style, here's a quick guide to help you understand how it works.

It's easy... just start in the top right panel and follow the numbers. Have fun, and look for more 100% authentic manga from TOKYOPOP®!